The History of Dei

The History of Democracy

A Marxist Interpretation

Brian S. Roper

PlutoPress
www.plutobooks.com

First published 2013 by Pluto Press
345 Archway Road, London N6 5AA

www.plutobooks.com

Distributed in the United States of America exclusively by
Palgrave Macmillan, a division of St. Martin's Press LLC,
175 Fifth Avenue, New York, NY 10010

British Library Cataloguing in Publication Data
A catalogue record for this book is available from the British Library

ISBN 978 0 7453 3190 4 Hardback
ISBN 978 0 7453 3189 8 Paperback
ISBN 978 1 8496 4713 7 PDF eBook
ISBN 978 1 8496 4715 1 Kindle eBook
ISBN 978 1 8496 4714 4 EPUB eBook

Library of Congress Cataloging in Publication Data applied for

This book is printed on paper suitable for recycling and made from fully managed and
sustained forest sources. Logging, pulping and manufacturing processes are expected to
conform to the environmental standards of the country of origin.

10 9 8 7 6 5 4 3 2 1

Designed and produced for Pluto Press by Curran Publishing Services, Norwich
Simultaneously printed digitally by CPI Antony Rowe, Chippenham, UK and
Edwards Bros in the United States of America

Contents

Preface and acknowledgements

The growing problems and inequalities generated by advanced capitalism and the liberal democratic states that have implemented neoliberal policies since the late 1970s have provoked increasingly global resistance to capitalism and neoliberalism. Every time that mass resistance breaks out it raises the question of whether there is an alternative to how the world is currently organised socially, economically and politically. Some simply want to see immediate improvements to the prevailing arrangements through short-term reforms, while others consider that a fundamental transformation of capitalism is necessary to create a better world. Despite the existence of many intellectual and political differences on various issues, the bulk of those on the left, whether socialists, feminists, anti-racists, anarchists, environmentalists, global justice campaigners, anti-war activists or cosmopolitan social democrats, consider that it is necessary to make the governance of society more democratic at global, regional, national and local levels in order to more effectively address the major problems confronting humanity in the twenty-first century.

Informed by the conviction that the present, and possible futures, are determined by what has happened in the past, this book contributes to the collective search for a democratic alternative to capitalism by clarifying the role that democracy has played, and is likely to play, in a variety of historical and societal contexts. This analysis will demonstrate that capitalism is only compatible with very limited forms of democracy, and consequently that the democratisation of social life can only be achieved through the collective transformation of capitalism to create a fundamentally more democratic, egalitarian, environmentally sustainable and socialist world.

The importance of considering democracy's past, present and future has never been greater. Because of the length of time that it has taken to complete the book, I have rewritten the preface on several occasions. The version before this started with a short critique of Bush's proclamation in his 2002 National Security Strategy that 'The great struggles of the twentieth century between liberty and totalitarianism ended with a decisive victory for the forces of freedom – and a single sustainable model for national success: freedom, democracy, and free enterprise.' It noted that the rhetoric of democracy has played, and continues to play, a key ideological role in justifying US imperial ambitions. Although Obama's (2010: ii) rhetoric differs substantially from that of Bush, he still argues in the 2010 National Security Strategy that his administration aims to 'maintain the military superiority that has secured our country, and underpinned global security, for decades', and asserts that 'democracy does not merely represent our better angels, it stands in opposition to aggression and injustice, and our support for universal rights is both fundamental to American leadership and a source of our strength in the world'.

Writing late in 2011 there is fortunately a better place to start than with a brief critique of the rhetorical deployment of a commitment to democracy promotion to justify the geopolitical hegemony of the United States. 2011 was the worst year for global capitalism since 1968 – a year of crisis, revolutions, revolts and global anti-capitalist protests. On December 17, 2010 in Tunisia, Mohamed Bouazizi, a 26-year-old street vendor with no other means of supporting himself and his family, set himself on fire to protest against having his cart and produce confiscated by a public official. This sparked a revolutionary uprising that toppled the corrupt dictatorship of Zine El-Abidine Ben Ali by mid-January. In February, Alexander (2011: 11) observed that the fall of the Ben Ali regime 'demonstrates that the stresses imposed on the states of the region by the combination of neoliberal reforms and global economic crisis have potential to fracture regimes by triggering popular revolts which can neither be managed by co-option nor broken by repression'. This potential was soon to be realised. Inspired by the events in Tunisia, a revolution centred on the mass occupation of Tahrir Square in Cairo led to the departure from Egypt of the hated Hosni Mubarak dictatorship, which had been in power for 30 years, on February 11, 2011. A wave of revolutionary upheavals swept across the Middle East, with uprisings against authoritarian regimes in Bahrain, Yemen, Libya and Syria and related mass protests taking place in Algeria, Iraq, Jordan, Morocco, Oman and Lebanon. These revolutions provided inspiration across the world to those in other countries wanting, among other things, more equality and democracy, and less austerity, unemployment and poverty. It appeared to many that resistance was no longer futile and that revolution was possible.

The global financial crisis and ensuing prolonged recession – universally recognised as constituting the most severe crisis of the world capitalist economy since the Great Depression – have been managed by governments around the world, initially with the injection of fiscal stimulus and huge bailouts of failing financial institutions, and secondly through the subsequent imposition of neoliberal fiscal austerity to reduce the resulting greatly increased levels of government debt. The crisis has greatly exacerbated long-running trends and patterns of historically poor economic performance, mass unemployment, growing inequality and poverty. It has provoked resistance to neoliberal fiscal austerity throughout the world.

In Europe protests and strikes against austerity policies occurred during the period from September 2010 to the end of 2011 in Croatia, France, Italy, Ireland, Portugal and Spain. Perhaps most importantly for the rest of Europe, both politically and economically, the national debt crisis in Greece led the Pasok government, under pressure from the European Union, the European Central Bank and the International Monetary Fund (IMF), to push through severe austerity measures, which provoked staunch resistance by the Greek working class in the form of a succession of general strikes and mass protests. In the

United Kingdom, where the Conservative-led coalition government attempted to implement the largest cuts to public spending since 1945, resistance took the form of mass student protests and occupations in November and December of 2010, around 500,000 participating in a Trades Union Congress (TUC) anti-cuts protest on March 26, 2011, coordinated strikes by public sector unions against the government's attacks on pensions on June 30, a wave of riots that swept across the country in August, and a public sector general strike and associated protests on November 30.

The deep and prolonged recession in the United States also provoked resistance. In response to the Wisconsin republican governor, Scott Walker, attacking workers' rights and cutting public spending, public sector workers and students engaged in mass strike and protest action, culminating in the occupation of the Capitol building in Madison in March 2011. Then in mid-September several hundred protestors successfully occupied Zuccotti Park near Wall Street to take a stand against corporate greed and the dominant influence of business on government policy making. Their main slogan was: 'We are the 99 percent that will no longer tolerate the greed and corruption of the 1 percent' (*New York Times*, October 24, 2011). This acted as a spark, with related protests and occupations rapidly spreading across the United States, and then giving rise on October 15 to the largest internationally synchronised protests since the global mobilisation against war on February 15, 2003. Although estimates vary, it is likely that over a million people participated in these protests in more than 900 cities across the world.

At the time of writing there is no way of knowing precisely how the Occupy movement will play out. The most common criticism is its failure to outline a coherent programme of progressive political change because it is a rainbow coalition encompassing socialists, anarchists, feminists, environmentalists, social democrats, unions, anti-racists, global justice activists and others. But widespread agreement prevails amongst the participants regarding the central issues that the movement is highlighting.

The implementation of neoliberalism on a global scale has had a devastating impact on the majority of the world's people. The shift from the Keynesian policy regimes of the 1950s and 1960s to the neoliberal regimes of the 1980s, 1990s and 2000s in the advanced capitalist societies from the late 1970s onwards dramatically increased inequality in the distribution of income and wealth. Several interrelated areas of policy change contributed to this. Regulatory control of financial institutions and activity facilitated the global integration of capital markets, massive expansion of debt, and the growth of finance relative to agriculture and manufacturing. Taxation systems were extensively remodelled in favour of the wealthy, with tax cuts for corporations and high-income earners, and tax increases for low- and middle-income earners, particularly through increases in consumption taxes. Anti-union industrial relations reform undermined the bargaining power of trade unions and legislative protection for workers with respect to minimum wages, working hours, holidays, unfair dismissal and workplace safety. Mass unemployment was deliberately allowed to rise and become entrenched as a mechanism to control inflation and undermine the collective organisation and bargaining power of workers. In addition, government spending on health, housing, education and welfare has been subject to fiscal restraint throughout the neoliberal epoch. Consequently, poverty, homelessness and malnourishment increased in most of the advanced capitalist societies, and 'almost all global indicators on health levels, life expectancy, infant mortality ... show losses rather than gains in well-being since the 1960s' (Harvey, 2005: 154).

For three decades governments around the world justified these neoliberal policies, which mainly benefited the top 10 per cent while impacting negatively on low and middle-income earners, ethnic minorities and women, by claiming, among other things, that governments could no longer afford the generous welfare states of the Keynesian period from 1945 to 1974. The spectacle of governments suddenly displaying the capacity to spend enormous sums of money to bail out financial corporations provoked the Occupy movement, and greatly exacerbated the tensions between nation-states. Long before the global financial crisis the US Treasury–Wall Street–IMF complex became expert at generating debt crises in order to provide a pretext for the imposition of so-called structural adjustment. In this respect, 'crisis creation, management, and manipulation on the world stage has evolved into the fine art of deliberative redistribution of wealth from poor countries to the rich. ... These debt crises were orchestrated, managed, and controlled both to rationalize the system and to redistribute assets' (Harvey, 2005: 162). Since 1980 over US$4.6 trillion has been sent from less-developed countries to western financial institutions (2005: 162). This massive transfer of wealth centrally involves interest payments on debt and the repatriation of profits from the assets acquired by the greatly increased direct foreign investment of transnational corporations based in the major advanced capitalist countries (McNally, 2006: 37–58). Widespread recurring famine in Africa and other impoverished parts of the world has been the result of a global financial order driven by the profit seeking of western financial institutions.

The implementation of neoliberalism on a global scale has also had a devastating impact on the environment, accelerating capitalist depletion of non-renewable resources, deforestation, and pollution of the atmosphere (ozone depletion and the accumulation of greenhouse gases in the upper atmosphere), waterways with effluents, soil with pesticides, and oceans with outfalls, shipping and oil spills. As the twenty-first century marches on and is increasingly punctuated by environmental disasters such as the 2010 Deepwater Horizon oil spill in the Gulf of Mexico and the 2011 Japanese nuclear disaster at the Fukushima power plant, as the effects of global warming become increasingly evident, and as the responses of the world's most powerful states appear patently inadequate, more people are being prompted to question whether in the long-term capitalist civilisation can survive the environmental devastation it is causing.

In all of the advanced capitalist countries, but perhaps most markedly in the United States, business is able to exert a disproportionate influence over government policy making. Consider, for example, that in the US presidential election year of 2004 business contributed $1,503 million to political parties compared with $61.6 million from trade unions, while in the congressional election year of 2006 the respective figures were $527 million from business and $69.5 million from unions (Selfa, 2006: 23). According to the Centre for Responsive Politics (2011), for the 2007–08 election cycle business contributed $1,999.8 million and labour $74.9 million, and the figures for 2009–10 were $1,367 million and $96.6 million respectively. As these figures and the notoriously pro-business bias of the US corporate media suggest, the capacity of business to exert a highly disproportionate influence over the political system is a central characteristic of the particular form of representative democracy that exists in the United States.

Business influence has recently been further enhanced by the Supreme Court's decision in the 2010 case of Citizens United versus Federal Electoral Commission, which permits corporations to 'make independent expenditures in relation to federal elections [advocating the election of the candidates which they prefer] and to fund electioneering communications' (Federal Electoral Commission, 2011: 1). This decision was justified on the grounds that corporations are for legal and constitutional purposes regarded as citizens, so their freedom of speech, including spending vast sums of money to intervene in federal elections, is protected by the First Amendment.

There is now a widely shared recognition that the major problems faced by humanity in the twenty-first century, such as poverty, unemployment, inequality, racism, women's oppression, war, global warming, and the extensive absence of effective democracy in both national and global governance, are interconnected and therefore must be combated by united campaigns and movements, bringing together a wide range of intellectually and ideologically disparate individuals and organisations. This was one of the most inspiring contributions of the global justice movement that emerged following the Seattle protests that shut down the World Trade Organization (WTO) negotiations at the end of 1999, and it has been continued and further developed by the Occupy movement.

It is true that these movements have to date generated more questions than answers, but they are the most important questions of the twenty-first century. Why has capitalism spread to engulf the globe? How can we explain inequality within and between capitalist nation-states? What can we do about it? Why does capitalist development generate recurrent crises characterised by declining profitability, economic stagnation and mass unemployment? Why does competition between capitalist elites often culminate in military conflict between nation-states? Why is it also destroying the natural environment, to the extent of threatening the continued existence of human life on the planet? What social forces are capable of successfully pushing for change within capitalism and potentially transforming capitalism in a revolutionary manner? In this respect, does the working-class majority, within which ethnic minorities and women are concentrated, have the collective capacity and power to defeat capitalists and governments defending capitalist interests? The evident deficiencies of capitalism, neoliberalism and US foreign policy suggest that there is a need to explore alternatives. Is it possible to transform capitalism in an emancipatory manner while retaining liberal representative democracy as the institutional framework for societal governance? If not, is there a feasible and desirable alternative to capitalism and representative democracy? Does socialist participatory democracy constitute such an alternative?

These questions form a guiding frame of reference for this book's exploration of the history of democracy from its origins in Athens around 508 BC to the present. Above all else, my aim is to explore the dynamic interconnections between the social and economic arrangements prevailing in various societies and the democratic state forms that emerged and governed these societies. Enhancing our understanding of how this has worked in the past will in turn help us to understand the configuration of social, economic and political changes required to create fundamentally more democratic societies in the future. The book has been written for all those, whether students, academics, workers and/ or activists, who want to know more about the history of democracy, and who are not only critical of capitalism but also open-minded about the possibility that a democratic, socialist and environmentally sustainable world will be created in the future. I hope it will encourage further discussion and research into the history of democracy.

I believe the book demonstrates that Marxism remains indispensable to those who want to better understand the past in order to clarify how we might collectively create a world that is qualitatively more democratic. I hope non-Marxist readers will also discover much that is of value in it. Open-minded and intellectually honest criticism is always welcome. Marxists do need to incorporate the scholarly advances and insights of non-Marxist traditions of thought, including liberalism, feminism and neo-Weberian historical sociology. This book provides a potent counter to those who want to misrepresent the Marxist tradition as contributing little of value to the task of investigating the history of democracy in order to inform the struggle for a better world.

I started working on this book while on sabbatical in 1996, and since then more people have assisted this project in various ways than I can acknowledge here. Special mention must be made of Barry Hindess, who made it possible for me to be a visiting fellow in the Political Science Programme in the Research School of Social Sciences (RSSS) at the Australian National University (ANU) on several occasions during the early years of the project. His warm encouragement of the project, despite his reservations about classical Marxism, is greatly appreciated. Although he is unlikely to agree with the book's central argument, I hope that he finds something of value in these pages.

David McNally also provided generous encouragement and support for this project. Thanks to his help I was a visiting fellow in political science at York University during the first half of 2005. My discussions with David, George Comninel, Colin Mooers, Leo Panitch, Geoff Kennedy and David Camfield were valuable. In the United Kingdom David Renton provided some useful advice at various points in the project. The University of Otago made this study leave possible and provided a research grant. Closer to home in the Australasian context I benefited from discussions with Rick Kuhn, Tom Bramble, David McInerney, Dougal McNeill, David Bedggood, Janet Bedggood, John Freeman-Moir, David Neilson, Andrew Tait, Jim Flynn, Mark McGuire, Rosemary Du Plessis, Philip Nel, Brett Nichols, Vijay Devadas, Vicki Spencer, Paul Ramaeker and many others.

Without doubt my greatest intellectual debt is owed to Marxists who passed away while I was working on this book: Geoffrey de Ste Croix, Tony Cliff, Paul Foot, Chris Harman, Christopher Hill, Brian Manning, Ernest Mandel and Ralph Miliband. The book is built on foundations laid by their work. My greatest personal debt is to my partner, Rebecca Stringer, who has commented on chapters in draft, discussed many of the central issues at length, inspired me with her own work, and made it possible to continue working on it by sharing the care of our young son Dylan.

My father, David Alphonsus Roper, taught me to value both socialism and democracy. Therefore it is fitting that I dedicate this book to him.

Brian Roper
August 2012

Introduction

Writing about the history of democracy is a difficult and controversial exercise. There is widespread disagreement over definitions of 'democracy' and the particular forms of government that deserve the label. As Green (1993: 2) observes, democracy 'is not only a contested concept but also a remarkably ambiguous one'. Intellectuals spanning the ideological spectrum from neoliberalism to revolutionary socialism all claim some kind of adherence to 'democracy', and define it in ways consistent with their broader political philosophies.

Democracy 'is a very old word .... It came into English in the sixteenth century, from a translation of *demokratia*, Greek, from the root words *demos* – people, and *kratos* – rule. It is at once evident from Greek uses that everything depends on the senses given to *people* and to *rule*' (Williams, 1993: 19). As this suggests, there is no general agreement as to what democracy, *defined as rule by the people*, means precisely because conceptions of 'rule' and 'people' differ according to the more general philosophical theory of democracy within which such conceptions are embedded. For the purposes of this book I define 'democracy' as denoting, in a minimal but necessary sense, a form of governance (or self-governance) that provides meaningful avenues through which the majority of citizens can exert a significant degree of influence over government decision making and policy making.

This book establishes that three distinctive and important forms of democracy have emerged during the course of its history – Athenian, liberal representative, and socialist participatory democracy. Most liberal political theorists will have trouble accepting this because they assume that representative democracy is the only genuine form of democracy, often in conjunction with the equally disputable assumption that there are no important intellectual and political differences between classical Marxism and Stalinism. In contrast, a much healthier starting point for considering the past, present and future of democracy is recognising that liberal representative democracy is not the only form of democracy that has existed in the past and that may be created in the future. As I hope to show, the contemporary competing conceptions of democracy that are at the heart of the conflicts and debates generated by the widely held desire to create a better world have historical lineages that can be traced back to one or more of these three forms of democracy.

If we are interested in the question whether another more democratic world is possible, we need to explore the history of democracy. This will show the social, economic and political forces that have propelled the emergence and development of the major forms of democracy in the past, and make us better prepared to participate in the struggle for a more democratic world in the future. The social forces that have most consistently fought for, and defended, democracy are the 'poor and middling folks' in various societies: peasant citizens in the Athenian city-state; the middle classes, urban petite-bourgeoisie (sans-culottes), poorer members of the clergy, wage labourers and sections of the peasantry in France during the 1790s; workers and peasants in Russia during the first two decades of the twentieth century; workers, students, farmers and members of the middle classes in the advanced capitalist societies during the twentieth century.

The importance of exploring the history of democracy becomes clear once it appreciated that it has been characterised above all else by the changeable and transitory nature of democratic state forms. Athenian democracy, the Roman republic, the first revolutionary experiment with republican democracy in France, and the ill-fated attempt to create socialist participatory democracy in Russia: each collapsed in dramatic fashion, albeit for very different reasons. The liberal democratic governance of most advanced capitalist societies cannot be viewed, in the context of the broad sweep of human history and in the wake of two world wars, as anything other than unstable and fragile. As Eagleton (1999: 33) observes, 'those with their heads truly in the sands or the clouds are the hard-nosed realists who behave as though chocolate chip cookies and the International Monetary Fund will be with us in another three thousand years time'.

Finally, exploring the history of democracy helps to identify, imagine and clarify potential democratic alternatives to a world dominated by neoliberal capitalism and the United States. Socialist participatory democracy, in my view, constitutes a realistically possible, feasible and desirable alternative to capitalism and representative democracy. I hope this history of democracy will highlight the extent to which it incorporates elements of Athenian and representative democracy, while transcending them in order to facilitate, arguably for the first time in history, the direct participation of the majority of citizens in the governance of society.

MAKING SENSE OF THE PAST, PRESENT AND FUTURE OF DEMOCRACY

In at least seven key respects, historical materialism provides valuable theoretical and methodological resources that can be employed fruitfully in considering democracy's past, present and future. These relate to the aspect of Marxian methodology that makes it possible to maintain both breadth and depth of focus in historical inquiry; the methodological distinction between transhistorical and historical concepts that enables systematic comparisons between different societies and forms of government to be made in a manner that avoids the problems of sweeping generalisation based on the analysis of a particular society, as evident in considerations of history based on neoclassical economic concepts, and the associated underestimation of the importance of historically specific research; the central heuristic impulse of historical materialism; the dialectical insight that social reality is always in a constant state of flux and that all forms of democracy exist only in fluid movement; the provision of a rigorous critique of capitalism and representative democracy; the recognition and consideration of possible historical trajectories beyond capitalism; and the articulation and defence of socialist participatory democracy as a feasible and desirable alternative to capitalism and representative democracy.

First, Marx provides a sophisticated methodology to investigate the history of democracy. Despite the considerable and continuing controversy concerning central features of Marx's method, particularly with respect to its relationship with Hegel's method, few would deny that the process of abstraction is absolutely central to it. In this respect, Ollman (1990: 71) argues that 'using the force of abstraction … is Marx's way of putting dialectics to work'. The process of abstraction, centrally involving 'boundary setting and bringing into focus', operates simultaneously in three different but closely related modes in Marx's method: extension, level of generality, and vantage point (1990: 41). Put simply, extension refers to the process of defining the temporal and/or spatial scope of analysis. 'In abstracting boundaries in space, limits are set in the mutual interaction that occurs at a given point in time. While in abstracting boundaries in time, limits are set in the distinctive history and potential development of any part, in what it once was and is yet to become' (1990: 41). Second, every abstraction not only defines the scope of analysis through extension, it also 'sets a boundary around and brings into focus a particular level of generality for treating not only the part but the whole system to which it belongs' (1990: 41). Third, establishing an extension and level of generality then sets up a vantage point 'for comprehending the larger system of which it is part, providing both a beginning for research and analysis and a perspective in which to carry it out' (1990: 42).

If Ollman is correct, Marx uses the process of abstraction to constantly focus and refocus his enquiry. This involves, for example, zooming in to examine a particular aspect of capitalism such as 'the value-form of the product of labour' which 'is not only the most abstract, but is also the most universal form, taken by the product in bourgeois production, and stamps that production as a particular species of social production, and thereby gives it its special historical character' (Marx, 1967a: 81). Thus Marx commences Volume One of *Capital* by analysing the value-form of the commodity with respect to use-value and exchange-value, then later in the same work he zooms out with his historical lens in order to show how the distinction between use-value and exchange-value corresponds to the distinction between the transhistorical qualities of things, and the historical social relations that govern their production in any particular context. Zooming out still further he demonstrates that the production of use-values can be used to measure the relative wealth of the different societies that have existed in history; '[use-values] constitute the substance of all wealth, whatever may be the social form of that wealth' (1967a: 36). Hence the level of abstraction that is being employed always delimits the scope of Marx's enquiry, and he uses many different levels of abstraction when investigating relationships, processes and events. Finally, and this is where the zoom lens metaphor inadequately conveys the full richness of Marx's method, he also uses the process of abstraction to view relationships and processes from different angles, viewing one relationship from the perspective of another, or viewing a single relationship from the vantage point of one and then the other side of that relationship.

The relevance of this brief reflection upon the process of abstraction in Marx's method to studying the history of democracy becomes particularly clear when we seek to understand state forms by 'putting states in their place' (Jessop, 1990: 365–7). The history of democracy is, in part, the history of those state forms generally held to be in some significant respects 'democratic'. In the considerable body of Marxist writing on 'the state', the full significance of the distinction between transhistorical and historically specific theoretical concepts in Marx's method is not widely recognised. Nor is Marx's methodological injunction that any particular mode of production and 'corresponding specific form of the state ... can be ascertained only by analysis of the empirically given circumstances' (Marx, 1967b: 791–2). Empirical and historical research is essential because political institutions, practices and principles assume widely varying concrete forms in different societies.

The point of this research is not, however, merely to describe these concrete forms but to use the process of abstraction to identify the underlying structural mechanisms and resulting class struggles that generate and shape them. If the critical realist interpretation of Marx's method is correct, this necessitates a conception of ontological depth in which reality is stratified and differentiated. Accordingly, Bhaskar argues that 'social phenomena ... are the product of a plurality of structures. But such structures may be hierarchically ranked in terms of their explanatory importance' (1989: 3; see also Archer, 1998: xi–xiii; Collier, 1989: 43–72). As this suggests, a related heuristic impulse of historical materialism is the drive to analytically penetrate the surface appearances of social reality in order to identify the underlying causes that generate these phenomenal forms and this centrally involves a complex process of retroduction – of working back from phenomenal forms to unobservable causal mechanisms (Bhaskar, 1989: 19; Sayer, 1983: 115–35). It is this process of the 'working-up of observation and conception into concepts' – analysing necessary relations, underlying structures and generative mechanisms – that enables us to accurately depict the concrete as 'a rich totality of many ... relations' and 'the concentration of many determinations, hence unity of the diverse' (Marx, 1973a: 100–1). Sayer (1998: 127) usefully observes in this regard that 'The concrete, as a unity of diverse determinations, is a combination of several necessary relationships, but the form of the combination is contingent, and *therefore only determinable through empirical research.*'

As this interpretation of Marx's method implies, there are very few convincing generalisations that can be made about 'the state' at the level of abstraction of the materialist conception of history. Within classical Marxism one of the more significant attempts to do so is Engels's *Origins of the Family, Private Property and the State*, in which he argues that:

the state arose from the need to hold class antagonisms in check, but because it arose in the midst of the conflict of these classes, it is, as a rule, the state of the most powerful, economically dominant class, which, through the medium of the state, becomes also the politically dominant class, and thus acquires new means of holding down and exploiting the oppressed class.

(Engels, 1968: 577–8)

In Marx and Engels's general theory of history, the state is, as Miliband puts it, 'an essential means of class domination' (1977: 67). But as with the transhistorical definition of exploitation, this amounts to little more than a preliminary hypothesis containing a heuristic injunction to engage in historically specific analysis of 'the empirically given circumstances' in which any particular state is embedded. There is, of course, no such thing as 'the state', any more than there is such a thing as 'the class'. 'The state' is always a particular institutional ensemble (state form) located in a specific historical context and defined in relation to other state forms. In a similar vein, Marx always defined each class in relation to other classes within a specific social formation and historical context. It is, therefore, fundamentally inconsistent with Marx's method to suggest that the relative autonomy of any particular state can be identified independently of a systematic historically specific analysis of that state and the mode of production in which it is embedded.

The relevance of this to investigating the history of democracy is clear: precisely how 'the specific economic form, in which unpaid surplus-labour is pumped out of direct producers', and which generates recurrent struggles between classes, 'determines the relationship of rulers and ruled', is something that can only ever be ascertained by remaining 'constantly on the real *ground* of history' (Marx, 1967b: 791; Marx and Engels, 1976: 61). In so far as any state form may be considered 'democratic' it exists within a totality in which the state 'reacts upon [the specific economic form] as a determining element' (Marx, 1967b: 791). This does not entail either a crude economic determinism or simplistic class reductionism, because societies are conceived of as complex historical totalities (Rees, 1998: 78–118). As Marx and Engels put it in *The German Ideology*, a society which encompasses, *inter alia*, a mode of production, 'theoretical products and forms of consciousness', class struggle, politics and the state, should always 'be depicted in its totality (and therefore, too, the reciprocal action of these various sides on one another)' (Marx and Engels, 1976: 61).

There is a stark contrast between the historical sensibility of Marxist considerations of democracy and the largely ahistorical consideration of representative democracy in the work of many contemporary liberal political theorists (see for example Rawls, 1993). In opposition to this tendency, Wood advocates a critical historical materialism 'in which the origin of capitalism – or any other mode of production – is something that needs to be explained, not presupposed, and which looks for explanations not in some transhistorical law but in historically specific social relations, contradictions and struggles' (1995: 6).

In order accurately to identify what is genuinely unique in capitalism and representative democracy it is necessary to recognise the unique qualities of pre-capitalist societies and the fundamental differences between these societies and capitalism. A failure to do this results in flawed and misleading conceptual interpretations of both capitalist and pre-capitalist societies. So, for example, the liberal conceptual separation of the 'economic' and 'political' spheres, 'while it reflects a reality specific to capitalism, not only fails to comprehend the very different realities of pre- or non-capitalist societies but also disguises the new forms of power and domination created by capitalism' (Wood, 1995: 11). In opposition to the 'teleological tendency to see capitalism in all its historical predecessors', Wood develops a sophisticated interpretation of the history of democracy in which systematic comparisons are drawn between Athenian democracy, the Roman republic, feudal absolutism and representative democracy (1995: 14). These comparisons enable Wood to identify the specific characteristics of representative democracy, and subject this particular form of democracy to a persuasive and powerful critique.

In emphasising the specificity of capitalism, Wood is drawing upon a crucially important distinction within Marxian methodology. At various points in their writings, Marx and Engels define clearly the different methodological functions of theoretical concepts deployed at distinctively transhistorical and historical levels of abstraction (see Marx, 1967a: 18–19, 167–70; 1967b: 814–31; 1970: 27–32; 1971: 453–519; 1973a: 83–8, 100–8; 1975a: 201, 207; 1975b: 141–2; Marx and Engels, 1975: 34, 293, 393.) Within the materialist conception of history, transhistorical concepts such as the forces and relations of production are used, first to identify and distinguish the various forms of society that have emerged in the broad sweep of history, and second to act as an initial heuristic guide for the historically specific analyses of particular societies that Marx considered necessary in order to discover the 'historical laws which are valid only for a particular historical development' (1975a: 34). In other words, it is only possible to develop a systematic Marxist understanding of a particular society, characterised by a specific mode of production, through an empirically grounded analysis of the 'real, transitory, historic social relations' (1975a, 34). This is necessary because 'events strikingly analogous but taking place in different historical contexts' can lead to 'totally different results' (Marx and Engels, 1975: 294). As Marx observes: 'By studying each of these forms of evolution separately and then comparing them one can easily find the clue to this phenomenon, but one will never arrive there by using as one's master key a general historic-philosophical theory, the supreme virtue of which consists in being supra-historical' (Marx and Engels, 1975: 294).[1] The heuristic role of transhistorical concepts within the materialist conception of history is thus both crucially important, providing preliminary conceptual guidance for historical research, and strictly limited, since historical explanation requires us

---

1 Sayer (1987: 12) observes that 'this passage … is much cited … but without due consideration for how it affects the interpretation of [Marx's] methodological fundamentals'.

to bring out 'empirically, and without any mystification and speculation, the connection of the social and political structure with production' (Marx and Engels, 1976: 41).

Marx's (1967b: 791) theorem that understanding the underlying process of exploitation 'in which unpaid surplus-labour is pumped out of direct producers' is the key to understanding 'the relationship of rulers and ruled' in a particular society combines a transhistorical definition of exploitation as the appropriation of surplus product by a non-producing class from a producing class, with a powerful methodological injunction to engage in historically specific analyses of particular social forms of exploitation. This is exemplified by Marx's own critical analysis of capitalist exploitation in Volume One of *Capital*, and Ste Croix's (1981) unsurpassed analysis of the forms of exploitation in the ancient Greek world. The point is that the potential fruitfulness of historical materialism is most clearly evident, not at the transhistorical level of abstraction required to apply it as a general theory of history, but rather in the historically specific analyses heuristically guided, in the first instance, by the transhistorical concepts of the general theory.

The continuing vitality of the central heuristic impulse of historical materialism is the third respect in which the Marxist tradition provides a potentially illuminating foundation for considering democracy's past, present and future. The inescapable reality is that all forms of democracy rest upon specific social and economic infrastructures and can only be understood adequately in relation to these infrastructures. But what historical materialism contributes that is distinctive and of value is not simply, or even primarily, a heuristic emphasis on the importance of analysing this relationship empirically and historically. Rather, sophisticated historical materialists insist that any particular democratic state form can only be properly analysed as part of a dynamic totality that is internally complex, mediated and contradictory. Whether or not, and if so how and why, the relationship between rulers and ruled is ultimately determined by an underlying process of exploitation can only be ascertained through theoretically informed historically grounded analysis of the specific totality within which a particular democratic state form is situated. This facilitates and guides detailed historical research which focuses, among other things, upon the level of development of the forces of production, the relations of production, process of surplus extraction, formation and structural differentiation of social classes and class fractions, class consciousness, the 'political forms of class struggle and its results, such as constitutions established by the victorious class after a successful battle', juridical forms, ideologies, religion, political parties, and the ensemble of institutions and practices constituting any particular state form (Marx and Engels, 1975: 394–5).

Fourth, historical materialism's breadth of historical focus helps to establish that social reality is in a constant state of flux and that all forms of democracy exist only in fluid movement. With respect to the broad sweep of history this movement involves the rise, persistence and eventual decline of particular democratic state forms; within a given epoch it can involve the progression, stagnation or retrogression of democracy. This change is generated by fundamental contradictions internal to societies understood as historical totalities. The precise ways in which these contradictions generate developmental tendencies and recurrent crises are complex because the relationships within totalities are highly interactive and mediated. Nonetheless, the recognition of the 'reciprocal action' within historical totalities does not imply indeterminacy because contradictions involve clashes between real forces in society (Bhaskar, 1989: 120–1). This makes the identification of causal relationships possible through theoretically informed and historically grounded analysis. Finally, the contradictions within historical totalities that generate change unify opposites. For example, the bourgeoisie and the proletariat exist as conjoined yet antagonistic classes in which there is contradictory interaction and conflict between them, and this interaction and conflict is characterised by a degree of directionality that can be ascertained through analysis.

Fifth, developing a rigorous critique of capitalism and representative democracy necessarily involves the deployment of both breadth and depth of historical focus. Depth of historical focus is required in order, among other things, to demonstrate the extent to which capitalism limits and constrains democracy. Breadth of historical focus is necessary in order to appreciate the historical brevity of all earlier and contemporary modes of production and democratic state forms. Further, adopting a broad view of history, and of the place of capitalism and representative democracy within it, helps us to remain genuinely open to the realities and potentialities of change, not just small incremental change, but that resulting from qualitative societal transformation. As Korsch observes:

> Bourgeois society may contain the relations of earlier societies in a further developed form. It may contain them as well in degenerate, stunted and travestied forms .... It like-wise contains within itself the germs of future developments of present society, though by no means their complete determination. The false idealistic concept of evolution as applied by bourgeois social theorists, is closed on both sides, and in all past and future forms of society rediscovers only itself. The new, critical and materialistic Marxist principle of development is, on the other hand, open on both sides.
>
> (Korsch, 1971: 35)

The reformist view that capitalism could be changed in an emancipatory and egalitarian direction either through, or at least while retaining, liberal representative democracy as the institutional framework for governance rests on a closed view of historical development. The notion that somehow it would be possible to transform, or even radically alter, the capitalist infrastructure while retaining essentially the same state form is fundamentally unrealistic in view of the historical persistence of inextricably close connections between democratic state forms and the underlying social and economic infrastructures which sustain them. In reality what lies beneath this notion is the much more banal bourgeois assumption that there is no conceivably feasible and desirable future beyond capitalism. History ends with capitalism. In this respect Fukuyama's (1989, 1992) central contention continues to prevail amongst the bulk of the western intelligentsia – both those politically to the right and, more surprisingly, a section of the left as well.

This alludes to the sixth respect in which historical materialism remains indispensable, not only for the investigation of the history of democracy, but also for those engaged in the struggle for a more democratic world than that which we currently inhabit. Marx (1967a: 21) wrote in 1872 that 'There is no royal road to science, and only those who do not dread the fatiguing climb of its steep paths have a chance of gaining its luminous summits.' But what did Marx see from the vantage point of the luminous summits of his historical social science? There is no simple answer because what is so spectacular about the view from the top of a mountain is precisely the breadth of vision – not only can we see for a considerably greater distance than at sea level, we can also see for a greater distance in every direction. In this respect, Marx had a uniquely broad historical vision because he could see beyond capitalism. In a justly famous comment on Hegel's dialectical method, Marx (1967a: 20) wrote that this method was a 'scandal and abomination to bourgeoisdom and its doctrinaire professors ... because it regards every historically developed social form as in fluid movement and therefore takes into account its transient nature no less than its momentary existence'. Thus as Ollman (1990: 32) accurately observes, 'history for Marx refers not only to time past but to future time. Whatever something is becoming – whether we know what that will be or not – is in some important respects part of what it is along with what it once was.' If we view the broad sweep of history from this perspective, the historical terrain occupied by capitalism is no longer all that we can see, because the temporal horizon stretches from distant past to distant future.

This is not to suggest that the view from Marx's luminous summits is necessarily pretty. Viewing capitalist history reminds us that 'capitalism is at one and the same time the best thing that has ever happened to the human race and the worst' (Jameson quoted by Callinicos, 1995: 153). We will consider the respects in which capitalism can be considered historically progressive shortly. Here it is important to note the respects in which capitalism is the worst thing that has happened to the human race. Marx and Engels analysed and highlighted the contradictory nature of capitalist development, in which, among other things, the advancement of human productive powers simultaneously advances human capacities to destroy other people and the natural environment. But they did not live to witness the horrors that capitalism would unleash on humankind and the environment during the twentieth century.

Leading figures in classical Marxism, particularly Lenin, Luxemburg and Trotsky, from 1914 to 1917 had to contend with nationalist hysteria, the leaderships of social democratic parties throughout Europe betraying the most basic principles of international socialism, and the ensuing mechanised killing of millions of workers and peasants during the First World War. Luxemburg (1970a: 262) observed:

> Business is flourishing upon the ruins. Cities are turned into shambles, whole countries into deserts, villages into cemeteries, whole nations into beggars, churches into stables; popular rights, treaties, alliances, the holiest words and the highest authorities have been torn into scraps; every sovereign by the grace of God is called a fool, an unfaithful wretch, by his cousin on the other side; every diplomat calls his colleague in the enemy's country a desperate criminal; each government looks upon the other as the evil genius of its people, worthy only of the contempt of the world. Hunger revolts ... misery and desperation everywhere. Shamed, dishonoured, wading in blood and dripping with filth, thus capitalist society stands.
>
> (Luxemburg, 1970a: 262)

Although Lenin, Luxemburg and Trotsky shared the view that the fall of capitalism was inevitable, their concrete experiences as revolutionaries led them to reject the idea that the victory of the proletariat was also inevitable. Capitalist crises, inter-imperialist rivalries, and war created circumstances that could culminate in proletarian revolution and the creation of socialism, but it could also create circumstances culminating in the collapse of civilisation and historical retrogression to barbarism. The choice that confronted the international proletariat in the historical long term was 'either the triumph of imperialism and the destruction of all culture, and, as in ancient Rome, depopulation, desolation, degeneration, a vast cemetery; or the victory of socialism, that is, the conscious struggle of the international proletariat against imperialism, against its methods, against war' (Luxemburg, 1970a: 269).

This conception of capitalist development culminating in either socialism or barbarism constitutes a significant advance upon the conception of proletarian revolution in *The Communist Manifesto*. In the *Manifesto,* Marx and Engels observe:

> Freemen and slaves, patrician and plebeian, lord and serf, guild-master and journeyman, in a word, oppressor and oppressed, stood in constant opposition to one another, carried on an uninterrupted, now hidden, now open fight, a fight that each time ended, either in a revolutionary reconstitution of society at large, or in the common ruin of the contending classes.
>
> (Marx and Engels, 1998: 35)

But this non-teleological conception of historical and revolutionary change stands in tension with another, more optimistic and teleological conception: 'What the bourgeoisie therefore produces, above all, are its own grave-diggers. Its fall and the victory of the proletariat are equally inevitable' (Marx and Engels, 1998: 50).

Those Marxists who endured the rise of fascism and Stalinism, and the Second World War, were confronted with the repeated triumph of barbarism over the kind of socialism envisaged by the classical Marxists. This calls to mind Benjamin's depiction of the angel of history – eyes staring, mouth open, wings spread, face turned toward the past, seeing instead of a chain of events, 'one single catastrophe which keeps piling wreckage upon wreckage and hurls it in front of his feet' (Benjamin, 1992: 249). Although this angel would like to 'awaken the dead, and make whole what has been smashed', he cannot because the storm blowing from paradise 'has got caught in his wings with such violence that [he] can no longer close them. This storm irresistibly propels him into the future to which his back is turned, while the pile of debris before him grows skyward. This storm is what we call progress' (1992: 249). In the wake of Hiroshima, holocaust and gulag, historical materialism envisages a range of possible futures beyond capitalism, without clinging to the optimistic teleological conception of the inevitability of socialism. In this respect, historical materialism is, as Callinicos (1995: 163) aptly puts it, 'a theory of historical trajectories' which holds that 'each historical crisis has more than one possible outcome, and the general course of history does not follow a predetermined linear path. The actual, contingent outcome of progress may be catastrophe, "the common ruin of the contending classes".' From this perspective, 'the suffering consequent on the development of the productive forces is not denied or explained away; at best it may be redeemed when revolution allows the victims of progress, or their proletarian descendants, to take control of these forces' (1995: 163).

Capitalism's brief historical existence has been characterised by constant change, rapid development, recurrent crises, class struggle, two world wars, and revolutionary upheavals. There is no reason to suspect that it will persist longer than earlier civilizations that were characterised by a considerably greater degree of internal stability, and indeed the weight of evidence suggests that its historical life will be considerably shorter. Once it is fully appreciated that what is will not always be, we can begin to understand the respects in which the present is a mediating moment between the past and future, and see in it 'the tendencies out of whose dialectical opposition [we] can *make the future*' (Lukacs, 1971: 204).

This leads us to consider the seventh respect in which historical materialism remains indispensable to making sense of the past, present and future of democracy. Marx, Engels and the major figures in classical Marxism made what remains a profoundly original contribution to the consideration of democracy in western political thought: a systematic defence not only of the basic principles of direct participatory democracy with a lineage that can be traced back to Athenian democracy, but of the desirability, feasibility and necessity of self-governance by labouring citizens in order to transcend all major forms of exploitation, oppression and alienation.[2] For Marxists, this

---

2 Wolff (2000: 117) correctly insists, 'Only insofar as democratic movements commit

is not a utopian dream because the internal contradictions of capitalism undermine it from within, not only driving the capitalist system into crisis, but simultaneously creating the collective agency that has the social structural capacity to transform it. In stark contrast to this vision of the possible transcendence of capitalism and representative democracy through the establishment of a radically democratic socialist society, all of the 'great thinkers' in western political philosophy, from the Socratic philosophers of classical Antiquity to Nietzsche and the poststructuralist philosophers of the late twentieth century, have denied the feasibility and/or desirability of self-governance by the associated producers.

When viewed historically the positive achievements of capitalism and representative democracy are clear, including tremendous development of the forces of production, the extension of citizenship rights and civil liberties to a substantial majority of the adult population, and establishing an elective principle in the selection of representatives. But these have always been encapsulated in the classical Marxist conception of the transcendence of representative democracy. The concept of transcendence implies, not simple abandonment, but the incorporation of the best elements of the lower form of democracy in a higher, more developed form – in this case, socialist participatory democracy. Of course, the concept of transcendence is currently unfashionable. But those who abandon or reject Marxism risk losing the field of vision that is obtainable only if we retain a sophisticated historical sense of the dynamic and transitive nature of all social and political forms, and a clear conception of the creative powers and potentialities of the associated producers to collectively transform and transcend capitalism and representative democracy in the twenty-first century.

GUIDE TO READING THIS BOOK

The broadly chronological structure of this book means that it can be used to provide an introduction to a particular period in the history of democracy, or read in its entirety in order to provide a condensed overview of democracy from its origins to the present. A guide to further reading at the end of each chapter identifies the major works in the area, and alerts the reader to the range of alternative interpretations both within and beyond the Marxist tradition. In order to grasp the overall conceptual analysis of the history of democracy, you will need to read the book in its entirety. Although it is not divided into parts, Chapters 1 (Athenian democracy) and 2 (Roman republic) focus on the origins of democracy in classical Antiquity, Chapters 3 (transition from feudalism to capitalism), 4 (English Revolution), 5 (American Revolution), 6 (French Revolution), 7 (1848 revolutions), and 8 (democratisation during the twentieth

---

to including the class structures of a society (the particular ways in which surplus labour is organized and its fruits distributed) among the actual objects of demo-cratic decision-making do they include ... the distinctive Marxist contribution to the democratic project.'

century) focus on the history of liberal representative democracy, and the final two chapters outline the Marxist critique of capitalism and representative democracy and the history of socialist participatory democracy respectively. The final chapter also serves as the conclusion to the book, because the history of socialist participatory democracy as a fully functioning system of societal governance is yet to be made.

GUIDE TO FURTHER READING

The best discussion of the difficulties associated with defining the term 'democracy' is in Williams (1993); also see Held (2006: 1–5). For general accounts of the history of democracy in the Marxist tradition, Novack (1971) is useful and Therborn (1978) less so. Wood (1995: 181–237) presents a Marxist interpretation of the history of democracy that is congruent with my own. There are a number of excellent general histories written from Marxist perspectives: Anderson (1974a, 1974b), Harman (1999), Hobsbawm (1962, 1975, 1987, 1995) and Wallerstein (1974, 1980, 1989). While these are not centrally or specifically focused on the history of democracy, they identify the broad historical contexts within which the major episodes in the history of democracy can be situated. Held (2006) and Dahl (1989, 1998) provide useful general accounts from non-Marxist perspectives. Callinicos (1991) provides the best Marxist critique of those who have interpreted the collapse of East European Stalinism as constituting a world-historic failure of Marxism. Holden (1993) provides the best textbook style defence of liberalism and representative democracy against the kind of arguments that I will be making throughout this book.

An extremely useful and reliable general introduction to Marx is provided by Callinicos (1983). Ollman (2003: 9–83) provides the clearest account I know of Marx's method of rational abstraction, which he considers to be 'Marx's way of putting dialectics to work'. A somewhat less clear but more comprehensive discussion of the employment of the dialectic in the Marxist tradition is provided by Rees (1998). While it is not entirely reliable, the best account of Marx's delineation of the distinctive methodological roles of transhistorical and historically specific concepts is still Sayer (1983: 77–149; also see 1987: 126–49). Critical realist interpretations of Marx's method abound, but one of the most important statements remains Bhaskar (1989: 66–88; also see Callinicos, 1983: 114–26; Collier, 1989; Mepham and Ruben, 1979). For a useful introduction to Marx and Engels's view of the state see Miliband (1977: 66–106).

1
Origins: democracy in the ancient Greek world

INTRODUCTION

Democracy was introduced into the Athenian city-state with the reforms of Cleisthenes in 508–7 BC, reaching its height while Pericles was a leading political figure from around 461 to 429, before being suppressed briefly in the wake of the defeat of Athens by the oligarchic city-state Sparta in the Peloponnesian War in 404. Democracy was soon revived, however, in 403 and persisted in a modified form until 322–1.

There is doubt whether this constituted the first democratic city-state in history, since there is some evidence that democratic institutions, practices, and principles emerged even earlier in Sparta and amongst the Phoenicians (Hornblower, 1992: 1–2). Keane (2009: xi) confidently argues that democracy was certainly 'not a Greek invention.' But even if it is the case, as Keane (2009: xi) argues, that the bulk of existing historical scholarship is wrong in claiming that democracy was a Greek invention and in fact popular self-government originated in western Asia, invented by peoples and lands that 'geographically correspond to contemporary Syria, Iraq and Iran', there can be no doubt that Athenian democracy was easily the most significant, advanced and influential form of democratic governance to emerge in classical Antiquity. It is of world historic significance, among other things because since its suppression in 322 BC, it has been viewed by intellectuals, political rulers and advocates of participatory democracy as the first fully fledged and sustained system of democracy in history (Ste Croix, 1981: 284; Raaflaub, 2007a: 1–14).

THE HISTORICAL EMERGENCE OF ATHENIAN DEMOCRACY

Why did democracy emerge in the Greek city-states of classical Antiquity? Why did Attica, as the Athenian city-state was then known, rise to prominence in the fifth and fourth centuries BC as the most culturally, intellectually and politically advanced and democratic of these city-states? The background to the emergence of democracy in Attica was the prolonged re-emergence of Greek civilization from rudimentary peasant communities from 800 to 500 BC. There is insufficient evidence for us to be certain of the underlying causes of the revival and growth of Greek civilisation during these centuries, but there seem to be several interrelated and mutually reinforcing key factors. First, 'The eighth century is the period when iron replaces bronze as the main working metal in Greece' (Osborne, 2004: 24). Because iron can be produced much more cheaply than bronze, it makes possible the large-scale production of weapons and tools. In particular the scratch plough and other iron tools were used to cultivate 'lighter rain-watered soils', and this meant that 'settled agriculture, rain watered and not dependent on artificial irrigation, was boosted, and the peasant farmer grew as an economic and military power' (Mann, 1986: 185). This led to an expansion of trade and greater interaction with other societies, which might also have helped peasant farmers to discover, or rediscover, more effective agricultural tools and techniques. The absence of extensive irrigation, unreliability of rainfall in the Aegean zone, and existence of a wide range of microclimates due to the geographical location and hilly topography of the classical Greek city-states, meant that crop specialization was rare: a mixture of grains, pulses, olives and vines was typically planted (Millett, 2000: 27).

As Anderson observes, 'The classical world was massively, unalterably rural in its basic quantitative proportions. Agriculture represented throughout its history the absolutely dominant domain of production, invariably furnishing the main fortunes of the cities themselves' (1974a: 19). Consequently, increasing agricultural productivity was of crucial importance and a necessary precondition for urbanisation, because 'The Graeco-Roman towns were never predominantly communities of manufacturers, traders or craftsmen: they were, in origin and principle, urban congeries of landowners' (1974a: 19).

The second set of material factors that contributed to the revival of Greek civilisation arose from the strategic geographical location of the Greek city-states in general, and Attica in particular. As Mann (1986: 196) observes, 'What distinguished Greece was its marchland position between Europe and the Near East. The closest of the European ploughed lands to Near Eastern civilization, with its promontory and islands it was most likely to intercept trade and cultural exchange between the two.' As this suggests, the Greek city-states were predominantly coastal precisely because 'marine transport was the sole viable means of commodity exchange over medium or long distances' (Anderson, 1974a: 20). The growth of sea trade from the eighth to the fifth centuries stimulated the development of well-placed coastal cities, some of which came to enjoy periods of progressive growth. Athens had a seaport strategically located at the centre of the Aegean zone. As Raaflaub (2007b: 118) observes, by the mid-fifth century Athens had 'developed into a large, economically and demographically diverse community that became the economic centre of the Greek world. A vast infrastructure and a whole industry, encompassing many trades, was created to build and maintain three hundred ships and to support the required personnel.'

The growth of agricultural output in the lands surrounding the Mediterranean and an associated growth of sea trade underpinned the emergence of the urban pattern of classical civilization from 800 to 500 BC (Anderson, 1974a: 29).

By the mid-sixth century 'there were some 1,500 Greek cities in the Hellenic homelands and abroad – virtually none of them more than 25 miles inland from the coastline' (1974a: 29). Essentially these cities were:

> residential nodes of concentration for farmers and landowners: in the typical small town of this epoch, the cultivators lived within the walls of the city and went out to work in the fields every day, returning at night – although the territory of the cities always included an agrarian circumference with a wholly rural population settled in it.
>
> (Anderson, 1974a: 29-30)

These cities not only acted as service centres for their rural hinterland, they were also nodal points for trade because Greek ships did not directly traverse the Mediterranean, but rather 'preferred to keep in sight of land for navigational and supply reasons, creeping around coasts and islands, calling in at a series of ports and staging posts' (Mann, 1986: 205).

The rise of Attica as the pre-eminent city-state or *polis* was also due to the mines in Laureion (south-east Attica), which worked the largest deposits of silver-bearing ore in the ancient Greek world. As Osborne (1985: 111) observes, 'silver was certainly "the most important Athenian resource, exported in substantial quantities" and it is possible that it was the only significant Athenian export'. These mines were worked by the heaviest concentration of chattel slaves in Attica, 10–20,000 out of an estimated total slave population of 80–100,000 (Millett, 2000: 36; Osborne, 1985: 111; cf. Anderson, 1974a: 40; Wood, 1988: 43). Silver mining not only provided raw material for a coin currency, the profits also flowed into the public treasury (the precise mechanisms are unclear) and enabled the construction of a powerful navy early in the fifth century (Millett, 2000: 37). A substantial proportion of the aristocratic propertied class derived at least some of their wealth from owning and/or leasing silver mines (Osborne, 1985: 112–26). According to Millett: 'mining operations were largely the preserve of the wealthiest members of the population …. Details of approximately 180 leases survive in inscriptions from the fourth century, and the lessees include a high proportion of Athenians (about one third) known to be wealthy and prominent in other fields, including politics'(Millett 2000, 36–7).

Attica's strategic location, these highly profitable silver mines and the comparatively productive system of agriculture go some way towards explaining its growing prominence, but do not explain why it was in this city-state that democracy first emerged. Of the other growing city-states in the region, Crete and Sparta, for example, were oligarchic and Macedonia had a monarchy. To find an explanation we need to focus on the unique internal social, economic and political developments in Athenian society that helped to give it a different historical trajectory.

Little is known about the largely peasant communities that survived the mysterious collapse of the Mycenaean kingdom around the twelfth century BC and the 'Dark Age' that persisted until the eighth century. But as Wood

(1988: 90) observes, 'When Greek society re-emerges from the obscurity of the Dark Age, one feature is especially striking: the presence of a clearly defined ruling class, a privileged nobility based on individual property.' This class accumulated its wealth through the exploitation of peasants by means of a range of tributary relations including tenancy, serfdom, debt bondage and chattel slavery (a process about which we shall have more to say shortly). Ste Croix (1981: 112) observes that 'The ownership of land and the power to exact unfree labour, largely united in the hands of the same class, together constitute, therefore, the main keys to the class structure of the ancient Greek communities.' As this suggests, wealthy landowners exerted ongoing political as well as economic dominance over the city-states that emerged from the eighth to the fifth centuries, and as far as we know, reproduced themselves as hereditary aristocracies.

By the late sixth century this hereditary landowning aristocracy was being besieged, both by upwardly mobile and wealthy members of the dominant propertied class who did not belong to the nobility, and by an increasingly disgruntled and militant *demos* consisting of middling and poor peasants, as well as free labourers and artisans. In sum, during this period society became increasingly divided between 'the hereditary ruling aristocrats, who were by and large the principal landowners and who entirely monopolised political power' and, at least initially, 'all other social classes sometimes together called the demos' (Ste Croix, 1981: 280).

The struggle within the ruling class, as the newly wealthy increasingly challenged the political dominance of the aristocratic ruling families, as well as the struggles between these affluent groups and the peasant farmers, intensified between the mid-seventh and late sixth centuries (Ste Croix, 1981: 280). Surplus extraction in Athens during this period seems to have increasingly taken the form of debt bondage (1981: 136–7, 162–70). A growing portion of the peasant farmers were becoming impoverished because, as tenants, they were forced to pay one-sixth of their produce to the landowner. Thorley observes that:

> The system almost certainly originated from the transfer of the land of owner farmers under some kind of mortgage to rich creditors as a result of debt. The *hektemorioi* [tenant farmers] then agreed to pay as rent one-sixth of their produce to the landowner, and markers were fixed in the ground to indicate that the land was held in this fashion. In the latter part of the seventh century many *hektemorioi* had found themselves unable to pay the sixth part to the landowner, and been forced to sell themselves and their families as slaves to the landowner. By about 600 the situation was one of seething unrest.
>
> (Thorley, 1996: 10)

A bitterly internally divided ruling class was in no position to respond effectively to this dramatic rise in struggle from below. Furthermore, it could not rely on a strong centralised state with a large standing army to suppress the masses. 'Athens in the seventh century ... was firmly governed by the aristocracy through the archons backed by the Council of the Areopagos' (Thorley, 1996: 10). Archons were the principal administrative rulers with responsibility for directing civil, military and religious affairs. By the mid-seventh century, there were nine archons and they held these positions for a maximum term of ten years. Representatives of the most prominent aristocratic families gathered in the Council of the Areopagos, which was the central governing body because it had 'oversight of the laws, the magistrates, the politically active citizens, and the general conduct of all Athenians, and it could pronounce judgement, [including] the death sentence, in political trials' (Hansen, 1991: 37). Nonetheless, despite its political dominance of the Athenian city-state, the aristocracy lacked the kind of extensive repressive apparatus required to decisively crush an increasingly rebellious peasantry. Since the bulk of the Athenian army was composed of peasants, this meant that the peasants possessed arms and military experience. For this reason, if members of the aristocracy wanted to suppress internal rebellion, they had to enlist an outside military force, such as the Spartan army. Such a course of action risked further fanning the flames of revolt and so was generally avoided.

In this context, the more politically astute members of the ruling class were prepared to accept a substantial degree of reform in order to ensure the continued viability of Athenian society, and hence of their own privileged position. Solon, who was part of the aristocracy but a merchant rather than a landowner, which distanced him from the feuding noble families, was appointed an archon in 594. Either then, or more probably during the years following his appointment, he introduced a comprehensive set of economic and constitutional reforms.

There is no doubt at all about Solon's perfectly serious conception of his own role, as a would-be impartial arbitrator in a situation of severe class strife, who was pressed by the demos to make himself tyrant, but refused. Although Solon also refused to make a general redistribution of the land, as demanded by the impoverished lower classes, he did take the extraordinary step of cancelling all debts, and he forbade for the future not merely the enslavement for debt but also any kind of debt bondage, by the simple expedient of prohibiting the giving of the body as security.

(Ste Croix, 1981: 281–2)

The central economic reform, cancelling the debts of tenant farmers, was captured in the phrase 'shaking off the burdens'. The hated markers on the land of the *hektemorioi* were removed, there could no longer be enslavement for debt, no foodstuffs could be exported except for olive oil, and other measures aimed at stimulating economic growth were introduced.

Debt bondage involved more than a purely financial arrangement between wealthy landowners and poor peasants because the peasants agreed to fulfil a set of rent or tribute obligations. As Wood (1988: 94) emphasises, 'in Solon's day Athens could hardly be considered a money economy'. Consequently, 'the "debts" which Solon cancelled were the obligations of rent or tribute owed by a dependent peasant to a lord. The practice of enslavement for debt [was thus] part of a more general system of dependence.' For this reason Wood (1988: 95) considers that Solon's reform 'constitutes a more substantial structural change than the cancellation of debt in the narrow sense would suggest, abolishing the last remaining forms of dependence and tribute to which Athenian peasants were subject'.

  While Solon's economic reforms involved major concessions to the peasantry to stave off revolutionary tumult, his constitutional reforms also addressed the tension between factions in the propertied classes:

> In reforming the constitution Solon saw it as essential to break the hold of the aristocratic families on the government of the state. So far the power of the archons, who were always chosen from members of the noble families and backed by the Areopagas, had been in effect absolute. Solon was intent on broadening the power structure of government, to include especially those who had substantial wealth and property ... but who were not from the noble families.
>
> (Thorley, 1996: 13)

He began by codifying four classes of Athenians: the *pentakosiomedimnoi*, who owned estates which produced annually at least 500 *medimnoi* (both a dry and a liquid measure of produce); the *hippeis*, 'horsemen, knights', who produced 300–500 *medimnoi*; the *zeugitai*, who produced 200–300 *medimnoi* and who were wealthy enough to pay for their own armour, and constituted the *hoplitai*, or fully armed infantrymen; and the *thetes*, who produced less than 200 *medimnoi* per year. As Thorley (1996: 14) observes, the word *thetes* 'originally meant a serf, a man bound to his master and to his land, but later the word referred to any hired labourer. ... this class must have included at least half, and in Solon's time probably considerably more, of the total citizen population'.

  Chief among the reforms was the establishment of a new Council of Four Hundred, consisting of 100 members from each of the four tribes, drawn from the top three classes (Hansen, 1991: 30–1; Thorley, 1996: 13–14). Second, 'The Assembly was now open to all four property classes, that is to all male citizens' but the powers of the Assembly, including the scope of its decision making, remained very limited, and the aristocratic Council of the Areopagas consisting of all ex-archons remained in place (although henceforth archons were elected from amongst the entire *pentakosiomedimnoi* class rather than being appointed by the nobility) (1996: 15–16). Third:

> A new court system was introduced in which all property classes were included as jurors, and any citizen could appeal to these new courts against

the decision of one of the archons. The new courts did not replace the legal function of the archons [who acted as judges presiding over serious cases], but they were a democratic check on their powers.

(Thorley, 1996: 15)

Finally, Solon provided a codification of law that formed the juridical foundation of Athenian society until the abolition of democracy in 322 (Hansen, 1991: 31).

It seems likely that Solon's reforms succeeded in re-establishing and maintaining the political stability of Athenian society, primarily because they granted major concessions to the peasantry, thus averting the revolutionary seizure of the wealth of the aristocratic families. At the same time, the reforms made the ownership of property rather than aristocratic descent the basis of political office holding. Nonetheless, in the years following Solon's reforms 'there was considerably turmoil, not because [they] were in themselves unworkable but because the most powerful noble families continued to contend amongst themselves for control of the system' (Thorley, 1996: 17). In 560 BC Peisistratos, who was a determined and skilled leader of his ruling class faction, took power as tyrant. Although Peisistratos was challenged on several occasions, he remained in power until his death in 527. The length of his rule was due to his skill in ostracising the Alkmeonid family and its supporters from Attica, and his ability to develop popular support amongst the peasantry (primarily by retaining the substance of Solon's reforms and extending them – he offered peasants state loans paid back at the rate of 10 per cent of their produce). His eldest son, Hippias, assumed the mantle of power following his death. However, he lacked his father's political acumen, and became a brutal and hated tyrant who was eventually removed in revolutionary circumstances.

CLASS STRUGGLE IN THE ANCIENT GREEK *POLIS*

As Ste Croix observes, the rise of the tyrants such as Peisistratos and Hippias was ultimately an expression of the intensified intra- and inter-class struggles that occurred during the century that preceded the establishment of democracy in Athens. Tyrants were generally upwardly mobile and wealthy members of the dominant propertied class who did not belong to the nobility, and therefore had limited political influence. In challenging the traditional political dominance of the aristocracy, they could often draw on the popular backing of the *demos:*

For Aristotle, there was an essential distinction between the two Greek forms of *monarchia* (*one-man-rule*), namely *basileia*, traditional kingship according to established forms of law, and *tyrannis*, the rule of tyrant. They differed in their very origin. Kingship, says Aristotle, 'came into existence for the purpose of helping the better classes ... against the demos ... whereas tyrants arose 'from among the common people and the masses, in opposition to the notables, so that the demos should not suffer injustice at their hands …. The great majority of the tyrants began as demagogues, so to speak, and won confidence by calumniating the notables.

(Ste Croix, 1981: 283)

Eventually the struggles in which the tyrants took power and were subsequently deposed created a situation in which all members of the ruling class could participate in governing the *polis,* regardless of whether or not they belonged to the nobility.

When the rule of the Greek tyrants ended, as it usually did after a short period, of a generation or two, hereditary aristocratic dominance had disappeared, except in a few places, and had been succeeded by a much more 'open' society: political power no longer rested on decent, on blue blood, but was mainly dependent upon the possession of property (this now became the standard form of Greek oligarchy), and in many cities, such as Athens, it was later extended in theory to all citizens, in a democracy.

(Ste Croix, 1981: 279–80)

The fact that political power was extended to the entire citizen body in Athens was ultimately an outcome of what Ste Croix refers to as 'the class struggle on the political plane' (I discuss this concept at greater length later: see pages 30–3). The point to note here is that the struggles of the subordinate classes in the *demos* often underpinned the rise to power of a tyrant:

The movement might often begin as a simple revolt by the demos, or (more usually) some sections of it, against oppression and exploitation, simmering possibly for years and breaking out only when a willing and capable leader presented himself – a leader, perhaps, whose aims eventually turned out to be mainly selfish.

(Ste Croix, 1981: 281)

By 510, the tyrant Hippias was increasingly unpopular. Cleisthenes, a member of the aristocratic Alkmeonid family that had been sent into exile by Peisistratos, gained support from one of the Spartan kings (Cleomenes) to help him overthrow Hippias. They achieved this with relative ease but Cleisthenes immediately encountered opposition from the other prominent aristocratic families, led by Isagoras, who was staunchly committed to the continuation of the political rule of Attica by an aristocratic elite. Isagoras managed to get himself appointed as an archon in 508, then enlisted the support of the Spartans in order to overturn the constitution established by Solon's reforms and establish the rule of an aristocratic oligarchy. As Thorley observes, with Spartan support:

Isagora now exiled the Alkeonids [including Cleisthenes] … together with many other families, and tried to dismantle the constitution and set up a council of his own supporters. This [provoked] a riot in Athens, and Isagoras and his Spartan supporters found themselves besieged on the Acropolis by the angry populace, who saw all that had been gained by Solon's reforms fast disappearing.

(Thorley, 1996: 21)

Cleisthenes was reinstalled in power by this popular movement. He then proceeded to introduce to Athens 'the most radical democracy in the ancient world' (Thorley, 1996: 21). Essentially, democracy arose in Athens out of the fires of a revolutionary uprising by peasants, artisans and free labourers.

In an interesting account of these events, Ober (2007) convincingly argues that we should reject a 'great man' interpretation in which Cleisthenes is portrayed as cunningly manipulating the ignorant masses from above. Solon's reforms empowered the bulk of the peasantry by enabling citizens from all property classes to participate in the law courts. These reforms 'and the civic festivals sponsored by the tyrants had undercut traditional lines of authority and encouraged Athenian political self-consciousness. By 508 B.C.E. the ordinary Athenian male was no longer a politically passive client of a great house. He had begun to view himself as a citizen rather than as a subject' (Ober, 2007: 86–7). This account can be strengthened by adding an emphasis on the continuing tension and conflict between the landowning aristocracy and the peasantry, which had been contained but not extinguished by Solon's reforms, and persisted throughout the sixth century. The attempt by Isagoras and his aristocratic faction to overturn Solon's reforms was likely to have been perceived – accurately – by the peasant citizenry as motivated by a desire to increase the burdens that the landowning aristocracy could impose on the peasantry (for example, by increasing rents and re-establishing debt bondage). Consequently, it is likely that:

Cleisthenes' leadership and the successful implementation of the reforms associated with his name are responses to the revolutionary situation, and so it is not Cleisthenes but the Athenian demos (qua citizen body) that is the protagonist. ... The events of the year 508–7 constitute a genuine rupture in Athenian political history, because they mark the moment at which the demos stepped onto the historical stage as a collective agent, a historical actor in its own right and under its own name.

(Ober, 2007: 86)

CLEISTHENES'S REFORMS: ESTABLISHING *DEMOKRATIA*

To overcome the incessant feuding between the aristocratic families of the four Ionic tribes, and establish the foundations for the new democracy, Cleisthenes broke up the old tribes and established ten new tribes, 'each consisting of a section of the city of Athens, a section of the coastal area, and section of the inland region' (Thorley, 1996: 23). The *deme* or village became the basic unit of the new state. Wood argues that this is highly significant because

Cleisthenes' system of *demes* 'had the effect of reposing political power in the ordinary people of Athens, the demos, to a degree unprecedented in the known ancient world' (1988: 105). As Ober observes:

the reform was sweeping, amounting to a rupture in the way that public space and time were imagined. The new system of local authority at the level of the demes enforced a startlingly new conception of each man's claim to citizenship as directly dependent upon a decision of his fellow citizens as a voting group: one's claim to merit citizenship, based on one's legitimate birth, was now to be a matter judged by one's fellow demesmen. Thus, by making 'the inhabitants in each of the demes fellow demesmen of one another' [Aristotle], the new constitution placed directly in the hands of ordinary men the power to decide the momentous question 'Who is fit to be one of us?' From that moment on, at the highly charged moment at which he sought to have his son recognized by the community as an adult Athenian, and thus regarded as worthy of all the immunities and all the participation rights of the citizen, the wealthy aristocrat and the landless labourer alike were dependent upon the vote of their fellow Athenians.

(Ober, 2007: 96–7)

The *deme* was of crucial importance not only because a man's citizenship was defined by his membership of a particular *deme*, even if he subsequently resided elsewhere, but because it was through the *deme* that peasant-citizens could exert real political influence.

The deme was the basic constituent unit of the polis and not simply its subject. All demesmen had the same civic rights and were entitled to attend the central assembly and serve on the juries through which so much of what we would consider *political* business was done; there was no distinction between villager and townsman in this respect, or between peasant and landlord. Every citizen could become *demarch*, the chief official of the deme through whom the local administration of the polis was mediated – and, in fact, the evidence is that the demarchs were generally men of moderate means and relatively humble status.

(Wood, 1988: 105)

Membership of the *deme* was also important because in all 139 *demes* there were assemblies to select potential members of the Council of 500, or *Boule*, which was essentially the executive body in the new democratic state. The number of *Boule* members from each *deme* was determined by the citizen population of the *deme*, subject to the requirement that there be 50 *Boule* members together representing all the *demes* in a tribe (Hansen, 1991: 247–9; Thorley, 1996: 27). Each *deme* had to nominate for *Boule* membership at least double the number of members it was entitled to, so that the *Boule* members from each *deme* could be selected by lot centrally in Athens. This was done using the personal bronze plaques that were the ancient equivalent of ID cards, and the allotment machines or *kleroteria* that the Athenians developed in order to expedite the process of selection by lot (Hansen, 1991: 248). Members of the *Boule* held office for one year, and could not hold office more than twice during their lifetime.

The *Boule* met on a daily basis except on festival days and days of ill omen: that is, around 275 days per year. It was structured in accordance with Cleisthenes's division of Attica into ten tribes. Each tribe's contingent of fifty served as the executive committee of the Council for a tenth of the year: the members of this committee were called *prytaneis*, and their period of office a *prytany*. The order in which the tribal contingents became *prytaneis* was settled by chance, because at the end of each *prytany* lots were drawn to select the group that would be next in *prytany* (Hansen, 1991: 250; Thorley, 1996: 29). The *prytaneis* committee had a president at its head, chosen by lot, to preside over it for one day, and also over the *Boule* if the *Boule* was meeting that day. The president was the official head of state, holding 'the keys of the treasuries where the state's money and documents were kept' and acting as 'the head of the state of Athens in relation to other states' (Hansen, 1991: 250). Because of the daily rotation of the position, up to 36 of the 50 tribal representatives and an overall majority of *Boule* members would act in this capacity at some point.

The citizenry as a whole (consisting of the male population aged over 18 in the fifth century BC and 20 in the fourth, excluding foreigners and slaves) formed the key sovereign body of Athens, the Assembly (Hansen, 1991: 88–90). The *Boule* could not make major governmental decisions. This was the province of the Assembly, but because 'the Assembly was too large a body to prepare its own agenda, to draft legislation and to be a focal point for the reception of new political initiatives and proposals', these functions were performed by the *Boule* (Held, 2006: 18). Thus 'the central role of the [Boule] in the decision-making process was ... its right to prepare the agenda for the Assembly and consider in advance every matter to be put before the people' (Hansen, 1991: 256). Furthermore, once the Assembly had made decisions and/or enacted laws, it was the *Boule*'s responsibility to ensure that they were implemented. Nonetheless, the powers of the executive were tightly circumscribed:

the annual change of membership, the *prytaneis* system, and the selection by lot of the president on a daily basis made it virtually impossible for any of the tribes (themselves, of course, from three different parts of Attica) or any other groupings of individuals to dominate the working of the *Boule*. This lack of permanence undoubtedly had its drawbacks ... but it did avoid the worst excesses of political factions and of aristocratic domination, and most Athenians were happy to accept the drawbacks.

(Thorley, 1996: 31)

The Assembly met 40 times a year, possibly more frequently in some years, and had a quorum of 6,000 citizens (that is, the minimum number required for the proper or valid transaction of business). From around 460 BC to 322 BC it met on the hill of the Pnyx above the Agora where the markets and *Boule* house were situated, and around 500 metres across a shallow valley from the Acropolis. A visit to the Pnyx makes it immediately clear as to why this site was chosen for the Assembly meetings. Not only is it a short walk to the Pnyx from the Agora, it also has a clear view of the Acropolis. Still an impressive sight today, it must have been an inspirational visual presence upon the completion of the building programme during the 'golden age' of Athenian democracy (the Parthenon was completed around 432 BC). From the peak of the hill above the meeting area there is also a panoramic view of the surrounding countryside.

The role and functions of the Assembly were extremely broad during the fifth century. They were narrowed somewhat following the restoration of democracy early in the fourth century, but remained relatively broad. All major issues confronting the city-state, such as 'the legal framework for the maintenance of public order, finance and direct taxation, ostracism, foreign affairs (including assessing the performance of the military and navy, forming alliances, the declaration of war, the concluding of peace) came before the assembled citizens for deliberation and decision' (Held, 2006: 17). Although the *Boule* met immediately before each Assembly meeting and determined the agenda, including formulating proposals for decrees and laws, the Assembly itself could decide that an item should be placed on the agenda for discussion at its next meeting.

The Assembly aimed for unanimity and consensus, but where this could not be achieved issues were put to a formal vote with majority rule. The originality and importance of this can hardly be overstated. As Ste Croix (1981: 284) observes, 'even many Classical scholars have failed to realise the extraordinary originality of Greek democracy, which, in the fundamental sense of *taking political decisions by majority vote of all citizens*, occurred earlier than in any other society that we know about'. Whereas during the fifth century 'the people in their Assembly could pass decrees and laws and sit in judgement on all serious political trials', Hansen (1991: 167–70) argues that during the fourth century the Assembly itself did not directly pass laws. Rather, it issued decrees which could only be made into law if they were passed by a special popular court (*nomothetai*), whose members were appointed from among the 6,000 citizens selected each year to act as jurors (see below). As a result, 'After the two oligarchic revolutions of 411 and 404 the Athenians restored democracy in 403/2; but it was not Periklean democracy' (Hansen, 1991: 151). Depending upon the importance of the legislation, the size of the *nomothetai* could be 501, 1,001 or 1,501. All major decrees of the Assembly and laws passed by the *nomothetai* were recorded and published, either by inscription on marble which was displayed in a public place, or else by being written on papyrus (an ancient form of paper) and stored in a public archive situated in the Agora.

Of equal importance to the establishment of these democratic institutions was Cleisthenes' introduction of large popular law courts. Since the time of Solon's reforms citizens from all classes had been eligible to serve as *dicasts*: that is, to act as both judges and jurors (Ste Croix, 1981: 284). Cleisthenes created a system in which 6,000 citizens over 30 years of age were selected each year by lot, 600 from each of the ten tribes, to act as *dicasts* in large public courts (Thorley, 1996: 35). Courts were held on all days except Assembly days and on festival days: that is, approximately 200 days per year. The juries ranged in size from 201 to 501 *dicasts* depending on the seriousness of the charge. Decisions were made by ballot and were inapellable.

This legal system was accusatory, in that prosecutions were brought to court by an individual citizen accusing another citizen of having acted in an injurious manner towards them, and/or in a manner that was illegal and injurious to the public interest (Hansen, 1991: 191–6). Accordingly, there was a twofold distinction between private law suits and public prosecutions, with the penalties for the latter generally being greater than the former. Protection against malicious public prosecution was provided by the requirement that the plaintiff pay a fine of 1,000 drachmas and loss of rights if they failed to obtain at least a fifth of the votes of the jury. Pay for jury service was introduced nearly 50 years earlier than pay to attend the Assembly, probably as part of, or at least immediately following, Ephialtes' radical democratic reforms in 462. These greatly enlarged the powers of the courts and reduced the powers of the aristocratic council of ex-archons, the Areopagos, which had previously continued to play an important role in the legal system. The fact that *dicasts* were paid (from 462 to 322) ensured that the law courts were composed of large numbers of citizens drawn from all classes, as opposed to the aristocratic archons who had held a monopoly on judicial power prior to Solon's reforms in 594. This is highly significant because it ensured that the courts provided protection for the labouring citizens against oppressive and exploitative domination by the wealthy.

It is important to recognise that these courts did not focus exclusively on what we understand as being central to judicial activity – criminal prosecution and civil litigation. Hansen (1991: 179) observes that 'political trials were the largest part of the business that came before them'. He overstates the relative importance of political trials especially in the fifth century, but the courts did assume a much greater political role during the fourth century, because following the re-establishment of democracy in 403 BC they performed 'judicial review' of the decrees of the Assembly, activities of the *Boule*, and the performance of magistrates.

Another major innovation was the way in which the bureaucratic functions involved in running the state and implementing policy were organised. Six hundred magistrates (meaning public office holders rather than judges) were selected by lot or elected each year from men aged 30 or over in the top three of Solon's four classes. They could only hold office for one year, and their performance was subject to public review once their term of office was over.

No one could hold the same magistracy more than once in a lifetime, but it was possible to hold different magistracies in successive years. These magistrates were grouped into committees of varying size, although the most important committees generally consisted of ten members, one from each tribe.

Throughout classical Antiquity the various Greek city-states were periodically engaged in military conflicts, with either their neighbours or more distant foes. Hence the organisation and control of the military was a central concern of all citizens. Cleisthenes' new constitution provided for ten generals to be elected each year, one from each of the ten tribes, by the citizens gathered in the Assembly. The generals could be reappointed year after year, unlike members of the *Boule* or *dicasts*. Thorley observes that:

The generals had a given measure of autonomy in carrying out their responsibilities, especially when they were on active service away from Athens, but they were always accountable to the Assembly for their actions. Nevertheless, the role of general came to be one of the key power bases in the democracy, partly because Athens was always at war with somebody during the fifth century, but also because the position was the only formal state office filled on merit which could be held for more than one year.

(Thorley, 1996: 39)

This is perhaps best illustrated by the political career of Pericles. After playing a leading political role in the Athenian democracy from the time of Ephialtes' reforms in 462 to 443, he became a general for fifteen successive years until his death in 429 (Fornara and Samons, 1991: 24–36). During this latter period he was undoubtedly the most powerful political leader in Attica.

Finally, mention should be made of the practice of ostracism, which may have existed in the form of forcible exiling prior to Cleisthenes' ascension to power, but which he certainly put on a new constitutional footing. If any citizen became extremely unpopular, he could be banished from Attica for a period of ten years, although he could retain ownership of his property. In December each year the Assembly was given the opportunity of deciding to ostracise any citizen that it considered should be banished.

The procedure was that all those who wished to vote went by tribes into a specially constructed enclosure in the agora and there scratched the name of the person they wished to see removed from the state on a potsherd and cast this as their vote. The potsherds were then counted, and if there were at least 6,000 they were sorted by names and the person named on the largest number of potsherds was 'ostracised' and had to leave Attica within ten days and go into banishment for ten years.

(Thorley, 1996: 43)

This was another mechanism which gave the bulk of the citizen body the power to banish unpopular and politically influential members of the wealthy classes. The first successful ostracism was conducted in 487, the last in 417. Thereafter the practice was discontinued, reflecting the more limited democratic constitution of the fourth century.

Remarkably, there is no major ancient Greek democratic theorist to whose writings and ideas we can turn for the details and justification of the classical democratic *polis*. Plato and Aristotle were both highly critical of Athenian democracy.[1] However, the ideals and aims of Athenian democracy are strikingly recounted in the famous funeral speech attributed to Pericles, a prominent Athenian citizen, general and politician:

> Let me say that our system of government does not copy the institutions of our neighbours. It is more the case of our being a model to others, than of imitating anyone else. Our constitution is called a democracy because power is in the hands not of a minority but of the whole people. When it is a question of settling private disputes, everyone is equal before the law; when it is a question of putting one person before another in positions of public responsibility, what counts is not membership of a particular class, but the actual ability which the man possesses. No one, so long as he has in him to be of service to the state, is kept in political obscurity because of poverty.
>
> (cited by Held, 2006: 13)

Clearly, in the Athenian democracy citizens faced no major obstacles to significant involvement in public affairs based on social position or wealth (although members of the lowest two classes in Solon's classification were prevented from holding some positions of high public office).[2] The *demos* held sovereign power: that is, supreme authority to engage in legislative and judicial functions. Further, the Athenian concept of 'citizenship' entailed taking a share in these functions, participating directly in the affairs of state. Athenian democracy was marked by a general commitment to the principle of civic virtue: dedication to the republic, the city-state, and the subordination of private life to public affairs and the common good. The principle of government was the principle of a form of life: direct participation. The process of government was based on free and unrestricted discourse, guaranteed by *isegoria*, an equal right of all citizens to speak freely, and *isonomia*, roughly meaning equality before the law (Ste Croix, 1981: 285). The peculiarly modern distinctions that emerged with Machiavelli (1429–1527) and Hobbes (1588–1679) between state and society, specialised officials and citizens, 'the people' and

---

1   For a critical commentary which sets Plato's and Aristotle's views in the social and historical context in which they were formulated, see: Wood and Wood (1978). They argue that, above all else, the Socratic philosophers were concerned to defend the power, privileges and interests of the nobility, which were threatened by the labouring citizens in Athenian democracy.

2   See, for example, Aristotle's (1962: 236–8) famous description of the Athenian democracy in the *Politics*.

government, are not part of the political philosophy of the Athenian city-state. For this city-state celebrated the notion of an active, involved citizenry in a process of self-government; the governors were to be the governed. All citizens met to debate, decide and enact the law.[3]

So far my account of Athenian democracy has focused on the central institutional features of this form of democracy. Although there is not sufficient space here to provide a detailed chronologically organized account of the advances and retreats of democracy from 508 to 322 BC, it is important to note that the major advances took place through three major sets of reforms, those of Solon around 594 BC, Cleisthenes around 508 BC, and Ephialtes and Pericles in 462/1 and the years immediately following. The last of these initiated the practice of providing pay for the performance of political tasks. Ste Croix considers of all the reforms that followed the establishment of democracy in 508 BC:

> the most important reform was the introduction by degrees, between the middle of the fifth century and its closing years, of pay for the performance of political tasks: at first sitting in the jury-courts, and on the Council (*Boule*) which prepared business for the Assembly, and later (after 403) for attending the Assembly. Although the rates of pay were low (less than the wages of an artisan), this reform enabled even the poorer citizens to play a real part in the political life of the city if they so desired.
>
> (Ste Croix, 1981: 289)

Elements of the wealthy propertied class remained implacably hostile to democracy throughout the fifth and fourth centuries, and on several occasions conspired with the rulers of Sparta (the oligarchic city-state that vied with Attica for hegemony over the Greek world) in order to overthrow democracy and replace it with the oligarchic rule of the wealthiest class of Athenian citizens. Two abortive oligarchic conspiracies took place in 480–79 and 458–7, the democratic reformer Ephialtes was assassinated in 462–1, and a group of wealthy reactionaries successfully staged a coup and established an oligarchic Council of Four Hundred in 411, but this only lasted around four months before democracy was restored (Ste Croix, 1981: 291).

In 404 the narrow oligarchy of the Thirty was forced upon Athens by the victorious Spartan commander, Lysander, some weeks or even months after the capitulation of Athens at the end of Peloponnesian war, during which period the Athenian oligarchs had evidently found it impossible to force through a change of constitution on their own.

(Ste Croix, 1981: 291)

---

3 The need for brevity has prevented a fuller account. For more detailed descriptions see Arblaster (1994: chs 2–3), Crawford and Whitehead (1983, Part II), Dahl (1989: 13–33 and 213–24), Farrar (1988: ch.7; 1992: 1–17), Hansen (1991: ch. 4), Harrison (1993: chs 1–2), Ober (1996), Ober and Hedrick (1996), Roberts (1994) and Sinclair, (1988: chs 1, 4, 8).

The broad mass of Athenian citizens rose up against this externally imposed oligarchy and re-established democracy in 403. However, in the fourth century the status of democracy was precarious throughout the Greek world. Attica was only a partial exception because democracy there became less radical, and it was 'perpetually on the defensive. In both the economic and political spheres, then, the tide of development had turned by the beginning of the fourth century, and a slow regression had begun' (Ste Croix, 1981: 294).

PEASANT CITIZENS, CLASS STRUGGLE AND DEMOCRACY

In this section of the chapter I argue, following Ste Croix (1981), that the struggles for democracy in classical antiquity are best conceptualised as class struggle on the political plane. There are a number of important aspects of this, which have implications for the central argument running throughout this book. First, as Wood (1995: 204) convincingly argues, although perhaps not as originally as she may think, 'the ancient concept of democracy grew out of an historical experience which had conferred a unique civic status on subordinate classes, creating in particular that unprecedented formation, the peasant citizen'. Thus it is impossible to fully understand the nature of Athenian democracy without recognising that it rested on historically specific social foundations in which the peasant citizen played a central role. The peasant citizen was a 'free labourer enjoying the status of citizenship in a stratified society' with the juridical and political freedom that this implies (Wood, 1995: 181). Hence the landmarks along the road to the establishment of democracy in classical antiquity represent pivotal moments in the elevation of the *demos* to citizenship. This was highly significant because, to put the point bluntly, it meant that for the first and only sustained period in history the producers or labouring citizens ruled. As Wood (1995: 188) points out, 'the real distinctiveness of the polis itself as a forum of state organization lies precisely here, in the union of free labour and citizenship'.

In *The Class Struggle in the Ancient Greek World* Ste Croix analyses the rise and fall of Athenian democracy in terms of 'the class struggle on the political plane'. He makes four key points which are worth quoting at length.

- In an ancient Greek polis the class struggle in the basic economic sense ... proceeded of course without cessation in so far as it was between property-owners and those whose labour provided them, directly or indirectly, with their leisured existence: that is to say, chattel slaves in the main, but in a few places principally serfs ...; some hired labourers, relatively few in number ...; those unfortunates who were obliged by need to borrow at interest and (probably in the great majority of *poleis* other than Athens) might become debt bondsmen on default; and more indirectly their tenants. This struggle was of course very one-sided; it expressed the master's dominance, and its essence was his exploitation of the labour of those who worked for him.
- There were, however, very many Greeks who owned little property and no

slaves: the majority of these [were] 'peasants' ... and a good number of others will have been artisans or traders .... Collectively, these people were the 'demos', the common people, and they must have formed the great bulk of the citizen population in the vast majority of Greek *poleis* (Ste Croix, 1981: 285–6).

It is in relation to this second point that Ste Croix really comes to the essence of the matter. He investigates the way in which the *demos*, made up for the most part of labouring citizens, participated in class struggle. Because class is essentially a relationship of exploitation, the focus of the struggles of the labouring citizens to avoid, or at least reduce, their exploitation by the wealthy class of landowners, money lenders and merchants was control of the state, understood as the 'constitution', the fundamental laws and customs governing political life (1981: 286). It is important to recognise that 'the Greeks habitually expected an oligarchy to rule in the interests of the propertied class, a democracy mainly in the interests of the poorer citizens. Control of the state, therefore, was one of the prizes, indeed the greatest prize, of class struggle on the political plane' (1981: 286).

• Class struggle on the political plane, then, was above all in most cases for control of the state. If in a Greek *polis* the demos could create and sustain a democracy that really worked, like the Athenian one, they could hope to protect themselves to a high degree and largely to escape exploitation.
• When, on the other hand, the propertied class were able to set up an oligarchy, with a franchise dependent on a property qualification, the mass of poor citizens would be deprived of all constitutional power and would be likely to become subject in an increasing degree to exploitation by the wealthy (Ste Croix, 1981: 286).

This analysis highlights the extent to which the struggle for and against democracy was essentially a class struggle on the political plane. The propertied class preferred oligarchy because it could then use the power of the state to facilitate an increase in the exploitation of the subordinate classes; in contradistinction the subordinate classes preferred democracy for the very opposite reason. I will be arguing throughout this book that the struggle for democracy in Athens during the fifth and fourth centuries was by no means unique in this respect. When the peasants of the late feudal era, and the proletarians in capitalism, fight for democracy they are essentially fighting for changes in the political governance of society that are likely to reduce their exploitation.

Although it is important to recognise the unique status of the labouring citizen in the Athenian democracy, it is equally important to recognise its major limitations. In particular, Athenian democracy had an extremely active and participatory citizenry, but a citizenry that was defined very narrowly. Estimates vary, but as Thorley (1996: 77) observes, it is reasonable to assume that 'during the fifth century the number of adult male citizens varied between 30,000 and 50,000 out of a total population of around 250,000 to 300,000. There were perhaps 80,000 slaves (some estimates are over 100,000), and about 25,000 metics (men, women and their families)' (see also Hansen, 1991: 93; Sinclair, 1988: 223–4; Stockton, 1990: 16–17; Wood, 1988: 43). Athenian citizenship excluded slaves, who according to Wood's (1995: 185; 1988: 43) estimation comprised around 20–30 per cent of the total population. It was a democracy of the patriarchs; women had no political rights and their civic rights were strictly limited. Hence the achievements of classical democracy were directly dependent on the labour of slaves and the politically unrecognised work and domestic service of women. Foreigners, or *metics,* were also excluded from citizenship. In 451–50 Pericles introduced a law that restricted eligibility for citizenship to those whose parents were both Athenian citizens (previously it had been sufficient for a man's father to have been a citizen), and this had the effect of making the citizen body more exclusive.

Athenian democracy was sustained by the payments it received from other city-states within its empire, ostensibly exacted for protection against the threat of Persian invasion (Thorley, 1996: 60–4). Although Athens generally promoted democracy in the city-states under its control, and often enjoyed the support of the bulk of poorer citizens in these states, the substantial sums of money that these city-states had to pay generated resentment and revolt. These revolts were suppressed in order to maintain the rule of Athens over her allies. Once the empire collapsed following Athens's defeat in the Peloponnesian War, it never again reached the glorious heights of the fifth century, when it was the hegemonic power in the Greek world.

It is important to consider the extent to which wealthy citizens could exert a disproportionate influence in the democracy. The evidence suggests that it would be an overstatement to claim that the peasants and artisans dominated the governance of Attica. Wealthy landowners were likely to exert disproportionate political influence because they were more likely to be highly educated and articulate, could employ others to speak on their behalf, and had more time than peasant and labouring citizens to participate in the Assembly, *Boule* and magistracies. Wealthy citizens also funded festivals, maintenance of warships and construction of temples. This would have greatly enhanced their status and political influence amongst the wider body of citizens.

What, then, are we to make of the political influence exerted by the peasantry and artisans? Arguing against the view that 'slavery constituted the productive basis of Athenian democracy', Wood (1988: 10) convincingly demonstrates that peasants and artisans undertook the bulk of economic production, with the important exception of the silver mines where slave labour prevailed. However, she does not convincingly rebut Ste Croix's claim that although peasant farmers and artisans performed the bulk of economic production, slave labour was of crucial importance in generating the surplus product that was appropriated by the dominant propertied class. Indeed, the political freedom of the peasantry meant that the propertied class was very heavily reliant on slave labour. This consideration led Callinicos (1988: 126) to argue that 'the land and slaves of the upper class gave them social and political power which prevented the democracy amounting to a "smallholders regime"'. In my view this is correct. Like Callinicos, Anderson (1974a: 39) contends that 'the landowners remained the dominant class, but their position was contested and challenged by small producers able to take advantage of democratic institutions', but this loses sight of the extent to which the majority of non-wealthy citizens could do more than merely 'contest and challenge' the social dominance of the wealthy. At crucial points in the history of classical Greek democracy they were able to exert a decisive influence over the course of events. The radically democratic reforms of Ephialtes and Pericles, for example, are simply inconceivable unless we assume that the majority of citizens were able successfully to support and defend these reforms against the resistance of the wealthy landowners.

Clearly by participating in the class struggle on the political plane, labouring citizens could win important victories. Thus the political influence of the wealthy was substantially limited by the reforms during the second half of the fifth century that introduced payment for jury service, membership of the *Boule,* attendance at the Assembly and the performance of other public duties, because this payment enabled even the poorest citizens to participate.

The upshot is that although we should not fall into the trap of glorifying Athenian democracy, a trap that Wood comes perilously close to falling into, neither should we underestimate its achievements (see for example Callinicos, 1988; Harman, 1999: 67–8). I think that it is important that we recognise, indeed celebrate, its achievements not only because for the only prolonged period in history that we know of, the labouring citizens played a central role in governing a *polis,* but also because Athenian citizens invented practices, such as selecting citizens for public duties by lot, which could be revived in a future socialist participatory democracy.

THE SUPPRESSION OF DEMOCRACY FROM 322–1 BC

Under the skilful leadership of Philip II, who became king in 360, and his son Alexander the Great who took over the reins of power from his father in 336, Macedonia rose to prominence during the next three decades as the hegemonic Greek state. The imposition of Macedonian dominance over Attica was part of the expansion of the Macedonian empire led by Alexander the Great, which was built through successful military conquest from 336 to 323, initially of the other significant Greek city-states, then of the whole of the Near East.

When the Athenians received the news of Alexander's death in June 323:

they soon led a widespread Greek revolt, which they themselves referred to proudly as a 'Hellenic war', against Macedonian domination; but in 323 they were utterly defeated and compelled to surrender, and the Macedonians turned the constitution of Athens into an oligarchy, limiting the exercise of

political rights to the 9,000 citizens (out of, probably, 21,000) who possessed at least 2,000 drachmae [the amount of money required to be a hoplite].
(Ste Croix, 1981: 301)

Thereafter, 'Athens was subjected to a whole series of interventions and was never able to decide her own destiny for very long' (St Croix, 1981: 301). It would, however, be a mistake to conclude that democracy was instantaneously suppressed throughout the ancient Greek world. As Ste Croix (1981: 293) observes, 'Greek democracy, between the fourth century BC and the third century of the Christian era, was gradually destroyed.' The peasantry and other labouring citizens vigorously resisted the top-down imposition of oligarchic constitutional arrangements. It took nearly 50 years of class struggle on the political plane before democracy was definitively suppressed in Attica.

The Greek propertied classes, with the assistance first of their Macedonian overlords and then of their Roman masters, gradually undermined and in the end entirely destroyed Greek democracy, which before the end of the [Roman] Principate had become extinct. Of course the suppression of Greek democracy was gratifying to the Romans; but it is clear that the Greek propertied classes did not merely acquiesce in the process: they assisted in it – and no wonder, because they themselves, after the Romans, were the chief beneficiaries of the system.
(Ste Croix, 1981: 309)

It is crucial to note that Athenian democracy in particular 'did not just die out, let alone commit suicide: it was deliberately extinguished by the joint efforts of the Greek propertied classes, the Macedonians and the Romans' (Ste Croix, 1981: 293). The extinguishment of democracy centrally involved the reduction of the sovereignty and powers of the citizen assemblies, the attachment to public office of liturgies (the funding of expensive civic duties) which both excluded less wealthy citizens from public office and legitimated this exclusion, and the 'the gradual destruction of the popular law courts, consisting of panels of dicasts ... which had been such an essential feature of Greek democracy' (Ste Croix, 1981: 300-1).

The Macedonian empire, which had been partitioned into four zones – Mesopotamia, Egypt, Asia Minor and Greece – collapsed following Alexander's death (Anderson, 1974a: 46). In its wake, Hellenistic monarchies emerged in Mesopotamia, Egypt and western Asia Minor. The eastward expansion of Rome during the second and first centuries BC resulted in these Hellenistic monarchies and the Greek city-states being incorporated within the empire of the Roman republic (Macedon became a province of Rome in 146 BC; Athens was occupied by the Roman general Sulla in 86 BC). As this suggests, during the last three centuries BC:

there developed all over the Greek world a tendency for political power to become entirely concentrated in the hands of the propertied class. This development, or rather retrogression, which seems to have begun early in the Hellenistic period, was still by no means complete when the Romans took over, in the second century BC. The Romans, whose governing class always detested democracy, intensified and accelerated the process; and by the third century of the Christian era the last remnants of the original democratic institutions of the Greek *poleis* had mostly ceased to exist for all practical purposes.

(Ste Croix, 1981: 300)

The Roman republic is the focus of the next chapter. It is, however, worth noting at this point that following the suppression of democracy in the Greek world, nothing remotely approximating a democratic system of government was allowed to re-emerge by the ruling classes of Europe. In this respect, the suppression of democracy is a common theme in the historical trajectories of the Hellenic empire, the Roman republic and empire, and European feudalism.

CONCLUSION

As Held (2006: 13) observes, 'The development of democracy in Athens has been a central source of inspiration for modern political thought. Its political ideals – equality among citizens, liberty, respect for the law and justice – have influenced political thinking in the West.' All major contemporary interpretations of democracy rest on positive or negative evaluations of key features of the Athenian model of democracy. Prominent intellectuals who proclaim a commitment to 'democracy' provide distinctive, and frequently conflicting, accounts of the ancestry of their own particular model of democracy, tracing its lineage back to the Athenian model. In this regard, it can be argued plausibly that there are two fundamentally distinct but still interrelated traditions of democratic thought and practice. One originated in Athens during the fifth and fourth centuries BC, and was subsequently revived and further developed in popular movements by (among others) the Levellers, Diggers, Chartists, Communards, and Russian workers and peasants in 1917. The other originated in oligarchic Rome, and was revived and further developed with Magna Carta, the English constitutional settlement of 1688, the American Declaration of Independence of 1776 and Constitutional Convention of 1787 (Wood, 1995: 213 and 232). The former is the democratic tradition of labouring citizens; the latter is a tradition of the propertied classes.

Athenian and contemporary representative forms of democracy are clearly both characterised by major weaknesses and limitations. A key difference that is of vital importance lies in the status of the labouring citizen in the two forms of democracy. Here the full significance of the earlier model of democracy stands out in stark contrast, for it is only in this model of democracy that the labouring citizens exert genuine influence over the governance of society. As we shall see later in the book, Marx promoted a radical model of democracy that built upon, and extended, key elements of Athenian democracy, in opposition to the diminution of these in liberal forms of democracy.

GUIDE TO FURTHER READING

Held (2006: ch.1) provides a useful chapter-length introduction. Thorley's (1996) short book is also a good place for the uninitiated to start. For illuminating accounts of the revolutionary origins of Athenian democracy see Ober (1996), Raaflaub, Ober and Wallace (2007), and Stockton (1990). Within the Marxist tradition, Anderson (1974a: ch. 2) is a good starting point. Harman (1999: 63–70) provides a very short introduction. Ste Croix (1981) is the classic Marxist work on the ancient Greek world, and it is essential reading on both Athenian democracy (ch. 5) and the Roman republic and empire (see the reading guide at the end of Chapter 2). Ste Croix (2004), although aimed at a more specialist readership, is also well worth consulting, as is his account (1972) of the Peloponnesian War (cf. Strauss, 1986).

Wood (1988: ch. 4) provides an interesting and illuminating Marxist interpretation in which she (1988: 2) argues, in opposition to Ste Croix, that slavery only played a relatively minor role in agriculture, and consequently that 'in the most notable "slave society" of ancient Greece, classical Athens, the majority of citizens laboured for a living'. Wood's (1995: chs.6–7) comparative analysis of Athenian and representative democracy highlights, among other things, positive features of Athenian democracy frequently overlooked by both Marxists and non-Marxists. Mann (1986: ch. 7) provides a very useful neo-Weberian account of Athenian democracy. Dahl (1989: ch. 1) provides a contemporary liberal interpretation which argues for the superiority of representative democracy. Other useful non-Marxist accounts that describe the key features of Athenian democracy and society include Arblaster (1994: chs.2–3), Davies (1978), Findley (1973), Jones (1957), Hansen (1987, 1991), Hornblower (1992), Osborne (1985, 2000, 2010), Sinclair (1988: chs 1, 4, 8) and Starr (1990).

For a very useful collection of primary source material with commentaries see Robinson (2004). Wood and Wood (1978) place the political theory of Socrates, Plato and Aristotle in its social context. Farrar (1988: ch. 7; 1992) and Roberts (1994) are also useful in this regard. Ste Croix (1981: ch. 5, section 3) provides the best account of the decline of Athenian democracy, but also see Mosse (1973).

2
Democracy suppressed: the Roman republic and empire

INTRODUCTION

In 509 BC, around the same time that Cleisthenes introduced the reforms that established democracy in Athens, Tarquinius Superbus, the last Etruscan king to rule over the city of Rome, was expelled, and a republic declared (Ward, Heichelheim and Yeo, 1999: 51–3). The Roman republic aggressively expanded the territory under its influence and survived for nearly five centuries, until 31 BC when Octavian (Augustus) defeated Mark Antony's forces at the battle of Actium and secured his position as the first emperor ruling over Rome and the empire. Henceforth the principate, or early empire, was governed by a succession of emperors until the accession of Diocletian in 284/5 AD. Diocletian and Constantine presided over a series of reforms that simultaneously expanded the armed forces, the power of the emperor (or emperors where two or more held power simultaneously), the state bureaucracy, and the exaction of taxation from the peasantry and provinces. The epoch from 284 to the eventual decline and fall of the western Roman empire, as it succumbed to barbarian invasions from 395 to 493, is referred to as the dominate, or late empire.

It is not possible to provide a general historical account of the Roman republic and empire in the space of a single chapter.[1] Accordingly, this chapter is structured as follows. After tracing the scale of the territorial expansion of Roman civilization and identifying the central features of the economic and social structure of Roman society, it describes the central constitutional and institutional features of the republic. The extent to which the Roman republic can be described accurately as a democracy is the central focus of

---

1 Space constraints mean that in this chapter I cannot provide a general historical overview of the rise of the republic, the class struggles and main political and military events of the tumultuous final century of the republic (from the reforms of the Gracchi, 133 to 121 BC, to the final crisis and disintegration of republic government, 52 to 27), the constitutional settlement that founded the principate, and the fall of the western Roman empire. Accordingly it does not fully outline the complex interplay of class struggle, military developments and events, constitutional arrangements, and political institutions, actors and events. Readers who are unfamiliar with Roman history may want to read the chapter in conjunction with the chapter-length general accounts by Anderson (1974a: 53–103) and Harman (1999: 71–86).

the next section. I argue that although there were democratic elements in the constitutional and institutional arrangements of the republic, overall it was characterised by essentially oligarchic governance in which democracy appeared in form but not substance, and once the republic collapsed the limited democratic elements in Roman politics diminished following the establishment of the principate under Augustus. The causes of the decline and fall of the Roman empire are considered in the final section. The conclusion highlights the influence of the Roman republic on the thinkers and political actors who played key roles in the democratic revolutions of the seventeenth to eighteenth centuries, and contends that the historical antecedents of liberal representative democracy in classical antiquity reside in the Roman republic rather than Athenian democracy.

THE HISTORICAL ORIGINS AND DEVELOPMENT OF THE ROMAN REPUBLIC FROM 509 TO 27 BC

The history of the Roman republic traditionally covers the period from 509 BC to 31–27 BC, when its faltering life was terminated with the rise to power of the first Roman emperor, Augustus. Formerly known as Octavian, a nephew whom Julius Caesar designated as his heir, he had acquired undisputed mastery of the Roman world by 30, and was declared Augustus in 27, beginning the principate. As could be expected given the width of this span of history (around 480 years), it is difficult to do much more than skim the surface of events. Some of the more significant developments included the conflict of orders between the patrician aristocracy and plebeians (circa 494–287), the succession of wars, particularly the Roman victory in the first (264–41) and second (218–01) Punic wars which, among other things, resulted in the territorial expansion of the republic from the confines of the city-state itself to the entire Italian peninsula, Sicily, Spain, Corsica and Carthage (in North Africa), and the attempted reforms of Tiberius Cracchus (133 BC) and his brother Gaius Cracchus (123–2 BC) at the beginning of the tumultuous final century of the republic's existence. The prolonged crisis of the republic culminated in the autocratic rule of Julius Caesar, which was significant both because his astute skill as a military strategist (combined with the increasing superiority of the Roman military apparatus) facilitated the dramatic expansion of the empire, and because of the role that his rise to power played in the final destruction of the republic.

Roman territorial expansion

Geographically Rome was well situated for defence and expansion, being located centrally in the Italian peninsula on the banks of the Tiber river. Although the growth and development of the republican empire was never smooth and linear, the overall picture is one of massive territorial expansion.[2]

---

2 For a useful video representation of the expansion of the Roman empire, see: http://en.wikipedia.org/wiki/File:Roman_Empire_map.ogv.

From a small city-state comprising around 983 square kilometres of territory and a population of less than 500,000 in the earliest decades of its existence, it grew to an expansive empire encompassing around 6.5 million square kilometres with a population of at least 60 to 70 million by 114 AD (Bang, 2008: 86–91; Le Glay, Voisin and Le Bohec, 2001: 101; Scheidel and Friesen, 2009: 61–91).

Rome defeated its rivals and established supremacy over the bulk of the Italian peninsula, with the tremendous expansion of resources, territory and military capabilities that this implies, in a prolonged series of military campaigns from 509 to 264 BC. It then embarked on a succession of wars beyond the Italian peninsula that extended Roman territory on a qualitatively greater scale. The most important of these were the wars waged against Carthage. By 264, the two dominant powers in the western Mediterranean region were Rome, hitherto a land-based military power, and Carthage, hitherto the dominant naval power in the region. Carthage was a prosperous Phoenician (or 'Punic' in Latin) city-state using the advantages of its strategic location on a small peninsula jutting out from North Africa into the Gulf of Tunis in order to dominate maritime trade and commerce and to expand its territory around the perimeter of the western Mediterranean. Its territorial acquisitions provided it with fertile land for agriculture. In addition, 'Carthage controlled by far the richest mining resources of the western Mediterranean basin. Sardinia and Spain produced lead, zinc, copper, iron, and silver' (Ward et al., 1999: 85). Although Rome had previously avoided conflict with Carthage, by the mid-third century the imperial ambitions of both powers had developed to the extent that war was inevitable. The two Punic wars between Rome and Carthage, from 264 to 241 and 218 to 201, were titanic struggles both because of the scale of the forces that were mobilised (each side enlisting armies with over 50,000 and navies with over 70,000 men) and the heavy losses suffered on both sides, and also because of the stakes. The victor was assured of becoming the dominant power in the region, and the vanquished risked utter destruction. As it turned out, Rome emerged as the victor and Carthage was incorporated as a province into the Roman empire. Further wars of expansion were waged from 201 BC to 114 AD against the kingdoms occupying the islands and surrounding land areas of the Mediterranean (including those in the Iberian peninsula, Gaul and North Africa) and Western Europe as far as the British Isles.

It is not surprising, therefore, that 'the interest of Rome lies in its imperialism. It was one of the most successful conquering states in all history, but it was the most successful *retainer* of conquests. Rome institutionalized the rule of its legions more stably and over a longer period than any other society before or since' (Mann, 1986: 250). In my view Mann accurately emphasises the double-sided nature of the Roman achievement: through military conquest it both obtained and retained a large territorial empire. How was it able to do this? After all, Rome was almost continuously at war for nearly a thousand years, and at least before the western empire suffered its final defeat in 476 AD, it generally prevailed even in those wars, such as the Second Punic War, where it suffered major defeats and had to absorb huge losses. It was able to do so not simply or even primarily because of military superiority, which in any case it did not always possess. Rather, it was the Roman economic and social structure, the specific qualities of its ruling class and character of its state, that enabled Rome so successfully to obtain and retain territory, and build what 'eventually became a true territorial empire', with 'about as high a level and intensity of territorial control as could be attained within the logistical constraints imposed on all agrarian societies' (Mann, 1986: 250).

The economic and social structure of Roman society

As Brunt (1971a: 20) observes, 'Economic activity in antiquity was overwhelmingly agrarian, and every district aimed at self-sufficiency. Trade was circumscribed outside a narrow radius to the exchange of luxury or semi-luxury goods or to such essential commodities as iron or salt, which were not found within that radius.' As the territory under Roman control expanded, an extensive network of roads, navigable rivers and sea routes was developed, although waterborne transportation remained vastly cheaper than land, with the latter being used primarily for military purposes. 'It was cheaper to ship grain from one end of the Mediterranean to the other than to cart it 75 miles' (Brunt, 1971a: 24). This network provided the material infrastructure for the empire to function as an integrated monetary economy.

Land was by far the most important form of wealth because land ownership afforded high social status and provided the income flow required for an affluent lifestyle and a successful political career. Massive fortunes could also be derived from tribute in war, including slaves, money, art, precious metals and other valuable items, tax gathering in the provinces, and money lending (although neither industry nor trade were socially esteemed). Accumulation of wealth was highly valued because the culture of the Roman ruling class centrally involved high levels of conspicuous spending and 'opulent conservatism' (Anderson, 1974a: 70). Wealth of all kinds was codified and protected by the Roman legal system. As Ste Croix observes, Roman law was 'an elaborate system, worked out in extraordinary detail and often with great intellectual rigor, for regulating the personal and family relationships of Roman citizens, in particular in regard to property rights, a peculiarly sacred subject in the eyes of the Roman governing class' (1981: 329). Although all citizens enjoyed formal equality before the law, in practice the legal system was systematically biased in favour of the upper propertied class.

As Mann (1986: 252) observes, '"class" is a term that is 'derived from the Roman "classis", a gradation of obligation for military service according to rank'. The class structure and highly stratified organisation of the military were closely interconnected and mutually reinforcing. The main classes of Roman society, throughout the history of both the republic and the empire, were the land-owning nobility, peasants, proletarians and slaves.

The land-owning nobility that dominated Roman society economically, politically and militarily was remarkably adept at ruling. The specific characteristics of this class are central to explaining Roman success in retaining territory acquired through wars of expansion and integrating this new territory quickly and effectively into the empire. Two points are worth noting.

First, the land-owning nobility successfully achieved a high degree of continuity in its political dominance of Roman society.

> Archaic monarchy was overthrown by a nobility in the earliest epoch of its existence, at the end of the sixth century BC, in a change strictly comparable to the Hellenic pattern. But thereafter, unlike the Greek cities, Rome never knew the upheaval of tyrant rule, breaking aristocratic dominance and leading to a subsequent democratisation of the city, based on a secure small and medium agriculture. Instead a hereditary nobility kept unbroken power through an extremely complex civic constitution, which underwent important popular modifications through the course of a prolonged and fierce social struggle within the city, but was never abrogated or replaced.
>
> (Anderson, 1974a: 53)

Second, Roman citizenship was extensive in nature, and was bestowed on adult men in allied states and the provinces of the empire. This enabled the incorporation into the Roman ruling class of the ruling classes of the territories that Rome conquered, expanding and invigorating this class, while simultaneously reducing resistance to Roman imperial rule and facilitating the integration of new territory into the empire. In addition, because 'all the new citizens were bound, like the old, to pay taxes and fight in Rome's armies', 'it helped to give Rome numerical superiority over each successive enemy' (Brunt, 1971a: 3). As Brunt observes, 'This policy could only have succeeded because the Roman system was undemocratic', and therefore expanding the citizen population did nothing to threaten the interests of the ruling class (1971a: 9). Latin became the dominant language of the Roman empire in the west, especially among the land-owning elites that ruled the provinces, and literacy played a key role 'as an instrument of state power and as the cement of class solidarity' (Mann, 1986: 270). As a result of these developments, there 'emerged a universal ruling class – extensive, monopolizing land and the labour of others, politically organized, and culturally conscious of itself' (1986: 270).

Slavery played a central role in Roman society. As Brunt observes:

> Even as early as Hannibal's invasion [in 218] the number of slaves must have been considerable, for it would otherwise have been quite impossible for Rome to mobilize for the armies and fleets one in every two of the citizens of military age; the necessary food and other supplies could not have been provided year by year but for slave labour. Only the abundance of such labour made it possible for the state to continue calling up so many free men in ensuing generations. Most labour was inevitably employed on the land, and on many great estates it consisted entirely of slave gangs.
>
> (Brunt, 1971a: 18–19)

Furthermore: 'slaves laboured in the fields and in the workshops, as well as in domestic employment; they even predominated as secretaries, accountants and doctors. We do not know their numbers, but it may be guessed without implausibility that in 28[BC] there were about 3,000,000 as against 4,000,000 free persons' (Brunt, 1971a: 18). The slave population was heterogeneous. Roman conquest and slave capture brought together people from many different cultures and ethnic groups, with many different languages. Slaves were employed in a broad range of occupations. Although the overwhelming majority worked in brutal conditions on large farms and plantations, mines, workshops, building and civil engineering projects and so forth, the small minority engaged to perform what we today would describe as professional work were relatively privileged, with some even being able to engage their own slaves.

Slavery provided the economic underpinning for the territorial expansion of the empire from the beginning of the first Punic war in 264 BC to Trajan's extension of the empire to its outermost perimeter by 117 AD. The Romans did not invent large-scale slave-based agricultural production, but rather copied an innovation of the Carthaginians, whose 'slave plantations demonstrated that more intensive agriculture generating a larger surplus was possible than the small peasant plot could provide' (Mann, 1986: 260). The Romans, however, applied this form of production much more extensively and effectively. Thus the decisive economic factor that underpinned the expansion of the Roman empire was large-scale agricultural production by a slave population that was continually augmented by the capture of new slaves through successful military conquest.

'What distinguished Rome was neither economic inequality nor exploitation but the enormity in the scale of both' (Brunt, 1971a: 40). The Roman landowning nobility, as we have seen, excelled at ruling in its own interests. The members of this class were motivated by greed and a desire for power and glory. They were always prepared to use brutality in ruthlessly exploiting slaves and peasants, who always constituted a large majority of the population. Although neither the peasantry nor slaves were capable of generating the kind of collective organisation and political leadership necessary in order to transform Roman society in a revolutionary manner, they were able to resist the exploitation and political dominance of the nobility. The resulting class struggle took a variety of forms: banditry, piracy, urban riots, slave revolts, civil wars, political crises and religious schism (Mann, 1986: 263). Class struggle in these forms became particularly intense during the period of the late republic, from 133 BC to 27 BC.

Mann (1986: 252) convincingly argues that the success of Roman imperial expansion 'was based on fusing military and economic organization into the state, linking stratification and citizenship to the necessities of land warfare'. Although the Roman military generally, but not always, utilised better strategy and tactics than its enemies, its overall superiority was due to the economic and social structure of Roman society, rather than the military machine itself.

In this respect, the 'Roman ability to sacrifice revealed the militarism of social structure. For a period of about 200 years, about 13% of citizens were under arms at any one time, and about half served for at least one period of seven years' (Mann, 1986: 253). For example, the militarism of the social structure was the crucial factor enabling Rome to win the Punic wars despite sustaining heavy losses. 'In the second war (218–201) half the men between eighteen and forty-six qualified for legionary service were generally under arms, many for several years at a stretch; the average was seven' (Brunt, 1971a: 13).

Roman victory in the Punic wars facilitated a shift away from the loose federated structure of an empire of domination towards a territorial empire composed of provinces ruled by designated magistrates, backed by legionary garrisons (Mann, 1986: 259–80). These wars undermined the volunteer citizen army. Many peasants lost their land and were forced into the proletariat. Following the Punic wars, the state increasingly employed proletarians as mercenaries and provided them with weapons to serve in the military. In the late republic, and throughout the history of the empire, the legions were predominantly composed of full-time professional soldiers and the bulk of state expenditure was directed towards the military, although the proportion of military spending varied considerably, before rising steadily in the final centuries of the empire. From the mid-third century BC onwards the bulk of state revenue came from the provinces.

The legions played a key role in converting captured territory into an economically productive and integrated part of the empire. Consider, for example, the equipment carried by the legionary troops following the military reforms of the consul and general, Marius, from 105 to 102 BC:

The foot soldiers have a spear, and a long buckler, besides a saw, and a basket, a pickaxe, and an axe, a thong of leather, and a hook, with provisions for three days so that a footman has no great need of a mule to carry his burdens .... This odd assortment was tied around a long pole, carried like a lance, which Marius's commissariat devised. Only the spear and buckler were battlefield equipment. They are unremarkable, as are the three days rations. All the rest of the equipment is 'logistical weapons', designed to extend the infrastructure of Roman rule. Most were to build fortifications and communications routes: The basket was for earthmoving; the leather strap was for moving turves; the pickaxe with two different blades was for cutting down trees and digging ditches. Others were primarily for adding to the supplies: the sickle for cutting corn, the saw for wooden equipment and firewood .... Contrast this to the equipment of most troops of other empires or city-states – which had carried merely battlefield equipment. The Romans were the first to rule consistently through the army not only with terror, but also with civil-engineering projects.

(Mann, 1986: 275–6)

These projects made possible an integrated economy with interdependent flows of labour, commodity trade, coinage, law and literacy. It is perhaps an overstatement to argue that 'the state was largely an army' and 'the state-led economy was an army-led economy' because the bulk of economic activity was never conducted by the state itself, but there can be no doubt that the preservation of this economy 'required major and unrelenting expenditure and money and manpower' (Mann, 1986: 276, 278).

Imperial expansion contributed to the growing urbanisation of Roman society. The population of Rome had grown to 750,000 by the time of Caesar (60 to 44 BC). As well as being a major centre of commerce:

> the concentration of the riches of the empire in the hands of a few Romans also meant that it was at Rome that loans were most easily to be secured; it became the leading banking centre. Rome was parasitic on the whole Mediterranean world: it was quite untypical of Italy, and most Romans did not live in it. Those who did mostly drew their income from Italian estates, or directly or indirectly from imperial profits; food subsidies for the poor, like the public and private building activity, were ultimately a charge on provincials.
>
> (Brunt, 1971a: 30)

Because citizens had to be present at Rome in order to vote in the assemblies, this gave the poor citizens in Rome greater potential political influence than their counterparts in the countryside. For this reason, members of the ruling class frequently used bribery of the urban plebs as a tool to influence the elections of tribunes and consuls. The proletarian masses in Rome were kept quiescent with a state-subsidised grain ration or dole (320,000 were getting the dole in 46 BC). This contributed to the growing importance of grain imports; 'By AD 70 Rome depended mainly on the crops of Africa and Egypt in the proportion of 2 to 1' (Brunt, 1971a: 26).

The political institutions of the Roman republic and the 'conflict of orders'

The governing core of the Roman state was composed of magistrates (in descending order censor, consuls, praetor, aedile, quaestor), tribunes, the Senate, and popular assemblies (*comitia centuriata, concilium plebis, comitia tributa*), which were developed and modified from the early to the late republic.

When the republic was established, two magistrates called consuls who only held power for one year exercised the powers of a king (*imperium*), including command of the military (North, 2006: 263–4; Lintott, 1999: 144–6). They also acted as judges, and could place legislative and other proposals before the military and tribal voting assemblies (*comitia centuriata, comitia tributa*). Each consul had the power to veto the other's decision, although they rarely did this. Because they were annual magistrates 'they could be brought to account when they laid down office, and as they held it for so short a time, they were much more likely to defer to the will of the Senate' (Brunt, 1971a: 45). This will be discussed in more depth shortly. In times of emergency a dictator could be appointed for six months. He was bestowed with the *imperium* of both consuls, and all other magistrates were subject to his authority.

From 509 to the conclusion of the Second Punic War in 201, the military success of Rome was highly dependent on mobilising a high proportion of the citizenry to fight in the legions and navy. This was achieved, in part, through the establishment of the *comitia centuriata*, an assembly in which the various centuries of the armed forces bloc voted in units. The *comitia centuriata* did not frequently vote on legislation or declarations of war, its key role was to elect magistrates. This was, as Brunt (1971a: 46) observes, 'of the highest importance; elections not only decided who were to be the executive agents of the state; they gave the successful candidates lasting prestige in the counsels of the Senate'.

The Senate was the dominant governmental institution in the republic. It consisted mainly of ex-magistrates, '300 before 81 BC, 600 until 45 BC, then 900 until Augustus reduced it again to 600' (Brennan, 2004: 61). During the fifth century membership was the exclusive preserve of the patrician nobility. Once admitted, membership was for life and was passed down from father to son. As Ste Croix (1981: 333) observes, 'by the foundation of the Republic the Patricians had succeeded in becoming a closed "order", a group in the state having a special constitutional position (involving a monopoly of office), one that it had arrogated to itself, not one created by any "law"'.

This led to the emergence of the plebeians, 'consisting in principle of anyone who was not a Patrician' (Ste Croix, 1981: 333). All plebeians, including those who had acquired substantial fortunes, were excluded from the Senate and thus political power. This gave rise to the 'conflict of orders' from 494 to 287, during which the plebs refused to perform military service on several occasions in order to achieve greater representation within the republican constitution and government. The first of these military strikes led to the creation of the tribune of the plebs around 494 and 'an Assembly of the collective plebs (the *concilium plebis*), presided over by their tribunes' (Ste Croix,1981: 333). Voting in the *concilium plebis* was by geographical tribe, with four urban tribes from Rome and eventually 31 from rural areas. Members from each tribe voted as a unit, and their tribal unit had one vote in the assembly. This assembly elected the tribunes, originally two although this was increased to ten, and the plebeian aediles who assisted the tribunes.

The tribunes were protected against the possibility of violent attack by the threat that the plebeians would put the perpetrators to death. Initially, their key role was to protect the life, person and property of all plebeians against the arbitrary exercise of power of a patrician magistrate. They could represent the views of the plebs to the consuls and/or Senate, and also present proposals to the *concilium plebis*. If passed these plebiscites clearly expressed the view of the plebs on that issue and carried the weight of law. The tribunes also 'had the right of veto (*intercessio*) with regard to any official act, including all legislative bills, even (unless a lex [law] barred it) decrees of the senate, and elections (except for elections of tribune)' (Brennan, 2004: 65).

A major source of plebeian agitation concerned the complete dominance of the formulation and adjudication of the law, which was largely unwritten and a matter of custom, by the patricians. The plebeians successfully pressured the Senate into codifying the law in twelve bronze tablets that were placed in the Roman forum for all to see. The twelve tables, as they became known, allowed capital cases to be appealed to the *comitia centuriata*, abolished torture as a means of soliciting evidence from citizens, and established the formal equality of all citizens before the law, although in practice the legal system was generally biased in favour of wealthy citizens (Ste Croix, 1981: 330). Around 450 BC patricians were allowed to participate in the tribal assembly of the plebs; when they were present it constituted a distinct assembly – the *comitia tributa* – and this predominately plebeian assembly was empowered to pass laws that were binding on all.

As the republic expanded it became necessary to elect more magistrates to perform the administrative, judicial and military functions of government. There is no general agreement in the literature about the precise functions performed by these magistrates. The most senior magistrates to assist the consuls were praetors. While being constitutionally subordinate to the consuls, they held *imperium* – that is, the capacity to command lower-ranked magistrates – and they had 'significant responsibilities in the Roman legal system (including supervising civil law and, after 149 BC, presiding over standing criminal courts) as well in the military/provincial sphere' (Brennan, 2004: 63). The number of praetors increased substantially, with there being one from 366 to 247 BC, two from 247 to 229, four from 228 to 198, six from 197 to 81, eight from 80 to 47, ten for 46, and more than 14 thereafter (2004: 63). Quaestors were appointed as more junior magistrates to assist the consuls. From 421 BC onwards two of the four quaestors assisted the consuls on the battlefield while two remained in Rome to manage state finances. The number of quaestors was increased to eight by the mid-third century, and 20 after 81 BC. In conjunction with the plebeian aediles, the curule aediles assisted with municipal administration, maintaining archives of the assemblies and senate, 'supervising markets, weights and measures, public works, food and water supplies, and public games' (Ward et al., 1999: 59).

Finally, from 443 BC onwards, two censors were elected by the *comitia centuriata* every five years for an 18-month term of office. They were generally ex-consuls, and their key role was to compile the census: the official list of Roman citizens eligible for military service, voting and taxation. The various magistrates stood in relation to each other in a rank order of seniority, status and power. This rank order was referred to as the *cursus honorum* – 'The hierarchical course of offices ... that marked an aristocratic political career for centuries was now all in place: quaestor, aedile, praetor, consul, and censor, in ascending order' (Ward et al., 1999: 64–5).

By 287 BC wealthy plebeians had unfettered access to all of the important political magistracies. Hence 'the result of the "conflict of orders" was to replace the originally patrician oligarchy by a patricio-plebeian oligarchy, differing very little in outlook and behaviour' (Ste Croix, 1981: 337). This wealthy patricio-plebeian land-owning nobility remained overwhelmingly socially and politically dominant throughout the subsequent history of the republic and empire.

THE 'MIXED CONSTITUTION' OF THE ROMAN REPUBLIC – DEMOCRACY OR OLIGARCHY?

Polybius, a Greek historian writing in the second century BC, described the political structure of the Roman Republic as a 'mixed constitution':

> It was impossible even for a native to pronounce with certainty whether the whole system was aristocratic, democratic or monarchical. This was indeed only natural. For if one fixed one's eyes on the powers of the consuls, the constitution seemed completely monarchical and royal; if on that of the senate it seemed again to be aristocratic; and when one looked at the power of the masses it seemed clearly to be a democracy.
>
> (quoted by Mann, 1986: 259)

This depiction of the Roman constitution as involving a mixture of elements of monarchy (the powers of the two consuls), oligarchy (the dominant influence of the Senate) and democracy (the roles of the voting assemblies in passing laws and electing magistrates) is better at highlighting the constitutional complexity of Roman politics and government than the operation of its central features in practice. For example, a brief reflection upon the powers and role of the consuls highlights fundamental differences from the absolutist rule of monarchs. Unlike kings and queens, the consuls were elected for a year, beyond which they depended upon being re-elected. They could propose laws but these had to be passed by the voting assemblies, and they generally tried to act in ways likely to be approved of by a majority of the senate (Mouritsen, 2001: 6).

A wide-ranging scholarly consensus maintains that the oligarchic dimension of the republic predominated to such a degree that it should also not be characterised as a form of democracy. Although there were voting assemblies of various kinds, and in this sense sovereignty lay with the citizenry, 'various factors – economic, political, military and religious – ensured that the people deferred to their "betters", the leaders of the nobility who, in fact, controlled all aspects of life and government through the senate and the magistracies' (Shotter, 1994: 2). Ste Croix (1981: 340) puts the same point more brutally, but no less accurately: 'Rome, of course, was never a democracy or anything like it. There were certainly some democratic elements in the Roman constitution, but the oligarchic elements were in practice much stronger, and the overall character of the constitution was strongly oligarchical.' Similarly Ward and colleagues argue that:

> The Republic was controlled by a powerful oligarchy. It was made up of

those wealthy landowners from patrician and plebeian gentes who had held the office of consul and constituted a consular nobility within the senate, whose lower-ranking members were also wealthy patrician and plebeian landowners from the highest census class.

(Ward et al., 1999: 66)

This view has been challenged. Millar argues that in the late Roman republic:

public office could be gained only by direct election in which all (adult male) citizens, including freed slaves, had the right to vote, and all legislation was by definition the subject of direct popular voting. That being so, it is difficult to see why the Roman Republic should not be [considered as] ... one of a relatively small group of historical examples of political systems that might deserve the label 'democracy'.

(Millar, 1998: 11; see also 1998: 197–226)

In a similar vein, Yakobson (2006: 384) argues that the reluctance by modern scholars to describe the Roman republic as a democracy 'stems largely from an unrealistic, idealized concept of democracy in general, and, in particular, of how a modern democracy actually works'. Since modern representative democracies also involve 'huge disparities in wealth and social status' in which the wealthy are able to exert a disproportionate influence over electoral processes and government decision making, we should not refuse to describe the Roman republic as a democracy because the wealthy senatorial nobility dominated the Roman system of government (Yakobson, 2006: 384). Furthermore, he argues, because on a substantial number of occasions, especially from the late second century BC to the fall of the republic, the tribunes successfully proposed laws that the tribal assembly passed 'against senatorial opposition and obstruction', we should take seriously 'the popular aspect of republican politics' (2006: 385).

This challenge to the scholarly consensus has stimulated further research, creating greater clarity about the composition and role of the voting assemblies. It is now generally accepted by those on both sides of the debate that patronage played a smaller role than previously thought in securing the votes of citizens from classes below the nobility and equestrians. A broad range of other interconnected and mutually reinforcing factors were probably more important. The apparently democratic features of the Roman system of government pertain, above all, to the participation of citizens in public meetings and voting assemblies, regular election of all magistrates for annual terms of office, and the fact that the tribal assemblies (*comitia tributa/concilium plebis*) passed laws that were binding on the entire Roman people. It is easy to see this as a form of direct democracy in practice, in which the 'Roman people' plays a central role in determining the composition of government and the passage of laws.

The main problem with this emphasis on the democratic elements of the Roman constitution is that it completely fails to distinguish between 'the ideals of popular political institutions and their practical functioning' (Mouritsen, 2001: 8). *Libertas* was the 'key political concept of the Roman republic', 'the common ideal invoked by all Romans who aspired to power', and consequently all political acts and arguments took place within the ideological framework of the liberty of the republic and the Roman people (Mouritsen, 2001: 11). This particular concept of liberty was subject to widely varying interpretation and use by Roman politicians, but in essence it conveyed a sense of freedom from the rule of monarchs, and referred to the rights of Roman citizens, such as formal equality before the laws, some protection against the arbitrary and oppressive exercise of power by magistrates, and the rights to pass laws and elect magistrates. Those who seek to portray the Roman republic as a democracy lose sight, however, of the degree to which 'political rights do not exist in a vacuum, but are embedded in social and economic structures which determine the extent to which they can be realised in practice' (Mouritsen, 2001: 146). Key questions that need to be addressed are who the 'Roman people' were in reality, and the extent to which they could exert effective influence over the governance of Roman society. As Mouritsen observes:

'the people', who formally represented the primary source of political legitimacy in the Roman state, bore little relation to the people who exercised these powers in the popular institutions. There were two 'peoples' in Roman politics: the ideal and the actual. The people as a political concept were distinct from the people as physical reality, and the direct nature of participation meant that the two were effectively separated. There was a stark contrast between the *populus Romanus* as collective political agent and the restrictive way in which this role was performed in practice.

(Mouritsen, 2001: 16)

The distinction between 'the Roman people' as a political concept and the people who actually participated in public meetings and the voting assemblies is crucially important, because 'in Rome the people's institutions may have been powerful, but that does not mean that the people as a whole were' (Mouritsen, 2001: 17).

The first problem with the depiction of the republic as a democracy is the small scale of the public meetings and voting assemblies relative to the citizen population. Those gathering in the public meetings and voting assemblies are referred to as 'the Roman people' by Roman magistrates even if the assembled crowd only numbered several hundred or thousand citizens. Mouritsen (2001: 19) estimates that the Comitium, which was located in front of the Senate House (*Curia Hostilia*), where the tribal voting assembly met until 145 BC, probably held a maximum of 3,600 and certainly no more than 4,800. The area in the Forum in front of the Temple of Castor was larger (80 by 60 metres), but it could hold no more than 15,000 to 20,000 people standing, and when the time-consuming nature of the group voting procedures is taken into account, it seems likely the number attending the tribal voting assemblies was considerably less than 10,000. It would have taken an assembly of 10,000 15 hours to vote if all the tribes were called upon to vote, and 9.5 hours if only two-thirds of the tribes cast their votes (Mouritsen, 2001: 23).

The *comitia centuriata* met in the larger space of the Saepta (a large structure built of wood) on the Campus Martius, and probably following the introduction of the secret ballot in 139, the tribal assemblies moved there. Although it is estimated that as many as 55,000 voters may have assembled there, Mouritsen (2001: 32) convincingly argues that the actual number of voters is likely to have been much lower once the practicalities of the voting procedures are taken into account. But even if over 50,000 voters took part in the elections for higher magistrates, this only constitutes a very small percentage of the total citizen population. As Mouritsen (2001: 32) observes:

> until 145 hardly more than 1 per cent of the citizens could take part in legislation and perhaps also in the elections of lower magistrates. This proportion must have fallen even further with the expansion of the citizenry in the first century, despite the change to a larger venue. For the higher offices the capacity of the Saepta could hardly have accommodated more than 3 per cent of the approximately 910,000 voters registered in 70/69.
>
> (Mouritsen, 2001: 32)

In short, only a small minority of citizens voted. Even if Mouritsen's figure of 3 per cent is a serious underestimate, and we accept Mullen's estimate that as many as 55,000 voters assembled, this still amounts to just 6 per cent of the citizens eligible to vote in 70/69 (Mouritsen, 2001: 28).

The low levels of attendance were obviously considered acceptable by senate and the magistrates because there were no attempts to introduce a 'statutory quorum prescribing minimum levels of attendance required to pass laws or elect magistrates. Even the most far-reaching bills could be passed by any number of citizens, as long as the correct procedures were followed' (Mouritsen, 2001: 33). Note also that even though the total number of citizens increased dramatically, there was no move to a substantially larger venue, suggesting that the percentage of citizens who participated in voting declined as the total citizen population grew. Finally, the geographical centralisation of Roman politics had important practical implications for participation. As Mouritsen observes, 'the simple fact that the citizens of a sizable territorial state could deliver their vote only in one topographical location illustrates the extent to which large-scale participation was deliberately precluded through the institutional framework' (2001: 95).

Although Millar (1998: 210) stresses that the available evidence is too sketchy to be able to determine 'the levels or significance of participation by citizens' in the voting assemblies, nonetheless he confidently asserts that there could be 'participation and voting, in both elections and legislation, and Roman political life was conducted in full awareness that this was possible', so 'the exclusive right of the assemblies to pass legislation is by far the strongest reason why, in purely

formal terms, the Roman *res publica* has to be characterised as a democracy'
(1998: 210). But there are solid reasons to suspect that the participation of poor
and middling citizens was lower and more episodic than that of citizens from
the top two classes in Roman society (the nobles and *equites*). As the empire of
the republic expanded the gap between rich and poor widened. Although the
nobility experienced growing wealth, 'there are few signs of any improvement in
the living conditions of the lower classes, which generally present a bleak picture
dominated by economic uncertainty, poor housing, food shortages and debt'
(Mouritsen, 2001: 135). Consequently, 'simply making a living for themselves
would have been a pressing concern for most members of the lower classes. In
order to provide food and other necessities an income had to be earned on a daily
basis' (Mouritsen, 2001: 135). Because the majority of the Roman population
was engaged in a daily battle for economic survival, attending public meetings
and voting assemblies would have been very difficult. Participation required
money and time, neither of which peasants, waged workers and small business
owners possessed in abundance. This problem was compounded because unlike
Athenian democracy, there were no payments for poorer citizens to attend
meetings and assemblies. These less affluent classes 'de facto would have been
excluded from the political scene by the lack of public remuneration, which in
effect left the *comitia* in the hands of the propertied classes for whom political
activity did not entail any material sacrifices' (Mouritsen, 2001: 37).

Public meetings or *contiones* often preceded the voting assemblies. A *contio*
was a non-decision-making meeting called by a magistrate or a priest at which
speeches would be made to an assembled crowd of citizens. Supporters of
the view that the republic was a democracy consider that 'the institution
represents an incontrovertible manifestation of the people's crucial role in the
running of the *res publica*' (Mouritsen, 2001: 38). Only a tiny proportion
of the citizen population could take part, however, and the *contiones* were
held frequently and sometimes were lengthy, meaning that only more affluent
citizens were likely to have the time to participate. Citizens had no right to
speak. The presiding magistrate controlled the proceedings and determined
who could speak. Consequently, the 'contio was not designed as a forum
for open debate, not even between members of the political class. [It was]
essentially an official platform for politicians to present themselves and their
views to small, presumably influential audiences' (Mouritsen, 2001: 46). The
nature of the issues discussed 'would have militated against regular plebeian
participation' (2001: 45). These meetings were gatherings in which the wealthy
and influential predominated. As Mouritsen observes:

> the *contio* can be seen as a formal consultation of the people for whom
> politics mattered – and who mattered to the politicians. As such it may
> simply have extended the political process to a broad section of the elite
> outside the active political class of office-holders and senators, while at the
> same time paying tribute to the venerable ideals of citizenship and *libertas*.
> (Mouritsen, 2001: 45–6)

Consequently, it is reasonable to assume that 'the Forum belonged to the world of the elite rather than the populace in general' (Mouritsen, 2001: 45).

In the fifth century the *comitia centuriata* voting assembly was based on the army, and reflected the close relationship between the class structure and military hierarchy discussed above. Accordingly, the voting groups in this assembly were determined on a class basis. Although the precise details are not entirely clear, it is generally held that there were approximately 193 voting groups (centuries) of which 18 were of *equites* (men of the highest census class who were designated as cavalry) and 170 of infantry, divided into five classes based on the amount of property owned. Seventy infantry centuries (35 senior and 35 junior) also comprised members of the highest census class. The second class made up a further 20 centuries (ten senior and ten junior), so the top two census classes constituted 108 out of 193 centuries. Classes three through five made up approximately 80 centuries, while those below the fifth class made up five centuries (two for smiths and carpenters, two for trumpeters, and one for proletarians without any property).[3] As these figures indicate, the richest census class could always outvote the lower census classes unless it was divided, which was very rarely the case:

The effect of the system was to ensure that the older, richer citizens carried more effective voting weight, the younger and poorer less. It was a consciously contrived conservative system, insuring that the better-off voters would always determine the business, unless they were divided amongst themselves.

(North, 2006: 62)

Cicero admired the structure of this assembly because he considered that 'the *suffragia* should be in the control not of the *multitudo* but of the rich' (quoted by Millar, 1998: 200).

The explicit class bias in military assembly voting was less pronounced in the organisation of the tribal assemblies. The division of the population of Rome into four tribes predated the republic but was maintained and developed after the monarchy had been overthrown. Originally membership of a tribe was determined by both geography and genealogy. As Roman territory expanded and Roman citizenship was extended throughout the Italian peninsula, the number of rural tribes was increased until it reached 31 in 241. After 241, new Roman citizens were added to the existing rural tribes arbitrarily 'with no attempt to introduce a greater equality between them' (Brunt, 1988: 24). There were two main tribal assemblies in operation following the conflict of orders. The *concilium plebis* was the original assembly of the plebeians, which elected and was presided over by the tribunes, while the *comitia tributa*, a later

---

3 There is no fully consistent account of the numerical breakdown of the *comitia centuriata* in the available sources, see for example Beard and Crawford (1985: 50–1), Brunt (1988: 24), Lintott (1999: 55–61), Mouritsen, (2001: 94) and Ward et al. (1999: 63).

formation, was presided over by a consul or praetor and may have included patrician voters (although this seems unlikely (Lintott, 1999: 55). These assemblies passed legislation binding on all Roman people (Taylor, 1966: 6).

Although all citizens enjoyed formal voting equality within the tribes, regardless of whether they were rich or poor, in reality a strong bias in favour of the upper classes was also evident in the tribal assemblies. Wealthy citizens from the rural tribes, many of whom maintained houses in Rome, were more likely to participate and vote than peasant farmers. Even though the population of the city of Rome increased dramatically until it had around a million inhabitants in the late republic, the number of tribes for Rome remained set at four. The limited voting power of the urban citizenry was exacerbated because most freed slaves and their dependants were also placed in these tribes. Offsetting this to a degree, substantial rural to urban migration during the second and first centuries BC led to an increasing proportion of urban voters being enlisted in the rural tribes. Nonetheless, the overall structure, composition and operation of the assemblies clearly favoured the wealthy.

The procedures of all the voting assemblies were elaborate and time-consuming. Only magistrates and tribunes could convene the assemblies and propose laws. Proposed legislation and candidature for the magistracies had to be publicly announced at least three market days (that is, at least 17 days) in advance (Lintott, 1999: 44). Although the assemblies were often preceded by *contiones*, once they were convened there was no discussion, questioning or debate. The assembly could only accept or reject proposals – it could not amend proposals or take initiatives of its own. The assembly began with a prayer, and there may have been a short introductory speech by the presiding magistrate (Lintott, 1999: 45). If the assembly was convened to vote on legislation, the proposed legislation would be read aloud. Those present remained standing and were organised into centuries or tribal groups depending on the type of assembly. Although it is not entirely clear how these groups were kept separate, it seems likely that ropes were used for the *comitia centuriata* until the late republic, when a large wooden building provided long parallel corridors for the 35 tribes to pass through in order to cast their votes (Mouritsen, 2001: 26–32; Taylor, 1966: 46–58).

Voting always took place on a group rather than an individual basis, and a simple majority of votes in each group determined the vote of that group. In the *comitia centuriata* voting took place in the order of the classes, with the richest class voting first, and within classes selection by lot was used to determine the voting order. Voting in the *comitia centuriata* was also sequential, so members of the bottom three census classes and the proletarians were only called to vote if voting in the top two classes was evenly split. The order of voting in the tribal assemblies was again determined by lot and sequential, so once 18 votes were cast in favour of or opposition to proposed legislation, voting ceased even though the remaining tribes had not voted. As this suggests, these procedures were time-consuming, and elections could take from four hours to an entire day. Written secret ballots were introduced in 139 for elections and

131 for legislation (Lintott, 1999: 47). This enabled the process of voting to be completed more quickly because it made simultaneous voting possible within groups, but the votes still had to be collected and counted for each century or tribe, and the evidence indicates that the process still took most of a day.

Other features also cast doubt over whether these assemblies constituted a form of democracy. First, there are very few instances of rejection of proposals. Thus from the origins of the republic to the mid-second century the *comitia* might have been no more than 'an acclamatory body, which hardly ever exercised the formal choices put before it' (Mouritsen, 2001: 67). This changed in the late republic, when the *comitia* did regularly pass laws that were opposed by the Senate. Nonetheless there are only five certain cases of proposals being rejected for the last 150 years of the republic (2001: 64). Second, most of the issues addressed in the *contiones*, legislation proposed to the assemblies, and the election of magistrates were of limited relevance to the vast majority of citizens and did not address their pressing social and economic concerns. Third: 'the Roman plebs took to the streets whenever it wanted to assert its interests. Public demonstrations, often caused by food shortages, were a common occurrence in Rome, which in itself is a serious indictment of the ability of the assemblies to serve as outlets for popular grievances and concerns' (Mouritsen, 2001: 147). Fourth, formal property qualifications for the magistracies meant the overwhelming bulk of citizens could not stand for office. There is a dramatic contrast here with Athenian democracy, where all citizens who were old enough could perform as magistrates. Thus in the Roman Republic electoral choice was limited to selecting individuals from within the wealthiest class to perform as magistrates. Elections were largely fought on the basis of the attributes of the individuals rather than political issues.

Because the bulk of the citizen population probably viewed these elections as largely irrelevant to their lives, it took a great deal of effort by the candidates and their supporters to get people to turn up to vote. Bribery of voters was considered to be a common and normal aspect of the political process. It was especially prevalent in the elections of magistrates, which were generally considered more important than votes on legislation, with much greater effort and resources being expended by the elite to ensure higher levels of participation in the voting. Consequently, a political career necessitated a high level of spending on bribes, public entertainment, payments to clients and so forth. The connection between money and power was direct and transparent. By the first century AD, it was a common saying that 'a provincial governor needed to make three fortunes, one to recoup his election expenses, another to bribe the jury at his expected trial for misgovernment, a third to live off thereafter' (Crawford, 1978: 172).

There was a breakdown of tight senatorial control over the passage of legislation through the assemblies during the last 150 years of the republic, as poor and middling citizens started to exert greater influence in the voting assemblies. North observes that 'The popular will of the Roman people found expression in the context, and only in the context, of divisions in the oligarchy' (1990: 18). This is most evident in the support for the *populares* when they proposed legislation that was favourable to the interests of the poor and middling citizens and strongly opposed by the Senate. Bribery appears to have increased substantially from the 130s to the fall of the republic, but it is important to note that in view of the time-consuming nature of the voting procedures and the lack of public financial compensation, this often simply involved providing poorer citizens with the money they needed to participate. Interestingly, the Senate conspicuously failed to mobilise enough voters to counter the proposals that it found objectionable in the assemblies and focused its efforts elsewhere, such as issuing the *senatus consultum ultimum*, which effectively empowered designated magistrates to take whatever measures they considered necessary, including the assassination of offending magistrates and the violent suppression of their supporters, when it considered that magistrates with popular support threatened its interests and/or the traditional organisation of the Roman state (Lintott, 1999: 88–93).

Other key institutions of the Roman system of government were also not democratic. The tribunes of the plebs were wealthy plebeians who originally were meant to protect citizens against harsh treatment by members of the patrician nobility, but they became increasingly co-opted by the aristocratic and oligarchical elite that ruled Roman society:

As the number of plebeian families who held high office and joined the senate grew, many of the new tribunes tended to be young men from their ranks who were starting out on political careers. Naturally, most of them desired to cooperate with the consular nobles, who controlled the senate, and they were willing to exercise their vetoes over fellow tribunes in the interest of powerful nobles. Eventually, the tribunes seemed to be so tamed that they, too, were admitted to the ranks of senators, even though they were not strictly part of the *cursus honorum*.

(Ward et al., 1999: 67)

The business of the Senate was 'conducted along strict lines of seniority in rank', and accordingly the *princeps senatus*, the most senior and leading member of the Senate, would speak first, followed by the censors-elect and censors, and then others in descending rank order. The most junior members did not speak at all. Consequently, senatorial debate was 'framed by the consular nobility and would have proceeded along lines laid down by the early speakers' (Ward et al., 1999: 67). The consuls and other magistrates had powerful incentives to avoid acting in ways that were likely to antagonise the Senate.

Magistrates during their brief year of office were not really independent of the noble dominated senate. Not only were they dependent for advice on the collective wisdom of the ex-magistrates who comprised the senate, but also they … were looking to become senators if they were not already, and those who already were senators hoped to advance in rank. Even the consuls were dependent on the senate for funds and for appointment to prestigious or lucrative military commands and, after the acquisition of an overseas empire, provincial governorships. Accordingly, there was great pressure to conform to the wishes of the powerful *consulares* in the senate, who formed a virtual oligarchy.

(Ward et al., 1999: 67)

The Senate, being composed of ex-magistrates who held their positions there for life, with great collective experience in the accumulation of wealth, the legal system, public administration, religious affairs, military command and foreign policy, was immensely powerful despite the fact that its constitutional role was limited to issuing decrees rather than passing laws. It effectively managed the state's finances, the conduct of war and the formation of military policy, managed the governance of the provinces, took responsibility for law and order issues throughout Italy, determined much religious decision making and practice, and was responsible for Rome's foreign policy. Finally, although its formal constitutional role was limited, it was prepared to disregard these limits if it considered it necessary. Defending the *senatus consultum ultimum*, Cicero emphasised that the moral authority of the senate derived from its ruling class composition: 'When the senate, the *equites* and the *boni* acted in unison, any established convention could be over-ruled' (Mouritsen, 2001: 148).

In summary, the Roman republic was not a democracy as such. The wealthy nobility completely dominated the political system. This domination did not rest on one feature of the constitution and system of government, but arose because of a broad range of mutually reinforcing social, economic, military, religious and political factors. 'While there was no formal exclusion of the lower classes, the logic of the system naturally favoured people with time, resources, interest and a certain level of integration into the world of politics' (Mouritsen, 2001: 130). Above all else, the domination of public meetings and the voting assemblies by the magistrates, and the heavily skewed participation of citizens from different social classes, mark the Roman republic as a political system ruled by the few rather than the many. North observes that 'The assemblies were convoked, presided over, addressed and dismissed by elite members in their roles as magistrates, and conducted according to voting systems privileging the well-off and inhibiting the poor from engaging in any kind of conflict with them' (1990: 16).

In essence Roman civilisation was ruled by a patrician-plebeian nobility, encompassing those who derived the bulk of their wealth from the exploitation of slave labour on large agricultural estates and the *equites* who derived their wealth from commerce and tax collection in the provinces, throughout its history. As North puts it:

the Roman oligarchy exercised an inherited, unchallenged authority going far beyond anything we know of in Athens, including a virtual monopoly of all forms of political initiative. If there was such a thing as Roman democracy, it was non-participatory to an extreme degree, and therefore in many ways at the opposite pole to Athenian democracy. If we were to attempt to classify Rome as a Greek city, then we ought to ask where Aristotle would have put it, given its very high property qualifications for any form of participation other than voting and – when it came to voting – its savage system of weighting in favour of the better-off, at least in important elections.

(North, 1990: 15)

Furthermore, although the Roman ruling class paid lip-service to the democratic elements of the constitution:

The profound respect for a notional *populus Romanus*, professed by all Roman politicians, went hand in hand with a disdain for the actual people, highlighting not only the ambiguous nature of the concept in Roman politics but also the distance between the elite and the populace.

(Mouritsen, 2001: 141)

Roman government was government of the rich, for the rich and by the rich. 'The elevation of wealth as a source of personal virtue lay in the aristocratic belief that only the rich man had freedom of choice and thus was able to act according to moral principles' (Mouritsen, 2001: 139). Finally, 'the attitude of the upper classes to the common people seems largely to have been one of contempt. Like many other aristocracies throughout history, the Roman elite viewed the lower classes as morally and intellectually inferior' (Mouritsen, 2001: 139).

FROM THE PRINCIPATE TO THE FALL OF THE ROMAN EMPIRE, 27 BC TO 476 AD

Declared Augustus in 27, Octavian fundamentally remodelled the Roman state. This is referred to as the principate, from the word *princeps*, which was subsequently used as one of the emperor's titles up to 282 AD, and which meant first among equals within the senatorial nobility. The remodelled Roman state was, according to Ste Croix, 'one of the most remarkable constitutional constructions ever devised by man, and it was supremely successful in maintaining social stability, in a sense of the dominance of the Roman propertied classes' (1981: 360). It constituted 'a stable form of government that enabled the Roman Empire to enjoy a remarkable degree of peace and prosperity for two centuries' (Ward et al., 1999: 252). Although of great interest to historians of classical Antiquity, the details need not concern us here because it is generally recognised that the battle of Actium in 31 BC marks the end of the republic and the beginning of the end of the democratic elements within it.

Although the decline and fall of the Roman empire is not part of the history of democracy as such because the democratic elements of the Roman constitution were gradually but eventually comprehensively extinguished during the principate and dominate epochs, nonetheless it forms an important part of the historical backdrop to the emergence of feudalism and the transition from feudalism to capitalism. The internal and external causes of the decline and fall were interconnected and mutually reinforcing. As we have seen, the territorial expansion of the empire from the origins of the republic to Trajan's conquests was fuelled by the capture of slaves who were forced to work on large agricultural estates in Italy and the provinces, as well as performing a wide variety of other forms of productive labour. The harsh and oppressive exploitation of slaves engaged in agricultural labour was a key source of the surplus product appropriately by the ruling class, and contributed to the economic growth and prosperity needed to sustain the expansion of Rome's armed forces and civilisation. Slave labour obtained in this manner allowed for a very high rate of exploitation because it was cheap, easily replaceable, and did not require slave owners to bear the costs of its reproduction. 'With the final closure of the imperial frontiers after Trajan, the well of war captives inevitably dried up' (Anderson, 1974a: 76). As this suggests, a major internal cause of the decline and fall was the requirement, which gradually became more pressing from 180 to 476 AD, to provide material conditions sufficient for the generational reproduction of slave labour. Because this meant that slave owners had to provide more than the minimal amount of food, water and rest necessary for the daily replenishment of slave labour, the costs of slave owning increased and the rate of exploitation declined.

Externally, the Roman empire faced a qualitatively higher level of sustained pressure from hostile military forces than the republic. The specifics of this are extremely complex but the general pattern is clear. From around 175 to 284 'Rome had to mount prolonged defence of its eastern provinces and at the same time of its Rhine–Danube frontier' (Mann, 1986: 287). These wars were largely defensive and did not generate the large influx of slaves and booty that characterised Roman warfare during its expansive phases. The cost of military defence against its external enemies increased enormously, and placed crippling fiscal pressure on the Roman state. Emperors responded by increasing taxation of the peasantry. In addition to the declining surplus produced by slave labour, the Roman economy was not based on intensive technological innovation, aimed at getting more outputs from the same level of input; rather, as Mann observes, 'the major Roman inventions were *extensive*, extracting more outputs from more coordinated, organized inputs' (1986: 285). The Romans 'were ill-equipped for what we call technological development because all of their major achievements were built, not on reducing inputs but on *extending* and *organizing* them' (Mann, 1986: 285). Once it was no longer possible to obtain episodically, but very substantially, increased inputs (principally slave labour and land) for production though imperial conquest, economic stagnation was inevitable.

As a result of sustained external military pressure, 'between 235 and 284, the Roman fiscal-military system broke down with disastrous effects on the economy in general' (Mann, 1986: 288). The empire in the west could have collapsed but a series of important military victories in the 270s and 280s gave 'a breathing space of about fifty years. Diocletian (284–305) and his successors, principally Constantine (324–37), took full advantage' (Mann, 1986). The sweeping reforms brilliantly conceived and implemented by the Emperor Diocletian saved the empire in the west for another century, but simultaneously set in train a series of interrelated and mutually reinforcing developments that ultimately sealed its fate. Among other things, Diocletian introduced conscription on a permanent basis, doubled the size of the army (under Constantine the army was further expanded to 650,000), and fundamentally reorganised the tax-collecting capacity of the Roman state to meet the increased cost. The civil bureaucracy was increased very substantially in order to conduct systematic appraisals of the tax-paying capacities of all Roman citizens. The main land and poll taxes tended to rise steadily, until by the end of the empire the rates of land taxation were probably over three times those of the later republic, and the state was absorbing between a quarter and a third of gross agrarian output (Anderson, 1974a: 96).

The reform of the taxation system contributed to the decline of slavery and the rise of the *coloni* or serf form of unfree labour. The *colonus* was a dependent peasant tenant, tied to his landlord's estate, and paying him rents either in kind or cash. This probably involved a decline in the rate of exploitation, because of the higher reproduction costs than the slave labour of the empire's territorial expansion phase (Anderson, 1974a: 76-80). It also contributed to the 'decentralisation of the economy as local landowners attempted to increase their independence from imperial power through the self-sufficiency of an estate economy' (Mann, 1986: 292).

Diocletian's reforms, which excluded the senatorial nobility from military command, had the effect, from mid-fourth century onwards, of shifting the locus of political power away from Rome towards the military camps of frontier areas. As if this was not bad enough, 'the establishment of Christianity as the official Church of the Empire [begun under the rule of Constantine from 312 to 337] was henceforth to add a huge clerical bureaucracy – where none had previously existed – to the already ominous weight of the secular state apparatus (Anderson, 1974a: 91). This meant that the Roman empire of the fourth and fifth centuries was loaded with a vast increase in its military, political and ideological superstructures at the same time that its agrarian economy was in serious decline.

'The military pressure of the barbarians' precipitated the final phase of the decline (Mann, 1986: 293). The centuries of Roman rule and the increasing reliance of Rome on mercenaries and barbarian peoples forced to serve in Rome's legions had 'spillover' effects on the 'barbarian' peoples to the north and near east: they became better organised militarily, more centralised politically and more prosperous economically. At the same time the increasing taxation of the peasantry undermined their commitment to resisting barbarian invasion and led to an intensification of a variety of forms of class struggle such as banditry, peasant revolt and mutinies. The final Roman emperor in the west was defeated in 476, and the remnants of Roman civilisation disintegrated during the century that followed.

CONCLUSION

The rise and eventual decline of Roman civilisation was of world historic significance. It survived for nearly a thousand years in the west, much longer in the east, dominated a large part of the world for over 600 years, and left a historical legacy that profoundly influenced the subsequent course of European history. It is important to recognise that republican Rome exerted far greater influence than democratic Athens over the revolutionaries who overthrew the rule of absolutist monarchies and established representative democracy during the eighteenth and nineteenth centuries. As Sellers observes:

> The vocabulary of eighteenth-century revolution reverberated with purposeful echoes of republican Rome as political activists self-consciously assumed the Roman mantle. James Madison and Alexander Hamilton, the primary authors and advocates of the United States Constitution, wrote together pseudonymously as 'Publis' to defend their creation, associating themselves with Public Valerius Poplicola, founder and first consul of the Roman Republic. ... At every opportunity, American and French revolutionaries proclaimed their desire to re-establish the 'stupendous fabrics' of republican government that fostered liberty at Rome. ... American and French republicans thought of themselves as part of a 2,000-year-old tradition originating in Rome.
>
> (Sellers, 2004: 347)

Although this may overstate the case somewhat, there is little doubt that republican Rome was a key reference point for the revolutionaries who were seeking an alternative to the absolutist rule of monarchs, and at the same time wanted to prevent the majority of poor and middling citizens – peasants, artisans, waged workers and members of the petty bourgeoisie and lower professions – from exerting a dominant influence over the governance of society.

As Wood (1995: 225) observes, the American redefinition of democracy that culminated in the US Constitution of 1789 has a historical ancestry much more firmly rooted in SPQR (the senate and people of Rome) than in the participatory model of democracy created in Athens. In view of this, there are some striking similarities between aspects of the constitutional arrangements of the Roman republic and the US Constitution, such as developing forms of citizenship that were much more extensive and inclusive than in the Athenian democracy, but much more limited in terms of the actual capacities that citizenship conferred on the majority of people to exert effective influence over the judiciary and all levels of government. Therefore the Roman republic and the long-term historical trajectory of Roman civilisation are an important part of the historical backdrop to the historical revival of democracy in the English, French and American revolutions.

GUIDE TO FURTHER READING

For overviews of the history of the Roman republic and empire in single chapters see Anderson (1974a: 53–103), Harman (1999: 71–86) and Mann (1986: 250–300). Anderson and Harman provide Marxist accounts while Mann applies a neo-Weberian approach. The best short book-length introductions to the history of the republic are Brunt (1971a), Crawford (1978) and Shotter (1994). Numerous textbooks focusing on the republic and empire are available for students of classics and ancient history, including Constable (2003), Flower (2004), Le Glay et al. (2004), Rosenstein and Morstein-Marx (2006), Sinnigen and Boak (1977), Ward et al. (1999) and Woolf (2003).

Culham (2004) provides an account of the gender dimension of the republic. Dupont (1992) provides an illuminating account of daily life in Rome. Much has been published on the conflict of orders: Raaflaub (2005) brings together a useful set of recent accounts. Brunt provides a very useful account of the late republic (1988) and the role of slavery in it (1971b). Ste Croix's *The Class Struggle in the Ancient Greek World* is a contemporary Marxist classic, and is essential reading (see, in particular, 1981: 327–408, 453–503). For the argument that the Roman republic should be considered a democracy see Millar (1998) and Yakobson (1999, 2006). Brunt (1988: 23–32), Mouritsen (2001), and North (1990, 2006) provide the other side of the debate. Lintott (1999: chs 5–6) provides another contribution to the debate, and a useful account of the constitutional and institutional arrangements of the republic. Taylor (1966) remains a useful account of the voting assemblies.

3

The early Middle Ages and the transition from feudalism to capitalism

INTRODUCTION

The historical narrative in Chapter 2 concluded with the overthrow of the final western Roman emperor (Romulus Augustulus) in 476 AD. This chapter provides a condensed overview of the early Middle Ages and the emergence of feudalism in Europe, emphasising the scale of the social, economic and demographic decline from 476 to 800 as well as the prevailing social forms of agricultural production that were central to the emergence of feudalism from the ninth century onwards. By the thirteenth century feudalism had, as Anderson puts it, 'produced a unified and developed civilisation that registered a tremendous advance on the rudimentary, patchwork communities of the Dark Ages' (1974a: 182). The substantial population growth from the tenth to the thirteenth centuries, including the re-emergence of large towns, and the increasing weight of military, state and religious requirements, placed feudal agricultural production under mounting pressure. A generalised crisis of feudalism ensued, with famine becoming widespread during the early decades of the fourteenth century, followed by the Black Death that swept across Europe recurrently from the first outbreak of the bubonic and pneumonic plague in 1347–9 to the mid-fifteenth century.

This prolonged crisis ultimately had different outcomes in Eastern Europe, France and England (Brenner, 1985, 1990, 2007). In Eastern Europe the outcome was intensified exploitation of serfs and peasants by noble landlords, in France it involved the growth of an absolutist tax-gathering and office-providing state, and in England it gave rise to capitalist relations of production in the countryside between noble landlords, capitalist tenant farmers and agricultural wage-labourers. This set of developments is the focus of the second section of the chapter.

THE EARLY MIDDLE AGES AND THE EMERGENCE OF FEUDALISM IN EUROPE

Historical retrogression during the early Middle Ages

In recent decades it has become intellectually unfashionable to refer to the period from 476 to 800 as the 'Dark Ages' characterised by the collapse of

Roman civilisation and major historical retrogression. The rejection of the depiction of decline after 476 has been driven, on the right, by right-wing revisionist and Christian historians, and on the left, by the poststructuralist rejection of historical materialism and lack of interest in economic history. Determining the extent of the decline after 476 is important because if we accept that there was in fact the collapse of an advanced civilisation followed by a major decline from 476 to 800, then this highlights the extent to which all civilisations, including the civilisation of advanced capitalism, are impermanent and vulnerable to collapse. Little wonder that intellectuals who are profoundly wedded to the status quo wish to minimise the scale of the decline.

In fact, the collapse of the western Roman empire (WRE), with its centralised and highly militarised tax-gathering state, organised into provinces with layers of imperial, provincial and municipal administration, had a profound impact on the subsequent trajectory of societal development across the west of the European continent and the British Isles. According to Wickham (2005: 830) it led to 'the involution of fiscal systems' and, 'above all, the weakening of regional aristocracies, and thus of exchange systems and of material culture as a whole'. As this suggests, there was generalised decline across the entire area of the former WRE. Indeed, one of the remarkable features of the intellectual rejection of the conception of the Dark Ages is how little factual support it finds in the evidence provided by early medieval archaeology:

> the more attached historians become to continuity (or to 'transformation') rather than to sharp change, the further they diverge from archaeologists. Archaeologists see very substantial simplifications in post-Roman material culture in the fifth to seventh centuries (the exact date varies according to the region), which in some cases – Britain is one example, the Balkans another – is drastic; only a handful of Roman provinces, Syria, Palestine and Egypt, did not experience it.
>
> (Wickham, 2009: 9)

From 476 until around 800 there were major and closely interrelated declines in economic production and exchange, population and urbanisation. Economic decline was most rapid and severe in the former Roman province of Britain, where by the early fifth century it had 'reverted to a level of economic simplicity similar to that of the Bronze Age, with no coinage, and only hand-shaped pots and wooden buildings' (Ward-Perkins, 2005: 124). As could be expected, the economic decline in the area of the former Roman provinces surrounding the western Mediterranean and in Gaul was more gradual:

> starting in the fifth century (possibly earlier in Italy), and continuing on a steady downward path into the seventh. Whereas in Britain the low point had already been reached in the fifth century, in Italy and North Africa it

probably did not occur until almost two centuries later, at the very end of the sixth century, or even, in the case of Africa, well into the seventh.
(Ward-Perkins, 2005: 124)

Based on a survey of the available archaeological evidence, Ward-Perkins (2005: 126) concludes that 'by AD 700 there was only one area of the former Roman world that had not experienced overwhelming economic decline – the provinces of the Levant, and neighbouring Egypt, conquered by the Arabs in the 630s and 640s'. In concrete terms, this generalised economic decline involved the declining use of coinage to facilitate trade; slower and more hazardous transportation networks; less economic specialisation across different regions; less sophistication and lower output of artisan production; lower levels of productivity, specialisation and output in agriculture, including a deterioration in the availability and variety of foodstuffs (indicated among other things by the declining size of livestock); the construction of fewer, smaller, more poorly designed buildings made out of less robust materials (wood and thatch rather than brick, marble and tiles); widespread cessation of investment in the construction and maintenance of sewage and water infrastructure in the cities and towns; and a major deterioration in the availability and quality of pottery and tableware. Interestingly, a survey of data on 'the ratio of total harvest yield to seed replanted', which 'gives us an index of the level of development of forces of production, for it incorporates all improvements in techniques', finds that 'there was a substantial drop in yield ratio with the collapse of the empire in the West' and, further, that the economic achievements of the Roman empire in this regard were 'agriculturally unmatched in its own heartland [Italy] for a thousand years' (Mann, 1986: 265).

Foreign invasion, bubonic plague epidemics beginning in Constantinople in 541–2 and recurring periodically during the sixth to eight centuries, deteriorating medical knowledge and treatment, economic decline, and the possibility that the peasant population may have restricted its births, resulted in a substantial western demographic decline (Wickham, 2005: 550). Throughout the history of the republic and empire, Roman society was urbanised and its cities and towns played a key role in the overall social, economic and political arrangements of that society. From 476 to around 800 a trend towards deurbanisation characterises all of the successor kingdoms that occupied the territory of the former WRE. By 800 the bulk of the cities and towns had either become much smaller, including the largest cities of classical antiquity – Rome and Constantinople – or disappeared altogether. The collapse of the WRE also contributed to a long-term general decline of literacy. This affected not just the peasantry, where literacy was probably always less prevalent, but also the aristocracies, and even some of the monarchs, of the successor kingdoms during the sixth, seventh and eight centuries. By 800, reading and writing became increasingly the sole preserve of the church (Ward-Perkins, 2005: 166).

The origins of feudalism in Western Europe

Wickham (2005, 2009) convincingly argues that the origins of feudalism stretch back through the early Middle Ages to the growing decentralisation of the economy and rise of the *coloni* (or serf) form of unfree labour during the final two centuries of the WRE, with the more direct antecedents of feudalism becoming active during the ninth and tenth centuries. The dramatic expansion of the Carolingian empire from 717 to 814 and its break-up during the ninth century set in train a series of developments that eventually led to the emergence of feudalism throughout Western Europe and the British Isles during the period from around 850 to 1100 (Anderson, 1974a: 137).

Lacking a centralised tax-gathering state, the Carolingian kings (Charles Martel, 714–41, Pippin III, 741–68 and Charlemagne, 768–814) were largely dependent on extracting the surplus product of the peasants working on their lands, as well as the military and political support of the aristocracy, which could only be maintained through making regular grants of land to them (Brenner, 1990: 171). This was only sustainable as long as the empire was being expanded by successful wars of conquest. Once this momentum ground to a halt, the break-up of the empire was inevitable. But it helped to both spread and entrench a central feature of feudalism, a system in which aristocrats performed military services for the monarch in return for favours and protection. 'Grants of land by rulers thereby ceased to be gifts, to become conditional tenures, held in exchange for sworn services' and:

> the eventual result of this convergent evolution was the emergence of the 'fief', as a delegated grant of land, vested with juridical and political powers, in exchange for military service. The military development, at about the same time, of heavy armoured cavalry contributed to the consolidation of the new institutional nexus, although it was not responsible for its appearance. It took a century for the full fief system to be moulded and rooted in the West; but its first unmistakable nucleus was visible under Charlemagne.
>
> (Anderson, 1974a: 140)

The Carolingian period was also crucial because throughout much of the territory of the empire 'aristocratic local hegemony became in practice complete' and the autonomy of the peasantry declined, with a growing number of 'peasant families bound to the soil, owing dues in kind and labour services to their masters' (Wickham, 2001: 91; Anderson, 1974a: 141).

During the ninth and tenth centuries, Vikings from the north (beginning around 834), Hungarians (Magyars) from the east, and Muslims (Saracens) from the south repeatedly invaded the kingdoms of Western Europe and the British Isles by land and sea. Although the Saracens mainly returned to their homeland after conducting raids aimed at obtaining booty and slaves, eventually the Vikings settled in parts of the British Isles (particularly Scotland and Ireland) and in the area of West Francia that became Normandy, while the Hungarians settled in the area of present-day Hungary. The main effect of these invasions was to hasten the process of the fragmentation and localisation of political, juridical and political power. As Anderson observes:

> It was in the last decades of the ninth century, as Viking and Magyar bands ravaged the West European mainland, that the term *feudum* first started to come into to use – the full medieval word for 'fief.' It was then too that the countryside of France, in particular, became criss-crossed with private castles and fortifications, erected by rural seigneurs without any imperial permission, to withstand the new barbarian attacks, and dig in their local power. The new castellar landscape was both a protection, and a prison, for the rural population. The peasantry, already falling into increasing subjection... were now finally thrust downwards to generalized serfdom. The entrenchment of local counts and landowners in the provinces, through the nascent fief system, and the consolidation of their manorial estates and lordships over the peasantry, proved to be the bedrock of the feudalism that slowly solidified across Europe in the next two centuries.
>
> (Anderson, 1974a: 142)

As this suggests, the geopolitical situation prevailing in the west around 1000 was fluid, complex and fundamentally different from contemporary Europe's centralised nation-states with clearly defined and fixed territorial borders. Nearly conquered by the Vikings during the ninth century before King Alfred's army decisively defeated them in 878, England was dominated by an Anglo-Saxon kingdom in 1000 that would be overrun by the Norman conquest of 1066. Celtic-speaking Wales had four kingdoms in 800 but by 1000 was dominated by one (Wickham, 2009: 492–3), Ireland had a patchwork of kingdoms and Viking settlements, and Scotland one major kingdom (of Alba) with the Vikings controlling all of the north and the islands. The Treaty of Verdun of 843 had divided the Carolingian empire into three kingdoms; by 1000 West Francia, East Francia and the kingdoms of Burgundy and Italy were in reality loose confederations of principalities. The Islamic caliphate of Cordoba occupied most of the Iberian peninsular. But the important point to note is that despite the bewilderingly fluid and complex nature of the rule of, and military conflict between, these territorial kingdoms:

> in a chronologically sequential and geographically uneven process from roughly 900 to 1050, public power cascaded down the ladder of political units – from dukes, to margraves, counts, and vice-counts – until even the smallest landed lord, the castellan, had appropriated the erstwhile regalia power of the ban [that is, royal powers of command, taxation, punishment, adjudication, and decree]. 'Counts, castellans, knights were not merely landowners with tenants but sovereigns with subjects.'
>
> (Teschke, 2003: 86)

In short, the political and military power of kings was generally declining while the power of aristocrats was rising and becoming increasingly localised.

The central features of feudalism

By the end of the eleventh century AD feudalism had become dominant throughout Western Europe. There were major regional variations which we shall discuss shortly, but first it is important to identify the central common characteristics of early feudalism: that is, the feudalism that prevailed from around 1000 to 1300 in much of Western Europe. Whereas the barbarian kingdoms that occupied the territory of the former provinces of the WRE preserved a public political sphere, albeit in a diminished form compared with the western Roman polity, it 'is the public world in this sense that weakened in the tenth century and, in particular, the eleventh in the West, above all in the West Frankish lands. The parameters of politics changed' (Wickham, 2009: 563). In particular:

> the old public rights now taken over by local lords were seen as part of their property, and could be divided between heirs or alienated away. Lordship could be claimed by people who had never met a king; the title of the count could be assumed in some areas by anyone who was powerful enough, and passed on to his heirs.
>
> (Wickham, 2009: 563)

In settings where over 90 per cent of the population worked and lived in the countryside, towns generally being small, few and far between, political, juridical and military power was exercised at a predominately local level while the real power of the monarch rested on the maintenance of a complex network of hierarchical vassalage relationships.

As Anderson (1974a: 152) observes:

> The feudal mode of production in the West thus originally specified suzerainty: it always existed to some extent in an ideological and juridical realm beyond that of those vassal relationships whose summit could otherwise be ducal or comital potentates, and possessed rights to which the latter could not aspire. At the same time, actual royal power always had to be asserted and extended against the spontaneous grain of the feudal polity as a whole, in a constant struggle to establish a 'public' authority outside the compact web of private jurisdictions.
>
> (Anderson, 1974a: 152)

Consequently in all feudal societies there were forces pushing the polity in the direction of internal fragmentation, intra-ruling-class tension and conflict, and aristocratic contestation of the monarchy itself, and forces propelling the polity in the opposite direction, such as the aristocratic need for political and military unity to ward off invasion by foreigners and to suppress peasant revolts too powerful to be overcome at the local level.

Although during the ninth and tenth centuries in all regions aristocrats continued to make some use of slave labour, and in some regions a substantial number of peasants managed to hold on to their land, the dominant historical trend was towards 'the caging of the peasantry: more and more, the huge peasant majority of the population of Western Europe became divided up into localized units, controlled more and more by local lords' (Wickham, 2009: 530). The main forms of surplus extraction in early feudalism were either serfdom, in which peasant producers were subject to customary ties that bound them to the land and person of their lord, or various forms of tenancy. As Anderson points out:

> The peasants who occupied and tilled the land were not its owners. Agrarian property was privately controlled by a class of feudal lords, who extracted a surplus from the peasants by politico-legal relations of compulsion. This extra-economic coercion, taking the form of labour services, rents in kind or customary dues owed to the individual lord by the peasant, was exercised both on the manorial demesne attached directly to the person of the lord, and on the strip tenancies or virgates cultivated by the peasant. Its necessary result was a juridical amalgamation of economic exploitation with political authority.
>
> (Anderson, 1974a: 147)

The extra-economic coercion was both complex and repeatedly contested. Brenner (1985: 15) highlights the fact that 'the very distribution of ownership of the land between landlord and peasant was continually in question'. Furthermore, the rent that lords extracted from their serfs assumed a range of complex forms. It did so because:

> There is very little in the way of direct lease and contract. We have instead a theoretically fixed, but actually fluctuating, structure of customary rights and obligations that define landholding arrangements. These specify in the first place the regular (ostensibly fixed) payments to be made by the peasant to the lord in order to retain his land. But they often lay down, in addition, a further set of conditions of landholding: the lord's right to impose additional extra-ordinary levies (tallages and fines); the peasant's right to use, transfer and inherit the land; and finally, the very disposition of the peasant's own person, in particular his freedom of mobility.
>
> (Brenner, 1985: 19)

Nonetheless, certain key characteristics of these forms of surplus-extraction stand out. First, lords ruled over a manorial territory that could be divided in widely varying ways but:

> was typically split into two parts of unequal size: the lord's 'desmesne' and

the peasants' holdings, which in the aggregate were much larger. Neither farming practices nor technology distinguished them, however: similar crops were planted, livestock raised, rotations followed, and implements used on both parts.

(DuPlessis, 1997: 16)

Peasants produced their own means of subsistence on the small strips of land that the lord allowed them to cultivate, often paying rent in kind out of whatever surplus they might produce, while if they were serfs, they also owed labour services to the lord. Although the distinction was never entirely clear-cut, those owing labour services to the lord were regarded as unfree whereas those who were rent-paying tenants or free-holding owners were free.

Second, in so far as rent took the form of labour services on the lord's manorial demesne, there was a spatio-temporal separation of necessary and surplus labour. As Marx put it, 'every serf knows that what [she or] he expends in the service of [her or] his lord, is a definite quantity of [her or] his own labour-power' (1967a: 77). When rents were paid in kind (in the form of physical product), it was also clear to the peasant that rent absorbed a high proportion of any surplus product that they produced over and above their subsistence needs (and of course, rent frequently absorbed such a high proportion of the peasant's total output that even bare subsistence was threatened).

Third, as mentioned above, provided the peasants were able to pay the rent demanded by the lord, they had (widely varying) customary rights of land tenure. They had access to a specified plot of land on which to produce their subsistence. In respect to rights of tenure, the heritability of peasant landholding was a major and recurrent focus of struggle between nobles and peasants, and consequently varied widely over time and across different regions. Nonetheless, peasants often had limited rights of bestowal/inheritance.

Fourth, in addition to the virgate provided by the lord, peasants often had access to the common land of their village, the resources of nearby forests, and sometimes freely possessed small plots of land or 'allods'. Communal village land, forests and allods were important because they ensured that across Western Europe there 'always remained a significant sector of peasant autonomy and resistance, with important consequences for total agrarian productivity' (Anderson, 1974a: 148).

Fifth, during the tenth and eleventh centuries both serfs and tenants were increasingly subject to the juridical power of the local lord: 'The local powers that castle lords managed to enforce over the villages around were no longer illegal or quasi-legal, as opposed to the public law of kings, but instead became a new legality: in France, in particular, for a century in some regions, this is all there was' (Wickham, 2009: 563). From 1000 to 1300:

justice was the *central* modality of political power – specified as such by the very nature of the feudal polity. ... Mediaeval 'justice' factually included a much wider range of activities than modern justice, because it structurally occupied a far more pivotal position within the total political system. It was the ordinary name of power.

(Anderson, 1974a: 152–3)

Sixth, while the lord exerted tremendous power over the peasants he controlled:

at the same time, the property rights of the lord over his land were typically of degree only: he was invested in them by a superior noble (or nobles), to whom he would owe [military service]. His estates were, in other words, held as a fief. The liege lord in his turn would often be the vassal of a feudal superior, and the chain of such dependent tenures linked to military service would extend upwards to the highest peak of the system – in most cases, a monarch – of whom all land could in the ultimate instance be in principle the eminent domain.

(Anderson, 1974a: 148)

Seventh, the church was a major landholder, and the ecclesiastical aristocracy extracted the surplus of peasant producers on its land in an essentially similar manner to the lay aristocracy. Of even greater significance to its role as a large holder of land was the crucial ideological role the church played in legitimating the status quo:

The popes, bishops and abbots also devoted themselves to upholding the wider values they shared in common with the lords. The cathedrals, the greatest artistic creations of the period, were also the greatest symbol of the power of the ruling class, emphasising the God-ordained character of society, with heavenly hierarchies of angels, saints and humans corresponding to earthly hierarchies of kings, lords, abbots, bishops, knights and commoners.

(Harman, 1999: 148)

In sum:

the feudal economy was thus structured, on the one hand, by a form of precapitalist property relations in which the individual peasant families, as members of a village community, individually possessed their means of reproduction. ... On the other hand, under feudalism, the individual lords reproduced themselves by individually appropriating part of the peasants' product, backed up by localized communities of lords connected by various sorts of political bond, classically vassalage.

(Brenner, 1990: 172)

The most common forms of class struggle in feudal society arose from this basic division of property relations. On the one side, the nobility sought to increase dues in kind, labour services, and to generate additional revenue through other imposts (such as fines and levies). On the other, serfs and peasants resisted this and pushed for lower rent, freeholding rights, enhanced village autonomy with common rights to shared land, and greater freedom of mobility.

Although all feudal societies were predominately rural, towns played an important role even in early feudalism, and from the mid-fifteenth century onwards the towns became larger and their economic, political, religious and intellectual functions became increasingly significant. The extent and importance of the role that towns played in the transition from feudalism to capitalism is much debated, but the fact that they enjoyed a significant degree of autonomy from the aristocracy, church and king is beyond dispute. As Hilton (1992: 6) notes, 'The essential feature of towns, large or small, was occupational heterogeneity in an economy which produced, bought and sold commodities other than those necessary for subsistence.' The autonomy of the inhabitants of the towns arose because in order to perform their functions as artisans, manufacturers, merchants and moneylenders, 'they would at least need freedom of status and tenure, freedom of movement and freedom of access to the market' (Hilton, 1992: 7). Furthermore, as Harman observes, 'Early feudalism was … an almost entirely rural society. But the rise of the towns was not something extraneous to this society – it was the result of its internal development' (1998: 81).

Towns played a crucial role in the development of the forces of production, and also in providing an escape route for serfs and support for the peasant struggles with the aristocracy in the surrounding countryside. Anderson (1974a: 195) considers that 'in every country the mediaeval towns represented an absolutely central economic and cultural component of the feudal order'. Yet their existence was precarious. 'Cities were atolls of civilisation (etymologically "citification") on an ocean of rural primitivism. They were supported by a terrifyingly slender margin of surplus agricultural production which could be destroyed swiftly by drought, flood, plague, social disorder or warfare' (White, 1972: 145).

The growth of feudalism

Feudalism in Western Europe grew substantially, economically, demographically and territorially, from the beginning of the eleventh to the mid-fourteenth century (Anderson, 1974a: 182). There was an impetus to growth amongst both the aristocracy and the peasantry, but it was weak compared with capitalist market economies because the primary social forms of surplus extraction (serfdom and tenancy) in feudalism gave rise to struggles over the appropriation of the current surplus product which tended to undermine attempts to increase its future magnitude. Nonetheless, because on one side lords were motivated by a desire to increase the production of the surplus product that they could appropriate from peasants, and on the other, 'the feudal mode of production that had emerged in Western Europe generally afforded the peasantry the minimal space to increase the yield at its own disposal, within the harsh constraints of manorialism', 'both lords and peasants were objectively engaged in a conflictual process whose overall consequences were to drive the whole agrarian economy forward' (Anderson, 1974a: 185, 187-88).

Feudal relations of production stimulated the substantial growth of the productive forces and were, in turn, conditioned by the development of these productive forces (Harman, 1998: 79–81, 111–12; 1999: 141–58). From 1000 to 1300 there was a very substantial increase in agricultural productivity, and subject to the impact of fluctuating climate conditions on a fundamentally agrarian economy, the total surplus product. 'The technical innovations which were the material instruments of this advance were essentially the use of the iron-plough for tilling, the stiff-harness for equine traction, the water-mill for mechanical power, marling for soil improvement and the three-field system for crop rotation' (Anderson, 1974a: 183; see also Duby, 1972: 191–212; Harman, 1998: 79–81; White, 1972: 147–62). As White (1972: 157) observes, 'The forward surge of European machine technology from the eleventh century onwards must be understood not as an accumulation of isolated items but as a single phenomenon of prime historical importance.' The invention of the mechanical clock and its diffusion through Western Europe was particularly significant because 'it created an increasing corps of craftsmen to make and repair them, and able to carry their skills into related fields. From the middle of the fourteenth century – a dismal age in most ways – the velocity of European technical growth increases markedly' (White, 1972: 160).

Even if annual economic growth was only 0.5 per cent, 'over 300 or 400 years this amounted to a transformation of economic life' (Harman, 1999: 142). Among other things, it contributed to substantial population growth: 'The total population of Western Europe probably more than doubled between 950 and 1348, from some 20,000,000 to 54,000,000' (Anderson, 1974a: 190). In conjunction with the continuing development of new military technology, it also underpinned the geographical expansion of the territory governed and/ or pillaged by feudal aristocracies in the Baltic, the Iberian peninsula and the Levant from the eleventh to the fourteenth centuries (Hollister, 1998: 189–205).

There were major regional variations in the configuration of feudal society in different parts of Europe. Although there is insufficient space to consider these fully here, it is important to note the major similarities and differences between England and France from 1000 to 1350. It is worth emphasising that:

the similarities considerably outweigh the differences, even if one looks as far away from England as Provence. In both countries the overwhelming majority of the population was rural, and most were peasant cultivators. The core of the peasantry in both countries consisted of producers with enough land to provide for the subsistence of the family, with sufficient surplus for transference in the form of rent (labour, kind, money) to the landowner – and in taxation to the state.

(Hilton, 1992: 19)

We have already considered most of the central features of feudalism as it took shape in France, because it was 'the central home of European feudalism' – emerging earlier and developing faster there than anywhere else (Anderson, 1974a: 157). Aristocratic power in France was more fragmented and localised than in England, with intra-ruling-class competition and conflict being much greater. From the tenth to the twelfth centuries the peasantry in France was subject to the juridical power of the local lord, and there was no centralised royal administration of justice. There was also no unified kingdom in reality. Instead, 'The great dukes and counts had, in effect, what were independent principalities, of which the duchies of Aquitaine, Brittany, Normandy and Burgundy, and the counties of Toulouse, Flanders and Champagne were the most important' (Hilton, 1992: 23). The establishment of a central monarchy was a protracted process. As Teschke observes:

The Capetian monarchy had to deploy the whole arsenal of feudal expansionary techniques to establish its suzerainty over Francia during the course of four centuries – from outright war and annexation, through dynastic marriage policies, alliance building, and bribery, to simple confiscation and enfeoffment. The local aristocracy was suppressed, co-opted, intermarried, bought off, or tied to the king by unstable bonds of vassalage.

(Teschke, 2003: 107)

The disunity of the aristocracy and the fragmentation of political and military power weakened the monarchy while simultaneously making it possible for the peasantry successfully to resist the continued imposition of serfdom, and from the late twelfth to thirteenth centuries to push for various forms of freeholding.

From the tenth to the fourteenth centuries, England differed most strongly from France in its development of a much more unified polity while also maintaining a more extensive and prolonged use of unfree labour (slaves and serfs). The more centralised polity of England developed from around 840 to 1066 under the Anglo-Saxon kings in response to the Viking invasions and occupations of the ninth and tenth centuries (Wickham, 2009: 455). Whereas in '840 Anglo-Saxon England was more or less back to the situation it was in in 700, in fact, with four roughly balanced kingdoms', only King Alfred of Wessex was able to successfully defeat the Viking army and become 'by his death, the only Anglo-Saxon king' (Wickham, 2009: 456). Crucially for the subsequent historical development of England, he followed up the military victory of 878 with a systematic upgrade of the military defensive capacity of his kingdom, introducing a 'large-scale military levy from the population', establishing 'a dense network of public fortifications', and requiring military service from his followers (Wickham, 2009: 457).

Thereafter the strength of the monarchy was assured by a number of developments that were to be of enduring significance and impact. First, a tax system was established in 990s and by the 'eleventh-century English taxation was more elaborate than any other post-Roman state managed in the West until after 1200' (Wickham, 2009: 464). Taxation increased royal wealth and power as well as underpinning 'the enduring solidity of the English state' (Wickham, 2009: 465).

Second, the monarchy in England, initially Anglo-Saxon then Norman, was successful in securing direct control over a higher proportion of the total land area of the kingdom than the Frankish kings.

Third, these sources of wealth meant that English kings had an undiminished capacity for patronage because they were not entirely dependent on granting land to secure the loyalty of lesser aristocrats.

Fourth, a system of what can be loosely described as public justice was maintained in England from the tenth century onwards (Wickham, 2009: 462; Maddicott, 2010: 1–4). Whereas the administration of justice in the Frankish kingdoms from the fall of the Carolingian empire until the thirteenth century was towards the increasing localisation of justice, with justice being the key mechanism of aristocratic domination of the peasantry, in England royal centralisation of the administration of justice constituted a major underpinning of royal power and authority. In contrast to the Frankish kingdoms:

> there was no permanent regional breakdown in at least southern England, no equivalent to the increasingly separate marches, duchies, counties of the Continent. Nor did private lordships develop; the shire and hundred assemblies controlled nearly all justice right up to the Norman Conquest.
>
> (Wickham, 2009: 466)

Finally, vassalage (the obligation of inferiors to perform military service for their superiors) was present and greatly strengthened by the Norman kings after 1066, but it remained generally weaker than in France from the tenth century onwards.

Crucially for the specific configuration (economic, social, political, military and religious) of the feudalism that was to emerge and develop in England until the seventeenth century, there was 'a revolution in land tenure, in which not just unfree, but also free, peasants ended up paying not tribute to lords and rulers, but rents to landowners' (Wickham, 2009: 468). Whereas there was a reasonably extensive free landholding peasantry throughout the British Isles in the eighth century, the spread of exclusive rights to property meant that England shifted from:

> being the post-Roman province with the least peasant subjection, in 700, to the land where peasant subjection was the completest and most totalizing

in the whole of Europe, by as early as 900 in much of the country, and by the eleventh century at the latest elsewhere. The lordships of France based on private justice did not develop in England but they hardly needed to; peasants were already entirely subject to lords tenurially, and many were unfree and thus had not rights to public justice either.

(Wickham, 2009: 469)

This development at the very beginning of feudalism in England explains why 'it became the European country where aristocratic dominance, based on property rights, was most complete, while also being the post-Carolingian country where kings maintained most fully their control over political structures, both traditional (assemblies, Armies) and new (oaths, taxation)' (Wickham, 2009: 471).

THE CRISIS OF FEUDALISM AND THE EMERGENCE OF ABSOLUTISM IN FRANCE AND CAPITALISM IN ENGLAND

The crisis of feudalism

As mentioned above, throughout most of the tenth to thirteenth centuries the feudal societies of Western Europe grew strongly both economically and demographically. By the end of the thirteenth century population growth, urbanisation, aristocratic consumption and spending on warfare, and the growing sophistication and size of royal administrations, had not been sufficiently matched by the growth of agricultural productivity and output. Indeed, agricultural output had started to decline and there were mounting signs of crisis even before poor crops resulting from adverse climatic conditions led to famine in much of Western Europe from 1315 to 1317 (Hilton, 1985: 131; Nicholas, 1992: 401–5). With malnutrition widespread the population was vulnerable to the epidemics that swept across Europe from the mid-fourteenth to the mid-fifteenth centuries. The worst of these was the Black Death, which 'had spread through central France by the early summer of 1348, to southern England by that winter, and to the rest of England and the Low Countries by the end of 1349. It then moved northeast into Scandinavia and Slavic Europe' (Nicholas, 1992: 404). Most regions lost from a quarter to a third of their populations, the cities generally lost more than this, and there were further outbreaks of bubonic plague 'in 1358, 1361, one in 1368–69 that may have been more severe in the Low Countries than that of 1348–49 and another in 1374–75 that was especially virulent in England' where as much as half the population may have perished (Nicholas, 1992: 404). From the mid-fourteenth to the mid-fifteenth century, 'a hellish cycle' unfolded in which the growth of population and output during the preceding centuries was followed by 'ecological collapse and mass starvation' (Callinicos, 1987: 165).

War was always a central feature of feudal geopolitics but it became endemic, most notably with the Hundred Years War from 1337 to 1453, which was mainly a war between England and France but also partly a civil war in France between the Burgundians and the house of Orleans. The dukes of Burgundy were allies of the English Plantagenet kings, who had Norman ancestry and a hereditary claim to the French crown. The dukes of Orleans supported the Valois kings, who ruled the parts of France that remained neither occupied by the English nor controlled by the dukes of Burgundy (Hollister, 1998: 335–42). In conjunction with declining agricultural output and successive plagues, the war had a devastating impact on the French peasantry, while many aristocrats had their possessions pillaged by the English armies (Keen, 1991: 248–52).

In England, shortly after the war with France ended, a civil war (the War of the Roses) broke out between the aristocratic houses of York and Lancaster over possession of the English crown, and raged intermittently from 1455 to 1485.

The wars were also expensive. Royal taxation grew everywhere, and taxes became oppressively high in the cities which had to rebuild and strengthen their fortifications. Papal taxation was carried to new and refined levels. Taxation thus contributed substantially to a serious shortage of bullion by the fifteenth century that hindered liquidity in the economy.

(Nicholas, 1992: 404; see also, Mann, 1986: 424–30)

Little wonder that Bois writes that during the century from around 1350 to 1450 'the greater part of the Continent was ... in the throes of a deep depression', suffering from:

a massive decline in population and regression of productive capacity. In scope and duration the phenomenon had no known historical precedent. It took place in an atmosphere of catastrophe: ceaseless epidemics, endemic war with its train of destruction, spiritual disarray, social and political disturbances.

(Bois, 1984: 1)

This generalised crisis soon generated an intensification of class struggle in which the landowning nobility sought to increase their exactions from the peasantry, and in which the peasantry attempted to use labour shortages to establish freehold title over their land and to push for lower rents. As Anderson observes:

these accumulated disasters unleashed a desperate class struggle on the land. The noble class, threatened by debt and inflation, was now confronted by a sullen and diminishing labour force. Its immediate reaction was to try to recuperate its surplus by riveting the peasantry to the manor or battering down wages in both towns and countryside.

(Anderson, 1974a: 201)

The aristocratic and royal attempts to make the peasantry pay for the crisis with varying combinations of increased tax and/or rent and/or seigneurial obligations provoked the largest peasant revolts in the history of European feudalism up to this point. 'The muffled, localized conflicts that had characterised the long feudal upswing suddenly fused into great regional or national explosions during the feudal depression, in mediaeval societies that were by now much more economically and politically integrated' (Anderson, 1974a: 202).

Although peasant resistance and revolt swept across the whole of the west, much of it small-scale and poorly recorded, three major revolts were particularly significant. In western Flanders, peasant revolt and the rebellion of the city of Bruges from 1323 to the popular movement's suppression by a French royal army in 1328 assumed an increasingly radical and egalitarian form, 'refusing to pay dues to the Church and dues to the lord' and ultimately seeking the abolition of serfdom (Harman, 1999: 150). A generalised peasant revolt in the area surrounding Paris, the *Grande Jacquerie* of 1358, arose in response to the severe depredations caused by the Hundred Years War and the imposition of a levy in order to pay the English a ransom for the release of French captive lords (Nicholas, 1992: 416). It was brutally suppressed by royal forces in June.

Responding to the royal imposition of a poll tax in 1380, 'coming after a sequence of heavy taxes' in previous years, in May and June of 1381 a revolt erupted in the south-eastern counties of England and London (Hilton, 1985: 152). It was by no means exclusively a revolt of the peasantry, but rather, as Hilton demonstrates, it brought together peasants (with richer peasants providing much of the leadership), merchants, petty traders, craftsmen, unskilled workers and thus the poor and middling strata of the towns and the city of London (1985: 216–18). The movement demanded an end to feudalism:

the end of all homage and service to lords; the distribution of all lordship (except the King's lordship) amongst all – in effect the abolition of lordship; the establishment of popular policing (the law of Winchester); the end of the control of labour; the division of church property amongst the commons; the clergy to have no property but only their subsistence.

(Hilton,1985: 219, 222)

This revolt was violently suppressed by an army summoned by King Richard II in June and July, with prominent participants continuing to be hunted down and executed for several years thereafter.

Although all of the major popular uprisings of the fourteenth century were successfully suppressed by royal armies based on the aristocracy, in conjunction with declining agricultural productivity and output, endemic war, and the devastating impact of successive epidemics, these struggles had a major and lasting impact on the subsequent course of European history.[1] The crisis of

---

1 The general crisis of feudalism during the fourteenth and fifteenth centuries, and the role that it played in emergence of capitalism in the English countryside, have been subject to wide ranging interpretations even within the Marxist tradition. Of course, non-Marxists reject the central thrust of the Marxist accounts, particularly the focus

feudalism during the fourteenth and fifteenth centuries was followed by a period of recovery from the mid-fifteenth to the end of the sixteenth centuries and then another major crisis in the seventeenth century. These crises prompted a generalized intensification of class struggle, which ultimately produced different outcomes across Europe. In Eastern Europe the nobility successfully expropriated the lands of peasant freeholders and tightened the grip of serfdom over the peasantry. In France and western Germany serfdom was successfully overthrown by the peasantry but peasants then became subject to the extraction of surplus from the absolutist state (in addition to the rents that many peasants still had to pay to local lords and the tithes that almost all peasants owed to the church). In England the outcome of the first generalised crisis of feudalism was the creation of conditions conducive to the emergence of capitalism: the gradual of achievement of absolute property ownership of land by the nobility, but a nobility which increasingly derived its income from the rents paid by capitalist tenant farmers, who in turn were able to exploit the growing class of agricultural wage labourers (Brenner, 1985, 1990, 2003a, 2007). It is worth focusing in more depth on France and England because the remainder of this chapter and the next focuses on the revolutions that subsequently unfolded in these two countries.

French absolutism

The absolutist state in France emerged from the crisis and class struggles of the fourteenth and fifteenth centuries.[2] It was developed as a response by the monarchy and sections of the ruling class to the peasant gains that:

> were significant at the beginning of the fifteenth century; in many areas of France, village communities had won corporative status and the right to enforce their claims to common lands. In addition, individual peasants had won heritability rights over their tenures. ... In short, for the peasantry as a whole this was a period of significant prosperity and economic advance.
> (Mooers, 1991: 47)

In contrast, the aristocracy found itself in a seriously weakened state of 'disarray, shaken in its fortunes and mentally ill-prepared for the effort of adapting to an unprecedented situation .... The lords were slowly being impoverished' (Bloch, quoted by Mooers, 1991: 47).

---

on exploitation, classes and class struggle (see for example Nicholas, 1992: 414–15). Perhaps to a greater extent than any other topic covered in this book, whatever is written here is likely to meet with disagreement from those wedded to other interpretations. See the guide to further reading for a brief discussion of the various Marxist interpretations.

2 For a highly illuminating and convincing account of the rise of absolutism and the background to the 1789 revolution in France see Mooers (1991: 47–64). In my view, this important work has not received the attention that it deserves. The next two paragraphs draw heavily upon it.

During the sixteenth century the gains that the peasantry had made in the previous century were rolled back through 'a combination of exorbitant new exactions, indebtedness to urban creditors and the growing burden of both royal and ecclesiastical tithes' (Mooers, 1991: 48). The peasants fought back, most famously in the mass revolts of the 1590s. Preferring 'royal authority to social anarchy', the aristocracy had no choice other than to support Henry IV (king from 1589 to 1610), and 'this was the basis on which Bourbon absolutism was constructed' (Salmon, quoted by Mooers, 1991: 49). In this respect, the absolutist state was 'a redeployed and recharged apparatus of feudal domination, designed to clamp the peasant masses back into their traditional social position' (Anderson, 1974b: 18). Absolutism also constituted the most historically advanced organisation of feudal society, as 'the absolute monarchies introduced standing armies, a permanent bureaucracy, national taxation, a codified law, and the beginnings of a unified market' (Anderson, 1974b: 17).

In essence, the French royal state, driven by its dire need to fund its military campaigns, dramatically increased the taxation of the peasantry, thereby intensifying intra-ruling-class competition, tension and conflict, since the aristocracy and monarchy were vying to obtain shares of the finite surplus produced by the peasantry. The potential for intra-ruling-class conflict was endemic since 'in so far as the absolutist state was forced to compete with the local nobility for a portion of peasant surplus, the Crown was naturally predisposed to the protection of the peasantry against intemperate exploitation by landlords' (Mooers, 1991: 49). Thus the absolutist state became dependent on the persistence of peasant ownership, but it also needed to maintain a degree of ruling-class unity sufficient to ensure the survival of the prevailing royal family and the continued exploitation of the peasantry by the aristocracy, church and state.

Eventually it achieved this through the creation of a large number of lucrative offices. 'By 1778 'there were no fewer than 51,000 venal offices in the law courts, the municipalities and the financial apparatus of the state' (Mooers, 1991: 54). These offices originally involved tax farming, but even though the administrative and military functions performed by office holders broadened considerably, office holding centrally involved revenue raising of some form for both the holder and the state. Furthermore, many of the offices became hereditary and 'office-holders thus came to see their positions as part of their rightful patrimony, resenting any arbitrary measures taken by the Crown which might threaten either the value or heritability of venal offices' (1991: 51). The sale of these offices became an important source of revenue, and also wedded the aristocracy to the state.

The absolutist tax/office state thus succeeded in establishing itself in France, as the outcome of much conflict over an extended period, not only by attacking sections of the aristocracy, but also by 'effectively reorganising much of the aristocratic class within the state itself, precisely by means of constructing a vastly expanded monarchical patrimonial group, composed of proprietors of offices and other beneficiaries of royal largesse' (Brenner, 2003a: 654).

In sum, as Brenner observes, in:

much of later medieval and early modern Western Europe (France and parts of Western Germany), although peasants succeeded in strengthening peasant possession, winning their freedom and destroying forms of surplus extraction by extra-economic coercion by individual lords, the lords succeeded, in response, in maintaining themselves by means of constituting a new, more potent form of now-collective surplus extraction by extra-economic compulsion, the tax/office state.

(Brenner, 1990: 183)

As the bourgeoisie emerged as a capitalist class its most wealthy members actively sought a share of the surplus produced by the peasantry. They did so by purchasing land and state offices while also seeking ennoblement – a trend aptly dubbed 'feudalisation of the bourgeoisie' (Mooers, 1991: 57). The upshot was that 'much bourgeois wealth, though not all, took on essentially the same character as noble fortunes. Proprietary wealth, comprising rents from land and the financial rewards of office made up approximately 80 per cent of all wealth in the late eighteenth century' (Mooers, 1991: 57). In contrast, the bulk of the peasantry was driven into poverty by rents, church tithes and state taxes that were 'generally so high that the majority of peasants were barely able to support their families, let alone retain anything to put to market' (Mooers, 1991: 49).

The situation of the peasantry was not helped by the necessity to have large families in order to provide security for illness, disability and old age (Brenner, 2007: 68–9). This led to the increasing fragmentation of peasant landholdings and contributed to the growing impoverishment of the peasantry. In France and much of western Europe this trend militated against the concentration of absolute property ownership of land. Aristocrats attempted to increase their ownership of forests and fisheries during the sixteenth and seventeenth centuries and this exacerbated peasant poverty. In view of the extraordinarily high rate of exploitation, peasants had little economic incentive to invest in specialisation and the introduction of new, more productive agricultural practices and techniques. The result was stagnation in both per-capita output and productivity.

One of the major problems generated by the sluggish growth of France's overwhelmingly agricultural economy was the increasing inability of the French state to compete militarily with the other major European powers, particularly England. The one obvious exception, the American War of Independence, merely proves the rule because, as we shall see in Chapter 6, although France and the United States emerged victorious militarily, the French state was virtually bankrupted by its involvement. The increasing inability of the French state adequately to fund its military activities – in addition to racking up taxes on the peasantry it borrowed enormous sums of money and became increasingly indebted – was caused by a deep-seated crisis in the entire system of surplus extraction that it presided over and derived its revenue from. This is of crucial importance because a 'central aspect of the dynamic of political accumulation which lay at the heart of absolutism, was the ability of the state to wage war. If this was disrupted, the whole structure of productive relations upon which the state rested was bound to be thrown into severe crisis' (Mooers, 1991: 63).

Explaining the emergence of capitalism in England

Appropriately, this takes us to a consideration of the very different outcome of the general crisis of feudalism in England. Brenner and other Marxists have developed a 'new social interpretation' of the transition from feudalism to capitalism, which provides an indispensable guide to the long-term sociopolitical trends from the mid-fourteenth to the seventeenth centuries that eventually propelled English society towards revolution.[3] The starting point of Brenner's interpretation is his compelling observation that:

> capitalism developed in England from the end of the medieval period by means of the self-transformation of the landed classes. As a result, the rise of capitalism took place within the shell of landlord property and thus, in the long run, not in contradiction with and to the detriment of, but rather to the benefit of the landed aristocracy.
>
> (Brenner, 1989: 2003a: 649)

This, he argues, is the key to understanding:

> the specific path of long-term political evolution in early modern England and helps to explain why this evolution did not take place without profound conflicts – conflicts that revolved around a far from capitalist monarchical state and that involved the powerful intervention of social forces outside the landed class.
>
> (Brenner, 1989: 303–4)

In no small part such conflicts arose because 'the "commercial classes", far from uniformly capitalist or ideologically unified, were divided from, and indeed in crucial ways set against, one another in consequence of their diverse relationships to production, property, and the state' (Brenner, 2003a: 649). This conflict generally focused on constitutional, economic, religious and foreign policy issues. It is crucial, Brenner argues, to recognise that the 'differing political and religious outlooks of the major socio-political actors'

---

3 See, for example: Brenner (1989: 271–304), Callinicos (1989: 113–72), Hill (1980: 109–40), Harman (1998, 1999, 2006), Mooers (1991, ch. 4) and Wood (2002). Although there are some major disagreements amongst these authors, they all attempt to overcome the problems and limitations of what Brenner describes as 'the traditional social interpretation' (2003a: 638–44).

in seventeenth-century England are shaped by 'their differing interests and experiences rooted in their differing relationships to capitalist development and its effects – or, more precisely, to the new forms of social-property relations and the new form of state that were the product of the transition to capitalism' (2003a: 650).

Brenner provides an illuminating analysis of the political and ideological ramifications of the changing form of surplus extraction that was central to the transition from feudalism to capitalism:

> What the transition from feudalism to capitalism on the land thus amounted to was the transformation of the dominant class from one whose members depended economically, in the last analysis, on their juridical powers and their direct exercise of force over and against a peasantry that possessed its means of subsistence, into a dominant class whose members, having ceded direct access to the means of coercion, depended economically merely on their absolute ownership of landed property and contractual relations with free, market-dependent commercial tenants (who increasingly hired wage workers), defended by a state that had come to monopolise force.
>
> (Brenner, 2003a: 650)

Feudal lords successfully transformed themselves into capitalist landlords, collecting commercial rents from tenant farmers producing for the market. Hence they no longer relied on extra-economic relations of politico-military coercion. Indeed, the landed aristocracy, far from being sent by these processes into a tailspin of economic decline, adapted remarkably successfully – 'because of their self-transformation – partly imposed on them, partly implemented by them – the greater landed classes thus succeeded in accumulating their great wealth and social power directly on the foundations of capitalist property and capitalist development' (Brenner, 2003a: 651).

Perhaps Brenner's most innovative insight concerns what he refers to as the 'immanently problematic' nature of the new form of state that emerged during the fifteenth to seventeenth centuries. The relinquishment of the lords' coercive capacities was a small price to pay for the establishment of a much more efficient form of surplus extraction. Whereas from the late twelfth century to the early fourteenth century the English aristocracy had enjoyed a period of unparalleled prosperity because they had been able, with the assistance of the monarchical state, to 'impose a tighter form of serfdom, of feudal domination, upon their tenants', the crisis of feudalism from the mid-fourteenth to mid-fifteenth century enabled the peasantry successfully to struggle for their freedom (Brenner, 2007: 96). Once free, peasants were endowed with the protection of the King's courts and thus no longer subject to the exertion of seigniorial power at local level. But in the struggles that unfolded from the mid-fourteenth to late sixteenth centuries:

> English lords succeeded in cutting short peasants' push to win not just

their freedom, but fixed payments and rights of inheritance to their land. They thereby at once established their property rights in the land and, by separating their tenants from their full means of subsistence, rendered them dependent upon the market.

(Brenner, 2007: 98; 2006)

The aristocracy thus relied on the monarchical state not to conduct the process of surplus extraction on their behalf, as was increasingly the case in France during this period, but to provide a juridical system that facilitated the shift towards and subsequent entrenchment of private property rights in land ownership. In this crucial respect 'landed-class elements contributed to and benefited from the creation of a new form of unified state with an unprecedented level of jurisdictional and legal unity and a novel monopoly of the legitimate use of force' (Brenner, 2003a: 651).

This state form was riddled with contradictions, tensions and conflicts because 'whereas capitalism and landlordism developed more or less symbiotically', 'the relationships of capitalist landlords and of the patrimonial monarchy [to this new state form] were essentially ambiguous and ambivalent and ultimately the source of immanent fundamental conflict' (Brenner, 2003a: 651). Several factors contributed to the emergence of conflict in the relationship of the aristocracy (acting as a class of capitalist landlords) to the monarchy, as well as in the different but related enmeshments of the aristocracy and monarchy with the central institutions of the English state during the fifteenth, sixteenth and seventeenth centuries.

One key aspect of the strengthening and unification of state power during the fifteenth and sixteenth centuries was the concentration of 'massive new, especially landed wealth in the hands of the monarch' (Brenner, 2003a: 653). As great patrimonial lords, English monarchs 'inherited political (prerogative) rights to economic resources sufficient to maintain themselves and to constitute their own political following' (Brenner, 2003a: 653). Based on this group of wealthy and powerful supporters, 'as well as the substantial power they derived from their formal control of the state as a whole – its operation and the appointment of its officers – English monarchs derived the power to pursue their own interests and those of their followers' (Brenner, 2003a: 653).

The combination of the substantial wealth of the monarchy and the concentration of coercive capacities in a centralised state was inherently problematic from the perspective of the parliamentary classes, because the monarch was therefore capable of threatening the interests of the landed classes – particularly the sanctity of absolute private property in the land and the unhindered exaction of rent from tenants. It should therefore come as no surprise that the royal levying of taxation without parliamentary approval became one of the major focal points of political and religious conflict between the landed classes and the monarchy. The carve-up of the social surplus product was of vital concern to them both, and the capacity of members of the parliamentary classes to exercise control over the collection of the bulk of the state's revenue was a pivotal element of their class power. The state as it developed in England prior to the revolution required collaboration between the capitalist landed classes (aristocratic landlords, minor gentry and yeomen farmers) and the monarchy while simultaneously generating tension and conflict between them. While cooperation was necessary 'in operating the state and governing the country', conflict was immanent because 'state action had become crucial to meet the needs of both the monarchy and the landed classes' (Brenner, 2003a: 657). In waging this conflict both sides had distinctive and potentially antagonistic sources of power, because while 'socio-economic power in the country generally remained in the hands of the landed class', government continued to be led, and to a considerable degree controlled, by the monarch (Brenner, 2003a: 657). More generally, during the same historical period, 'coercive powers and jurisdictional rights were, for the first time, clearly separated from the private property and private proprietors, to which and for whom they had historically been integral, and concentrated in a unified state structure, formally possessed by the patrimonial monarchy' (Brenner, 2003a: 657).

Brenner's (2003a: 665) essential point is that the 'differing socio-political positions within the state and with respect to private property' endowed the patrimonial monarchy and the parliamentary classes 'with conflicting interests and conceptions concerning the proper nature of the state, its constitution, and to lead them to differing general perspectives on foreign policy and religion, as well as state finance and administration'. Thus, while the monarchy initially had no long-term aim for an absolutist state and the parliamentary classes no conscious goal of parliamentary sovereignty – and while both certainly saw unity as a fundamental ideal and disunity a major danger – each was almost obliged to pursue its policy goals and defend its own conception of mixed monarchy (the prerogative and rights there defined) in ways that could easily lead in one or another of those directions (Brenner, 2003a: 665).

Brenner's account of the long-term causes of the English Revolution is not entirely adequate because of what he leaves out of his account. In particular this account fails consistently to maintain a sense of proportion with respect to the overall configuration of seventeenth-century English society, and as a consequence fails to place sufficient emphasis on the crucial role played by the 'middling sort of people' in the English Revolution (Manning, 1996: 8–15). Brenner's interpretation lurches dangerously in the direction of conceptualising the developments that resulted in the outbreak of the Civil War as largely taking place between the ruling class and the monarchy. Manning observes that:

Traditionally the events in England in the middle of the seventeenth century – collapse of government, civil war and revolution – have been seen as arising from divisions within the ruling class. Although true up to a point, this does not justify historians studying only the nobility and the gentry, and perhaps the clergy, lawyers and merchants, to explain these events. A vast amount of research has been devoted to discovering the causes of the divisions amongst the nobility and gentry, and the characteristics of those who took different sides, as if the other 97 per cent of the population did not exist or did not matter. More recently it has been recognised that people other than lords and squires did play parts worthy of investigation – for one thing they did most of the fighting and dying – and they did not always follow blindly the lead of their social superiors.

(Manning, 1996: 1)

The key point is that both 'the poorer classes' and the 'middling sort of people' played major, and at times decisive, roles in the English Revolution, and Brenner's conceptual framework seems to veer in the direction of neglecting this.

CONCLUSION

This chapter focused on such a broad period (476 to around 1640) of European history for three key reasons. The first was to highlight the extent to which the collapse of the WRE was historically regressive, centrally involving social, economic, demographic and intellectual decline. Among other things, this decline highlights the fact that when civilisations collapse, the outcome can be disastrous for the majority of the population, and the negative effects can persist for centuries.

Second, an understanding of the specific features of the societies of the barbarian kingdoms that came to occupy the British Isles and Western Europe after the collapse of the WRE is necessary in order to understand the emergence of feudalism.

Third, feudalism centrally involves forms of surplus extraction that necessitate extra-economic coercion of a politico-military nature. It thereby entails an even more vigorous suppression of democracy than that which prevailed in the Roman Empire. The only partial, but nonetheless important, exception was the cities that became increasingly independent throughout the feudal era (particularly those in northern Italy). In short, feudalism is inherently undemocratic.

Finally, the central theme of the analysis of the historical revival of democracy in the next three chapters is that democracy emerged concurrently with the emergence of capitalism in Western Europe and North America from the seventeenth to the nineteenth centuries. It is no grand coincidence of history that capitalism and representative democracy emerged concurrently. In essence, the emergence of both involved two interrelated and mutually reinforcing developments within complex and contradictory processes of historical change. The decline of feudalism and emergence of capitalism created social and economic conditions conducive to the emergence of representative democracy, and once established, this state form facilitated the further development of capitalism.

There was nothing inevitable about this process because the emergence of capitalism could also be associated with and facilitated by authoritarian political regimes, as in Germany, Russia and Japan during the nineteenth century. But wherever it emerged, capitalism created necessary, if not sufficient, conditions for the emergence of representative democracy. It did so by supplanting feudal relationships between serfs and/or peasants on one side, and noble landlords, church and state on the other, in which the appropriation of the agricultural surplus product of the former by the latter depended crucially 'on a superior coercive power, in the form of juridical, political and military status' (Wood, 1995: 209).

In place of the widely varying but generally coercive class relationships that characterised feudalism, capitalism gave rise to relationships in which the majority of the adult population, increasingly losing direct access to the means of production, would eventually become subject to a socio-economic compulsion to sell their capacity to work for a specified period of time to an employer for a wage or similar form of payment. Labour-power emerged as a commodity that could be bought and sold on so-called 'labour markets'. This was a revolutionary development because it removed the sticky web of relationships (social, economic, religious, political and military) that effectively ensnared the bulk of the population in oppressive ties of subjection to the authority of lords, church and state, and made possible the eventual bestowal of democratic citizenship rights upon the legal owners of labour-power who worked as 'employees' for 'employers'.

Furthermore, even though the elected assemblies that emerged during the course of the English, French and American revolutions were overwhelmingly dominated in composition (and much else) by wealthy property-owning men, it was widely assumed by these men and their followers that they were best placed to act as the representatives of those less fortunate than themselves. More importantly, even though these revolutions did not immediately create fully developed liberal representative democracies but rather democratised the relationship of socio-economically dominant classes to the state, they simultaneously created constitutional principles and forms of political representation that would become the focus of the struggles of workers and/or peasants for a much more extensive democratisation of the state in the more advanced capitalist societies. It was the demolition of feudalism by capitalism from the sixteenth to the nineteenth centuries that made the democratisation of these states historically possible.

GUIDE TO FURTHER READING

For Marxist accounts of the break-up of the Roman Empire, the ensuing retrogression of civilisation in the area of the former Roman empire that can still legitimately be called the 'Dark Ages', the post-Roman west from 550 to 750, and the origins of feudalism in the eighth and ninth centuries, see Anderson (1974a), Harman (1999: 103–5, 117–35, 140–4) and Wickham (2005, 2009). Ward-Perkins (2005) provides a valuable account of the Dark

Ages, effectively rebutting the arguments of those who downplay the scale of the decline after 476.

The transition from feudalism to capitalism has been extensively investigated and debated within the Marxist tradition. The first major debate focused on Dobb's (1963) *Studies in the Development of Capitalism* published in 1946, with the major contributions brought together in the collection edited by Hilton (1976). The second major debate was stimulated by Brenner's (1985, 1989, 1990, 2007) analysis of the transition, with an early set of responses in the collection edited by Aston and Philpin (1985). Wood (2002) defends and elaborates upon Brenner's approach in her account of the origin of capitalism (see also Wood, 1991). Harman (1998, 2006, 2008) convincing argues that Brenner and his followers have underemphasised the importance of the development of the productive forces under feudalism. Anderson (1974b) and Mooers (1991) provide the best accounts of the role played by absolutism in the transition from feudalism to capitalism. DuPlessis (1997) provides one of the best non-Marxist accounts of the transition from feudalism to capitalism.

4

The English Revolution and parliamentary democracy

INTRODUCTION

Representative democracy was not established through a prolonged process of peaceful reform but rather by revolutionary means. A series of revolutionary upheavals, economic and political crises, wars and civil wars, from the first Dutch revolt in 1565 to the end of the American Civil War in 1865, transformed previously existing states and established representative democracy.[1] Although Bismarck's 'revolution from above' in Germany and the Meiji Restoration in Japan are also of great historical significance (Mooers, 1991: 103–53; Akamatsu, 2010; Anderson, 1974b: 435–61; Jansen, 1995), three revolutions – the English (1640–89), American (1776–90) and French (1789–95) – played world-historic roles in reviving democratic forms of governance from the seventeenth century onwards and have been the most influential intellectually and politically. Accordingly, this chapter focuses on the English Revolution from 1640 to 1689, while the next two chapters focus on the American and French revolutions respectively.

The most basic aim of this chapter is to establish that what occurred in English society during this period was in fact a revolution. Even though Coward (2003: 185) accepts much of the revisionist critique of Marxist accounts of the revolution, he argues that 'the dramatic and unique nature of [the events of the 1640s] is incontrovertible'.

Within less than a decade the power of the monarchy was first drastically reduced, and then extinguished, the king executed and monarchy abolished, along with the other pillars of traditional society, bishops and House of Lords. The downfall of the crown and the established church meant the collapse of effective censorship of the press, and the emergence of radical ideas about religious toleration, political democracy, economic reform, fundamental restructuring of education and the law, and the imposition of new social values. What is more, these ideas were often voiced by men and

---

1 There is no space to consider the Dutch revolt against foreign rule by the Spanish Habsburgs in this book. For useful accounts of varying length see Brandon (2007), Harman (1999: 194-202), Parker (1977) and Van der Linden (1997).

women of low social status, whose views were only rarely heard in England before 1640 and after 1660. In these circumstances 'the English Revolution' does not seem to be an unreasonable term to use.

(Coward, 2003: 185)

As this suggests, the English Revolution was by no means simply and exclusively a revolutionary upheaval directed against absolutism and for democracy. It centrally involved the revolutionary assertion by a minority of the aristocracy and upper gentry, together with a majority of the staunchly protestant 'middling sort' of the people, of the rights and role of Parliament in governing England against the absolutist aspirations and catholic sympathies of Charles I (Manning, 1991; 1996: 6–11). But constitutional and political considerations only formed one part of a complex and dynamic array of closely interwoven issues encompassing political and constitutional reform, fiscal policy, ecclesiastical reform and religious divisions, social and economic questions (popular revolt, the sanctity of property rights, resistance to enclosure, taxes and tithes), English policy towards Ireland and Scotland and the mutually interactive impacts of events in the three kingdoms, England's foreign policy with respect to the other European powers, and military strategy, tactics and logistics in the various wars from 1642 to 1690.

This chapter provides a chronologically organised description of the social context, historical backdrop and main events in England during the seventeenth century, not only to highlight the revolutionary nature of these events, and the role played by class forces in the revolution, but also to highlight the extent to which it ultimately created a system of government that was substantially more democratic by the 1690s than that which prevailed during the 1630s.

THE ENGLISH REVOLUTION AND CIVIL WAR, 1640–59

English society in the mid-seventeenth century: population, class, gender and religion

It is important to have a sense of the scale and structure of English society in the seventeenth century. The population at this time was small compared with the present day. According to the Cambridge group's estimates, it increased from 2.3 million in 1522–3 to 2.774 million in 1541, 4.110 million in 1601 and 5.281 in 1656 (Coward, 2003: 8).[2] English society was also overwhelmingly rural, with the provincial towns and villages generally being small (Jack, 1996: 168–84). As Coward observes:

even at the end of the seventeenth century only about 5 per cent of the

---

2 According to Muldrew (2003: 150), the population of Wales increased from 250,000 in 1550 to 400,000 by 1650, the population of Scotland grew from 700,000 to 1,000,000 during the same period, and by the end of the seventeenth century the population of Ireland had reached 1,100,000.

population lived in towns of over 5,000 inhabitants outside London. Before 1650 there were only a handful of provincial towns in this category, including Norwich and Bristol, which had between 10,000 and 20,000 inhabitants, and Exeter, Plymouth, Worcester, Coventry, Ipswich, Colchester, York, and Newcastle upon Tyne with between 5,000 and 10,000.

(Coward, 2003: 32)

In view of this, it is remarkable that London 'grew at an exceptionally rapid rate in the sixteenth and early seventeenth centuries and by 1650 its economic and social importance was greater than before or since' (Coward, 2003: 29). The total national population grew rapidly from 1550 to 1600, and the population of London grew even more rapidly from 80,000 to 200,000. 'In 1650 London's population had reached 400,000, by which time it was about twenty times bigger than the largest English provincial town' (Coward, 2003: 29). The development of London into a city vastly larger than any other urban centre in the British Isles was highly significant for a number of reasons, not least the influence that the mass of the London population was able to exert over the central political institutions of the state at crucial points in the revolution (Beier and Finlay, 1986; Carlin, 1999: 43–5, 112–13; Lindley, 1997; Manning, 1991: 13–15, 49–180). Not only was it the case that 'compared with the rest of Europe, England had a highly integrated and centralised political system', London was the main trading and financial centre as well (Hughes, 1991: 33).

Although much is known about the major classes in English society during the seventeenth century, it is impossible to do more than roughly estimate the distribution of the population across the main social classes. The intricacies of a hierarchically ordered agrarian society make it exceedingly difficult to conceptually define and empirically identify the dividing lines between the peerage and gentry, wealthy and less wealthy gentry, less wealthy gentry and peasantry, and the peasantry and wage labourers (Wrightson, 1982: 17–38). As Manning observes:

at the top of English society there was a hierarchy of peers (dukes, marquises, earls, viscounts and barons – members of the House of Lords) and gentry (baronets, knights, esquires and gentlemen). 'Gentleman' had two meanings: it was the title of a man in the lowest rank of the gentry, but it also described the status of all peers and gentry and that which distinguished them from all the rest of the population, the plebeians. While all the peers may be allocated to the ruling class, the gentry were more diverse, differing greatly in wealth and power. Greater gentry, like peers, were big landowners who lived off the rents of tenants, but minor gentry had much smaller estates and were mostly farmers. The ruling class largely consisted of peers and greater gentry, and these will be termed the aristocracy.

(Manning, 1996: 6)

If we define the ruling class in these terms, then it constituted a small percentage of the total population. In 1600, Thomas Wilson estimated that there were 16,000 members of the gentry and 561 members of the nobility (Coward, 2003: 44). This may well be a very substantial underestimation of the actual sizes of these groups. Nonetheless, making the generous assumption that the 16,561 gentlemen were all married with three children and taking into account that important social groups such as the wealthiest merchants, financiers and lawyers should also be incorporated within the ruling class, this still suggests that it constituted substantially less than 5 per cent of the total population in 1600 (see also Stone, 1965: 21–128; Carlin, 1999: 119).[3]

The 'middling sort' is the term used to categorise those between the ruling class above, and the peasantry and the emerging working class below. It encompasses yeomen farmers, relatively affluent craftsmen, moderately affluent lawyers and small merchants, and made up somewhere between 20 per cent and 40 per cent of the population (Manning, 1991: 181–241, 1996: 8–11; Muldrew, 2003: 149; Richardson, 1998: 151). The ruling class and the middling sort formed what has aptly been termed 'the broad political nation': that is, the sections of English society most directly concerned with affairs of church and state (Hughes, 1991: 69–72). The remainder of society, perhaps making up somewhere between 55 to 65 per cent of the population, were poor tenant farmers of varying status, wage labourers (generally estimated to compose somewhere from a quarter to a third of the total population), and struggling craftsmen (Coward, 2003: 50–8; Manning, 1999: 9).

The role played by the main classes, and class fractions, in the English Revolution is particularly complex because members of the propertied classes had 'diverse relationships to production, property, and the state' (Brenner, 2003a: 649). Nonetheless it is mistaken to conclude that 'the allegiances of individuals do not appear to have been determined by their social status or wealth. There were prosperous and declining landed gentry, merchants, and lawyers on both sides' (Coward, 2003: 186). Although there were both royalists and parliamentarians amongst the aristocracy, gentry, merchants and lawyers, there were still significant class differences between royalists and parliamentarians, and important social and economic determinants of political allegiances. As Manning observes:

Parliamentarians were a small minority in the ruling class. Of the richest 23 peers, with gross rentals over £6600 a year in 1641, only seven were parliamentarians, and since two of these changed sides, only five were consistent parliamentarians. ... at the outbreak of the Civil War there were 700 gentry with estates of £1000 a year or more: out of these, parliamentarians numbered 197 in 1643, falling to 172 two years later due to defections. All the rest were not royalists because many remained

3   Assuming that all of the 16,561 gentlemen have wives and three children gives us 66,244, which is 1.61 per cent of the Cambridge Group's estimate of the English population in 1601 (4.11 million).

uncommitted to either side, but in the ruling class royalists probably outnumbered parliamentarians by two to one.

(Manning, 1996: 41)

It is clear that a substantial section of the landed aristocracy rallied in support of Charles I, preferring monarchy to the perceived dangers of the London mob and the potential threats to their power and privileges posed by an enlargement of parliamentary democracy and the growing unrest of 'the poorer classes' and the 'middling sort of people' who supported Parliament during the civil wars (Manning, 1996: 1; 1991: 319–25; Hill, 2002: 117–42).

Although the franchise was complex, and varied considerably across the counties and boroughs in different parts of England, Hirst estimates that the total electorate numbered somewhere from 200,000 to 300,000, the latter figure being at least 27 per cent and maybe as much as 40 per cent of the adult male population (1975: 105; also see Coward, 2003: 102). Although 40 per cent is probably a substantial overestimate, it still indicates that the franchise was much wider than the aristocracy and wealthy gentry, encompassing the bulk of the middling sort. Note, however, that 300,000 male voters only equates to 6.67 per cent of the total population in 1641 if we use Hirst's estimate of a one to five ratio of adult males (900,000) to the rest of the population (4.5 million). Clearly the operation of property requirements for voting debarred the bulk of the population from voting. Furthermore, voting was not by secret ballot but rather by open ballots, so the wishes of the wealthy could influence the voting of the less well off (Hirst, 1975: 109–31; Kishlansky, 1986: 12–48).

Class was not, of course, the only prominent feature of English society. The family-households of all social classes were organised patriarchally; fathers were expected to and generally did rule over their wives and children. Of course, there were substantial differences between classes, with the family-households of farmers, craftsmen and small traders typically acting as sites of both productive and reproductive labour, while ruling-class households performed an entirely different set of functions, maintaining the male line of descent in order to maintain the family heritage across the generations, facilitating and reflecting 'the obsession of the landed classes with expensive displays of wealth and status' (Coward, 2003: 46), socialising male and female children into more marked cultural forms of masculinity and femininity than were found among the men and women of the lower classes, and so forth. Gender inequality and the subordination of women was both legitimated by and reflected within religion and politics. Nonetheless, women of the middling sort, peasantry and emerging working class were actively involved in the protests and riots of the 1640s and 1650s, and 'elite women had the wealth, time and social contacts throughout the Stuart period to engage in political activities' (Foyster, 2003: 122; Rowbotham, 1972: 15–35).

Religious principles, ideas, practices and buildings shaped the daily lives of all members of society to varying but generally substantial degrees. The

Church of England was a protestant state religion. Attending a service in the local parish church every Sunday was legally obligatory, with regular absentees liable to be fined. Likewise all male members of the parish had to pay tithes, set at one-tenth of their income, produce or profit. Church courts imposed sanctions not only for church non-attendance and failure to pay tithes, but also for sexual immorality and heresy.

In order to understand why puritanism played such a large role in the revolution it is necessary to take some account of puritan attitudes towards the protestant Reformation in England. Because Henry VIII had driven the Reformation from the top down during the 1530s, with the support of the aristocracy who benefited greatly from the ensuing seizure and sale by the state of church land, it had taken a different and more moderate course than the protestant Reformation in continental Europe. Prior to the revolution the Church of England retained more aspects of catholicism than its European counterparts, including episcopacy, the wearing of clerical vestments, and bowing during church services. England only became a protestant country through 'a long, painful period of adjustment and conversion in the later sixteenth and early seventeenth centuries', and consequently by 1640 it was still a relatively new religion and 'on-going project' (Coward, 2003: 80; Carlin, 1999: 52).

Puritans did not differ from other protestants in their fundamental theological principles, but rather in the intensity and proselytisation of their theological beliefs (Hughes, 2003: 351). They considered that the Reformation was incomplete and that more fundamental reform of the church was required. Thus, for example, the London Root and Branch Petition of December 1640 'catalogued the alleged evils of bishops and demanded that "the said government [of bishops] with all its dependencies, roots and branches, may be abolished"' (quoted by Coward, 2003: 195). Hence the religious policies of Charles I and William Laud, who was appointed by Charles as the archbishop of Canterbury and head of the church in 1633, were an anathema to puritans, who saw them as returning the church to aspects of its pre-Reformation past. Nonetheless, for the most part, during the eight years prior to the revolution 'the vast majority of critics of the Church wanted to change it, not to leave it' and considered that 'there could be only one church in England, to which everyone born in England belonged, or ought to belong' (Carlin, 1999: 48). As the revolution unfolded from 1640 to 1660, 'Puritan hopes for the completion, at long last, of the reformation of the English church' became frustrated and ultimately largely unfulfilled (Hughes, 2003: 350). As English protestantism fragmented irrevocably, 'a remarkable range of religious sects and radical speculations developed – to the marvel of some and the horror of many; and a robustly self-conscious 'Anglican' commitment to a Protestant but not Puritan Church of England emerged, perhaps for the first time' (Hughes, 2003: 350).

Religious issues became highly charged politically during these decades because they were interwoven with economic, political, constitutional and foreign policy concerns such as widespread fear of internal threats (the catholic queen and the king's other 'wicked advisers', most of whom were suspected of being catholic sympathisers) and external threats (catholic France and Spain, catholics in Ireland). Furthermore, 'when the head of the state, the monarch, was also head of the Church religious nonconformity was not only heresy; it was treason' (Coward, 2003: 127–8).

As we shall see, the positions that the members of the various classes of English society adopted with respect to constitutional, political, foreign policy and religious issues often shifted fundamentally during the course of the revolution. When the Long Parliament was convened in November 1640 there was broad consensus among the propertied classes that constitutional reform was required to remove the worst features of Caroline government, and at this moment there was no straightforward correspondence between the class circumstances of parliamentarians and their support for or opposition to the king. Class location was, however, an important factor in determining the political directions taken by parliamentarians, members of the aristocracy and wealthy gentry, the 'middling sort', peasants and wage labourers as the revolution unfolded. As Manning observes:

> revolutions commonly begin with alliances between diverse social groups against an existing regime, and as the revolution develops the different and conflicting interests of these groups emerge. In the English Revolution opposition to Charles I and the royalists brought together a few aristocrats, some gentry and merchants, numerous farmers and artisans as well as labourers, leading historians to jump to the conclusion that it was not a class struggle. But it was with the progress of the revolution that class differences and class conflicts emerged, shaping the course and outcome of the revolution.
>
> (Manning, 1999: 15)

This is not, however, to deny that seventeenth-century English society was profoundly and extensively religious. In fact, religious ideas were consistently at the centre of revolutionary events. People of all classes made use of religious concepts in order to interpret, justify and provide prescriptions for their involvement in political developments. Royalists and parliamentarians both claimed that God was on their side. Nonetheless:

> while it is clear that religious issues were very important, they do not explain everything, for religious conflicts coexisted with political, social and economic conflicts, and each influenced the other. Where consciousness of class differences emerged from the economic and social situation in which people found themselves, and their relations to the system of production, it shaped religious and political conflicts.
>
> (Manning, 1996: 4)

Thus although the conflicts of the English Revolution were thoroughly imbued with religious concerns throughout, these conflicts and the ultimate political outcome (representative democracy within the framework of a constitutional monarchy) cannot be understood adequately without reference to the class structure and class forces of English society in the seventeenth century.

The historical origins of the English Parliament

Conservative intellectuals who do not accept the portrayal of the events from 1640 to 1689 as a revolution emphasise the institutional continuities in the historical evolution of the English system of government (Richardson, 1998: 206–7). In fact, there were elements of continuity in the development of the constitutional framework and political institutions of the English state from the origins of Parliament in the assemblies of the Anglo-Saxon kings of the tenth and eleventh centuries, through the development of these assemblies in the wake of the Norman conquest (1066), with the Norman kings recurrently convening a council of feudal magnates to advise them, and after Magna Carta (1215), to consent to pay taxes to the king (Maddicott, 2010: 1–156). More formal organisation of Parliament and the increasing importance of petitioning became a characteristic feature of the operation of parliaments during and following the reign of Edward III (1327–77), with the nobility and bishops (together constituting the Lords) meeting separately from knights, burgesses and gentlemen (the Commons) from 1341 onwards (Linebaugh, 2008: 21–45; MacKenzie, 1950: 9–21).

The kind of assembly from which the English Parliament emerged was not unique to England, and during the reigns of the last Anglo-Saxon kings it was influenced by Carolingian government (McKitterick, 2001: 40–3). England was unique, however, in the early emergence and continuing extent of the monarch's reliance on Parliament for the approval of legislation and granting of taxes, and the centralisation of the state and the representation of the nobility within it (Anderson, 1974b: 113–16; Wickham, 2009: 464).

Background and context, 1603–40

Like all revolutions the English Revolution was an historical phenomenon of immense scale and complexity. A brief narrative of events can obviously do little more than skim the surface, but it can anchor the discussion to broad factual reference points.[4] When Queen Elizabeth died in March 1603 leaving no heirs, the Scottish king, James VI, succeeded her as James I, king of England. James's proposal in 1604 to integrate the Scottish and English kingdoms was rejected by Parliament, and his relations with Parliament were not harmonious throughout his reign, with Parliament being suspended for most of the period from 1610 to 1621. A clash between the king and Parliament early in his reign, concerning whether the king had the right to exclude MPs from the Commons, 'led the House of Commons to declare that their privileges were inherited of right, and were not due to the King's grace' (Hill, 1980: 10). Furthermore, there was continuing conflict over foreign policy, with the Commons wanting

England to take the side of protestant Bohemia in the Thirty Years War against the catholic Spanish-Austrian Habsburg alliance. When in 1622 the protestant Parliament made the vote of taxation conditional on the king declaring war on catholic Spain, James I responded by dissolving it.

As mentioned above, the Elizabethan constitution had a major weakness that was the source of increasing conflict between the crown and Parliament in the decades leading up to the outbreak of revolution in 1640. Although the monarch had executive authority with respect to foreign policy and war, Parliament controlled the taxation revenue required in order to fund England's military activities. This source of tension, and the resulting fiscal crises of the English state, became increasingly acute as Elizabeth I, James I and Charles I were forced to sell royal estates, and consequently 'the average annual income [from these estates] dropped from £200,000 in the 1530s, to £72,000 in 1619, and to only £10,000 in the 1630s' (Coward, 2003: 108). This involved, from the perspective of the crown, a downward spiral in which inadequate funding from taxation approved by Parliament forced sale of crown land, reducing the annual revenue flow from this land, and increasing the financial dependence of the crown on parliamentary taxation.

The tension and conflict between king and Parliament escalated after Charles I became king, with Buckingham as his chief adviser, following the death of James I in 1625. Charles 'had none of his father's political ability and proved to be inflexible and uncompromising' and was 'the most inept monarch to have occupied the English throne since Henry VI in the fifteenth century' (Coward, 2003: 158). Russell and other revisionists argue that Charles's political incompetence was one of the major causes of the revolution (Underdown, 1996: 3). Although Charles's flaws of character, including his chronic incapacity to compromise regardless of the political circumstances, lack of intelligence, inability accurately to judge the strengths and weaknesses of his allies and opponents, duplicity, inarticulateness and arrogance, consistently fanned the flames of revolution, his personal failings must be placed amongst the broad range of long- and short-term causes of the revolution (Carlin, 1999; Hughes, 1991).

In fact, the entire period from 1625 to the outbreak of the revolution was characterised by escalating tension and conflict between Charles I and Parliament. Although it is not possible to provide a full account here, several points are worth noting. First, England's protestants did not view positively Charles's marriage to the catholic sister (Henrietta Maria) of King Louis XIII of France in 1625. Second, Charles committed England to a series of unsuccessful and costly military adventures which greatly exacerbated his financial problems and fiscal dependence on Parliament. Third, the imprisoning of five wealthy financiers for their refusal to provide him with a loan (the Five Knights case) led parliament to pass the Petition of Right in 1628, which declared illegal both arbitrary imprisonment and the collection of taxes without parliamentary consent (Hill, 2002: 12).

Fourth, Charles appointed William Laud as bishop of London in July 1628 and archbishop of Canterbury (head of the church) in 1633. Laud propounded the view that 'God's grace was open to all and that an individual could attain salvation by good works', that church governance should be in the hands of the king and bishops, and that emphasis should be placed on the 'sacramental and ceremonial aspects of the church service' (Coward, 2003: 174). During the 1630s Laud made sure that 'men of his faction were promoted, in Church and state' and that his vision of the church was fully implemented (Hill, 2002: 12). As a result, Laudians were seen 'as revolutionaries threatening the status quo in Church and society. [They] came to be seen as a group with a coherent doctrinal position and aims that were completely opposite to those held by most fellow English Protestants' (Coward, 2003: 174). Laud 'became the most hated archbishop of Canterbury in English history', and by supporting him Charles antagonised and alienated a large majority of protestants (Coward, 2003: 174).

Finally, developments in Ireland compounded Charles's other problems. Acting as lord deputy of Ireland from 1633, Thomas Wentworth (earl of Strafford) was determined to assert royal authority in Ireland in order to ensure that it would cease to be a financial drain on the English exchequer and become a source of revenue instead. He eventually achieved this but at the considerable political cost of uniting all of the major ethnic groups, and the corresponding fractions of the dominant class, in Ireland against his rule (Scott, 2004: 6–8, 13–15).

The immediate political backdrop to the outbreak of revolution in 1640 was the eleven years of 'personal rule' that commenced with Charles's dissolution of Parliament in March 1629 after Parliament passed resolutions against the royal imposition of taxes without parliamentary approval and Laudian religious innovations. Developments at the king's court, particularly the perception by parliamentarians of the growing influence over the king of a catholic faction led by Queen Henrietta, led to mounting suspicion and concern, especially after she started to work closely with the papal representative at court in 1637 and abandoned her previous support for an Anglo-French alliance against Spain. Laud appeared to be introducing elements of catholic religious practice into the church, such as moving the communion table from the nave, where it was located in most parish churches, to the east end and surrounding it by rails, which was widely seen as ushering in the mass. He then ruthlessly imposed these new practices as a strict religious uniformity throughout England. Critics of these reforms of the church were savagely repressed, most notably in 1637, when Prynne, Burton and Bastwick 'were mutilated, heavily fined, and imprisoned for life' (Coward, 2003: 174; Hill, 2002: 13). In order to alleviate his financial difficulties, the king imposed ship money (originally an occasional tax on port towns in lieu of providing a ship for the navy) throughout England and maintained it each year from 1635 to 1639. It was widely viewed as a regular tax not voted by Parliament, and generated increasing resentment amongst the bulk of the propertied classes.

Developments in Scotland during the 1630s had a major impact on England.

James I had re-established episcopacy in Scotland. Attempts by Charles at the beginning of his reign to recover church lands from the Scottish nobility evoked hostility, and when he also attempted to impose a modified version of the English Prayer Book on Scotland it sparked a national resistance movement. Elections to a Scottish National Assembly were held in November 1637, and in February 1638 'the National Covenant abolishing the Book of Common Prayer was signed all over Scotland and an army was raised' (Hill, 2002: 13).

When the Scottish National Assembly abolished bishops in November 1638 it provoked military intervention by Charles, known as the first Anglo-Scottish Bishops' War. Without the support of Parliament, however, Charles did not have the money to pay his reluctant army. Militarily, the English war effort was a debacle. As Woolrych (2002: 116) observes, 'there had been a strong element of theatre in [Charles's] military preparations, which had been planned more to frighten the Scots into submission than to fight them in the field'. The conflict was brought to a temporary halt with the Treaty of Berwick, but Charles's refusal to accept the abolition of episcopacy and the Scottish Parliament's completion of 'the ecclesiastical and constitutional revolution' in the months following the first Bishops' War made the resumption of conflict inevitable (Coward, 2003: 181).

The leaders of the English opposition to Charles were in communication with the Scots, and when he convened his fourth Parliament in April of 1640 it refused to accede to his demands and was dissolved after sitting for only three weeks (convened April 13, dissolved May 5), hence it is called the Short Parliament. Prominent parliamentary leaders were arrested. Breaking with historical precedent, the assembly of the clergy – Convocation – continued to meet after Parliament was dissolved. It agreed to preach the divine right of kings, place rails around altars, and gifted the king £20,000. This demonstrated the subservience of the upper echelons of the church hierarchy to the king. Furthermore, the Convocation:

> began by affirming that 'The most high and sacred order of kings is of divine right, being the ordinance of God himself'; moreover the Scriptures accord kings 'a supreme power' and commit to them 'the care of God's Church'. 'Tribute, and custom, and aid, and subsidy' are due from subjects to kings for the public defence 'by the law of God, nature and nations', and this obligation does not conflict (so it was affirmed) with subject's right to their property.
>
> (Woolrych, 2002: 141)

Starved of funds, Charles was unable to pay the army and it became mutinous. When the Scots crossed the border in the second Anglo-Scottish Bishops' War they were easily able to occupy Newcastle and completely defeat the English army by mid-October 1640. Hoping to force the king to convene Parliament, the Scots successfully demanded £850 per day until a settlement was reached. The humiliating military defeat of the English army and the ensuring fiscal crisis forced the king to convene his fifth Parliament in November 1640, decisively bringing the eleven years of personal rule to an end. Since it sat with intermissions for around twenty years it is called the Long Parliament.

Parliamentary rebellion, civil war and the Levellers, 1640–49

The Long Parliament, led by Bedford, Brooke, Essex, Mandeville, Saye and Brooke in the House of Lords and Pym, St John, Hampden and Holles in the Commons, impeached the King's two main advisers – Wentworth, whom the king had promoted to earl of Strafford and lord lieutenant of Ireland in January 1640, and Archbishop Laud – executing the former in May 1641 and imprisoning the latter (Laud was subsequently executed in 1645). Prominent dissenters (Prynne, Burton, Bastwick, Lilburne) who had been imprisoned during the personal rule were released, with rapturous support from the London crowds that assembled to greet them. As Coward observes, 'Judging by the volume of petitions to parliament and parliamentary speeches', the opening debates of the Long Parliament were:

> 'one long outburst of suppressed complaint'. The comprehensiveness of the legislation of the first session of the Long Parliament and the speed with which it was enacted (the last major measures were passed in August 1641) testify to the strength and unity of agreement among MPs in favour of abolishing the royal financial expedients of the 1630s ... and [in July 1641] the prerogative courts (star chamber, council of the north, the ecclesiastical court of high commission).
>
> (Coward, 2003: 191)

In addition, a Triennial Act was passed in February 1641 setting a maximum gap of three years between parliaments, and an Act against Parliament being dissolved without its own consent was passed in May 1641. Thus it became for the first time 'a permanent part of the constitution' (Hill, 2002: 53). Non-parliamentary taxes were declared illegal and further collection prohibited without parliamentary consent.

The mounting grievances generated by Wentworth's heavy-handed rule and the opportunity afforded by revolutionary tumult in England led to an uprising in Ireland starting in October 1641. From 1641 to 1649 the Irish rebellion had major impacts on the course of the revolution.[4] 'Many hundreds, probably thousands, of Englishmen were killed. The opposition group in parliament refused to trust a royal nominee with command of an army to reconquer Ireland. So the question of ultimate power in the state was raised' (Hill, 2002: 110). In the ensuing panic caused by the Scottish defeat and Irish uprising the Grand Remonstrance was narrowly passed (159/148) by Parliament on November 22, 1641. It provided a comprehensive critique of royal policy.

---

4 Ireland was only subdued when the New Model Army (NMA) led by Cromwell crushed resistance from 1649 to 1652.

Much to the horror of the conservatives in Parliament, it was printed and made available to the public (Coward, 2003: 201).

The Irish rebellion had to be suppressed in order to re-establish English rule. But in order to do this an army had to be raised, and this led to the question whether the king or Parliament was to exercise control over it. The key point is that Parliament did not trust the king sufficiently to approve the tax increases required to pay for this army and the navy that had to transport it without greatly increasing parliamentary control over the armed forces, something that was completely unacceptable to Charles.

After a popular demonstration in London prevented the twelve bishops from entering the House of Lords in December 1641, the bishops declared that all the proceedings that had taken place in their absence were invalid. A majority of the Lords interpreted this as an attack on their privileges, and supported a Commons vote of impeachment of the bishops. In response, the king charged five leaders of the Commons with treason, and on January 4, 1642 he personally led an armed band into the Commons to arrest them. Having been informed of the king's impending arrival, Pym, Hampden, Hazelrige, Holles, and Strode left before the King arrived. The MPs responded to his attempt to arrest the five members with shouts of 'privilege! privilege!'

When the king rode to the seat of London municipal government, the Guildhall, he was shocked by the hostility of the crowds, and his demand that the city hand over the five members had the opposite effect to what he intended – it further provoked Parliament and its supporters amongst the London masses. In response to an alarm on the night of January 6 that Charles was sending cavalry and foot soldiers to arrest the five members, their 'supporters went around the streets, knocking from door to door and shouting "arm! arm!" It was reckoned (no doubt with some exaggeration) that 40,000 citizens turned out completely armed, while 100,000 more stood to in their houses with halberds, swords, or clubs' (Woolrych, 2002: 213). In the midst of this popular rising in defence of Parliament against the brazen attempt of the king to infringe upon its long-standing constitutional privileges, Parliament was able to take control of the city's armed forces. Fearing for the safety of his wife and himself, Charles fled from London on January 10, 'never to see it again until he was brought back seven years later as a prisoner' (Woolrych, 2002: 213).

This was the turning point in the conflict between the king and Parliament. These events led Parliament to accelerate the implementation of reform, and so in February 1642 it passed legislation excluding bishops from the House of Lords and giving Parliament control over the appointment of commanders of the militia, forts and the Tower of London (the Militia Ordinance). This involved a major break with previous constitutional practice because this legislation came into effect without the assent of the king. Parliament now claimed the right to appoint the king's most important advisors. In the same month, the king began making preparations for war and Queen Henrietta Maria left England to seek foreign support for the royal cause.

A split started to develop within the ruling class. The parliamentary leadership, fearing the violent suppression of Parliament by the king, appealed to the people and tried to lead and contain them. During 1642 a majority of the ruling class either supported Parliament or remained neutral, but a growing minority were concerned that 'the political crisis was associated more and more with the breakdown of order, with huge political demonstrations, with enclosure riots, and disturbances in churches' (Coward, 2003: 203). In other words, they were frightened by the prospect of revolt from below that would directly threaten their wealth, power and privileges.

The focus of conflict became the competing attempts of the royalists and parliamentarians to mobilise the militia to fight on their side. The king responded to parliament's Militia Ordinance (finally passed by the Lords without the king's assent in March 1642) by issuing royal commissions of array in June, which called upon gentlemen in the counties to take command of the local militia on behalf of the king. The competing attempts to gain control over as much of the militia as possible gave rise to armed clashes as the king's forces attempted to get control of local stores of weapons and ammunition. Following several skirmishes of this nature, the civil war officially started when Charles I raised his standard at Nottingham in August 1642.

In October the first major battle at Edgehill ended without a clear victor, and in November a royal army headed by the king marched on London. The king's march was halted, after a significant royalist victory at Brentford, by the remnants of the parliamentary army commanded by Essex and a mass mobilisation of the London trained bands at Turnham Green. The parliamentary forces numbered around 24,000 men, the largest number fielded by either side throughout the remainder of the civil war (Woolrych, 2002: 240–1).

The early success of the royalist armies surprised parliamentary leaders, most of whom had been expecting a quick and easy fight, and so Parliament agreed to open peace negotiations with the king. As it turned out, the peace negotiations between the king and Parliament, held at Oxford from February to April 1643, were unsuccessful. War resumed in the spring and continued throughout the summer. The royalist armies scored a succession of victories throughout June and July of 1643, with the parliamentary armies providing more effective resistance in August and September (Woolrych, 2002: 259–67). Nonetheless, it appeared to a growing number of parliamentarians that royalist forces might defeat the parliamentary armies, enabling the king to impose terms of surrender on Parliament.

Parliament responded by establishing an alliance with the Scottish Parliament in August 1643 (the Solemn League and Covenant), and in January a Scottish army (slightly over 20,000 strong) under experienced military command entered England to join its parliamentary allies. 'The Scots demanded as the price of their alliance the introduction into England of a [Presbyterian] religious system like their own, together with persecution of sectaries' (Hill, 2002: 126). In the first combined action, the parliamentary and Scottish armies besieged York in June 1644. The first major defeat of the royalist armies by the combined Scottish and parliamentary forces took place at Marston Moor, Yorkshire later in June. This success was offset by the decisive defeat of the parliamentary army led by the earl of Essex at Lostwithiel, Cornwall, in August 1644, resulting in the loss of all of the parliamentary army's weapons and the surrender of the remaining 6,000 troops.

The military leadership of the earl of Manchester at the Battle of Newbury was inept. His army arrived too late in the field, and this contributed to the loss of an opportunity to inflict a major defeat on the royalist army. Oliver Cromwell was furious, and there was open conflict between himself and Manchester over the question of military leadership in October and November 1644. One of their exchanges reveals the differences between those who ultimately wanted a negotiated settlement with the king, and those who wanted a complete military victory. After Newbury, Manchester stated that 'The king cares not how often he fights but it concerns us to be wary, for in fighting we venture all to nothing. If we beat the king ninety-nine times he would be king still; but if he beat us once we should be hanged, and our posterity be undone.' 'My lord', Cromwell replied, 'if this be so, why did we take up arms first? This is against fighting ever hereafter. If so, let us make peace, be it never so base' (Woolrych, 2002: 291).

The dispute between Cromwell and Manchester became the subject of parliamentary debate in November. The heated nature of the debate was a manifestation of the growing split in the parliamentary ranks, based on both class and religious concerns. During the course of the war the differences grew between those, generally from the aristocracy and upper gentry, who 'favoured a defensive war and a negotiated peace' (led by Holles, Essex, Clarendon and Stapleton), and those who tended to come from more modest class locations, who formed what Hill aptly terms the 'win-the-war party' (led by Cromwell, Vane, Marten, Hazelrige and St John), which 'everywhere looked to London for a lead and for organisation, to the middling sort within the county for support' (Hill, 2002: 125). In between the 'peace party' and the 'win-the-war party' was the 'middle group' (led by Pyms, Saye and Wharton), which unlike the peace party was:

> not willing to trust the King until he had been defeated militarily and forced to accept limitations on his power. Consequently, they allied with the 'war group' in securing parliamentary approval for measures for an effective prosecution of the war. Yet, unlike the 'war group', [it] wanted an eventual constitutional settlement that was of the traditional sort with the novel features introduced in 1641 grafted on to it.
>
> (Coward, 2003: 210)

The parliamentary armies were mainly led by members of the aristocracy concerned about the threat of unrest from below and wanting a negotiated peace with the king. In contrast, the military officers drawn from the middling sort were committed to winning the war decisively (Hill, 1980: 124–6; Manning 1991: 242–358; Woolrych, 2002: 234–330, 401–33). Despite the fact that Parliament potentially had far greater resources of money, weapons and men at its disposal, the royalist armies more than held their own from mid-1643 to early 1645. This was due to the royalist armies being better led by officers who were more determined to win the war than their parliamentary counterparts (Woolrych, 2002: 292). As the war dragged on, Cromwell and the win-the-war party were increasingly determined to reorganise the parliamentary armies and replace the aristocratic officers, who were not committed to winning the war and had provided ineffective military leadership, with officers who were strongly committed to the parliamentary cause and more effective military commanders. Cromwell stated that he would rather 'have a plain russet-coated captain that knows what he fights for, and loves what he knows, than that which you call a gentleman and is nothing else' (Manning, 1991: 356).

The growing divide between the peace and win-the-war parties was inextricably tied to a religious split between political presbyterians and political independents. As mentioned, in order to secure the support of the Scottish army Parliament had agreed to the establishment of a presbyterian church in England and Ireland (Woolrych, 2002: 271). The more conservative MPs shared the Scottish desire for a unified state presbyterian church and the suppression of heterodox protestant sects. The independents were not opposed to the establishment of a presbyterian church but 'for religious, political, and military reasons they supported religious toleration' through the imposition of more relaxed rules on parish attendance which would have allowed for participation in other forms of protestant worship (Hill, 2002: 126).

From the commencement of the Scottish and parliamentary alliance in August 1643 to the end of the war in June 1646, the Scottish Covenanters shifted away from allying themselves with the win-the-war party and the middle group, and towards the political presbyterian peace party and the king. In the process the Scots became increasingly hostile to the political independents' win-the-war party. The political independents, led by Cromwell among others, became increasingly hostile towards the Scots, especially as the military usefulness of their army declined. As Hill observes, 'The "Independents" were those who wanted an all-out war fought to a decisive conclusion. … They wanted appointment by merit, irrespective of social rank, and the full mobilisation of Parliament's vastly superior resources in men and money' (2002: 125).

The Scots, presbyterians and the earl of Essex initiated a new set of peace proposals which Parliament sent to the king in November 1644. The resulting discussions held at Uxbridge in January were unsuccessful and collapsed in February, strengthening support amongst the middle group for the war party's proposals to reorganise the parliamentary armies. Parliament responded with a fundamental reorganisation of its army, passing the Self-Denying Ordinance on December 19 (Woolrych, 2002: 303). Crucially, it removed the automatic right of peers and members of the Commons to act as officers in the army. Under extreme pressure from the Commons, the Lords passed the New Model

Ordinance on February 15, 1645, and a revised version of the Self-Denying Ordinance on April 3.

The New Model Ordinance aimed to create for the first time a genuinely national, rather than regional, army. Amalgamating the dilapidated armies of Manchester, Essex and Waller, and supplementing this with further conscription of the poor (2,500 from London and 1,000 from Norfolk, Suffolk, Essex and Kent), it created an army of 22,000 men (6,600 cavalry, 1,000 dragoons and 14,400 infantry) which was to be better funded, equipped and paid than any other that had played a role in the civil war up to this point (Scott, 2004: 87–8; Woolrych, 2002: 301–8). The Self-Denying Ordinance was necessary for the formation of the New Model Army (NMA) because it was only by removing the aristocratic officers who were not committed to fighting for absolute victory over the royalist armies that the parliamentary armies could be reorganised fundamentally to achieve this kind of victory. The formation of the NMA was a decisive moment:

> the army which became the instrument of victory was different from previous armies; it was one in which promotion was determined increasingly by professional merit rather than social rank; in which there was a leaven of ideological commitment to the cause; and in which 'middling sort' and plebeian elements gained voices in the affairs of the nation.
>
> (Manning, 1996: 77)

Sir Thomas Fairfax, who was only 32 years old, was appointed general of the NMA in January, along with Philip Skippon as major-general in charge of the infantry. On June 8 Fairfax decided to appoint Cromwell to the position of lieutenant-general in charge of the cavalry. Although the Commons immediately endorsed Cromwell's appointment, the Lords opposed it, but to no avail, as Cromwell with an additional 700 horse joined the NMA the day before the battle of Naseby. The victory at Naseby on June 14 was decisive, with the NMA (composed of around 15,000 infantry and cavalry) losing only 200 troops while killing over 1,000 and taking prisoner 4,500 of the 9,000 men in the King's army. This victory was followed with another decisive victory at Langport on July 10, 1645, and after this military operations were largely an exercise in 'mopping up' the royalist forces. The first civil war ended with the surrender of the royalist HQ at Oxford in June 1646. In addition to the serious military defeat, the capture of the king's secret papers, including correspondence with the queen:

> laid bare his hopes of bringing an army of native Irish into England and of obtaining money and mercenaries from foreign princes, as well as his readiness to consider granting toleration to English papists. These letters, published as *The King's Cabinet Opened*, created a sensation and did him immense harm.
>
> (Woolrych, 2002: 319)

'As soon as the Civil War ended, the Political Presbyterians began a political campaign against the NMA, which they disliked as a major obstacle to a settlement with the king and as the seedbed of religious extremism' (Coward, 2003: 229). In February and March 1647, they pushed measures through Parliament 'to reduce the NMA in size without satisfying its demands for payment of wage arrears or for indemnity against prosecution for actions committed during the war' (Coward, 2003: 229). Political and religious radicalism was becoming increasingly prevalent in London. On March 20 a petition promoted by a London-based movement called the Levellers was intercepted by Parliament 'asserting that a just government was one based on the supremacy of the representatives of the people, and demanding the abolition of the power of the king and the House of Lords to veto acts of the House of Commons', as well as greater toleration of diversity in protestant religious theology and practice, reform of the legal and prison system, and some provision of sustenance to 'keep men, women and children from begging' (Manning, 1996: 89; Woolrych, 2002: 355–6; Aylmer, 1975: 76–81). This outraged the presbyterians in Parliament and they condemned it as treasonable.

Ten days later Parliament became aware of a petition addressed to Fairfax circulating within the NMA:

It emerged as the 'The petition of the officers and soldiers of the army', and it asked for just five things: a parliamentary ordinance to guarantee their indemnity, security for the payment of their arrears before they were disbanded, regular pay while still in service, no compulsion on those enlisted voluntarily to serve outside the kingdom and no conscription of cavalrymen into the infantry, and finally some provision for maimed ex-soldiers and for the widows and children of the fallen. These were all fair requests, respectfully expressed, and confined to the soldiers' interests as soldiers.

(Woolrych, 2002: 354)

In response, Parliament expressed 'high dislike' of the petition, stating that those who promoted it would be 'looked upon and proceeded against as enemies of the state and disturbers of the public peace' (2002: 355). This *Declaration of Dislike*, which Fairfax was instructed to have read aloud to all of the regiments, provoked outrage within the army and had a profoundly radicalising impact:

The soldiers were infuriated by the denial of their right to petition (even their own general on matters concerning them as soldiers) and the slur on their honour to be branded 'enemies of the state and disturbers of the public peace' by the parliament for which they had just won victory in the Civil War.

(Manning, 1996: 90)

The presbyterian majority in Parliament wanted to disband the NMA in its entirety, but an army was still required to suppress the Irish uprising. Accordingly from March to April negotiations were conducted between parliamentary commissioners, on one side, and Fairfax and the large number of officers he assembled to meet with the commissioners, on the other. On April 15, a parliamentary delegation meet with over 200 officers and told them that the demands in the March petition were unacceptable and that the expedition to Ireland would be led by Skippon and Massie rather than Fairfax and Cromwell. In response 151 officers signed the *Vindication of the Officers of the Army*, which reaffirmed the demands of the March petition. It indicated clearly that the solidarity between the officers and their men in the army was high, and defended the right of soldiers to petition Parliament: 'We hope, by being soldiers we have not lost the capacity of subjects, nor divested ourselves thereby of our interest in the commonwealth; that in purchasing the freedom of our brethren, we have not lost our own' (Manning, 1996: 90; Brailsford, 1983: 180).

From mid-April the radicalisation of the army assumed an organisational form, with the election of two agents or 'agitators' from each regiment, starting with eight cavalry regiments. In May similar elections were held in the infantry regiments and the remaining cavalry regiments. 'The representatives of the regiments formed a committee to promote the organisation of the rank-and-file throughout the army, to coordinate the actions of the regiments, and to direct resistance to parliament's terms for recruiting some regiments for Ireland and disbanding others' (Manning, 1996: 90; Woolrych, 2002: 359). Parliament was alarmed that the soldiers had taken this initiative, and sent MPs who were also officers (Skippon, Cromwell, Ireton and Fleetwood) to ascertain their grievances and placate them with an assurance that 'an ordinance for their indemnity would be passed shortly' (Woolrych, 2002: 359). The officers refused to report to Parliament until the regiments had been given time to report on the grievances of the men. The reports provide a clear indication of the politicisation of the army. Alongside demands for payment of the wages that were in arrears (which amounted to nearly £3 million), indemnity, due parliamentary acknowledgement of the achievements and honour of the army, were demands for religious toleration, the abolition of bishops, and democratic rights and freedoms. 'General Fairfax's own regiment of horse did "declare our averseness to the business of Ireland or disbanding till the real freedom of the free people of England be established"' (Manning, 1996: 359).

Cromwell read the consolidated statement based on the regimental reports to the Commons on May 21. Four days later Parliament voted to disband the entire New Model infantry between June 1 and June 15 with only eight weeks' arrears of wages to be paid. In late May and early June effective command of the army passed, in large part though not entirely, into the central committee of the agitators. It pushed for a general rendezvous of the army, and in response Fairfax held a council of war on May 29 where the vote was overwhelmingly in favour of a general rendezvous at Newmarket. The central committee of agitators also issued instructions to Rainsborough's regiment to secure the army's artillery train and ammunition in Oxford, and it probably directed Cornet George Joyce to prevent the king from being moved from Holmby House, which then led to Joyce relocating the king to Newmarket where the army was meeting. Most importantly of all, the committee called upon the soldiers 'to refuse to obey the orders of parliament to disband' (Manning, 1996: 92).

Although Oliver Cromwell approved of the arrest of the king he did not order it, and he left London to join the army at Newmarket. The officers were uncomfortable with disobeying Parliament but they sympathised with their soldiers' grievances and wanted to prevent the revolt from moving completely beyond their control. The rank and file and their elected agitators were becoming influenced by the radical ideas of the Levellers, and increasingly were acting independently of their officers, effectively deposing the presbyterian minority of officers that remained loyal to Parliament, while putting intense pressure upon the remaining officers to lead the army in action to ensure that their demands were met. This accelerated the tendency that had started with the Self-Denying Ordinance for the class composition of the army's officers to become decreasingly aristocratic and increasingly drawn from the 'middling sort'. As Manning observes,

One vital factor that was to influence the actions of the army from now on was that its officers were no longer predominantly peers and greater gentry as they had been in the armies with which parliament began the Civil War. In the conflict between parliament and the NMA, about a quarter of the officers of the rank of captain-lieutenant and above supported parliament and either left or were driven out by their men. Eight colonels, two lieutenant colonels, and seven majors were replaced by men who 'were on the whole less socially distinguished and more politically militant'. Half of the officer corps now consisted of men who 'came from backgrounds so obscure that no information can be recovered about them'.

(Manning, 1996: 96)

The general rendezvous of the army on June 4 and June 5, 1647, attended by six regiments of cavalry and seven of infantry, constituted a crucial turning point in the revolution and marked the beginning of its most radical phase. It issued *A Solemn Engagement* pledging that the army would not be divided or disbanded until its grievances had been met and neither the army nor the other '"freeborn people of England" would remain subject to oppression and injury through the continuance in power of the men who had abused parliament in its past proceedings against the army' (Woolrych, 2002: 370). The NMA was now to be headed by a General Council composed of two officers and two elected delegates from the lower ranks of each of the regiments.

The army commenced a slow march towards London. Once it reached St Albans, around 20 miles from London, Fairfax set up his HQ. Cromwell's son-in-law, Henry Ireton, emerged at this point as a leading figure in the formulation of army policy. 'He had the keenest and most original political mind in the army, though as a tactician and debater he had his limitations' (Woolrych, 2002: 369). In conjunction with Cromwell and Lambert, Ireton drafted A Declaration of the Army on behalf of the General Council. Issued on June 14, it announced that the army 'was "not a mere mercenary Army", but a political force with a political programme: a purge of the present Parliament, future parliaments of fixed duration, guaranteed right of the people to petition Parliament, and liberty of tender consciences. They were an army dedicated to "the defence of our own and the people's just rights and liberties"' (Coward, 2003: 230). More specifically, the army planned to impeach eleven presbyterian MPs for leading what was, in effect, a counter-revolution.

In July the army moved to Reading. Ireton and Cromwell drafted a programme for a constitutional and religious settlement, in consultation with leading independent MPs, including Saye, Wharton, Northumberland, Vane, St John, Pierrepont and Fiennes, and presented it to the General Council in July. Entitled the Heads of Proposal, it proposed:

> a constitutional settlement with the king that provided for regular biennial parliaments, rational reform of parliamentary representation which was linked accurately to regional variations in population and wealth, parliamentary control of the army and navy, and parliamentary appointment of the great officers of state for ten years.
>
> (Coward, 2003: 231)

The religious settlement was to maintain a national church with bishops, but the bishops would not have the coercive power and jurisdiction they possessed prior to the civil war. Penalties for failure to attend the parish church were to be removed, the use of the Book of Common Prayer was to be allowed but not imposed (a measure designed to appease the king), and no one would be forced to subscribe to the presbyterian covenant (Woolrych, 2002: 375; Coward, 2003: 230). The General Council received the Heads of Proposal positively but cautiously, and the agitators insisted that a list of matters requiring Parliament's early attention be appended to it, including 'tithes, the excise, the general inequality of taxation, and an assortment of legal abuses' (Woolrych, 2002: 376). Finally, although the Heads were composed for negotiations with the king, he remained obstinately opposed to a settlement involving compromise.

Although the Levellers were the most influential political current on the left of the revolution, they were neither the only nor the most radical current. Whereas the Levellers mainly focused on the form of government that was to emerge from the revolution, the far left in the revolution, of which the Diggers led by Gerrard Winstanley were the most significant movement, was focused on the social conditions of the poor (encompassing both wage labourers and peasant farmers with smallholdings) and the redistribution of wealth that they considered was necessary in order to secure the liberties and well-being of the majority of the population who were positioned in society beneath the 'middling sort' and the aristocracy. Winstanley inaugurated 'the Digger communes as models of a society in which there would be no rich and poor, no paying of rents to landlords, no working for wages, no buying and selling, but all would work cooperatively to till the land, which they would hold in common, and share their produce according to need' (Manning, 1999: 62). The ultimate goal was to create an egalitarian and democratic society based on common ownership of the land, and this was to be achieved through a two-pronged strategy: all labourers were to refuse to continue working for landlords and large farmers, and poor tenant farmers were to cease paying rents. As Manning observes:

> The combination of a labour strike and rent strike would have accomplished an economic and social revolution, but it would have required a vast amount of organisation and a legion of local leaders, far beyond the capacity of the small band of Diggers, and there would still have been the questions about the control of state power.
>
> (Manning, 1999: 65)

Nonetheless, the emergence of the Diggers and the receptivity of the rural labouring poor to their ideas, together with the activities and ideas of other leaders and groups on the far left of the revolution, underlines the importance of recognising that the revolution was not the exclusive business of the 'political nation' composed of the middling sort and the aristocracy, but also radicalised the thinking of at least a substantial minority of the labouring poor (Brockway, 1980; Manning, 1999; Wood and Wood, 1997: 65–93).

In late July there was an upsurge of conservative sentiment in sections of the London population, particularly amongst those apprentices who resented the high levels of taxation necessary to fund the army. The political presbyterians in Parliament and the city saw an opportunity to channel this disgruntlement with the parliamentary cause towards their own ends. 'On 26 July, apparently with the connivance of Holles, Waller, and Sir John Clotworthy, a mob invaded the chamber of the Commons and forced the House to pass a resolution inviting the king to come to London' (Coward, 2003: 232). The army responded by marching into London, and without any significant resistance it occupied Westminster and the City from August 6 to August 8, easily defeating the attempted counter-revolution.

In August the *Heads of Proposal* were published and debates began within the General Council of the NMA concerning possible settlement of the issues at stake in the civil war. In early September 1647, the army headquarters were shifted to Putney, and the General Council started to meet weekly. During this time agitators with Leveller links appeared in five cavalry regiments. They presented *The Case of the Army Truly Stated* to Fairfax on October 18. It was critical of what they saw as being the excessively conciliatory and moderate approach being taken by the army leadership, especially with respect to its negotiations with the king and its failure to take decisive action against the counter-revolutionary presbyterian MPs.

The positive demands of *The Case of the Army* were based on the principle that all power rested originally in the whole body of the people, and that supreme authority, both legislative and executive, lay in their elected representatives. It called for an immediate and drastic purge of the present parliament, a dissolution within nine or ten months, and thereafter biennial elections at an appointed date in which 'all the freeborn' aged twenty-one or over should have the vote.

(Woolrych, 2002: 384)

Another document entitled *An Agreement of the People*, which concisely outlined the key principles for a post-war constitutional and religious settlement, soon followed. It was presented to the General Council on October 28 (Aylmer, 1975: 32) and in conjunction with the *Heads of Proposal* provided the basis for what subsequently became known as the Putney debates in late October and early November. The debate centred on two proposed constitutional settlements: first, the *Heads of Proposal*, favoured by the generals which as we have seen promoted the establishment of a constitutional monarchy in which the king and the Lords would retain a right of veto over legislation passed in the Commons, and second, the much more radical *Agreement of the People* formulated and advocated by the Levellers, which proposed that the Commons, elected on the basis of an extended franchise and biennial election, be made the supreme governmental authority, no longer subject to the power of veto by the Lords and king. In addition, the *Agreement* called for the dissolution of the current Parliament and redistribution of the franchise so that the 'Counties, Cities and Burroughs, for the election of their Deputies in Parliament, ought to be more [fairly] proportioned, according to the number of Inhabitants' (Aylmer, 1975: 90). It called for freedom of religion, immunity from conscription, equality before the law for all, and legal indemnity for those who had fought in the civil war.

Much of the debate focused on the question of the extension of the franchise. Was it to include all freeborn Englishmen or only to those who owned sufficient property? Speaking in defence of *The Agreement*, Thomas Rainsborough argued 'that the poorest he that is in England hath a life to live as the greatest he' and therefore 'that every man that is to live under a government ought first by his own consent to put himself under that government' (Aylmer, 1975: 100). Ireton opposed extending the franchise, counter-arguing that 'no person hath a right to an interest or share in the disposing of the affairs of the kingdom, and in determining or choosing those that shall determine what laws we shall be ruled by here', 'that hath not a permanent fixed interest in this kingdom' (Aylmer, 1975: 100). By the later Ireton meant that the people who elect MPs should be 'the persons in whom all land lies, and those in corporations in whom all trading lies' (Aylmer, 1975: 101). Rainsborough, in turn, replied, 'I do not find anything in the law of God, that a lord shall choose twenty [representatives], and a gentleman but two, or a poor man shall choose none' (Aylmer, 1975: 102). Most of the Levellers were not advocating a fully universal male franchise because being of the middling sort, they 'held that servants – apprentices and labourers as well as domestic servants – were represented by the head of the household no less than were his womenfolk and children. "Free" Englishmen were those who could freely dispose of their labour, of their property in their own persons' (Hill, 2002: 128).

There was growing support for *The Agreement* in the army, and by the end of October it probably had the support of 16 regiments (Woolrych, 2002: 392). Before the Putney debate reached a conclusion, however, the army was forced to respond to a new wave of counter-revolution that arose following the king's escape from custody on November 11, 1647. In December he formed an alliance (the Engagement) with the Scots and rejected parliamentary peace proposals (the Four Bills). Parliament passed the Vote of No Addresses in January 1648, which stated that 'the Lords and Commons do declare that they will make no further addresses or applications to the King' (Coward, 2003: 234). From March to June 1648 anti-parliamentary revolts broke out, in part due to widespread dislike of parliamentary policies with respect to taxation and religion. This marked the beginning of the second civil war. The NMA eventually suppressed all of these regional revolts. In July, the Scottish army invaded England, and was easily defeated by the NMA brilliantly led by Cromwell and Lambert on August 17 – it 'was not merely beaten, it was annihilated' – with little loss of Cromwell's troops (Woolrych, 2002: 418).

Before the victory of the English army in the second civil war was complete, the presbyterian MPs, who had only reluctantly declared the invading Scottish army to be their enemies (the Lords refused to do so), succeeded in overturning the Vote of No Addresses on August 24, 1648. Parliament then started negotiations for a settlement with the king in September at Newport on the Isle of Wight. At this juncture the influence of the Levellers was crucial in leading popular opposition to a settlement with the king, both within the army and amongst anti-royalist popular forces in London. They organised a comprehensive petition – *To the Commons of England in Parliament Assembled* – with 40,000 signatures and submitted it to Parliament on September 11. It called for 'the removal of the King's and the Lords' power of veto, regular elections (this time annual, not biennial), freedom of religion, equality before the law, abolition of tithes, enclosures, and the excise [a consumption tax], and much more' (Woolrych, 2002: 421). Condemning Parliament for being prepared to sacrifice their freedom and rights as freeborn subjects in negotiations with the king for a 'slavish peace', it had an immediate impact on the army. 'A flood of petitions from the regiments and garrisons of the army demanded that the king be put on trial, and more than half of them expressed support for the Leveller petition of September 11' (Manning, 1996: 107).

Anger in the army directed against the king and his presbyterian supporters in Parliament had by now reached boiling point. The experience of the second civil war and, as they saw it, more treachery from Parliament, had unified the army and narrowed the gap between the army, including its most influential senior officers, and the Levellers. Ireton emerged from the war determined to oppose parliamentary negotiations with the king, 'bring the king to trial, and secure the early election of parliament' (Woolrych, 2002: 423). In October he drafted *The Remonstrance of the Army*, and after considerable debate between the officers who supported it and the Levellers, *The Remonstrance* was approved on November 18. It was a reaction to the Commons declaration three days earlier 'that the king shall be settled in a condition of honour, freedom and safety, agreeable to the laws of the land' (Woolrych, 2002: 423). Among other things, *The Remonstrance* endorsed the programme of reform outlined in the Levellers' September petition, and demanded that the king be executed for his role as 'the principal author ... of our late wars' (Woolrych, 2002: 424).

Late in November, the army marched on London and occupied it for the second time. The Commons defiantly voted to continue negotiations with the king, and troops under the command of Colonel Pride took control over Parliament and purged it of supporters of a settlement with the king ('Pride's purge'). Slightly more than half of the 471 MPs were excluded. The Levellers and officers led by Ireton worked on a new *Agreement of the People*, which was presented to the General Council of the army on December 11. The Levellers thought that agreement had been reached on the final wording of the agreement, but when it was finally presented to Parliament on January 20, 1649, after five weeks of debate in the General Council (the 'Whitehall debates'), it had been substantially modified (hence it is referred to as the 'Officers' Agreement'). On December 15 the General Council resolved to put the king on trial, and army officers then 'drove forward the trial of the King and his execution on January 30, 1649, the abolition of the monarchy and the House of Lords [in February], and the establishment of a republic [in May]' (Manning, 1996: 109).

The republic and protectorate of Oliver Cromwell, 1650–59

This settlement was extremely unstable, and now rested ultimately upon the capacity of the army, under the increasingly strained leadership of Cromwell, to subdue mounting opposition from both the right and the left. Cromwell was able to do this, and was installed in power as lord protector by the army in December 1653. He managed to retain power until his death in September 1658, but his son Richard could not secure control over the army, and it removed him from power and then recalled the Rump Parliament: that is, the little that remained of the Long Parliament that had first met in November 1640.

In January 1660 the English army in Scotland, led by George Monck, declared its support for the Rump Parliament and marched south to London. Once in London Monck allowed the MPs excluded from Parliament by the army in 1648 to return. In March the Rump Parliament dissolved itself and ordered new elections. A pro-royalist Convention Parliament was elected, and met from April 26 until it was dissolved on December 29, 1660. It restored the House of Lords and the monarchy between April and May of 1660. The restoration of the monarchy did not, however, involve a restoration of the constitutional set-up that had prevailed prior to 1640:

> After 1660 no doubt Charles II (from time to time) and James II (more seriously) dreamed of building up the absolute monarchy that their father had failed to achieve. But, thanks to the revolution, there was never any chance that they could succeed. Without an army, without an independent bureaucracy, absolutism was impossible.
>
> (Hill, 1980: 120; 2002: 138–41)

FROM THE RESTORATION OF 1660 TO THE GLORIOUS REVOLUTION OF 1688–89

A wave of pro-royalist sentiment swept across the propertied classes early in 1661. 'Men of property were pleased to feel that law, order and social stability, liberty and property, were being restored with the King, discipline with the Bishops' (Hill, 2002: 140). Consequently they elected the even more pro-royalist Cavalier Parliament, which first met on May 8, 1661 and was not dissolved for 18 years until January 1679. Nonetheless:

> [not] even in the atmosphere of royalist euphoria of 1660–1 were MPs prepared to abandon all the constitutional gains of the early 1640s. Charles I's financial expedients of the 1630s remained illegal, and Star Chamber, the court of high commission, council of the north, court of wards, and feudal tenures remained abolished. It is often, correctly, said that the monarchy that was restored in 1660 was that of 1641 not 1640.
>
> (Coward, 2003: 290)

In essence, the restoration merely established another highly unstable and transitory settlement between the monarchy and the classes supporting Parliament, in which there was recurrent conflict over taxation, religion and foreign policy (Coward, 2003: 285–344; Hill, 2002: 138–41). As Coward (2003: 285) observes, 'The "Restoration Settlement" is a misnomer. The series of ad hoc decisions made in the early 1660s by the Convention and Cavalier Parliaments, which are traditionally called "the Restoration Settlement", settled very little.'

Despite the assurances provided by Charles II in the Declaration of Breda, which he issued from exile in April 1660, once restored to the throne he was intent on maximising the power and resources at his disposal. The

Convention and Cavalier parliaments obliged by restoring many of the king's prerogative powers: the king could call and dissolve Parliament, veto and suspend legislation, exempt individuals from the provisions of parliamentary statutes, appoint privy councillors and other state officials, determine who would fill church and local government positions, exercise overall command of the armed forces and play the leading role in foreign policy making. In addition the Cavalier Parliament passed an act against 'tumultuous petitioning' in 1661, gave the king extensive powers of censorship in 1662, and weakened the provisions for regular parliaments with the Triennial Act of 1664. It also passed a series of statutes (the Clarendon Code) aimed at restoring the pre-revolutionary Anglican Church and crushing religious and political dissent (Coward, 2003: 292–3).

Underpinning these political developments was the declining influence of the middling sort and revival of the pre-eminence and power of the landowning aristocracy and upper gentry with respect to the affairs of church and state. The members of this class were inclined to consider that 'The Government of a king though tyrannical is far better than the usurping tyranny of many plebeians' (excerpt from a 1660 parliamentary speech cited by Manning, 2003: 196).

Even the Cavalier Parliament was not, however, prepared to grant the king sufficient regular income to sustain his extravagant lifestyle and military adventures. When the second Dutch war (1665–67) was unsuccessful and coincided with the Great Plague of 1665 and the Great Fire of 1666 in London, the resulting fiscal crisis generated increasingly strained relations between the king and Parliament. In 1670 Charles II reached a secret agreement with the French King Louis XIV in which Charles promised that he would eventually declare himself a catholic in return for financial support from the French crown. He issued the Declaration of Indulgence in 1672 which allowed catholics freedom to worship in their own homes and greater toleration for protestant dissenters. Parliament responded to Charles II's religious and foreign policies, which it found objectionable, by starving him of funds. This was crucial in enabling Parliament to exert a substantial degree of power over the king. The king's fiscal dependence on parliamentary taxation was intensified by the unsuccessful third Dutch war from 1672 to 1674.

A wave of anti-catholic sentiment swept the country in the late 1670s, and the attempts by Parliament to exclude Charles's catholic brother James II from the succession to the crown generated the exclusion crisis from May 1679 to March 1681, when Charles dissolved the Cavalier Parliament. Although the details need not concern us, it is important to note that from 1681 until 1688 first Charles II, then (following Charles's death in 1685) James II, made concerted efforts to strengthen royal power and authority. During this period relations with Parliament deteriorated still further, so much so that on June 30, 1688 'seven leading Protestants, representing Whig and Tory opinion ... wrote to William of Orange, pledging their support if he brought a force to England against James' (Coward, 2003: 341).

The 'Glorious Revolution' of 1688–89 was less of a genuine revolution than the events of 1640–49, resting on the external military invention of William III in November, supported by internal provincial risings in Cheshire, Nottingham and York (finally consolidated with William III's victory over James II at the battle of the Boyne in July 1690). But it has aptly been referred to as the 'final settlement' because it established the essential foundations of the constitutional monarchy that was to survive in Britain for the next three centuries (Hallas, 1988: 17). As Hill astutely observes:

> The Revolution [of 1688–89] demonstrated the ultimate solidarity of the propertied class. Whigs and Tories disagreed sharply about whether James had abdicated or not, whether the throne should be declared vacant, whether Mary alone or William and Mary jointly should be asked to fill it, or declared to have filled it. But these differences were patched up, and the Declaration of Rights – as successful a compromise as the Elizabethan Prayer Book – simply stated both positions and left it to individuals to resolve the contradictions as they pleased.
>
> Nevertheless, if 1642–49 was not forgotten, neither were the mistakes of 1660. The Revolution Settlement set down in writing the conditions which had been tacitly assumed at the Restoration. The House of Commons resolved that, before filling the throne, it would secure the religion, laws, and liberties of the nation. The Declaration of Rights was the result.
>
> (Hill, 2002: 274, 275)

Henceforth the monarchy retained considerable powers, but the constitutional, and even more importantly the fiscal, limits to the sovereign's power were 'real and recognised' (Coward, 2003: 360; Hill, 2002: 275). The 1688 settlement attempted to remove the king's claim to suspend laws without parliamentary consent, tightly circumscribe the collection of revenue through unparliamentary taxation, prevent the king from maintaining a standing army during peacetime, and prohibit excessive bail or fines and 'cruel and unusual punishments'. During the same period measures were introduced to enshrine freedom of election to Parliament, freedom of speech in Parliament, and frequent elections. In particular the Triennial Act (1694) 'provided not only that Parliaments should meet every three years but also that they should not last longer than three years. Henceforth parliament was a necessary and continuous part of the constitution, in closer dependence on the electorate' (Hill, 2002: 275). This had a very real effect on the frequency of parliamentary elections and the size of the electorate. Indeed: 'the most startling contrast in the nature of political life during the reigns of William III and Queen Anne, and one which sets it apart from both the preceding and succeeding periods, is the frequency of general elections. From 1660 to 1688 there were only five; from 1689 to 1715 there were eleven' (Coward, 2003: 348). The electorate numbered at least 200,000, or approximately 4.3 per cent of the total population, during the reign of William III (2003: 349).

CONCLUSION

When focusing on the role played by the English Revolution in the historical re-emergence of democracy from the seventeenth to the nineteenth centuries, it is clear that complexities and ambiguities abound with respect to the anti-authoritarian and pro-democratic dimension of the revolution. The English Revolution was not a revolution for democracy, as we understand that term today, even in the limited liberal sense of the rule of the majority of citizens within the constitutional and institutional framework of representative democracy. As understood by the supporters of Parliament, they fought for 'religion, liberty and property' against the catholic sympathies, absolutist aspirations and corrupt fiscal practices of Charles I. Even the Levellers were not advocating social and economic equality or the abolition of property. In so far as parliamentary government was democratic and ensured liberty, it was a democracy of, by and for property owners, who by virtue of this ownership had a 'permanent interest' in the affairs of the kingdom, and it was their liberties and property rights that it helped to entrench. After the revolutionary period from 1640 to 1690 was over, Parliament maintained a dominant protestant state religion that legitimated a highly unequal society, and a system of government that excluded a higher proportion of the population from participation in elections and public office than the systems of government created by the French and American revolutions.

In what sense then did the English Revolution nonetheless contribute historically to the revival of democracy? First, the revolution was decisive in defeating the aspirations of the English monarchy to create an absolutist state broadly modelled on those of continental Europe. Second, the revolution established key features of representative democracy operating within the confines of a constitutional monarchy. These including the limitations on the powers of the monarchy established by the Bill of Rights (1689), the Triennial Act (1694) and the Act of Settlement (1701). Although leaving the monarch with considerable powers, these acts ensured that the monarch would remain dependent on parliament for taxation revenue; 'standing armies in peacetime had to be approved by parliament'; laws passed by Parliament could not be suspended by the monarch; freedom of speech within Parliament was protected; the independence of the judiciary was enhanced by 'making permanent the tenure of offices'; and the right of free Englishmen to petition Parliament and the king without fear of retribution was established (Coward, 2003: 451).

Coward claims that the wars of William III and Queen Anne's reigns were more significant in driving forward the centralisation, expansion and more effective tax-gathering capacity of the English state, but England's involvement in these wars would have been unlikely without the religious and constitutional changes brought about by the revolution (see Braddick, 1996; Wheeler, 1999).

Third, 'the court of wards and liveries and all feudal tenures were formally abolished in February 1646' (Coward, 2003: 191). As we have seen, feudalism centrally involves a form of surplus extraction that necessitates extra-economic coercion of a politico-military nature. It thereby entails the brutal suppression of all overt expressions of popular democracy. The revolution hastened the demise of the elements of feudalism that were still in existence when it broke out in 1640. In doing so it contributed to the emergence of social and economic conditions that were more conducive to the extension of the citizenship rights that are constitutive of representative democracy to a much larger proportion of the population than was enfranchised in 1640.

Fourth, even though the elective principle was limited to a small percentage of the adult population (wealthy property-owning men), the revolution had a lasting impact on the consciousness of 'the middling sort' and those less well off whose descendants in subsequent generations would eventually press for the extension of the franchise. The Chartists in the 1830s referred back to the arguments of the Levellers and demanded the same right to vote in parliamentary elections as had been so long enjoyed by the wealthy (Foot, 2006: 91–2). They were arguing that the principles and rights that became entrenched following the victory of Parliament in the civil war should be enjoyed by all men aged 21 and over regardless of wealth and status. In this sense the revolution helped to lay the political and constitutional foundations for the creation of a more developed and inclusive form of representative democracy.

Fifth, the revolution had significant international impacts, among other things, influencing the thinking of those who played leading roles in both the French and American revolutions. As it expedited the further development of capitalism in England it thereby increased the competitive pressures on geopolitical rivals such as France, Spain and the German states to match England's economic success and growing military power.

Finally, the English Revolution was a bourgeois revolution because, like all bourgeois revolutions, it was a decisive moment in the dialectical process of the long-term historical transformation of societies from feudalism and the rule of absolutist monarchies to capitalism and the prevalence of representative democracy as the dominant state form in advanced capitalism. In this respect, the revolution's course was shaped by the continuing presence of what the society had once been as well as by elements of what it was to become. The English Revolution was in large part caused by the prior development of capitalism, and had the effect of accelerating the further development of capitalism, within the British Isles, on the European continent, in the North American colonies, and eventually throughout much of the British Empire.

GUIDE TO FURTHER READING

The best Marxist introductions to the English Revolution are Harman (1999: 203–18), Hill (1980, 2002) and Manning (1996). Coward (2003) provides an excellent textbook overview from a non-Marxist perspective. Woolrych (2002) provides a meticulously detailed account of the revolution from 1625 to 1660. Richardson (1998) provides a comprehensive survey of the intellectual debates about the revolution from the seventeenth century to the revisionist critique of Marxist accounts during the 1980s and 1990s. Carlin (1999) and Hughes (1991) provide reliable overviews of the major accounts of the causes of the Revolution. Manning (1991) provides a superb account of the social forces involved in the revolution.

Brenner (2003a: 638–716) provides the most influential contemporary Marxist social interpretation of the revolution, an interpretation that rejects the earlier social interpretation developed by Hill (1941). For accounts of the Diggers, Levellers and other radical currents see: Aylmer (1975), Brockway (1980), Brailsford (1983), Foot (2006: 3–44), Manning (1999) and Wood and Wood (1997: 65–93). For an account of 'voting and voters under the early Stuarts' see Hirst (1975).

5

The American Revolution and constitutional redefinition of democracy

INTRODUCTION

When the War of Independence broke out at Lexington in April of 1775, 87 years had passed since the Glorious Revolution of 1688. After the military victory over British forces, with a formal cessation of hostilities in 1783, the so-called 'Founding Fathers' engaged in a constitutional redefinition of democracy from 1787 to 1791. Thus the American Revolution immediately preceded and partly coincided with the French Revolution of 1789 to 1793. The American Revolution was not completed, however, with the ratification of the Constitution by the 13 states in 1791. Delegates to the Philadelphia Convention that drafted the Constitution in 1787 compromised on the key issue of slavery, with the legality of slavery being left to the states to determine. The growing conflict between the northern and southern states over slavery, and the struggle of the north-eastern bourgeoisie for continental political hegemony, culminated in a civil war from 1861 to 1865. Although it somewhat disturbs the broadly chronological sequencing of the narrative in the book, I also consider the civil war in this chapter, albeit very briefly.

This chapter has three key objectives. First, it provides a condensed historical account of the revolution, focusing on the period from the early 1760s to 1791. Second, it analyses the central features of the historically unique form of democracy created by the US Constitution. Third, it describes the key respects in which the civil war was not just a civil war but also a bourgeois revolution which completed the constitutional redefinition of democracy from 1787 to 1791 by eliminating slavery.

THE AMERICAN REVOLUTION 1775–87

Background and context

By the mid-1770s the territory of the 13 American colonies 'was already vast by European standards. Its 867,980 square miles ... stretched about 1500 miles from a northerly point on the frontier with modern Canada to a disputed southern border with Florida ... and up to 1200 miles from the Atlantic Ocean westwards to the Mississippi river' (Bonwick, 1991: 12).

The Appalachian mountain range, running from present-day Maine in the north to Alabama in the south, separated the extensive area of established white settlement that ran from the mountains to the Atlantic seaboard, from the area to the west of the mountains that was at this time still only lightly settled by whites, and which remained largely under Amerindian control. The area of white settlement can be divided into four major regions: the New England colonies/states (New Hampshire, Massachusetts, Rhode Island, Connecticut), which constituted a unified area east of the Hudson river; the mid-Atlantic colonies (New York, New Jersey, Pennsylvania and Delaware); the upper south, formed by Maryland, Virginia and parts of North Carolina, grouped round Chesapeake Bay; and the rest of North Carolina, South Carolina and Georgia, which constituted the lower south (Bonwick, 1991: 14).

The fact that communications, travel and freight movement between Britain and the American white settler colonies had to transverse a distance of 3,000 miles across the Atlantic ocean conferred the colonies with a considerable degree of economic and political autonomy. Consequently, 'under eighteenth-century communications conditions, America could not be run from London' (Mann, 1993: 137). Because land transport was considerably more expensive and slower than sea-borne transportation, transportation and communications conditions prevailing in the late eighteenth century also enhanced the political autonomy of the colonies/states relative to each other, and simultaneously created logistical difficulties for the development of centralised government on a continental scale.

The climate and fertile soils of this part of the continent provided favourable conditions for agriculture. The growing agrarian economy sustained rapid population growth, due to both European immigration and a high internal birth rate, from approximately 275,000 whites and blacks in 1700 to 2,500,000 in 1775, 3,929,214 by 1790, and 5,296,990 in 1800 (Bonwick, 1991: 17). The majority of the non-Amerindian population originated from the British Isles (67 per cent in 1790), despite the growing ethnic diversity of the white population during the eighteenth century due to immigration from other parts of Europe (1991: 19). African-Americans constituted around 20 per cent of the non-Amerindian population, numbering approximately 500,000 in 1775 and 757,208 in 1790 (Bonwick, 1991: 19). European settlement had a devastating impact on the Amerindian population; it fell from approximately 10 million prior to settlement to less than 4 million by the mid-1770s (Bonwick, 1991: 16).

'The colonial economy was unique – fundamentally agrarian, even primitive, yet highly capitalistic' (Mann, 1993: 138). It is only possible to develop an adequate understanding of the American Revolution if the centrality of capitalist agriculture (augmented in the southern colonies by the exploitation of slave labour) to economic production, social life and politics is fully recognised. The bulk of the white population was either directly engaged in capitalist agriculture or else indirectly dependent on those who were. According to Bonwick:

about two-thirds of all white men were farmers. Throughout the colonies as little as 50 or even 25 acres could provide a minimal living for a family, though much would depend on the location, quality and tenure of the land. All but about 10 to 15 per cent of landholders farmed between 50 and 500 acres.

(Bonwick, 1991: 36)

Perkins (2000: 55) notes that 'The occupational profile of the colonial work force reveals that about 80 per cent of all free males were involved primarily in agricultural pursuits.'

The wealth generated by capitalist agriculture was unequally distributed. The richest 10 per cent of colonists 'owned more than half the total physical wealth' and 'within that fortunate group the richest one per cent owned almost 15 per cent', with this inequality being most pronounced in the southern colonies and least pronounced in the mid-Atlantic colonies (Bonwick, 1991: 31–2; Perkins, 2000: 53–4). This points to two vitally important facts: land ownership together with other forms of wealth in property was highly unequally distributed and concentrated in the richest 10 per cent of the white population, yet at the same time small or middling farmers for whom property ownership was the primary source of income and social status constituted the majority of this population.

American society before and during the revolution was profoundly patriarchal. The framers of the US Constitution are aptly referred to as the 'Founding Fathers'. Whereas 'during the French Revolution, many people raised and debated questions about women's political role under the banner of [equality]', in the American Revolution the subordination of women to men was taken-for-granted rather than being contested (Crane, 1987: 258). Crane provides a convincing explanation of why this was so. Women in late eighteenth-century America, although identified in law as a largely homogeneous category, were in fact divided by the class structure in a manner that:

precluded a common bond on the basis of gender alone. Similarly, ethnic and geographic divisions created schisms between blacks and whites, Northerners and Southerners, just as they did for men. ... Quite simply, there is no evidence that most women shared much sense of consciousness of common problems as women, and those who did were foreclosed from action by the broadly shared agreement about the position of women with late eighteenth-century American society.

(Crane, 1987: 257)

Consequently, 'unlike French revolutionary women, who insisted on bearing arms and forming their own republican societies, American women never claimed universal rights for themselves' (Bloch, 2000: 608).

Although women's oppression was never a major focal point of political activity during the revolution, nonetheless gender was central to American society, the struggle for independence and the revolutionary creation of a historically unique form of democracy. Most obviously and importantly, women, who significantly outnumbered men within the white population, performed much of the labour that was essential to keep the society and military running.

There were few ladies of leisure in late colonial America. Most women worked, and worked hard. They grew vegetables, raised and butchered fowl, preserved food, cooked meals, tended the fire night and day, combed flax, carded wool, spun thread, wove and dyed cloth, sewed shirts and skirts, knitted socks and caps, washed and mended clothes, hauled water, made soap and candles, doctored the sick, gave birth to babies, tended toddlers, and instructed children in practical duties and moral obligations.

(Raphael, 2001: 107)

Once the War of Independence broke out and men enlisted in the Continental or Loyalist armies, women were expected, in addition to their already considerable unpaid workload, to take on traditionally male work in a predominantly agrarian economy, such as planting and harvesting the fields, cutting wood, fixing fences, repairing houses to keep out rain and snow, forging and sharpening tools, selling crops, and managing farm and household finances. Women also provided vital labour in the military sphere, not only working to produce garments for the army at home, but also as 'camp followers' who 'served the army as cooks, washerwomen, and nurses; during battles they carried messages and supplies and assisted with the artillery' (Raphael, 2001: 120). During the eight years that war was waged across the territory of the American colonies, with each side advancing and retreating, women were vulnerable to looting, violence including rape, being widowed and losing their homes (Raphael, 2001: 136).

Although women generally did not organise collectively to promote their interests and rights, they were politicised by the war and revolution, and this politicisation was reinforced as women took on work and responsibilities previously reserved for men, and traditional gender roles began to fracture. In March 1776, Abigail Adams wrote to her husband John Adams, who was serving as a delegate to the Continental Congress, 'If particular care and attention is not paid to the Ladies we are determined to foment a Rebellion, and will not hold ourselves bound by any Laws in which we have no voice, or Representation' (quoted by Raphael, 2001: 115). While radical political consciousness of this nature was relatively rare, the increasingly active involvement of women in political activity was common. Not only did women engage in a broad range of patriotic activities ranging from spinning circles and boycotting goods to fundraising for the army, they were also key participants in anti-Loyalist activities, and led nearly one-third of the food riots during the revolution, thereby engaging in 'collective action that made a difference' (Raphael, 2001: 119).

As Mann (1993: 139) observes, 'the dual horror of Indian genocide and African enslavement remained central to North American society'. White settler colonialism in North America, and other parts of the British empire such as Australia, New Zealand and South Africa, centrally involved the systematic appropriation of communally owned tribal land, which then deprived indigenous peoples of the traditional material and economic foundation of their existence because it destroyed the pre-capitalist tribal mode of production upon which their societies were based. Simultaneously, it laid the foundations for the emergence of capitalism because it commodified all of the major means of production in the form of labour-power and private property rights. Precisely because 'the expropriation of the mass of the people from the soil forms the basis of the capitalist mode of production', there are important similarities in all historical transitions from pre-capitalist to capitalist modes of production (Marx, 1967a: 768). Just as the emergence of capitalism in England during the seventeenth and eighteenth centuries centrally involved the mass of poor peasants being deprived of the small plots of land upon which they produced their subsistence, and being denied access to the village commons, the emergence of capitalism in America centrally involved both Amerindian peoples and the poorer European migrants being deprived of their lands (McNally, 1993, pp.7–24). As mentioned above, the Amerindian population declined precipitously as a result of white settler colonialism through war, mass murder, disease, the deliberate use of smallpox to devastate indigenous populations, alcohol, poverty, incarceration, capital punishment, and cultural and spiritual disorientation.

Amerindian tribes and tribal nations adopted a variety of complex strategic and tactical responses to the Seven Years War and War of Independence, which are not easy to summarise briefly. With the exception of the Mohawks in the north and the Chickasaws in the south, most tribes sided with the French in the Seven Years War, which is why it is also referred to as the 'French and Indian War'. This war ended in 1763 with the Peace of Paris signed on February 10, with Britain gaining Quebec, Florida, and all of North America east of the Mississippi. On May 7 a young Ottawa leader launched a successful attack on a British garrison near Detroit. As word spread, this 'prompted uprisings elsewhere, until by summer's end every British post in the West had been attacked', with most major forts falling into the hands of Amerindian forces (Hinderaker, 2000: 96). Thus although the French army departed, 'Amerindian warriors still commanded fear and respect' (Marshall, 2000: 160). Realising the impossibility of suppressing Amerindian resistance by force, the British government on October 7 issued its Proclamation of 1763 prohibiting white settlement beyond the Appalachians.

Deteriorating relations between the British government and its American colonies gave the latter plenty of scope to continue to encroach upon Amerindian territory. Consequently, during the War of Independence most tribes sided with the British. As Merrell (2000: 413) observes, 'while abandoning neutrality was often a difficult and painful decision, choosing between Britain and America was not. The British had a history of trying to protect Amerindian land from encroachments; the Americans had a history of making those encroachments.'

Although slavery existed in all the colonies in the 1760s, it was predominantly concentrated in the south. According to Bonwick (1991: 20–1), 89 per cent of blacks lived in the south, and 'of the populations of Maryland and Virginia 39 per cent were black, as were 35 per cent of North Carolina, 45 per cent in Georgia and a massive 61 per cent in the coastal parishes that formed the principal populated area of South Carolina'. The concentration of slave plantation agriculture in the south was central to the emergence of fundamental social, economic and political differences between the southern colonies and the other regions. Whereas in the other regions, both economic production and the social structure were organised around family farms, mainly freehold farms but also including a significant minority of tenant farms, in the south slave plantation agriculture was the predominant form of economic production, generating substantial exports of cotton, rice and tobacco.

As this suggests, the relationship between slave owners and slaves was central to the social structure, requiring the former to maintain the coercive enslavement of the latter. This could not be taken for granted as slaves generally resented their exploitation and desired freedom, generating widespread resistance such as working slowly, injuring crops, feigning illness, disrupting work routines, running away and, much less commonly, collective revolt (Ashworth, 1995: 4–8). In the context of the War of Independence where the British offered slaves their freedom if they fought against the Patriots, thousands of slaves escaped from their masters to join the British army, with South Carolina losing around one quarter of its slave population (Frey, 2000: 411).

Slavery also had a significant political impact on the American Revolution. In explaining why southern Republicans such as Jefferson were critics of the northern Federalist vision of a highly restrictive form of democracy, with extensive and high property qualifications for the franchise and office-holding, and were committed to establishing a more expansionist form of democracy for the white population, Ashworth argues that: 'the crucial factor was the different alignment of class forces in the slave South, in which the masters, exploiting their slaves, had been able to reach a modus vivendi with the non-elite whites. It was this modus vivendi which had profound consequences for the development of democracy in the United States' (Ashworth, 1995: 32). Chief among these is the fact that whereas the wealthy Patriot elites in the northern colonies were mainly concerned with potential revolt against their rule from poor and middling farmers, possibly in combination with non-property-owning wage labourers, in the southern colonies the elites were much less concerned about this, and primarily concerned to maintain coercive dominance over their slave populations.

The intellectual and ideological influences on, and currents within, the American Revolution included Lockean liberalism, Protestantism, the juridical rights of British subjects, republicanism, the Enlightenment and key figures in the Scottish Enlightenment such as David Hume, Adam Smith and Adam Ferguson (Kramnick, 2000). The relative weight of these influences is much debated and difficult to ascertain precisely, but Lockean liberalism, work ethic Protestantism and early-modern republicanism appear to be the most important.

The influence of Lockean liberalism on the revolution is most obvious with respect to the Declaration of Independence of 1776, which was drafted by Thomas Jefferson. The Declaration asserts that men are endowed 'with certain unalienable Rights' including 'Life, Liberty and the pursuit of Happiness'. In order to secure these rights, 'Governments are instituted among Men, deriving their just powers from the consent of the governed.' This consent is conditional upon the performance of government and can be withdrawn when government fails to respect and preserve the rights of the governed; 'whenever any Form of Government becomes destructive of these ends, it is the Right of the People to alter or to abolish it, and to institute new Government'. This echoes Locke's (1966: 122) argument in *The Second Treatise of Government* that to protect their rights to life, liberty and property men form government, that the legislative and executive powers of government rest upon the consent of the governed, and that the governed have a right to dissolve government and 'erect a new form [of government], or under the old form place it in new hands', if it fails to protect their rights and abuses its authority.

Republican ideas also influenced the thinking and conduct of the framers of the Constitution (Appleby, 1984, Kramnick, 2000; G. Wood, 2003: 91–5). The Revolution centrally involved 'a republican commitment to the renovation of virtue' (Pocock quoted by Kramnick, 2000: 92). Drawing upon the ideas of thinkers from classical antiquity, Renaissance Italy and the English Revolution such as Aristotle, Cicero, Plutarch, Machiavelli, Ireton and Harrington, the Anglo-American republican tradition: 'conceives of man as a political being whose realisation of self occurs only through participation in public life, through active citizenship in a republic. The virtuous man is concerned primarily with the public good, res publica, or commonweal, not with private or selfish ends' (Kramnick, 2000: 91). In contradistinction: 'corruption is the absence of civic virtue. Corrupt man is preoccupied with self and oblivious to the public good. Such failures… fuel the decline of states and can be remedied only through periodic revitalization by returning to the original and pristine commitment to civic virtue' (Kramnick, 2000: 91).

American society at the time of the Revolution was highly religious, with church membership 'ranging from about 56 per cent of the population in the South to as much as 80 per cent in the North', and predominantly protestant (Bonwick, 1991: 42). The protestant work ethic was pervasive in the American colonies, and closely allied with Lockean liberalism and the Republican emphasis on civic virtue:

Central in work ethic Protestantism was the vision of a cosmic struggle between the forces of industry and idleness. ... Work was a test of self-sufficiency and self-reliance, a battleground for personal salvation. All men were 'called' to serve God by busying themselves in useful productive work that served both society and the individual. Daily labour was sanctified and thus was both a specific obligation and a positive moral value.

(Kramnick, 2000: 89)

According to this view, 'virtuous man is a solitary and private man on his own, realizing himself and his talents through labour and achievement; corrupt man is unproductive, indolent, and in the devil's camp. He fails the test of individual responsibility' (Kramnick, 2000: 89).

As Bonwick (1991: 67) observes, 'continental unity was much more a product than a precursor of the American Revolution'. Each of the 13 independent colonies had formal political ties with Britain but none with its sister colonies, and hence 'the highest level of community for pre-Revolutionary Americans was not the continent but the empire' (Bonwick, 1991: 67). With respect to political structure, each colonial government was loosely modelled on the British machinery of government:

with traditional functional divisions between executive (the governor), legislature and judiciary, and distinctions between governor, upper house (except in Pennsylvania and Georgia) and lower house that mimicked the social balance of monarchy, aristocracy and democracy manifested in England by the king, lords and commons.

(Bonwick, 1991: 44)

Important differences existed between the nature of colonial and British government, with the power of the governors being circumscribed by their dependence on colonial assemblies for revenue and political support necessary to implement policies, even though their formal powers were considerable (control of the military, right to veto legislation, dissolve the assembly, nominate members of the upper house, and make appointments to the higher judiciary) (Bonwick, 1991: 45).

The specifics of the institutions of colonial government are, however, much less important than the fact that in all cases the colonial governments were dominated by white, male, wealthy capitalist elites. In all 13 colonies:

Possession of property was the primary qualification for the franchise. Ownership of freehold land had triple merit. It demonstrated possession of a stake in society, in an agricultural society it was held to demonstrate particularly admirable social virtue, and it gave its owner independence in the broader economic, social and therefore political sense.

(Bonwick, 1991: 47)

The qualification was highest in the upper and lower south, where voters were required to own 50 acres of land; in the other colonies voters had to own land worth between 40 shillings and £50 in value (Williamson, 1960: 12–15). Even though landownership was unequally distributed amongst the white population, nonetheless it was much more equally distributed than in Britain, which meant that at least 50 per cent of the white male population was entitled to vote (Mann, 1993: 142). Property qualifications for office were set at a much higher level, however, and consequently most members of the colonial assemblies 'were great planters, merchants or lawyers drawn from the upper tenth of the population' (Bonwick, 1991: 47).

Mann (1993: 143) argues that because 'the mass electorate accepted its political powerlessness, failed to turn out to vote, and accepted the patronage and deference networks of the colonial notable regime', it was 'a speaking aristocracy in the face of a silent democracy'. Although this is true with respect to electoral politics, Pennsylvania being the one notable exception, the poor and middling folk by no means meekly accepted their political powerlessness. Instead of using electoral channels to influence the colonial governments, they protested, marched, tarred and feathered their opponents, and formed popular militias to close courts and resist authority.

As we shall see, before, during and after the American Revolution the rich ruled. Before the Revolution 'stable British rule depended on an alliance between the crown and local-regional notables', but during the Revolution the colonial elites split along Loyalist and Patriot lines, with the majority rejecting British rule (Mann, 1993: 146). As Foner (1976: xvi) observes, leadership of the revolution 'was, in general, conducted and controlled by an alliance of the colonial ruling classes – merchants, lawyers and large landowners in the northern colonies, slaveholding planters in the South'. After the revolution, the rule of the rich was secured through a historically unique constitutional redefinition of democracy, discussed on pages 138–42.

The clash of French and British imperial ambitions in North America gave rise to the Seven Years' War from 1756 to 1763. The British were only able to defeat the French and their Amerindian allies by enlisting substantial military, logistical and financial support from their American colonies, particularly Virginia, Massachusetts and New York. By the end of the war, 71,000 colonists had fought in the war alongside 21,000 British redcoats. However, although the British and Anglo-Americans had emerged victorious, the victory had come at considerable cost to the British government and the English aristocracy and landed gentry, which bore the bulk of the tax burden:

The aristocracy and landed-gentry ... endured [tax] levies on their rent rolls that peaked at 25 per cent of annual income. Britain's national debt moreover nearly doubled from £72,289,673 to £129,586,789 by 1764, with annual interest charges exceeding £5,000,000, while the accumulated colonial debt was about £1,000,000 in 1764.

(Purvis, 2000: 114)

This pushed the British government to impose increased taxation upon the American colonies, and this in turn generated the hostility and resistance from the colonists that ultimately led to the War of Independence. Despite this resistance, the British government repeatedly attempted to impose new taxes on the colonists because it 'believed American principles were a smoke screen for unwillingness to pay their fair share for imperial defence and it was reluctant to [further] increase the burden of taxation in Britain' (Mann, 1993: 147).

Narrative of events

The unequal distribution of land ownership, other forms of wealth, income, and political and judicial influence, generated recurring incidents of class-based conflict. As Zinn (1999: 59) says, 'by 1760, there had been 18 uprisings aimed at overthrowing colonial governments. There had also been six black rebellions, from South Carolina to New York, and 40 riots'. In the aftermath of the Seven Years War, the emerging capitalist elites in the colonies, encompassing rich landowners, merchants, financiers, lawyers and slave plantation owners, 'saw the possibility of directing much of the rebellious energy against England and her local officials. It wasn't a conscious conspiracy, but an accumulation of tactical responses' (Zinn, 1999: 59). Zinn places a little too much weight on this aspect of the revolution. In my view, Mann (1993: 146) is correct to argue that 'because there were fewer impoverished "dangerous classes" among whites', with less than a third of the settler population being proletarianised and tenant farming much less common than freeholding, 'notable Patriots were less disciplined by the fear of revolution from the "populace" below than were their counterparts in most of Europe'. However, as Mann also recognises, and as all Marxist accounts of the revolution rightly emphasise, although the fear of revolution from below amongst the colonial Patriot elites may have been less than that prevailing within the ruling classes of Europe, it was still an important factor in the revolution.

It is widely recognised that 'the wealthy notables who proclaimed rebellion in the name of the "people" were not democrats' because they were consistently opposed to a system of democracy in which the majority of people would be enfranchised and able to be elected to positions of power (Mann, 1993: 151). As we have seen, not only were women, Amerindians and slaves excluded from their vision of democracy, so too were white men without property. Nonetheless, in order 'to combat the world's dominant superpower they needed to mobilize the mass of small property owners on their side – most of whom were used to carrying arms' (Mann, 1993: 151). 'Just about every white male had a gun and could shoot. The revolutionary leadership distrusted the mobs of poor. But they knew the Revolution had no appeal to slaves and Indians. They would have to woo the armed white population' (Zinn, 1999: 78). In order to do this, the Patriot leaders of the revolution used 'a language inspiring to all classes, specific enough in its listing of grievances to charge people with anger against the British, vague enough to avoid class conflict among the rebels, and stirring enough to build a patriotic feeling for the resistance movement' (Zinn, 1999: 68). But this was a difficult game for the Patriot leaders to play because it required a balancing act, maintaining broadly popular support for the War of Independence and revolution by appealing to universal notions of liberty and democracy, on one hand, while simultaneously defending the sanctity of property and the rule of a rich capitalist minority, on the other.

As we shall see, this balancing act lies at the heart of the American Revolution. It explains why the revolution eventually created a form of democracy that constituted a world-historic advance on the British parliamentary democracy of the 1770s. As Mann (1993: 151) puts it, 'The petite bourgeoisie, led uniquely by small farmers, achieved mass democracy in advance of anywhere else in the world.' Less obviously, it also explains, at least in part, why American representative democracy was highly effective in institutionally entrenching capitalist relations of production and securing the interests of the rich capitalist minority that would continue to dominate politics and policy making at both federal and state levels into the twenty-first century. Throughout the revolution, and especially when framing and ratifying the US Constitution from 1787–91, the wealthy Patriot elite was concerned to create a form of government that, although formally democratic, would protect their interests and power against 'mob rule' or even, in Madison's justification of the Constitution, against the possible influence of poor and middling folk, who constituted a majority of the population, over the legislative, executive and judicial branches of government.

A dramatic increase in social and political unrest occurred from the early 1760s to 1775. This unrest was channelled in three major directions: internally towards the wealthy governing elites in the various colonies; externally towards the British government; and internally towards the latter's troops, appointed American agents, and domestic Loyalist supporters, who constituted between 20–30 per cent of the white settler population.

White settlers and their colonial governments were outraged at the British Proclamation of 1763 prohibiting white settlement beyond the Appalachians. In 1764, several hundred white settlers known as the 'Paxton Boys' slaughtered some Amerindians then marched on Philadelphia, demanding both aid against the Amerindians and better western representation in the state legislature. As relations with the British government deteriorated, imperial control over colonial western expansion diminished, and ongoing settler encroachment on Amerindian territory accelerated. Thus colonial resistance to British authority was motivated, in part, by settlers' desire to expropriate Amerindian land.

In order to increase the taxes paid by the American colonies, the British government in 1765 passed the Stamp Act on March 22, and it took effect from November 1. Resistance to the Stamp Act quickly emerged throughout the colonies, with the strongest opposition in Boston. On August 14 an angry crowd of Bostonians hung the stamp collector (Andrew Oliver) in effigy from a Liberty Tree and burned his house. Affluent American Patriots formed the Sons of Liberty in order to coordinate opposition to the Act. They enlisted poor and middling folk in the movement while simultaneously trying to control their involvement. Patriot leaders wanted boycotts and protests directed against the British, but they also wanted these to be disciplined and to respect the sanctity of property. As Sam Adams put it, 'No Mobs or Tumults, let the Persons and Properties of your most inveterate Enemies be safe' (Zinn, 1999: 66). The non-importation movement that promoted and policed the boycott of British goods was significant because, in contrast to other forms of protest and resistance to British rule, 'it involved the majority of free Americans in one manner or another' (Raphael, 2001: 31). As Raphael observes:

> It is the engagement in collective and purposive activity that turns ordinary people into revolutionaries. American patriots from New Hampshire, Massachusetts, Rhode Island, Connecticut, New York, New Jersey, Pennsylvania, Delaware, Maryland, Virginia, North Carolina, South Carolina, and Georgia were willing to wage war in 1775 and declare their independence in 1776 because they had participated for the better part of the decade in what would appear as a simple and non-violent political protest: an economic boycott of British imported goods.
>
> (Raphael, 2001: 31)

In May of 1766 tenant farmers rose up against their wealthy landlords in the Hudson Valley. The Regulator movement, which started in North Carolina and then spread to South Carolina, emerged as 'a powerful movement of white farmers who organised against wealthy and corrupt officials in the period from 1767 to 1771' (Zinn, 1999: 63; Raphael, 2001: 25). In 1769, armed white settlers in the Green Mountain region of north-eastern New York, 'Green Mountain Boys' as they came to be called, formed an unauthorised militia to defend their property titles against the conflicting claims of rich New York speculators, and effectively controlled the west side of the mountains until they joined the Continental Army in 1775. Raphael provides a useful summary of the significance of these movements.

> The 1766 uprisings in New York foreshadowed the greater conflict that followed: angry farmers, apparently powerless, stood tall in the face of their rulers, who had to be bailed out by the British Army. The tenant rebellions of the middle colonies, along with the Regulator movements in the South, contributed indirectly to the coming Revolution by chipping away at the notion that a few men of prestige and privilege could exploit those beneath them with impunity.
>
> These pre-revolutionary disturbances advanced a social climate conducive to violent confrontation. Tenants who wielded axes against their landlords or poor folk who tore apart theatres were not protesting against Parliament, but they were becoming accustomed to expressing rage, resisting authority, and taking public policy into their own hands. They

questioned, they challenged, they refused to submit. Modern historians call it an end to deference; in the minds of the contemporary elite, it seemed like insolence. The hierarchical society which Euro-American colonists had brought with them from the Old World was beginning to crumble. Many common people on the eve of the Revolution would not accept conditions that were presented to them by those with more power, status, or money. They were primed to become rebels.

(Raphael, 2001: 27–8)

Simmering tensions in Boston between British troops and civilians reached a climax on March 5, 1770 when the troops opened fire on a band of boys who had been harassing them verbally and throwing snowballs at them. Five boys were killed in what became known throughout the colonies as the 'Boston massacre'. This action further radicalised the populace of Boston, numbering around 16,000 at this time, and generated the cadre who played a key role in the Boston Tea Party, which took place on December 16, 1773. The importation and taxation of tea had been an enduring source of conflict since the early 1760s. As Raphael puts it:

The boycott of tea, the most enduring component of American resistance, was imbued with class connotations. ... Although some common folk might enjoy a sip now and again, the major consumers of tea participated in a ritual activity which was prohibitively expensive for the vast majority of colonists. ... Tea was an easy target, a symbol both of Parliament's arrogance and a crumbling social hierarchy. By identifying the British and their loyalist allies as purveyors of a decadent European culture – tea-drinking theatregoers who dressed in fancy clothes and enforced oppressive laws – Whig leaders and street fighters were able to unite around a common enemy.

(Raphael, 2001: 16–18)

When the British government decided to allow the East India Company to sell tea in America through its own agents, rather than by public auction as previously, Patriot leaders in the ports of New York, Philadelphia, Charleston and Boston were determined to prevent the landing of tea. This led to a stalemate in Boston where three British ships were anchored but unable to offload their cargo. A carefully selected group of radicals, 'a contained and disciplined cadre' numbering less than 100, disguised as Amerindians, boarded these ships and dumped 90,000 pounds of tea in the harbour.

This act outraged the British Parliament, which responded by introducing four Coercive Acts in 1774 aimed at suppressing the rebellion in Massachusetts and sending a clear message to the other colonies that further resistance would be suppressed forcibly. These acts closed the port of Boston until compensation was paid for the destroyed tea, restructured the Massachusetts government to increase British control over it, allowed those charged with resisting the importation of tea and the collection of customs duty to be tried in courts outside of the province, and authorised the governor to billet British troops in unoccupied private buildings without the permission of the owners. The Coercive Acts, labelled the 'Intolerable Acts' by colonists, only succeeded in further fanning the flames of revolt.

> Each harsher measure of British control – the Proclamation of 1763 not allowing colonists to settle beyond the Appalachians, the Stamp Tax, the Townshend Taxes ... the stationing of troops and the Boston Massacre, the closing of the port of Boston and the dissolution of the Massachusetts legislature – escalated colonial rebellion to the point of revolution.
>
> (Zinn, 1999: 70–1)

From May to August 1774 angry crowds in Boston closed the court houses in response to the Coercive Acts and forced judges to resign in humiliating public ceremonies. This drew wide support from across the colonies since the Coercive Acts appeared to introduce 'a complete system of tyranny', which could be easily applied to the other colonies.

Rapidly rising resistance to British tyranny over the American colonies was given further impetus when in May 1774 General Thomas Gage was made commander-in-chief in America and given three additional regiments of soldiers (an extra 3500 troops). In response to a call from Massachusetts for a Continental Congress on June 17, all colonies except Georgia elected delegates. The first Continental Congress then met in Philadelphia from September 5 to October 26, resolving to reconvene in May 1775. The Congress warned Massachusetts to avoid aggression but also promised aid if the British escalated its military campaign to suppress rebellion. It issued a Declaration of Colonial Rights and Grievances, opposing the Coercive Acts and asserting the rights of colonial assemblies to legislate and impose taxes, on October 14. It criticised the policies and conduct of the British government around the themes of 'no taxation without representation' and defending American liberty against the imposition of British tyranny. Military training and preparedness was advocated. Most importantly, Congress formed the Continental Association to promote and enforce, via local committees of inspection, non-importation of British products; non-importation was to begin on December 1, 1774, non-consumption on March 1, 1775, and non-exportation on September 1, 1775 (Bonwick, 1991: 82). The idea was to create a powerful source of opposition to the government's American policies amongst the British public.

On April 14, 1775, General Gage received a letter from the British government directing him to use military force to implement the Coercive Acts, while at the same time denying his request for 20,000 troops to restore order.

> Prodded by the British government to be more active, General Gage dispatched an expedition to capture colonial military supplies stored at Concord, a few miles west of Boston. Early on the morning of 19 April this foray encountered about 70 American minutemen drawn up on Lexington

green. Sweeping them aside and killing 8, the British troops continued onwards. They were repulsed by American militia at Concord and were forced to retreat under continual fire. The British lost 273 casualties and achieved nothing. Nearly 4000 American militiamen participated in the fighting.

(Bonwick, 1991: 84)

Thus began the War of Independence. A Second Continental Congress convened several weeks later on May 10, 1775. It quickly evolved into a de facto national government. It resolved on May 15 to put the colonies in a state of defence, and formed the Continental Army (June 15), appointing George Washington as commanding general (July 3). The navy was formed on November 28. On August 23, King George III proclaimed the colonies in 'open and avowed rebellion', declaring 'the die is now cast. The colonies must either submit or triumph' (Sarson, 2000: 727).

It is not possible to provide a detailed account of the course of the War of Independence here, but three points are noteworthy. First, this was a major conflict, spanning a period of eight years from 1775 to 1783, and affected the entire white settler population. 'In fact, a greater percentage of the American population perished in the Revolutionary War than in WWI, WWII, or the Vietnam War; only the Civil War was more deadly' (Raphael, 2001: 6). Second, it was also a civil war, 'pitting neighbours against neighbours and splitting families apart. Much of the violence, unsanctioned by any formal military organisation, took place in houses and barns and public streets; even in some of the major battles, British troops were conspicuously absent' (Raphael, 2001: 4). In a similar vein, Mann (1993: 150) observes, 'During the war, the participants used extremely socially, and politically, directed violence. ... Loyalists were as likely to have their property expropriated and were almost five times as likely to flee into exile as were Royalists in the French Revolution.' Third, the scale and duration of the conflict had important unifying and centralising effects, with governmental and military organisations being formed on a continental basis for the first time.

The mass radicalisation of the white settler population contributed to the outbreak of the War of Independence, and in turn was given further impetus once the war was underway. Thomas Paine published *Common Sense* in January 1776. In the three months that followed it sold over 120,000 copies. As Foner comments, it was:

a forceful and brilliant argument for the independence of the American colonies from Great Britain and the superiority of republican government over hereditary monarch, [which] had an enormous impact on the subsequent decision for independence. ... In an age of pamphleteering, *Common Sense* was unique in the extent of its readership and its influence on events.

(Foner, 1976: xi)

After prolonged debate during the first half of 1776, Congress finally resolved to break from Britain, and declared independence on July 2, issuing the Declaration of Independence on July 4. The Declaration provided a critique of the alleged crimes of the British Crown; 'The history of the present King of Great Britain is a history of repeated injuries and usurpations, all having, in direct object, the establishment of an absolute tyranny over these states.' This served to justify the revolt against British rule and the Declaration of Independence.

We, therefore, the representatives of the United States of America, in general Congress assembled, appealing to the Supreme Judge of the world for the rectitude of our intentions, do, in the name, and by the authority of the good people of these colonies, solemnly publish and declare, that these united colonies are, and of right ought to be, free and independent states; that they are absolved from all allegiance to the British Crown, and that all political connection between them and the state of Great Britain is, and ought to be, totally dissolved.

(quoted in Brown, 2000: 172)

The opening philosophical preamble declared that all men are created equal and possess inalienable rights to life, liberty, and the pursuit of happiness. Governments are formed in order to secure these rights and depend on consent of the governed. However, 'whenever any Form of Government becomes destructive of these ends, it is the Right of the People to alter or abolish it, and to institute a new Government' (quoted in Brown, 2000: 170).

Congress intended that following the Declaration of Independence in 1776 it would introduce the constitutional framework for a national government in the form of Articles of Confederation. This took much longer than expected, with the Articles of Confederation finally being ratified by all the states in 1781. In the interim the growth of central government was shaped by the imperatives of war and the pragmatic decision making of the members of Congress. Congress itself was an assembly of delegates from the 13 provincial governments, which later became states. Although each state government could determine the size of its delegation, each state possessed only one vote. A unicameral assembly, the United States in Congress as it was called officially, both formulated and implemented policy. Funding the war was the major problem that it faced. The war cost somewhere between $158 million and $168 million, of which the states raised half (Bonwick, 1991: 103). Given its inability to raise money by taxes, Congress issued vast quantities of coins and notes. Not surprisingly this generated rampant inflation, which further exacerbated the financial, military and political difficulties that it faced.

In contrast to the protracted development of national government, change took place much more rapidly at the provincial/state level. Each colony transformed its government from a colonial government headed by a governor appointed by the British Crown, and with no formal links to the governments of the other colonies, to a state government set up according to republican principles, formally confederated, albeit loosely, with the other states via its representation in Congress. The written constitution was the mechanism used to 'set out the general principles of government, the structure of its machinery, and the extent and limits of its lawful authority' (Bonwick, 1991: 121). Central to these republican principles was the notion that sovereignty ultimately resided in the people, but 'the people' was generally defined to exclude men without property, women, Amerindians and slaves. Zinn (1999: 83) observes: 'The new constitutions that were drawn up in all states from 1776 to 1780 were not much different from the old ones. Although property qualifications for voting and holding office were lowered in some instances, in Massachusetts they were increased. Only Pennsylvania abolished them totally' (Zinn, 1999: 83). Like the more conservative Loyalists, the Patriot elites were convinced of the need for stable, orderly government, and the protection of property. They denied that the lower orders – those who worked with their hands – should be permitted to share in the administration of public affairs, and feared that if they were so permitted they would immediately launch raids on the property of the rich (Bonwick, 1991: 126).

This is a vitally important point because the constitution making at the state level constituted the immediate precursor for the development of the 1781 Articles of Confederation and the Philadelphia Convention that in 1787 drafted the US Constitution.

Four key issues caused division and conflict that prevented the states' delegations from quickly agreeing on the Articles of Confederation: how the representation of the states in Congress should be determined, taxation, control over western land, and the amount of power that central government should possess relative to the states. In the debates over these issues the small states prevailed with respect to the question of representation; the principle of state equality in which each state had one vote in Congress regardless of the size of its population was maintained. It was finally decided that states would contribute to the costs of national government according to the value of their settled lands, rather than the population of the states. The issue of congressional power over the setting of state boundaries and the lands that lay to the west of them was left unresolved. Most importantly, Congress accepted the amendment moved by Thomas Burke, a delegate from North Carolina, that each state would retain 'its sovereignty, freedom, and independence, and every power, jurisdiction, and right, which is not by this Confederation expressly delegated to Congress' (quoted by Rakove, 2000: 283). As Bonwick (1991: 148) observes, this amendment 'significantly altered the nature of the union by explicitly affirming the legal supremacy of the states and by reducing Congress to the status of an agent possessing strictly defined powers'.

The Articles of Confederation that were agreed upon by Congress in November of 1777 created a weak central government without the powers it really needed to respond effectively to the many challenges and difficulties it faced. Despite this, continuing disagreement between the states over the role of

Congress in adjudicating access to western land and territorial disputes between the states meant that even this very limited granting of power to Congress was not ratified by all the states until 1781. That the Articles were ratified at all was due to mounting pressure placed on both Congress and the states by the severe economic and fiscal crisis that resulted from the war. Rampant inflation and a huge national debt could be dealt with effectively only by central government. It soon became apparent that the Articles had not vested enough power in Congress to deal adequately with these and other problems.

In addition to this, one other factor pushed the Patriot elite to develop a centralised system of government with much more power than that granted by the Articles of Confederation; the fear of rebellion from below. Although there was significant social and political unrest throughout the course of the American Revolution, none was more significant for the subsequent development of central government and the US Constitution than the uprising of struggling farmers in the summer of 1786 in western Massachusetts. This became known as Shay's rebellion, named after Daniel Shay, a veteran of the Continent army who left military service in 1780 because he had not been paid, and returned to his farm where he faced insurmountable debts. This was a general problem faced by many of the small to middling farmers of western Massachusetts. Their frustration and anger was exacerbated by the stance of the Massachusetts legislature in Boston. As Zinn observes:

> The new [Massachusetts] Constitution of 1780 had raised the property qualifications for voting. No one could hold state office without being quite wealthy. Furthermore, the legislature was refusing to issue paper money, as had been done in other states, like Rhode Island, to make it easier for debt-ridden farmers to pay off their creditors.
>
> (Zinn, 1999: 91)

These farmers wanted the legislature to take action to assist them with their financial difficulties, especially given that these difficulties had arisen because of the sacrifices that most of them had made fighting for independence, but the courts were the immediate focus of their grievances. The court proceedings that were scheduled to take place in the towns of western Massachusetts, such as Northampton, Springfield, Worcester and Athol, were about to order the seizure of:

> the cattle of farmers who hadn't paid their debts, to take away their land, now full of grain and ready for harvest. And so, veterans of the Continental Army, also aggrieved because they had been treated poorly on discharge – given certificates for future redemption instead of immediate cash – began to organize the farmers into squads and companies.
>
> (Zinn, 1999: 92)

Hundreds of armed farmers then forcibly shut down the courts in town after town. Debt-ridden farmers and veterans in the other states started to take similar action as word of the rebellion in Massachusetts spread. But the success of the rebellion was relatively short-lived. Winter snows made it more difficult for the farmers to make it to the courts, and the legislature commissioned General Benjamin Lincoln, with an army funded by rich Boston merchants, to suppress the rebellion, which he eventually did.

Leading members of the Patriot elite quickly drew political conclusions from this rebellion. One was the importance of ruthlessly suppressing collective challenges to the power and privileges of wealth and property. In this vein, Sam Adams argued that the leaders of Shay's rebellion should be put to death: 'In monarchy the crime of treason may admit of being pardoned or lightly punished, but the man who dares rebel against the laws of a republic ought to suffer death' (quoted by Zinn, 1999: 95). The major problem, from the perspective of the ruling capitalist elite, was that Congress, as constituted under the Articles of Confederation, had proven itself to be entirely ineffective in responding to the rebellion. Although it called upon the states to provide money and men to help suppress the rebellion, only Virginia had responded with more than words.

This led the majority of the Patriot elite to the conclusion that the powers of central government were far too weak and that they needed to be greatly enhanced by further constitutional reform. On the one hand, they generally agreed with Alexander Hamilton's view that: 'all communities divide themselves into the few and the many. The first are the rich and the wellborn, the other the mass of people. ... The people are turbulent and changing; they seldom judge or determine right. Give therefore to the first class a distinct permanent share in government' (quoted by Zinn, 1999: 96). As we shall see, there was considerable disagreement as to how this state of affairs might be best achieved, but the desirability of the rich ruling was never in question. On the other hand, they faced a rebellious populace disgruntled that the privations of war had left the rich largely unscathed while falling heavily on the poor and middling folk who had done most of the actual fighting. In this vein, General Henry Knox wrote to George Washington observing with respect to Shay's rebellion that:

The people who are the insurgents ... see the weakness of government; they feel at once their poverty, compared with the opulent, and their own force, and they are determined to make use of the latter, in order to remedy the former. Their creed is 'That the property of the United States has been protected from the confiscations of Britain by the joint exertions of all, and therefore ought to be the common property of all. And he that attempts opposition to this creed is an enemy to equity and justice and ought to be swept off from the face of the earth.'

(quoted by Zinn, 1999: 95)

This, in combination with Congress's failed attempts successfully to manage rampant inflation and the huge national debt, prompted Congress to call a convention to draw up a new constitution that would establish a more powerful and effective central government for the United States.

THE CONSTITUTIONAL REDEFINITION OF DEMOCRACY, 1787–91

The Philadelphia Convention of 1787

It is widely recognised that the Philadelphia Convention, which met from May 25 to September 17 to draft the new constitution, was composed exclusively of white propertied (generally wealthy) men. As the neo-Weberian historical sociologist Michael Mann (1993: 150, 155) says, 'The leaders of the Revolution, the Founding Fathers, remained men of substantial property from beginning to end', and 'threatened by class radicalism, the notables organised to strengthen the [central] state'. When they met at the convention, 'their debates did not centre on class issues, on which delegates shared common unspoken assumptions'. They shared these assumptions because virtually all of them 'were planters, merchants or lawyers and possessed broad experience of commercial affairs, thus representing the country's major economic interests and dominant social groups, and they were members of the elite within their respective states whose interests they could therefore claim to represent' (Bonwick, 1991: 202).

The classic work establishing the highly unrepresentative composition of the convention is *An Economic Interpretation of the Constitution of the United States* by Charles Beard. Published in 1913, it surveys the economic status of all of the delegates, and determines that the majority of delegates owned substantial property in one or more of land, slaves, manufacturing, shipping and banking, and that 40 out of the 55 delegates held public securities and would therefore benefit from the establishment of a stronger central government that could guarantee the full value of these securities (Beard, 1913: 150). According to Beard (1913: 149), 'The overwhelming majority of [delegates], at least five-sixths, were immediately, directly, and personally interested in the outcome of their labours at Philadelphia, and were to a greater or less extent economic beneficiaries from the adoption of the Constitution.' He drew the 'profoundly significant conclusion that they knew through their personal experiences in economic affairs the precise results which the new government that they were setting up was designed to attain' (Beard, 1913: 150).

This conclusion has been subject to widespread critique from non-Marxist revisionist historians who dispute the claim that the delegates benefited financially from the Constitution, and highlight the strong ideological commitment of the delegates to the Republican notion of civic virtue. In doing so they miss the most important point of Beard's analysis. Whether or not the delegates benefited directly and personally from the greater centralisation of government that resulted from the Constitution is much less important than the fact that as successful participants in 'commercial affairs' they had a clear understanding that the new constitutional framework would have to, as one of its core tasks, successfully entrench and codify the rights and liberties of property. If it failed to do this, their own wealth and privileges would be undermined, and the rapid expansion of capitalist agriculture, industry, commerce and banking would be impossible. The Republican notion of civic virtue served their purposes admirably in this respect because it enabled them genuinely to believe that they were acting not in their own selfish interests but in the interests of property generally, interests that they equated ideologically and philosophically with those of the society as a whole.

The proceedings of the convention were conducted in secret and behind closed doors. While these 55 rich white men from twelve states debated the best constitutional framework for the United States, others were excluded and unrepresented: Amerindians, women, slaves, labourers, small business owners, small farmers and westerners. We shall now consider the extent to which these 'men of property' really did act in the interests of all or the interests of their class.

The delegates to the convention proceeded on the basis of several areas of broad agreement. First, as we have seen, they were convinced of the necessity of developing a central government powerful enough to curb what they considered to be the excessive democracy that had recently manifested itself in Shay's rebellion and other incidents of popular unrest directed at state governments. Consequently, 'they believed a republic could be made to work only by restraining popular influence' (Bonwick, 1991: 204). Second, this meant that the powers of central government had to be increased substantially through, among other things, enabling it to raise revenue through taxation, regulating international and inter-state commerce, establishing its own courts to adjudicate federal law, and maintaining Congress's existing control over foreign affairs and the military. Third, the underlying principles, key institutional structures and most important procedures of the new central government would be established, codified and maintained by an entrenched constitution having juridical supremacy over the legal codes of the states. To this end, the delegates quickly agreed to dump their original instructions from Congress to revise the Articles of Confederation and instead write an entirely new constitution.

As could be expected, despite general agreement prevailing on these issues, profound disagreements emerged on other issues as the proceedings unfolded in response to an initial set of 15 brief resolutions drafted by James Madison and proposed by Edmund Randolph on May 29, known as the Virginia Plan. This plan advocated a constitutional framework for strong national government with a national judiciary, a legislature made up of two houses, the lower being elected by the people, the higher elected by the lower, and the executive elected by the legislature. Although most elements of the plan would be rejected or else modified substantially, on May 30 the Convention agreed to support the development of a government that was 'national and supreme' (Kaplanoff, 2000: 472).

After considerable debate and disagreement, the convention decided that state representation in the legislature, together with the apportionment of internal taxes, would be based on the total free population plus three-fifths of the slave population. This alarmed the small states since they feared that the large more populous states would overwhelmingly dominate the new national government. A deadlock on this issue was broken early in July with the Connecticut Compromise, in which representation in the House of Representatives would be based on population, while each state would have equal representation in the Senate (ultimately set at two per state). Money bills would originate in the lower house and not be subject to amendment in the upper. Elections to the lower house would be held every two years, and the franchise was determined by the states: 'the electors in each State shall have the qualifications requisite for electors of the most numerous branch of the State legislature' (Brown, 2000: 411). The Senate:

> like its state counterparts, was expected to protect the property interest (especially land) against the political envy and levelling spirit of the masses. Achievement of this end required senators to be insulated to some extent by allowing them a longer term of office than was customary for representatives in state legislatures. The issue was resolved by allowing them a six year term.
>
> (Bonwick, 1991: 208)

For electoral purposes the Senate was divided equally into three 'classes'. At the time of each election to the House of Representatives one of these classes, that is, one-third of the senators, would be elected by the legislatures of their states (this operated until 1913; since then senators have been chosen by the voting public in congressional elections).

There was considerable debate over the structure and functions of the executive. A small group led by James Wilson, Gouverneur Morris and Alexander Hamilton, who were inclined towards a more aristocratic vision of democracy with high property qualifications for voting and office holding, successfully promoted a strong and energetic presidency. As Kaplanoff (2000: 476) observes, 'Throughout the Convention these men fought to have the President elected independently of the legislature, to give him a veto, and to grant him considerable powers of his own.' Eventually, it was decided that a president would be elected, not by the legislature for a non-renewable term of seven years, as originally proposed, but for a renewable term of four years. The method of electing the president was highly controversial, and eventually a compromise was reached on the establishment of an electoral college. Each state was granted 'a number of electors equal to the state's combined representation in both houses of Congress' (Kaplanoff, 2000: 476). The president was made commander-in-chief of the armed forces, authorised to conduct diplomacy including making treaties with other nations (subject to approval by two-thirds of the Senate), could recommend legislative measures to Congress and veto legislation (it would then be sent back to Congress but could be passed nonetheless if two-thirds of both houses voted in favour), and granted power 'with the advice and consent of the Senate, shall appoint ambassadors, other public ministers and consuls, judges of the Supreme Court, and all other officers of the United States' (Brown, 2000: 416).

Establishing a national judiciary was less controversial than establishing the other two branches of government. A Supreme Court was established, with judges being appointed for life, and Congress was empowered to establish inferior courts. However, the Constitution left large gaps in the structure and functions of the judiciary. As Kaplanoff observes:

> details about the judiciary were so sketchy in the Constitution that the work was only truly completed by the Judiciary Act of 1789 .... This Act not only defined the structure of the federal courts and their particular jurisdiction but established an appellate jurisdiction whereby federal courts could review state court decisions that [allegedly] conflicted with the federal Constitution or laws. In this final refinement of American federalism, federal courts adjudicated federal laws, state courts adjudicated state laws, but federal courts had the final say in resolving conflict between state and national authority.
>
> (Kaplanoff, 2000: 478)

The Constitution did not explicitly grant the Supreme Court the power of judicial review, in which the court has the capacity to determine the constitutionality of state and federal laws. This was established during the three decades that followed the ratification of the Constitution in 1790, in part through Section 25 of the Judiciary Act, which permitted appeals from state courts to the Supreme Court on matters of constitutionality, and in part through the landmark decisions of the court itself. By 1816 the Supreme Court 'had emerged as fully independent – both of the states and of the other branches of the national government – as the possessor of the power of judicial review, and as entitled to exercise some measure of judgement and statesmanship as well as the technical arts of law' (Diamond, Fisk and Garfinkel, 1966: 227).

The Philadelphia Convention agreed that the Constitution should create a separation of powers 'producing a divided central state designed to appeal to radical decentralisers as well as to conservatives by preventing equally despotism and sudden expressions of popular will' (Mann, 1993: 156). The Constitution created a system of checks and balances in which power in the federal state was divided between the executive, legislature and judiciary, and each could, to a degree, exert influence over the other two branches of government. Furthermore, 'public powers were divided among no fewer than five representative institutions – the presidency, the two houses of congress, the thirteen states, and the local governments' (Mann, 1993: 156). In this respect, the Constitution created a division of powers between federal government and the state governments in which 'federal government and individual state governments were intended to be parallel authorities; each was to be supreme within its own sphere, but both were subordinate to the United States Constitution' (Bonwick, 1991: 216). Amendments to the Constitution could be made if supported by two-thirds of each house in Congress, and if subsequently ratified by three-quarters of the states.

As mentioned above, the new federal government had much greater power than Congress under the Articles of Confederation. Being elected independently of the state governments (with the exception of the Senate), it could raise taxes, thereby removing the former fiscal dependence of Congress on the states, regulate international and inter-state commerce, enabling it to create an increasingly unified national economy, exercise exclusive powers in the areas of foreign and military affairs, and pass laws that would be directly binding on citizens and enforceable through the federal judiciary. Nonetheless, 'the states retained the right to regulate their own intrastate or internal commerce, and continued to exercise jurisdiction in many important areas of civil, criminal and family law; for many decades to come the daily life of citizens was impinged upon far more by state than by federal law' (Bonwick, 1991: 2).

Much is made of the conflict between large and small states at the Convention, but this is generally overstated. As James Madison, who played a leading role in the proceedings, accurately observed:

States were divided into different interests not by their difference of size, but by other circumstances; the most material of which resulted partly from climate, but principally from the effects of their having or not having slaves. These causes concurred in forming the great division of interests in the United States. It did not lie between the large and small states: It lay between the Northern and Southern.

(quoted in Diamond et al., 1966: 50)

Whereas in the northern states, 'the combination of blacks in the military, the lack of powerful economic need for slaves, and the rhetoric of Revolution' led to the gradual elimination of slavery, in the southern states slavery remained central to economic production and the key source of wealth for the southern Patriot elites (Zinn, 1999: 88). The bitter debate on the issue of slavery occupied three weeks during the Convention and was ultimately resolved when delegates from the northern states agreed that the Constitution would not prohibit slavery, that it would provide for the return of fugitive slaves to the states from which they had escaped, and that the southern states would be able to continue importing slaves until 1808.

Ratification of the Constitution: federalists versus anti-federalists

On September 16, the Constitution was accepted by a unanimous vote of all the state delegations to the Convention and sent to the states for ratification when the Convention adjourned on September 17, 1787. The process of ratification was protracted, and provoked widespread and often heated public debate. The states had to stage ratification conventions, with delegates either being directly elected by voters or else appointed by the state legislature. It took until June 1788 before the requisite number of states (nine) ratified the Constitution so that it could take effect, and not until Rhode Island ratified on May 29, 1790 was it ratified by all the states.

The Federalists, led by James Madison, Alexander Hamilton, John Jay, James Wilson and others, had major advantages in campaigning for the Constitution. The bulk of the delegates to the Philadelphia Convention supported ratification, and they had developed strong informal ties with each other that enable them to coordinate their activities on a national basis. The Constitution was supported by a majority of the wealthy Patriot elite, and consequently the bulk of the newspapers were biased in favour of Federalist arguments. The Constitution itself constituted a positive plan for creating a strong national union of the United States. The opponents of the Constitution, who became known as 'Anti-Federalists', promoted the idea of a much more limited form of federal government in which the powers of the federal government would be greatly diminished, and the rights of the states enhanced considerably. To many, it appeared as if this would merely recreate a weak federal government suffering from all of the disabling weaknesses that had afflicted the old Congress.

The Anti-Federalists considered that republican democracy could only work effectively in a relatively small community defined by territory and population, as the states were. For this reason, they argued that the state legislatures were more genuinely representative of the people than the federal government proposed under the Constitution. Furthermore, they considered that 'the Constitution was calculated to increase the power and wealth of those who already had it, and they contended that under a consequent aristocracy the liberty of the common people would disappear' (Bonwick, 1991: 224). Whereas the elective principle ensured in the state governments substantial representation of the 'middling class', composed of 'the yeomanry, the subordinate officers, civil and military, the fishermen, mechanics and traders, many of the merchants and professional men', 'in the federal government under the Constitution, election is bound to produce a largely if not exclusively aristocratic body' composed of 'governors, members of Congress, the superior judges, the "most eminent professional men" and the wealthy' (Dry, 2000: 485).

We shall consider shortly the opposing Federalist argument, which ultimately prevailed. Here it is important to note that the Anti-Federalist arguments on this and other issues were sufficiently reflective of the concerns of both the masses and the delegates to the state conventions about the very substantial power that the Constitution placed in the federal government that the Federalists were forced to make a major concession. They promised to append a Bill of Rights to the Constitution protecting the rights of individual citizens against the powers of the federal government. This promise, initially given at the Massachusetts Convention but then repeated at subsequent conventions, was essential to the Constitution being ratified. The Bill of Rights, taking the form of ten amendments appended to the Constitution, was passed by Congress and ratified by the states during the second half of 1791.

The historical novelty of representative democracy

Wood (1995: 214–15) argues that 'representative democracy', an idea with no historical precedent in the ancient world, is essentially an American innovation. Since it is the United States that has given the modern world its dominant definition of democracy, a definition in which the dilution of popular power is an essential ingredient, it is worth clarifying the respects in which this particular form of democracy is historically unique. The Federalists, developing the Constitution in the context of the American Revolution, faced the historically unprecedented task of preserving what they could of the division between the mass of 'poor and middling folk' and the wealthy Patriot elite, with the latter dominating the former, in the context of an armed citizenry that was becoming increasingly politically active and rebellious. In a revolutionary context where it was no longer possible to maintain an exclusive citizen body, the framers of the Constitution embarked on the first experiment in designing a set of political institutions that would both embody and at the same time curtail popular power. Where the option of an active but exclusive citizenry (classical republicanism, Athenian democracy) was unavailable, it became necessary to create an inclusive but passive citizen body with limited powers (1995: 218–19).

How was this achieved? Primarily through establishing historically unique principles of representation. You will recall that in Athenian democracy the process of government was based on free and unrestricted discourse, guaranteed by *isegoria*, an equal right to speak in the sovereign assembly. This meant that, as Plato observes in a passage that is highly critical of Athenian democracy: 'when it is something to do with the government of the country that is to be debated, the man who gets up to advise them may be a builder or equally well a blacksmith or a shoemaker, merchant, or shipowner, rich or poor, of good family or none' (quoted in Wood, 1995: 193; Held, 2006: 23–7). The situation that prevails in the form of representative democracy created by the US Constitution differs fundamentally from this. As Alexander Hamilton wrote in *Federalist Paper* no. 35, 'The idea of actual representation of all classes of the people, by people of each class, is altogether visionary' (quoted in Wood, 1995: 215). In essence, he considered that it was the man of substantial property who was best qualified to speak on behalf of the labouring multitude, including not just wage labourers but also farmers with small landholdings.

Hamilton argued that there were three key classes, or interests, in American society – the commercial, the landed and the learned professions. As the merchant is the natural representative of the mechanics and manufacturers, so the large landholder is the natural representative of the small landholder; and the men of the learned professions, lawyers especially, will have the confidence of all parts of society (Dry, 2000: 486).

In response to Anti-Federalist arguments that members of the 'middling class' are best placed to represent those of society as a whole, because 'the interests of both the rich and the poor are involved in that of the middling class (sic)', Hamilton argued that 'as riches increase and accumulate in few hands ... virtue will be ... considered as only a graceful appendage of wealth' and, further, that 'the advantage of character belongs to the wealthy. Their vices are probably more favourable to the prosperity of the state than those of the indigent, and partake less of moral depravity' (Melancton Smith and Hamilton, quoted in Dry, 2000: 486–7).

Representation was required in order to, as Madison put it, 'refine and enlarge the public views, by passing them through the medium of a chosen body of citizens' (quoted in Wood, 1995: 216). Hence representation is considered to be a filtering mechanism and preferable to selection by lot, which was the preferred method of selecting political functionaries in the Athenian democracy, because the intense competition for a small number of government positions in representative democracy ensures that those with the greatest talent are selected. But Madison's primary concern was not with the quality of representatives; rather it was preventing the non-wealthy majority from being able to rule society in their own interests.

Economic development, [Madison] warned the Constitutional Convention, would inevitably produce a society with a non-propertied majority and class conflict between rich and poor. How could government resting on the popular will survive when a democratic majority, resenting its propertyless status, might seek to despoil the rich? For Madison, the answer was to structure government so as to prevent any single interest from achieving power. With its elaborate system of checks and balances and divided sovereignty, the Constitution was designed, in part, to enable republican government to survive the rise of economic inequality (and to render unequal concentrations of property immune from governmental interference).

(Foner, 1998: 22)

This is a vitally important point. In *Federalist Paper* no. 10 Madison is crystal clear in arguing that the protection of the 'rights of property' is 'the first object of Government' (Madison in Brown, 2000: 441). His argument starts from the premise that 'the most common and durable source of factions, has been the various and unequal distribution of property. Those who hold, and those who are without property, have ever formed distinct interests in society' (in Brown, 2000: 441). Consequently, 'the regulation of these various and interfering interests forms the principal task of modern legislation, and involves the spirit of party and faction in the necessary and ordinary operations of Government' (in Brown, 2000: 442). The major problem in this regard is the possibility that a majority faction may use 'the form of popular government' to 'sacrifice to its ruling passion or interest, both the public good and the rights of other citizens' (in Brown, 2000: 442).

Pure participatory democracies, such as Athenian democracy, are fatally flawed as a solution to this problem because they are 'spectacles of turbulence and contention', which 'have ever been found incompatible with ... the rights of property' (Madison in Brown, 2000: 442). In contrast, 'A Republic, by which I mean a Government in which the scheme of representation takes place, opens a different prospect, and promises the cure for which we are seeking' (in Brown, 2000: 443). It does so both because, as just mentioned, 'the delegation of Government ... to a small number of citizens elected by the rest' refines and enlarges public views 'by passing them through the medium of a chosen body of citizens' (in Brown, 2000: 443), and also because the extensive separation of powers in a federal republic ensures that although 'factious leaders may kindle a flame within their particular States', they 'will be unable to spread a general conflagration through the other States' (in Brown, 2000: 444). This secures 'the national Councils' against populist pressures such as 'a rage for paper money, for an abolition of debts, for an equal division of property, or for any other improper or wicked project' (in Brown, 2000: 444).

As Wood observes:

> We have become so accustomed to the formula, 'representative democracy', that we tend to forget the novelty of the American idea. In its Federalist form ... it meant that something hitherto perceived as the *antithesis* of democratic self-government was now not only compatible with but constitutive of democracy: not the *exercise* of political power [by the citizens themselves] but its *relinquishment*, its *transfer* to others, its *alienation* [from the populace].
>
> (Wood, 1995: 216)

Representation not only acts as a filtering mechanism, it acts to distance the people from direct involvement in politics and government. 'The American republic firmly established a definition of democracy in which the transfer of power to "representatives of the people" constituted not just a necessary concession to size and complexity but rather the very essence of democracy itself' (Wood, 1995: 216).

This leads to the next important point, that the American definition of citizenship and democracy is completely devoid of the social meaning that citizenship and democracy had in the Greek context. The full significance of this only becomes apparent through comparison with classical definitions of democracy based on the Athenian experience. First, consider again Aristotle's classic definition of democracy as a constitution in which 'the free-born and poor control the government – being at the same time a majority' (Aristotle, 1962: 155). This contrasted with an oligarchy, in which 'the rich and better-born control the government – being at the same time a minority' (Aristotle, 1962: 155). As Wood (1995: 220) rightly emphasizes, 'the social criteria – poverty in one case, wealth and high birth in the other – play a central role in these definitions'. The framers of the Constitution very carefully constructed a system of government in which 'the rich and better-born control the government', despite being a small minority of the population. Participation of the poor and labouring citizens in the process of government is not only no longer a defining feature of democracy, it is seen as being fundamentally antithetical to the form of representative democracy created by the US Constitution.

In the system of government created by the Constitution, the judiciary has emerged as one of the most important lynchpins of capitalist property, wealth and power:

> The final separation of powers created the Supreme Court. This proved a stroke of genius, but it was less conscious strategy than a consensus about the nature of rights that proved to have enormous unintended consequences. It stemmed from the predominance of notable lawyers-cum-property owners in the Revolution and in the drafting of the Constitution itself – at least 33 of the 55 delegates had practised law, but only 4 of them had been only lawyers.
> (Mann, 1993: 156)

After Shay's rebellion and state government infringements on property law, delegates to the Convention 'thought it prudent to "entrench" their Constitution as the rule of law, supervised by a Supreme Court – if necessary … against executive and legislatures alike' (Mann, 1993: 157). They did not foresee the extent to which this branch of government would grow and develop until 'the law profession, up to the Supreme Court, became active regulators of private, corporate, and government agencies – a surrogate for a more centralized state administration' (Mann, 1993: 157). 'Private property became truly sacred, inviolate from state and anarchism alike' (Mann, 1993: 158). The legal profession plays this role because 'American law was then, as it is now, inseparable from capitalist property. These propertied lawyer notables had a distinctive conception of rights. They had been reared on that equation of personal human freedom and individual property rights labelled by McPherson as "possessive individualism"' (Mann, 1993: 157).

Representative democracy in late eighteenth and early nineteenth-century America constituted a significant advance on British parliamentary democracy because the rights of democratic citizenship were bestowed on a significantly larger minority of the adult population. Nonetheless, it remained a very limited form of democracy in two key respects other than those just mentioned. First, as Zinn observes with respect to the Bill of Rights:

> These amendments seemed to make the new government a guardian of people's liberties: to speak, to publish, to worship, to petition, to assemble, to be tried fairly, to be secure at home against official intrusion. It was, therefore, perfectly designed to build popular backing for the new government. What was not made clear – it was a time when the language of freedom was new and its reality untested – was the shakiness of anyone's liberty when entrusted to a government of the rich and powerful.
> (Zinn, 1999: 99)

Second, like Athenian democracy, this was designed to be a system of democracy in which both the citizenry and their representatives excluded slaves, women, men without property and Amerindians. As Crane observes,

> The phrase 'all men are created equal' in the Declaration of Independence at least suggested the possibility of a more equal status for women, and this suggestion was actually taken up by a few articulate women such as Abigail Adams. Ultimately, however, what is most impressive about the American Revolution in regard to women is that so few people of either sex pursued these implications to their ultimate conclusions, that they fought a war in the name of independence without generating any palpable demand for the independence of the more than half the population who remained – by virtue of their gender – so thoroughly dependent upon the male segment of the population.
>
> (Crane, 1987: 258)

The US Constitution 'solidified, regularized, made legitimate' women's confinement to and oppression within the private sphere, 'the inferior position of blacks, the exclusion of Indians from the new society, and the establishment of supremacy for the rich and powerful in the new nation' (Zinn, 1999: 89). In this, and many other respects, the American Revolution was the most predominantly bourgeois of the bourgeois revolutions.

COMPLETING THE REVOLUTION: CIVIL WAR 1861–65

In formulating and ratifying the Constitution, representatives of the wealthy elites in the northern and southern states compromised on the question of whether slavery should be prohibited or tolerated. As we have seen, this compromise was essential in order to avoid conflict over slavery preventing the formation of an effective national government. But far from subsiding, the conflict between the northern states and the slave states of the lower south became more intense, and gave rise to increasingly serious crises that threatened to tear the federal union apart.

Underpinning and propelling this conflict and crises were two fundamentally differently configured and opposed modes of production. Efficient capitalist farming and comparatively advanced and rapid industrialisation generated extraordinarily high rates of economic and population growth in the north. Exploitation took the social form of the production of surplus-value by 'free labour' and its appropriation by capitalists. In the south, capitalist and pre-capitalist relations of production prevailed in a mode of production in which capitalist farming and industry was combined with the widespread use of slave labour and large-scale slave plantation production of cotton, rice, tobacco and hemp. The most important social form of exploitation was the appropriation of the surplus product of slave labour by slave owners. Overall, although the southern states were growing throughout the first half of the nineteenth century, they were growing at a much slower rate than the northern states. As could be expected, the ruling elites in the southern states felt increasingly threatened by the north, and were appalled at what they considered to be the undue political influence of free labour. 'The great evil of Northern free society', insisted a South Carolina journal, 'is that it is burdened with a servile class of mechanics and laborers, unfit for self-government, yet clothed with the attributes and powers of citizens' (cited by McPherson, 1988: 197).

As white settlement rapidly spread across the continent, expedited by the genocidal expropriation of land from Amerindians, this conflict was mainly focused on the question of whether this new land, and the states formed on it, would become available to be worked by capitalist farmers and free labour as opposed to southern settlers using slave labour. In 1854 Congress passed the Kansas–Nebraska Act, which was 'the most important single event pushing the nation towards war' (McPherson, 1988: 121). The Act's key provision was that 'all questions pertaining to slavery in the Territories ... are to be left to the people residing therein' (McPherson, 1988: 123). As Harman observes, this:

Infuriated all those Northerners – however infected by racist ideas – who stood for 'free soil', for dividing the land of the West into small farms for new settlers. Both groups feared that the plantation owners, who controlled the presidency, Congress and the Supreme Court, would grab the whole of the West. This would destroy the hopes of would-be farmers, leave industrial capital dominant in only a handful of northeastern states, and give the plantation owners control of government for the foreseeable future.

(Harman, 1999: 347–8)

Armed conflict, resulting in over 200 deaths, broke out in Kansas between 'free-soilers' and pro-slavery 'settlers'. Thousands of 'border ruffians' were sent over the border from Missouri, encouraged by the Missouri Senator David Atchison and backed by wealthy plantation owners. Simultaneously, an Emigrant Aid Company was formed in New England to encourage free settlement and ensure that the free soilers in Kansas were well armed with new Sharps breech-loading rifles. The small-scale civil war in Kansas and other related events led to the formation and rapid growth of the Republican Party from 1854 to 1856 on an anti-slavery 'free soil' platform.

In 1860 the Republican candidate, Abraham Lincoln, won the presidential election. Although he had declared prior to the election that 'I have no purpose, directly or indirectly, to interfere with slavery in the States where it exists', the slave states of the lower south responded to his election with frenzied and ultimately violent hostility (McPherson, 1988: vii). They considered that the election of Lincoln was a catastrophe for the south. The recently formed Republican Party was driven by a 'profound fanaticism' to destroy 'the white man, in order that the black might be free' (McPherson, 1988: 230). Rejecting the notion that 'the Black Republican party is a moderate' party, the New Orleans Delta declared, 'It is, in fact, essentially a revolutionary party'

(Mcpherson, 1988: 233). Defending what they saw as their rights under the US Constitution, seven slave states (South Carolina, Mississippi, Florida, Alabama, Georgia, Louisiana and Texas) seceded from the Union between December 20, 1860 and February 1, 1861, lobbied the other southern states to do likewise, and began military preparations for war against the northern states. The slave-owning elites of these states were prepared to go this far because:

> as far as they were concerned their whole society was at stake. If it did not expand it was doomed – and Lincoln's presidency doomed expansion. Some also feared that unless they raised a storm their hold on the South as a whole might be undermined, since two thirds of the whites owned no slaves and might be attracted to the ideas gaining support in the North.
>
> (Harman, 1999: 348)

War broke out on April 12, 1861, when Confederate forces attacked Fort Sumter at Charleston, South Carolina. By the time that the war ended four years later with Robert E. Lee's surrender in April 1865:

> More than 620,000 soldiers lost their lives in four years of conflict – 360,000 Yankees and at least 260,000 rebels. The number of southern civilians who died as a direct or indirect result of the war cannot be known; what can be said is that the Civil War's cost in American lives was as great as in all of the nation's other wars combined.
>
> (McPherson, 1988: 854)

The ferocity and scale of the war pushed Lincoln from adopting a moderate and conciliatory posture in relation to the south, towards becoming the kind of revolutionary that the southern press had falsely accused him of being prior to the election. As McPherson (1988: vii–iii) notes, although the Congress in July 1861 proclaimed that it was not intent on disestablishing slavery in the South, 'both Lincoln and Congress had decided to make emancipation of slaves in Confederate states a Union war policy' within the following year.

By the time of the Gettysburg Address, in November 1863, the north was fighting for a 'new birth of freedom' to transform the Constitution written by the founding fathers, under which the United States had become the world's largest slaveholding country, into a charter of emancipation for a republic where, as the northern version of 'The battle cry of freedom' put it, 'Not a man shall be a slave.' 'Once the war ended, the Constitution was duly altered by the Thirteenth Amendment of 1865, which stated 'Neither slavery nor involuntary servitude ... shall exist within the United States.'

During the decade that the Union army occupied and 'reconstructed' the southern states, the franchise was extended to black men throughout the south, and 20 black congressmen and two black senators were elected. A Louisiana planter exclaimed in 1865 that 'Society has been completely changed by the war. The [French] revolution of '89 did not produce a greater change in the

"Ancien Regime" than this has in our social life' (Mcpherson, 1988: 861). It is true that, although the gains of reconstruction were rolled back by a violent racist backlash throughout the south, nonetheless the civil war completed the revolution of 1775–91, ensuring that the northern variant of capitalism and representative democracy would prevail throughout the United States. In this respect, the key aims of the northern bourgeoisie were achieved by the war; it resulted in a seismic shift in national politics that would last decades, and simultaneously entrenched, and provided for the rapid expansion of, a comparatively advanced capitalist mode of production centred in the north-eastern states. It thereby established the national hegemony of the northern industrial bourgeoisie over the western and southern regions of the United States. McPherson observes that it led to the powers of the federal government being expanded dramatically relative to the states, and further that it involved a radical shift of political power from south to north.

> During the first seventy-two years of the republic down to 1861 a slaveholding resident of one of the states that joined the Confederacy had been President of the United States for forty-nine of those years – more than two-thirds of the time. In Congress, twenty-three of the thirty-six speakers of the House and twenty-four of the presidents pro tem of the Senate had been southerners. The Supreme Court always had a southern majority; twenty of the thirty-five justices to 1861 had been appointed from slave states. After the war a century passed before a resident of an ex-Confederate state was elected president. For half a century *none* of the speakers of the House or presidents pro tem of the Senate came from the South, and only five of the twenty-six Supreme Court justices appointed during that half-century were southerners. These figures symbolize a sharp and permanent change in the direction of American development.
>
> (McPherson, 1988: 859–60)

CONCLUSION

The American Revolution, and the Civil War that followed 70 years later, constituted bourgeois revolutions because they created a democratic state form that facilitated the emergence of the United States as the world's dominant capitalist power. The political leaderships involved in both the revolution and the civil war were predominantly composed of capitalists (merchants, financiers, industrialists) and wealthy slave plantation owners. The mass of 'poor and middling folks', composed of farmers, wage labourers, and the self-employed and small employers, also played central roles in the revolution and civil war, not least doing the bulk of the actual fighting and dying, and also pushing ruling-class political elites to concede much more than they wanted to with respect to popular participation in various aspects of American politics. But this mass radicalisation was, for the most part, neither anti-capitalist nor radically democratic. Rather, it was channelled in directions that helped to entrench capitalism and representative democracy.

Representative democracy, as developed by the Founding Fathers, is a historically unique form of democracy which ostensibly embodies but actually curtails the rule of the majority of the people. As the United States steadily outgrew the other major capitalist countries, economically, demographically and militarily, representative democracy of the American type emerged as the world's dominant 'model of democracy'. Quite apart from the recurring bloody imperialist adventures of its duplicitous rulers, this is cause for concern because US representative democracy, even in comparison with other liberal representative democracies, let alone in comparison with socialist participatory democracy, is a highly limited and restrictive form of democracy which minimises effective popular influence over government at both federal and state levels. In short, it is a form of democracy that has, for more than two centuries, been highly conducive to the largely untrammelled, but never entirely uncontested, dominance of capitalist power over the lives of the working-class majority of US citizens.

GUIDE TO FURTHER READING

The literature on the American Revolution and the Civil War is absolutely vast and yet, despite this, surprisingly little appears to have been written on either from a Marxist perspective. Bonwick (1991: 299–315) provides a much longer and more detailed guide to the literature than I can here. In two chapters Zinn (1999: 59–102) provides the best introductory account of the revolution from a broadly Marxist perspective. Harman (1999: 265–76) also provides a chapter-length Marxist account. For a chapter-length radical account of the role that conceptions of freedom played in the Revolution, see Foner (1998: 3–28). Mann's (1993: 137–66) neo-Weberian account of the revolution is illuminating. The best book-length non-Marxist accounts of the Revolution are Bonwick (1991) and Countryman (1985). Novack (1976) is a useful set of Marxist essays on the revolution, and G. Wood (2003) is a representative example of contemporary revisionist accounts.

Greene and Pole (2000) is an extremely useful edited volume that contains chapters on virtually every significant aspect of the revolution, including a detailed chronology of events. Brown (2000) and Dahl et al. (2003) provide useful collections of primary sources and documents, together with essays providing contemporary commentary. Raphael's (2001) people's history of the revolution provides an invaluable account of the class dimension and also of women, loyalists and pacifists, Amerindians and African-Americans. On the Philadelphia Convention, in addition to those sources already mentioned, Beard (1913) is still worth a read, Kaplanoff (2000) provides a chapter-length account, and Novack (1976: 127–36) provides a Marxist account. See Marx and Engels (1961) for their writings on the American Civil War. McPherson (1982, 1988) provides the best non-Marxist account of the Civil War and Reconstruction.

6

The revolutionary revival of democracy in France

INTRODUCTION

This chapter describes the background and context of the French Revolution, identifies its major phases, provides a broadly chronological narrative of its main events, and outlines the world-historic role that it played in the re-emergence of democracy. The French Revolution encompassed the economic and fiscal crisis of 1787–89; the meeting of the Estates General on May 5, 1789; the establishment of the National Assembly by the Third Estate on June 20; the insurrectionary storming of the Bastille on July 14; the formal abolition of feudalism on August 4; the Declaration of the Rights of Man on August 26, 1789; the adoption of the liberal Constitution of 1791; the war with Austria (from April 1792), Holland and England (from February 1793); the rise of the Jacobins from September 1792 in which the still-born Declaration and Constitution of June 1793 marked the highpoint in the democratic advance of the revolution; the overthrow of the monarchy, King Louis XVI being executed on January 21, 1793; and the fall of the Jacobins and the conservative but not counter-revolutionary Thermidor beginning in July 1794 that culminated in Bonaparte's rise to power in 1799.

The French Revolution was a bourgeois revolution, not only in the limited sense that it contributed positively to the further development of capitalism in France and Europe, but in the fuller sense that the bourgeoisie itself played a central and leading role – albeit not as a united entity but rather as an internally socially differentiated and politically factionalised class that was still in the early stage of its historical formation. To a greater extent than either the English or the American revolutions, it was also a genuinely mass revolution, involving the bulk of the population, estimated at around 28 million by the 1790s (Lewis, 1993: 73). This is significant because:

The most indubitable feature of a revolution is the direct interference of the masses in historic events. In ordinary times the state, be it monarchical or democratic, elevates itself above the nation, and history is made by specialists in that line of business – kings, ministers, bureaucrats, parliamentarians, journalists. But at those crucial moments when the old order becomes no longer endurable to the masses, they break over the barriers excluding them

from the political arena, sweep aside their traditional representatives, and create by their own interference the initial groundwork for a new regime.
(Trotsky, 1980a: xvii)

The French Revolution is the bourgeois revolution in which the influence of the collective action of the masses over the unfolding of political events is most pronounced. Although the English Revolution played a pioneering role in the historical revival of democracy, the democratic rights it championed were essentially those of a tiny propertied male elite. The American Revolution was very much led from above, with the masses playing a variety of crucial but subordinate roles in the War of Independence, rather than being driven forward by mass disgruntlement and unrest below. The French Revolution was driven forward at pivotal junctures by the rural and urban masses, and proclaimed universal rights of man that remain enshrined in the constitutional arrangements of liberal representative democracies to this day. Furthermore, the liberal ideas that underpinned the revolutionary formation of a republican form of representative democracy in France from 1789 to 1794 had a major international, and eventually global, impact as they were adopted and further developed by the sociopolitical forces in other nations struggling for democracy.

BACKGROUND AND CONTEXT

The emergence, development and crisis of feudalism that propelled the rise of the absolutist monarchic state in France were considered at length in Chapter 3. There is no need to repeat this discussion here. Rather the focus is on the more immediate backdrop to the outbreak of revolution.

Classes, clergy, monarchy

Prior to the revolution French society was divided into three estates: the clergy (first estate), the nobility (second estate), and the remainder of society (the overwhelming bulk of the population) grouped together in the third estate. The class structure was highly complex because it involved a combination of nascent capitalist classes emerging within the context of an advanced feudal social structure. In a sense, the feudal classes (nobility and peasantry) no longer remained purely feudal, and the capitalist classes (bourgeoisie, petit (or petty) bourgeoisie and proletariat) were not purely capitalist (see pages 78–81). Nonetheless, it is possible to identify the major classes that existed prior to and during the revolution as long as we realise that the boundaries separating these classes from one another, although often clearly recognised by the members of the classes at the time, are also often blurred and difficult for the historical analyst to discern.

By the 1780s French society was divided into the nobility, a small minority at the top of society deriving the bulk of its wealth from landownership and state office; the peasantry, constituting a large majority of the population, who laboured on the land to produce enough to subsist after paying rent, a variety of other feudal dues, taxes and tithes; a nascent capitalist class or bourgeoisie that derived its wealth from mercantile, financial, legal, professional and rudimentary manufacturing activity; a large petit bourgeoisie of small traders, artisans and craftsmen; and a proletariat composed of wage earners which was in the earliest phase of its emergence as a distinctive class. As Rudé observes: 'we may picture French eighteenth century society as a kind of pyramid, whose apex was filled by the Court and aristocracy, its centre by the 'middling' classes or bourgeoisie, and its base by the 'lower orders' of peasants and urban tradesmen and craftsmen' (1988: 1). Although this depiction is accurate, a more detailed consideration of the class structure of eighteenth-century French society reveals that some class boundaries, such as those separating the nobility from the peasantry and the bourgeoisie from the proletariat, are much more clearly marked than others, such as those dividing the bourgeoisie from the petit bourgeoisie and the petit bourgeoisie from the emerging proletariat.

The nobility that formed the second estate were divided into two main groups: the traditional 'nobility of the sword', and the 'nobility of the robe' that incorporated wealthy members of the bourgeoisie who had brought themselves hereditary deeds of nobility via the purchase of offices in the royal bureaucracy. As discussed on pages 78–81, the nobility derived the bulk of their income from two sources: seigniorial dues and the proceeds from holding state office. It is important to note that the nobility were largely exempt from direct taxation, and that they resisted all moves from reforming ministers in royal ministries to increase their relatively light burden of taxation.

The relationship between the nobility and the monarchy was fraught with tension and conflict because of the role that the absolutist state had come to play in surplus extraction from the sixteenth to the eighteenth centuries. Whereas on the one side the nobility was dependent on the monarchy to roll back the peasant gains of the fifteenth century, suppress peasant revolt, and provide another mechanism to exploit the peasantry (tax offices and tax farming), on the other, this generated recurrent outbursts of conflict between the aristocracy and monarchy because they were vying to obtain shares of the finite surplus produced by the peasantry. As Mooers observes:

> The autonomy of the absolutist state was of a dual character: to the extent that it competed with other sections of the feudal ruling-class over the distribution of peasant surplus between rent and taxes, it assumed a class-like role in the relations of production. But to the degree that it won the allegiance of its competitors by absorbing them into its tax/office structure, it came to be seen as the vehicle par excellence for social advancement and the accumulation of wealth.
>
> (Mooers, 1991: 56)

In view of this, it should hardly come as a surprise that taxation and access to state office should have been central focal points of conflict not just between the 'privileged orders' composed of the nobility, upper clergy and wealthy bourgeoisie, on one side, and the monarchy on the other, but also among the privileged orders, as nobles and wealthy members of the bourgeoisie sought to limit or expand ennoblement and access to lucrative state offices.

Although in principle the clergy formed a separate order or estate, in reality the upper layers of the clergy formed part of the nobility. Indeed, as Rudé shows they enjoyed even greater privileges than the rest of the nobility because they enjoyed the same income from rents and dues as other landowners, while facing an even lighter tax burden from the state (discharged with regular voluntary gifts to the exchequer), and in addition they derived extra income in the form of tithes (which might amount to one-twelfth of the yield of the land) (Rudé, 1988: 3). The bulk of the clergy, however, were not so well off. The majority were parish priests with a standard of living that was similar to that of the average peasant and vastly inferior to the affluent lifestyles of the aristocratic bishops. As one priest observed, 'While the Bishop plays the great nobleman and spends scandalous sums on hounds, horses, furniture, servants, food and carriages, the parish priest has not the wherewithal to buy himself a new cassock' (quoted in McGarr, 1989: 18). As could be expected, the highly unequal distribution of income and wealth among the clergy gave rise to serious ideological and political tensions and conflicts between the parish priests and the bishops, which intensified during the course of the revolution.

At the time of the French Revolution, and in the years prior to 1789, there was no fully formed bourgeoisie comparable to those existing in advanced capitalist societies today. Precisely because capitalism was in the earliest stage of its development within an ageing feudal society, the existing feudal social relations profoundly shaped the emerging bourgeoisie. Members of the wealthy upper bourgeoisie typically initially gained their wealth through conducting financial and/or mercantile operations, then subsequently purchased both land and title. In this way they became entwined with the nobility. Hence in eighteenth-century French society the bourgeoisie did not form a homogeneous class:

> Some elements had found a place in the structure of the old regime and shared to greater or lesser degree the privileges of the dominant class, whether through the possession of landed wealth and seigniorial rights, through administrative office in the state, or through a commanding position in the traditional forms of commerce and finance.
>
> (Soboul, 1977: 16)

Just as the mercantile bourgeoisie in England retained the strongest links of any section of the bourgeoisie to the aristocracy and the crown, so too in France 'those elements of the bourgeoisie connected to commercial capitalism soon emerged as supporters of compromise solutions' (Soboul, 1977: 16).

There was a discernible but not entirely clear division between the lower reaches of the bourgeoisie and the upper reaches of the petit bourgeoisie. Despite the fact that 'in the society of the old regime ... the different social groups lumped together under the general heading of the Third Estate were not clearly distinguishable from each other', the small and middling bourgeoisie stood above the petit bourgeoisie or *sans culottes* (Soboul, 1977: 18). Soboul argues that although the system of handicraft production and retail distribution generated a series of fine social distinctions and gradations, 'at the top of the hierarchy these almost imperceptible distinctions gave way to a sharp cleavage' separating the bourgeoisie from the petit bourgeoisie on the basis of 'the scale of their business or by some connection with the liberal professions, or by the special privileges and rules of their trade' (1977: 19). It is also important to recognise that:

> one of the distinctive characteristics of French society was the existence of a large class of small and middling bourgeois. Most local production was still in the hands of artisans, independent producers, and dealers. But the class of artisans was marked by an extreme diversity and legal and social status; an infinite number of gradations separated the middling bourgeoisie from the 'little people' who worked with their hands.
>
> (Soboul, 1977: 17–18)

The petit bourgeoisie or *sans culottes* were in the main shopkeepers, independent artisans, small merchants and traders. As McGarr accurately observes, they constituted 'a vast petty bourgeoisie who had a much greater social weight than they do today' (1989: 24). This group played a key role in the revolution. Along with the peasantry, the petit bourgeoisie was a mass social force that intervened in the maelstrom of political conflict between monarchy, nobility and the bourgeoisie.

Although the bulk of the peasantry shared the experience of grinding poverty, it would be misleading to assume that the peasantry remained socially undifferentiated. As Rudé indicates, the peasantry was divided into a number of different strata:

> By the end of the *ancien régime*, perhaps one in four peasant families owned their land outright – comparatively few were prosperous *coqs de village* ('village roosters'), some were relatively prosperous *laboureurs* (yeomen farmers), and others ... were 'poor and miserable, much arising from the minute division of their little farms among all children'. Half or more of the peasants were poor *metrayers* (sharecroppers) who owned no capital and shared their produce with their landlords on a fifty-fifty basis; and a quarter or more were landless labourers or cottagers working for wages and renting tiny plots.
>
> (Rudé, 1988: 2)

Despite this differentiation, there is little doubt that by the 1780s the vast bulk of the peasantry was firmly opposed to feudalism as they understood it – the complex system of exactions through a combination (principally) of seigniorial dues, church tithes and state taxes. The strength and persistence of peasant opposition to feudalism which, among other things, periodically generated mass revolts, arose because:

> the French peasant bore a heavy burden of taxation: he paid tithe to the Church; *taille* (direct tax on income or land), *vingtième* (a 'twentieth' tax on income), *capitation* (income tax per head) and *gabelle* (salt tax) to the state; and to the seigneur (lord) of his manor, whether lay or ecclesiastical, he discharged a varying toll of obligations, services and payments ranging from the *corvée* (forced labour on roads) and the *cens* (feudal rent in cash) to the *champart* (rent in kind) and the *lods et ventes* (tax levied on the transfer of property).
>
> (Rudé, 1988: 2)

When the climatic conditions were favourable and harvests plentiful, the peasantry could maintain a reasonable level of subsistence. In the years with harsh weather and poor harvests, however, famine became widespread and the majority of peasants experienced dire poverty.

Why were the social tensions and conflicts so pronounced in France, and why did they generate a revolution? In part it was because by the 1780s, the class structure of French society:

> was riddled with contradictions both within and between its constituent parts. For it had a monarchy that, although absolute in theory, carried within it the seeds of its own decay; an aristocracy that, though privileged and mostly wealthy, was deeply resentful of its long exclusion from office; a bourgeoisie that, though enjoying increasing prosperity, was denied the social status and share in government commensurate with its wealth; and peasants who (in part at least) were becoming more literate and independent, yet were still regarded as a general beast of burden, despised and over-taxed. Moreover, these conflicts and the tensions they engendered were becoming sharper as the century went on.
>
> (Rudé, 1988: 1–2)

Enlightenment philosophy

Like all revolutions, the French Revolution was ultimately caused by a complex array of long- and short-term factors encompassing economic, social, political and ideological developments. In particular, it requires more than 'economic hardship, social discontent and thwarted ambitions to make a revolution. To give cohesion to the discontents and aspirations of widely varying social classes there had to be some unifying body of ideas, a common vocabulary of hope and protest – something, in short, like a common "revolutionary psychology"' (Rudé, 1988: 7). In this respect, Trotsky's brilliant insight that 'the dynamics of revolutionary events is directly determined by swift, intense and passionate changes in the psychology of classes which have already formed themselves before the revolution' (1980a: xviii) is crucial to understanding the actual events of the French Revolution and the importance of the role that the ideas of the Enlightenment played within them.

The ideas of Montesquieu (particularly the rule of law and separation of executive, legislative and judicial power in a constitutional monarchy), Rousseau (active citizen involvement in determining the general will, majority rule, popular sovereignty, separation of executive and legislative functions, the inalienable right of the people to change the government), Voltaire and others had become widely disseminated during the four decades leading up to the revolution. This is significant because, as McGarr observes:

> Though many of the individual *philosophes* [including Voltaire, Diderot and d'Alembert] were clergy or nobles, their ideas as a whole represented the coming of age of the bourgeoisie. The social and political order envisaged by the *philosophes* was one which would be free – in the sense of freedom from arbitrary power, freedom of speech, freedom of trade, freedom to realise one's talents, in other words a bourgeois freedom. Their ideas filtered down through the new academies, reading societies and public libraries that sprang up in most towns across France and in the salons of fashionable Parisian society. When the crisis which resulted in revolution came, the ideology of the old order had already been fatally undermined by the *philosophes*. The outlines of ideas that fitted a new bourgeois society were at hand.
>
> (McGarr, 1989: 20)

The specific manner in which these ideas were taken up, developed and applied during the mass struggles of the revolution is beyond the scope of this book. Note, however, that the 'French bourgeoisie, finding themselves in the late 1780s with the need to make a revolution, picked on Rousseau's theory of "popular sovereignty" and his "social contract" to provide an ideological justification for their rebellion against nobility and royal despotism', and that the '"lower orders" – in particular, the sans-culottes in Paris – learned their lesson and, having acquired the new idiom of revolution from the liberal aristocracy and bourgeoisie, adapted it in turn to their own uses and, on occasion, turned it to good account against their former teachers' (Rudé, 1980: 36).

Long and short-term causes of the revolution

There is no definitive and generally accepted explanation of why a revolution took place in 1789 in France. Nonetheless, it is clear that any compelling account must provide an integrated analysis of both the long-term transition from feudalism to capitalism and the short-term causes of the immediate crisis in the second half of the 1780s. In addition, it needs to focus on the external forces (economic, military and ideological) that impacted upon France. As Rudé observes:

> The French Revolution appears, then, to have been the outcome of both

long-term and short-term factors, which arose from the social-political conditions and the conflicts of the *ancien régime*. The long-standing grievances of peasants, townsmen and bourgeoisie; the frustrations of rising hopes among wealthy and 'middling' bourgeois and peasants; the insolvency and breakdown of government; a real (or, at least, perceived) 'feudal reaction'; the claims and intransigence of a privileged aristocracy; the propagation of radical ideas among wide sections of the people; a sharp economic and financial crisis; and the successive 'triggers' of state bankruptcy, aristocratic revolt and popular rebellion: these all played a part.

(Rudé, 1988: 10)

Let us consider some aspects of this in greater depth. First, as Callinicos argues:

One of the most important general propositions about bourgeois revolutions is their cumulative impact. Each revolution alters the terms for its successors. Thus the English Revolution, by forging a formidable expansionist state, increased the burden on the French monarchy, which in any case was embroiled in military and diplomatic rivalries with the other Continental powers.

(Callinicos, 1989: 141)

Hence the severe fiscal crisis of the French state, which precipitated the first phase of the revolution, was a direct result of France's victorious but costly intervention in the American War of Independence from 1778 to 1783. The French state was evidently becoming decreasingly capable of competing – either economically or militarily – with the countries where capitalism was developing most rapidly, England and Holland. This is evident from the facts not only that France lost the Seven Years War (1756–63) but that even in the case of the War of Independence, whereas England emerged economically unscathed (despite military defeat), France was economically crippled (despite military victory). McGarr puts it somewhat bluntly but nonetheless accurately: 'This inability of the French state to match the bourgeois states in England and Holland, militarily and economically, is a fundamental cause of the crisis which resulted in the revolution' (1989: 27).

It would however be misleading to focus exclusively on the external causes of the crisis that precipitated the revolution. Economically France remained an essentially agrarian society, albeit one in which there was growth in manufacturing (much of it on a putting-out basis), and growing reliance on international trade. But the growth of agricultural production remained sluggish compared with England. As we have seen this was owing in no small part to the continued dominance of a state-imposed and enforced system of surplus extraction which acted as a fetter on the introduction of new agricultural techniques utilisable with a more concentrated pattern of land tenure of the kind that was integral to the capitalist agricultural revolution in England. It meant that the French economy could not generate the surplus needed to fund military competition with other imperialist powers. It also resulted in economic convulsions and crisis. Indeed, Rudé argues that:

> it was precisely in these closing years of the *ancien régime* that the general prosperity of agriculture was grinding to a halt. This developed in two main stages. After 1778 ... there was a recession as a result of which prices fell, gradually in most industrial and farm products, but reaching crisis proportions in wines and textiles. ... Then, on top of the cyclical depression, came the sudden catastrophe of 1787–9 which brought poor harvests and shortages, with the price of wheat doubling within two years in the north and in mid-summer 1789.
>
> (Rudé, 1988: 6)

The bulk of the peasantry was hit by a brutal combination of falling prices for their produce and rising prices for food. The crisis spread to industry, with unemployment rising rapidly. Workers' wages failed to keep pace with major rises in food prices. This alerts us to the social antagonisms that were by the 1780s prevalent at different interstices of class relations, which the economic crisis intensified greatly. The rural and urban masses faced dramatically rising food prices in the years leading up to the revolution (and, of course, at various times during the revolution itself). This greatly fuelled discontent:

> The wage-earners and small consumers, in both villages and towns, were compelled by the rapid rise in food prices to increase their daily expenditure on bread to levels far beyond their means. Thus peasants and urban craftsmen and workers – not to mention manufacturers – were drawn together in a common bond of hostility to government, landlords, merchants and speculators.
>
> (Rudé, 1988: 7)

It was not only that opposition to the *ancien régime* was mounting amongst the peasantry, workers, and the petty bourgeois, there was simultaneously growing disgruntlement among the bourgeoisie. This was because the Crown had tightened access to state office, in no small part because of the pressure from the existing nobility, and this generated widespread angst. Towards the end of the *ancien régime* members of the bourgeoisie 'were suffering from an increasing sense of indignity and humiliation at the hands of government and aristocracy' (Rudé, 1988: 5).

NARRATIVE OF EVENTS

The revolution itself can be divided into four phases: the revolt of the nobility from 1787 to May 1789; the bourgeois revolution of 1789, culminating in the liberal Constitution of 1791; the rise and fall of the Jacobins from September 1792 to July 1794; and the reactionary, but not counter-revolutionary, Thermidor from July 1794 to 1799 which culminated in Bonaparte's *coup d'état.*

The revolt of the nobility

As we have seen, the French monarchy emerged from the War of Independence victorious but essentially bankrupt. This forced the finance minister to attempt to reform the system of taxation and tighten state expenditure. In response, 'the aristocracy rose in defence of its privileges' (Soboul, 1977: 97). Calonne was given the post of controller general of finances in 1783, and initially continued his predecessors' policy of borrowing to cover the fiscal deficit. This was necessary because it was impossible to raise taxes further. The nobility, which held the overwhelming bulk of the wealth in French society, was largely exempt from paying them, and the peasantry, labourers and petit bourgeoisie had already been bled dry through major increases in taxes during the eighteenth century, as well as by a substantial rise in food prices immediately prior to the revolution. There was a major popular revolt provoked by the rising price of bread in 1775, and it was clear that any further attempt to raise taxes substantially would have met with stiff popular resistance in the mid to late 1780s. In this context 'The only remedy was that of equality, the imposition of taxation on all Frenchmen regardless of rank' (Soboul, 1974: 99). Calonne proposed relatively modest reforms of the taxation system, the centrepiece of which was 'a direct land tax, a "territorial subvention", to be levied without exception upon all landowners' (Lefebvre, 1962a: 98). He was well aware that this measure would be firmly rejected by the bulk of the nobility, and in order to try to ensure its acceptance he hand-picked a group of 144 'notables' – including 'bishops, great landed aristocrats, *parlementaires, intendants,* and *counseillers d'etat,* as well as members of the provincial estates and municipal councils' (Soboul, 1974: 101).

Predictably even this carefully selected group of nobles rejected the proposed reforms when they convened on February 22, 1787. They tenaciously defended their existing privileges, and declared that 'it was not within their power to consent to taxes' and that the king should convene the Estates-General to discuss and resolve the fiscal crisis (Lefebvre, 1962a: 99). Other political bodies dominated by the nobility soon followed suit. 'The resistance offered by the Notables was followed by the equally unyielding resistance of the *parlements*' both in Paris and in the provinces (Soboul, 1974: 102). These *parlements* were not assemblies of the representatives of all propertied voters, as in England, but exclusive assemblies of nobles that had to register royal edicts and laws before they could become law in the locality over which they presided. They also acted as the highest level of law courts, administering, adjudicating and enforcing the imposition of complex feudal law and dues upon the social inferiors of the nobility. When the nobility was strongly opposed to the king on some issue, the nobility would use the *parlements* to remonstrate with him.

The royal ministry's refusal to summon the Estates-General provoked the aristocratic revolt that swept the country for almost a year: 'The revolt ended with the defeat of the Ministry and a total victory for the *Parlements* and aristocracy. Above all, the government was forced to concede that the States-General (through which the "privileged" hoped to solve the crisis at the commons' expense) should be summoned after all' (Rudé, 1988: 9). Not surprisingly, popular support for the nobility evaporated rapidly once their desire to shift the burden away from themselves on to the members of the third estate became apparent.

The bourgeois revolution of 1789

The aristocratic revolt forced the king to announce on August 8, 1788 a convention of the Estates-General for May 1, 1789. The Estates-General actually convened slightly later than this on May 5, 1789. In the intervening months both the 'privileged orders' and the plebeian masses engaged in greatly intensified political activity. The nobility were motivated by their desire to ensure a resolution of the fiscal crisis afflicting the state on terms most favourable to themselves, the bourgeoisie were determined to gain meaningful access to, and influence over, the state governance of society, and the peasantry, petit bourgeoisie and nascent working class sought some relief from the taxes and exactions they associated with 'feudalism' (exacerbated by what was popularly perceived as a feudal reaction in the decades preceding the revolution).

The elections for the Estates General:

provided a focus for all the grievances and discontent beneath the surface of society. And it forced various classes and groups to begin to define programmes for the resolution of the impasse in France. Crucially, there were to be national 'elections'. In effect the vast bulk of the population were entitled to attend primary assemblies where they would draw up lists of grievances and elect delegates to a higher body.

(McGarr, 1989: 28)

It meant people in every town and village were drawn into a discussion regarding the problems facing society and the possible solutions to these problems. Expectations were awakened among millions of people that change for the better would be the outcome of the Estates General (McGarr, 1989: 28–9).

'The privileged orders enjoyed direct male adult suffrage, while deputies of the Third Estate were chosen by a rather more restricted franchise as well as by a more complicated system of indirect election' (Rudé, 1988: 37). Without doubt, 'the system most certainly favoured the urban and professional bourgeoisie who dominated discussion and voting in the Third Estate' (Rudé, 1988: 37–8). Consequently, the leadership of the third estate's elected representatives was almost exclusively bourgeois.

When the Estates General convened on May 5, 'the old feudal structures were flaunted in the bourgeoisie's face. The King insisted that each order march in separately, appropriately attired – with the Third Estate bringing up the rear of course' (McGarr, 1989: 30). Debate between the three estates immediately focused on the question whether they should meet in common or separately. It was a vital issue because if the three estates met separately, the first two estates could always outvote the third, even allowing that the third estate had been granted double the number of representatives of each of the other two. Accordingly to Soboul (1974: 127–8), the first estate (clergy) had 291 deputies, the second estate (nobility) had 270, and the third estate had 578. McPhee (2002: 50–1) provides slightly different figures; of the 1231 deputies at Versailles, the first estate had 303, the second 282 and the third 646. According to Jones (1995: 54), at the time of the elections to the Estates General there were only between '110,000 and 120,000 individuals – or 25,000 families – [that] possessed incontrovertible nobility in 1789'. This meant that 'roughly 0.4 per cent of the population could legitimately claim noble status, a proportion comparable to that of the clergy'. Even if this estimate is too low, the clergy and the nobility combined did not constitute much more than 2 per cent of the total population, yet their combined deputies (585) constituted 47.6 per cent of those assembled at Versailles. Only votes on taxation issues were decided on the basis of a head count. On constitutional issues there was one vote per estate, so the first and second estates could outvote the third two to one. Hence the debate whether the three estates should meet and vote together or apart, which raged for five weeks, involved a struggle for power.

During the course of this debate the king failed to adopt a clear position and instead vacillated:

On the eve of its bankruptcy, the French monarchy was being harassed by the aristocratic opposition and thought that it could find a means of survival in the calling of the Estates General. But at the moment when its absolutist principle was under attack on two flanks, from both the aristocracy who intended to gain real power in the government of the country by returning to what they believed the ancient constitution of the Kingdom to be, and those committed to the new ideas of the enlightenment who wanted the nation to have certain rights of supervision over the administration of the State, the monarchy found itself with no specific programme to offer. Instead of being in command of events, it was following meekly in their wake, slipping from one concession to another along the path that led to Revolution.

(Soboul, 1974: 117)

Ultimately the king was too attached to the trappings of absolute power, and entwined with the feudal privileges of the aristocracy, to preside skilfully over a transition to a constitutional monarchy on the English model.

At the same time, mounting crisis and popular unrest was convulsing the wider society: 'In Paris, the price of bread was at almost twice its normal level; there had been bloody riots in the Faubourg St Antoine; and in the countryside the peasants had passed from words to deeds and were stopping food-convoys, raiding markets and destroying game reserves' (Rudé, 1988: 40). Failing to obtain agreement from the first and second estates on the question whether the estates should meet in common, and with mounting support amongst the masses, the third estate unilaterally declared itself the National Assembly on June 17 and invited deputies of the other estates to join it. (The vote was 491 to 89 within the third estate.) This first revolutionary act of the bourgeoisie was followed by the issue of two decrees. One provided that a dissolution of the new Assembly, for whatever cause, would invalidate all existing taxes; the other that as soon as a constitution had been determined, the public debt, instead of being levied locally, should be consolidated and underwritten by the nation as a whole (Rudé, 1988: 41).

This was soon followed on June 20 by the Oath of the Tennis Court, where every deputy of the third estate (with one exception) swore an oath that the National Assembly should not disperse until a new constitution had been ratified.

The king vacillated in response to this situation, and was subject to conflicting advice from different factions at court. Eventually, however, at an *séance royale* on June 23 he announced that 'The King wishes the ancient distinction between the three orders of the State to be preserved in its entirety as being essentially linked to the constitution of his Kingdom' (quoted by McGarr, 1989: 31). In essence, 'Louis XVI commanded the three orders to meet separately in their own chambers, overruled the decrees of the Third Estate, and, while agreeing to the principle of fiscal equality, expressly ruled that "tithes, rentes, and feudal and seigniorial dues" should be maintained' (Soboul, 1974: 134). Following the reading of these royal edicts, the king ordered all three estates to disperse. The nobility and much of the clergy followed him out of the hall. The third estate remained and proceeded to reiterate its own earlier resolutions. In effect, the political leadership of the bourgeoisie was directly challenging the power of the king.

From this moment the forward march of the third estate gathered momentum. A narrow majority of the clergy (parish priests rather than bishops) and 47 nobles joined the National Assembly (Lefebvre, 1962: 114). Faced with this, the king was forced on June 27 to order all three estates to meet jointly. This was, however, merely a tactical concession on the part of the king. He assembled loyal Swiss and German troops at Versailles, sacked the moderate reformer and relatively popular minister Necker, and replaced him with the arch-conservative baron de Breteuil on July 11. This was perceived both by the deputies of the National Assembly and the bulk of the bourgeoisie and *sans culottes* in Paris as foreshadowing the royal dissolution of the Assembly. A frantic search for arms began in Paris as the masses armed themselves to defend the revolution. The bourgeoisie was concerned to retain control of the situation, and on July 13 the 407 Paris electors of third estate deputies, who had formed a commune or city assembly, moved to form a National Guard. They carefully excluded the poorer petit bourgeoisie and propertyless labourers so that the National Guard could be used to support the National Assembly against counter-revolutionary forces, while remaining under the control of the bourgeois leadership of the revolution (Rudé, 1988: 43).

The popular movement was rapidly gaining momentum. Following the seizure of 30,000 muskets from the hotel des Invalides the cry went up 'To the Bastille!' The Bastille became the target for a range of reasons. It was thought to store a considerable amount of gunpowder, it was a hated symbol of absolutism because political prisoners were held there, and its guns were trained on the Rue St Antoine – leading to the Faubourg (or district) St Antoine of Paris where many militant *sans-culottes* resided. On the morning of July 14, a rumour spread rapidly that armed suppression of the popular revolutionary movement had started in this Faubourg the previous night (McGarr, 1989: 32; Rude, 1988: 54-6). The people of Paris, roughly and newly organized into the National Guard, stormed the Bastille on July 14. The storming of the Bastille was the culmination of a popular insurrection. Rudé observes that:

> the capture of the Bastille was the affair not of a few hundred citizens of the St Antoine quarter alone, but of the people of Paris as a whole. It has been said that on that day between 180,000 and 300,000 Parisians were under arms. Taking an even broader view, we should not ignore the part played, though less conspicuously, by the great mass of Parisian petty craftsmen, tradesmen and wage-earners – in the Faubourg St Antoine and elsewhere – whose revolutionary temper had been moulded over many months by high living costs and, as the political crisis deepened, by the growing conviction that the hopes raised by the calling of the States-General were being thwarted by an 'aristocratic plot'.
>
> (Rudé, 1988: 56)

This was the first major insurrection of the revolution. The National Assembly was now temporarily secure against the immediate threat of counter-revolution. Revolution spread throughout the country as the news of these revolutionary events spread from Paris to the provinces; 'it was this news, conveyed by word of mouth, or by letter, that in the following seven to fourteen days spurred the provinces into action in more or less close imitation of the great events in Paris' (Rudé, 1988: 44).

The intervention into political events of the armed masses of Paris prompted the emergence of divergent political tendencies within the bourgeoisie. On one side were the moderates or constitutional monarchists who were 'essentially the lawyers, merchants, former government officials and landed proprietors of the old Third Estate', who were frightened by the popular movement of peasants and *sans culottes*, and desperately sought a compromise solution (Rudé, 1988: 59). On the other side was a faction of the bourgeoisie, possibly differing in composition in that this was the 'middling and lower' bourgeoisie, thus its members were less likely to be merchants, holders of state office and/

or landowners. The members of this faction feared the aristocratic counter-revolution more than they feared the popular masses. Again and again all of the key bourgeois figures in the revolution would be motivated by fear of a counter-revolution and the popular movement.

It is not possible to provide a full account here of the popular movement. In the towns and cities *sans culottes* provided the backbone and militant core of the movement, but the peasantry also started to move during 1789. The peasant revolt culminated in the Great Fear. This fear was:

> not only that the Court and aristocracy had attempted to disperse the new Assembly (on which the peasants pinned great hopes) by force of arms, but also that the royalist troops disbanded after the fall of the Bastille were really 'brigands' who were preparing to seize their land and destroy their crops. So 'fear bred fear' and gave a new dimension to peasant unrest which, in the latter part of July, became generalized and spread over the greater part of France.
>
> (Rudé, 1988: 47)

The focus of the revolt was the chateaux and seigniorial *chartiers* that were at the heart of surplus extraction. The Fear began on July 20 and ended on August 8. Most importantly, it had the effect of forcing the National Assembly 'to pay immediate attention to the survivals of feudal privilege and to the pressing needs of the rebellious peasants' (Rudé, 1988: 49).

It was in these circumstances that the Constituent Assembly (as it had become) voted on August 4 to 'abolish feudalism in its entirety' (Soboul, 1974: 148). In reality, as Soboul (1974: 62) points out, the decrees 'were more a concession to the demands of the moment than the sign of a real desire to satisfy the grievances of the peasantry', and 'Feudalism had been abolished in its institutional and juridical forms, but it lived on as an economic reality.' The peasantry soon realised this and engaged in direct action to end feudalism throughout the revolution.

During the same period, the revolutionary government established constitutional principles known as the 'Principles of '89' – first enshrined in the Declaration of the Rights of Man on August 26 and subsequently given constitutional form in the constitutional settlement of 1791. Influenced both by the example of the American Declaration of Independence (if only to a minor degree) and by the liberal philosophical heritage of Locke, Montesquieu and Rousseau, the Declaration was 'remarkable in that it neatly balances a statement of universal principles with an evident concern for the interests of the bourgeoisie' (Rudé, 1988: 59). In terms of principle, it embraced liberty, equality and fraternity, but only through very specific (and inherently limited) application of these principles. Liberty implied in an economic sense, freedom to dispose of property, engage in trade, and sell the capacity to work as a commodity on a market for labour; and in a political sense, a notion of universal civic rights guaranteeing freedom of thought, writing and speech.

Equality meant equality before the law, and fraternity 'was about the creation of a unified national state and market. All were now French citizens. Internal barriers to trade and commerce were gone and class antagonism could be blurred under the patriotic ideal' (McGarr, 1989: 35). In sum, the Declaration provided for: 'protection of property; freedom of conscience, freedom of the press and freedom from arbitrary arrest; equality before the law; equal taxation and equal eligibility for office; and, to show the deputies' appreciation of practical realities, it implicitly sanctioned – *post factum* – the right of rebellion' (Rudé, 1988: 60).

The 'Principles of '89' were most fully enshrined in the Constitution of 1791. This Constitution established a framework for a constitutional monarchy in which the king had a right to veto legislation, appoint his own ministers, and engage in diplomatic relations with other states. But there was to be no upper house on the English model or the clear separation of powers evident in the American Constitution of 1789. Hence: 'the real power in the land was, in fact, to be the National Assembly itself. It was to be a unicameral body, untrammelled by 'checks and balances', armed with unlimited powers over taxation and with initiative and authority in all legislative matters, restricted only by the obligation to hold elections every two years' (Rudé, 1988: 61). The franchise was extended to all men over 25 who fulfilled a property qualification (paying direct tax equivalent to three days of unskilled labour), the old heredity offices were scrapped, public office was made open by either election or appointment (regardless of noble status), regional government was thoroughly reformed, civil liberties were guaranteed, the judiciary were made independent of the executive and all were to be treated equally before the law, fiscal policy was overhauled, the church's lands were nationalised and put up for sale, and titles and hereditary nobility were abolished.

The revolution of 1789 was led by the bourgeoisie through its deputies in the National Assembly, its domination of the Paris commune of electors and of the National Guard, and through the many publications and networks of political clubs that sprang up during the course of the revolution. The Constitution of 1791 that developed and codified the principles of '89 created a democracy of and for propertied men, and offered little to the urban or rural masses – neither peasants nor *sans culottes* were the chief beneficiaries. Women remained excluded from citizenship and from the democracy. Finally, it was an unstable settlement, increasingly pressured from either side by the forces of the counter-revolution and the popular movement.

The revolutionary Jacobin government and the popular movement, 1792–95

From August 1789 to June 1792 most of the bourgeois deputies favoured a constitutional monarchy and sought a compromise with the king. For example, the Legislative Assembly, which first met on October 1, 1791, 'consisted of 264 deputies who belonged to the Club de Feuillants' on the right, 136 deputies on the left, 'most of whom were members of the rival Jacobin Club', and the centre, which consisted of around 345 deputies who vacillated between right and left but who mostly favoured compromise with the monarchy (Soboul, 1974: 230–1). That no such compromise was reached was owing not only to the pressures on the government of the continuing economic crisis, the popular movement and (from April 1792) the war, but also to the king and queen's steadfast refusal to accept anything less than absolute power. I cannot consider this period in depth here, but it is important to focus on the most radical phrase of the revolution – the establishment of the revolutionary Jacobin government – because this was undoubtedly the high point of the French Revolution with respect to the progressive development of democracy.

It will help us to understand the second revolution and rise of a new revolutionary government if we recognise, as Callinicos argues, that:

> far from there being a profound discontinuity between 1789–91 and 1791–4 the entire period between the fall of the Bastille and Thermidor involves an increasingly radicalised version of the same pattern, in which popular movements, in the cities at least under the leadership of a section of the bourgeoisie, force through and defend changes against the opposition of counter-revolutionary forces whose strength is variable but which are always present.
>
> (Callinicos, 1989: 144)

More specifically, Callinicos (1989: 143–4) argues that there were three major sets of forces driving the revolution forward: first, the general economic crisis and in particular the rising food prices this generated, which fuelled recurrent outbreaks of urban and rural unrest amongst the masses; second, peasant risings and resistance directed at ending the seigniorial rights and dues which were left in place by the decrees of August 4–11, 1789; and third, the forces of counter-revolution. To this list we may add a fourth: the war that profoundly shaped the course of the revolution.

After much debate, the Legislative Assembly declared war against Austria in April 1792. It was hoped by those bourgeois deputies in the Assembly who promoted it that the war 'would allow the deepening social conflicts … to be diverted into unity behind the nation under a stronger regime and so help to stabilise the revolution' (McGarr, 1989: 45). In the event Robespierre, who had been the most consistent opponent of the war, was proven correct – France was ill prepared for war and immediately suffered severe reverses. The political ramifications of the military disaster were the opposite of those envisaged by the advocates of war – it strengthened the forces of the counter-revolution and 'exacerbated social and political conflicts within France' (McGarr, 1989: 46).

The Girondins, then the governing faction of the bourgeoisie in the Legislative Assembly, 'lurched from left to right desperately trying to regain control of the worsening situation' (McGarr, 1989: 46). Initially they sought a compromise with the monarchy and the Feuillant faction. Then having been rebuffed they were forced towards the popular movement in order to ward off the threat of a counter-revolution led by the king and the royalist

General Lafayette. Things came to a head on June 28 when Lafayette made a bid for power, appearing before the Convention and urging that it take strong measures against the popular movement and the Jacobins (Lefebvre, 1962a: 234; McGarr, 1989: 47). The political temperature in Paris reached boiling point amid rumours of an impending counter-revolutionary coup. 'The danger to the real gains of the revolution was awakening a massive popular movement' (McGarr, 1989: 48).

On June 20, 'a popular demonstration in Paris ... paraded in arms before the Assembly and broke into the [King's] Tuileries palace, where they obliged the reluctant Louis to don the Cap of Liberty and drink with them to the health of the nation' (Rudé, 1988: 77). This insurrectionary uprising in defence of the revolutionary government was a manifestation of the growing political radicalisation of the popular movement, especially the *sans culottes*. The Girondins had stirred the popular movement to save themselves from the forces of the counter-revolution, but a militant mass movement over which they had little control now confronted them.

> By this time [the Girondins] had surrendered the leadership of the popular movement to Robespierre and their Jacobin rivals. The truth is that, like the sorcerer's apprentice of legend and many other parties before and since, they were not prepared to face up to the consequences of the storm they had unleashed. Having demagogically aroused the sections and Faubourgs to demonstrate against the monarchy and having threatened to overthrow it, they now drew back in support of the King: they had not bargained for a republic that would be at the mercy of the voters and weapons of the hitherto 'passive' citizens, or *sans-culottes*.
>
> (Rudé, 1988: 78)

But it was too late. The popular upsurge continued – culminating in the insurrectionary overthrow of the monarchy on August 10. This was the second major insurrection of the revolution.

> When the victory of the insurrection was clear the Assembly voted to suspend the King and recognised the insurrectionary commune of Paris. The commune was enlarged and assumed effective power, at least for the moment. It was composed of hitherto unknown faces from the ranks of the popular movement with a sprinkling of bourgeois leaders, including Robespierre, who was elected to it. It allowed the Legislative Assembly to remain until a National Convention, elected by universal male suffrage, could decide on the fate of France, the revolution and the King.
>
> (McGarr, 1989: 49)

Elections to the new National Convention took place, and it met for the first time on September 20, 1792. Of its 749 deputies, who differed little in terms of social composition from the previous two national assemblies, the majority 'was generally formed by the great mass of independent deputies, with no permanent commitment to any particular faction or programme, known as the "March" or "Plain"' (Rudé, 1988: 80). To the right was a large minority of 178 deputies – the Girondins – who initially had enough support amongst the March to govern. To the left was a smaller minority of 148 deputies – the Montagnards (or 'Mountain' – so called because they sat in the upper tiers of seats in the assembly) – who included all but one of the 24 Paris deputies, who promoted a more radical political programme, and who were most closely aligned with the popular movement (McGarr, 1989: 104). Among the Montagnards, the delegates most militantly committed to the victory of the revolution against its internal enemies and of France against her external foes formed a faction known as the Jacobins.

According to Soboul:

The conflict between Girondins and Montagnards bears the mark of class antagonism, in spite of both groups' bourgeois origin, because of the different political choices that confronted them. As spokesmen of the commercial bourgeoisie, the Giroudins strove to defend property and economic liberty against the controls demanded by the sans-culottes – regulation of prices and production, requisitioning of essential commodities, a fixed rate of exchange for the assignats. Very sensitive in matters of social rank and status, the Giroudins instinctively recoiled from contact with the masses and felt that government should be a monopoly of members of their own class.

(Soboul, 1977: 87)

On the other side, the Jacobins:

reflected the interests of the lower layers of the bourgeoisie and those who had benefited from the sale of Church and noble lands confiscated by the revolution, that is, those for whom no compromise with, or restoration of the old order was conceivable. They came to understand the need for centralisation and a more controlled economy if the revolution was to be defended against internal and eternal enemies. The central aspect of their politics was the idea of the 'Republic One and Indivisible' – the defence of the bourgeois nation state against all attempts to fragment it or restore the old order.

(McGarr, 1989: 51–2)

One of the first major issues that confronted the convention concerned the king. The Girondins, reflecting the views of the majority of the bourgeoisie, yearned for a compromise solution, preferring a constitutional monarchy, and opposed Robespierre's proposal that the king be put on trial for high treason and if found guilty, executed. Despite their reluctance the king was put on trial, and following the discovery of a secret chest containing documents which conclusively proved that he had conspired with foreign powers to stage a counter-revolution, he was duly found guilty. The Girondins then attempted to avoid an execution by calling for a referendum on the issue. This failed, and the Jacobins carried the issue in the convention – the final vote was 380 to 310 against a reprieve (Lefebvre, 1962a: 272). The king was executed on January 21, 1793. The execution 'made a deep impression on the people of France and left Europe in a state of utter shock' (Soboul, 1974: 285). It was highly significant, both because it greatly increased the determination of monarchies throughout Europe to crush the revolution, and because it committed the bulk of the bourgeoisie to the revolution (Soboul, 1974: 285).

From September 1792 to May 1793 the wider society in France was convulsed by economic crisis, military reverses in the war, counter-revolutionary civil war in the Vendée region of western France, and riots over rising food prices in Paris. The Girondins, as the governing faction during this time, received most of the blame in the eyes of the popular masses, and particularly in the view of the Parisian *sans culottes*. Their declining popularity was owing to their doctrinaire adherence to laissez-faire solutions to economic problems (particularly their refusal to implement price controls on food) and their close association with General Dumouriez who, having failed 'to persuade his army to march on the Convention, disperse the Jacobins and restore the Constitution of 1791 with Louis XVII as King, deserted to the enemy' (Rudé, 1988: 83). The course of the war ultimately sealed their fate because 'while the Republican troops were marking up successes, the Gironde succeeded in staying in power; but they were lost as soon as the armies started to suffer reverses' (Soboul, 1974: 271).

The Jacobins under Robespierre's leadership skilfully manoeuvred in this situation in order to build their popular support and enhance their position within the convention. By April their support had reached the point where they were ready to make a play for power. They developed and proselytised their programme through the Jacobin Club. On April 5 'Robespierre publicly invited the sections to present themselves at the bar of the convention and "force us to arrest the disloyal deputies"' (Rudé, 1988: 85). The Paris commune invited its sections to form a Revolutionary Committee, which then proceeded to organise an insurrection that was conducted with military precision.

> The tocsin was sounded, workshops and points of entry to the city were closed, and ... the Tuileries were surrounded on 2 June by a combined force of National guards and armed *sans-culottes*. The 'named' deputies ... surrendered ignominiously to the insurgents' demands. Twenty-nine deputies and two ministers of the defeated party were place under arrest.
>
> (Rudé, 1988: 85)

Hence the third major popular insurrection of the revolution from May 31 to June 2 placed the Jacobins firmly in power by giving them a majority in the Convention.

This left the way clear for the Jacobins to assume leadership of the revolution. They were still a minority in their class and the Convention, but by allying with the *sans culottes* had pushed the majority, who shared their aim of winning the war and saving the Republic, into accepting their leadership. The revolution had moved sharply to the left on the base of another mass 'day', the best organised of any in the whole revolution.

(McGarr, 1989: 59)

The Jacobin Constitution of 1793

A full account of the revolutionary government of the Jacobins is not possible here. It is important however to highlight their greatest achievement, the Constitution of 1793. Despite its limitations:

the Declaration and Constitution of June 1793 marked the highpoint in the liberal phase of the revolution. Here for the first time in history a nation was given (on paper at least) a system of government, both republican and democratic, under which all male adults (with a few exceptions) had the right to vote and to a considerable measure of control over their representatives and rulers.

(Rudé, 1988: 87)

The 1793 constitution incorporated the basic rights of the 1789 constitution but greatly extended and augmented them. Its stated general aim was 'the happiness of all' within society. As we have just seen, it extended the franchise to all adult men 21 years and over. Among its declared rights it included:[1]

- equality, liberty, security, and property
- equality before the law
- accessibility of all citizens to public office
- 'liberty is the power which belongs to man to do all which does not harm the rights of another'
- 'the right to make known thought and opinion'
- freedom of religious worship
- 'the law must protect public and individual liberty against the oppression of those who govern'
- freedom from arbitrary arrest and other forms of state coercion
- 'the presumption of innocence'
- 'the right of property'
- 'All citizens have the right to concur in the establishment of taxes, to supervise their use, and to have an account rendered concerning them'
- 'society owes subsistence to unfortunate citizens, whether by finding them

---

1 All quotes that follow are from the original text as translated in Hardman (1981: 165–9); see also Jones (1988: 70–1).

work or by assuring the means of existence to those who cannot work'
- 'education is necessary for all'
- 'sovereignty resides in the people'
- 'when the government violates the rights of the people, insurrection is the most sacred of rights and the most indispensable of duties for the people and for each portion thereof'.

This is a remarkable declaration, not only because it was historically unprecedented in the extent of rights that it granted to the citizenry, and particularly the universality of its franchise, but also because it went far beyond the mere proclamation of narrowly political rights to incorporate social rights as well. Accordingly the Constitution of 1793 Act states:

> The Constitution guarantees all Frenchmen equality, liberty, safety, the rights of property, the inviolability of the national debt, freedom of worship, a common education, public assistance, unlimited freedom of the press, the right of petition, the right to assemble in popular societies and the enjoyment of all the rights of man.
>
> (quoted in Hardman, 1981: 169)

The second major achievement of the Jacobin government was the definitive abolition of feudalism, with an important law of June 17, 1793 that cancelled all that remained of seigniorial dues and obligations. This meant that 'at a stroke what the peasants had fought for since 1789 had been won by a combination of their own efforts and the needs of the bourgeois republic to secure itself' (McGarr, 1989: 60).

Third, the revolutionary dictatorship established by the Jacobins in October 1793 had the lamentable consequence that the new constitution was put into abeyance until the enemies of the revolution – both internal and external – had been defeated. But it did take the measures needed to win the war against the invading armies of *ancien régime* Europe, including greater state control of the economy, cracking down hard on counter-revolutionary forces through the terror, and reorganising and centralising the machinery of government.

Most important of all was the *levée en masse* issued on August 23, 1793 which called the entire nation to arms. Its first proclamation was that 'From this moment, until our enemies have been driven from the soil of the Republic, the whole French people is in permanent requisition for military service' (Soboul, 1974: 329). It was this provision that guaranteed victory against the smaller paid standing armies of the continental European monarchs. 'Thus the Republic, with nearly a million men under arms, began to clear the soil of the invader' (Rudé, 1988: 99).

Fourth, it was within the popular movement that supported the Jacobins that direct forms of democracy reached their highest point in the revolution. For example, in Paris where the city was divided into 48 sections, each with its own assembly, *sans culottes*:

conducted a long fight to gain the upper hand over the richer elements in the section assemblies. They were largely successful over the summer of 1793. The sections were meeting almost daily and direct democracy – through attendance at meetings, accountability of representatives to the section assembly and so on – was a distinctive characteristic of the sectional movement.

(Rudé, 1989: 61; Soboul, 1972: xxxvi)

1795: the fall of the Jacobins and the Thermidorian reaction

Ironically, military success paved the way for the fall of the Jacobins. The bulk of the bourgeoisie was only prepared to support them and their revolutionary measures as long as they considered them to be essential in order to win the war and decisively defeat the counter-revolution. When these conditions no longer applied they withdrew their support. The majority of the convention, known as the Plain, ended their rule in late July of 1794. The final wave of popular insurrection in March and May 1795:

one of the most stubbornly fought of the whole Revolution, was essentially a social protest, inspired by hunger and hatred of the new rich, yet it was accompanied by the political demands learned and absorbed since Thermidor: the release of 'patriot' prisoners, a freely elected Commune and the Constitution of 1793.

(Rudé, 1988: 117)

Because this movement lacked effective political leadership, its own political programme and clear objectives, military forces easily and brutally suppressed it at the behest of the Thermidorian majority in the National Convention.

A 'republic of proprietors' took over the reins of power and drew up the much more conservative Constitution of 1795. This Constitution, while it did involve a major retreat from the more radical provisions of the Jacobin Constitution of 1793, did not re-establish the monarchy or other trappings of feudalism. It was reactionary, but not counter-revolutionary. Nonetheless, it proceeded on the basis of the assumption that 'those most suited to govern are men of good education and endowed with great concern for the maintenance of order', who were only to be found amongst 'the ranks of the propertied', as one Thermidorian member of the Assembly put it (Rudé, 1988: 118).

CONCLUSION

First, the French Revolution clearly facilitated the demolition of feudalism, and less clearly and more ambiguously it facilitated the development of capitalism. That it did the former should be clear from the narrative above. The claim that it did the latter is more controversial, because while it is indisputable that the revolution brought fundamental achievements for capitalism, it also established peasant freehold ownership of the land – something that was to act as a major barrier to the kind of agrarian revolution that was central to the emergence of capitalism in England (Mooers, 1991: 70). Nonetheless, the overall impact of the revolution was favourable for accelerated capitalist development in the long term.

Second, the three constitutions of the French Revolution (in 1791, 1793 and 1795) provided a model of liberal democracy that was to be highly influential internationally and historically. The kind of democracy that was established was of a very specific kind. It was essentially a narrowly political (rather than social) form of indirect representative democracy that centrally incorporated specifically bourgeois notions of private property ownership into all of its various constitutional arrangements.

Third, the French Revolution was certainly unique in the extent to which the popular movement that drove it forward, in its more radical phases, utilized more direct forms of democracy. In this respect the French Revolution was more radically democratic than the English and American revolutions.

The bourgeoisie itself played a central and leading role in the French Revolution – albeit not as a united entity but rather as an internally socially differentiated and politically factionalised class that was still in the early stages of its historical formation. The empirical foundation of the revisionist critique of Marxist conceptions of bourgeois revolution is weak in this respect. As Lewis observes, in a book that carefully attempts to balance the arguments of both camps, to deny that the bourgeoisie played a central role in the revolution and that the revolution itself was of great importance in abolishing feudalism and facilitating the development of capitalism 'is to barter historical truth for ideological advantage' (1993: 72–3). We can therefore readily agree with Soboul that:

The Revolution marks the advent of bourgeois, capitalist society in French history. Its essential achievement was the creation of national unity through the destruction of the seigniorial system and the privileged orders of feudal society. Its final outcome, the establishment of liberal democracy, provides a further clue to its historical meaning.

(Soboul, 1977: 1)

The scope of this chapter has been considerable. Despite this, the broad thrust of the chapter can be summarised succinctly. The French Revolution achieved the definitive abolition of absolutism and feudalism. It created a republican form of government that would, despite the Thermidorian reaction and many subsequent changes, remain predominant in French history until the present day. The Revolution also established the majoritarian principle as central to representative democracy. As we have seen, the Constitution of 1793 stipulated that government should be elected on the basis of universal male franchise, inspiring popular movements in other countries to push for the extension of the franchise to encompass the bulk of the adult population. In conjunction with the American Revolution, the French Revolution established the constitutional codification of liberal democratic citizenship rights as a central feature of representative democracies. Finally, the international impact of the Revolution ensured that liberalism would be the dominant intellectual tradition providing the principal political, economic and ideological justification of capitalism in Western Europe and North America.

GUIDE TO FURTHER READING

For chapter-length introductions to the French Revolution see: Harman (1999: 277–302) and Hobsbawm (1962: 73–100). McGarr (1989), Rudé (1988), and Soboul (1977) are still the best short books on the subject for those on the left. Lefebvre (1962a, 1962b, 1989) and Soboul (1974, 1988) provide longer and more detailed Marxist accounts. Kropotkin (1971) and Guérin (1973) provide different anarchist accounts. On the Parisian popular movement see Rudé (1959) and Soboul (1972). Severe limitations of space have prevented a consideration of the important role played by women and feminist aspirations in the Revolution. Godineau (1998), Landes (1988), and Rose (1998) are useful in this regard. Cobban (1964) and Furet (1981) are the most influential revisionist historians of the French Revolution. Callinicos (1989), Heller (2006), Hobsbawm (1990a, 1990b), Mooers (1991), Wolfreys (2007) and Haynes and Wolfreys (2007) provide vigorous and illuminating defences of the Marxist social interpretation of the revolution. Lewis (1993) provides a superb non-Marxist introduction to the revolution and the debate between Marxists and revisionists. Hanson (2009) provides a more recent survey of the scholarly debate, albeit it one that is more sympathetic to revisionist than Marxist arguments. Comminel (1987) is highly controversial because of the concessions that it makes to the revisionist onslaught. Tocqueville (1955) remains a necessary port of call when considering liberal interpretations of the Revolution. McPhee (2002: 219–23) provides a substantially longer guide to further reading than I can give here.

7

The revolutions of 1848–49

INTRODUCTION

In 1848 the wave of revolutionary upheavals that swept across Western and Central Europe combined 'the greatest promise, the widest scope, and the most immediate initial success, with the most unqualified and rapid failure' (Hobsbawm, 1975: 37). But if these revolutions failed to achieve the creation of lasting republican democracies loosely modelled on those of the French and American revolutions, nonetheless they profoundly shaped the future course of European history, demolishing what remained of serfdom in Western and Central Europe, forcing monarchs to make liberal concessions that resulted in the prevalence and persistence of parliamentary forms of governance in which property owners were more widely represented than before 1848, and leading to the creation of constitutional, juridical and political arrangements that were significantly more favourable to the development of capitalism.

This chapter outlines the wider historical context and underlying causes of the 1848 revolutions, provides a brief descriptive overview of the main events in France, Germany, Austro-Hungary and Italy, considers the June insurrection of workers in Paris, describes the conservative counter-revolution that destroyed the new governments created during the initial phase of the revolutions, and finally identifies the common features and historical legacy of these revolutions.

BACKGROUND AND CAUSES

The revolutions of 1848 took place in the wider historical context of the transition from feudalism to capitalism, uneven development of capitalism across Europe, the rapid growth of industrial capitalism in Britain that provided the economic underpinning for the global expansion of the British Empire, and finally the growing pressure on France and Germany to introduce capitalist relationships in agricultural production and to industrialise in order to be able to compete with Britain's growing economic and military power. Much of this has been discussed earlier. Nonetheless, it is important to recognise that the persistence of serfdom and feudal relationships in Central and Eastern Europe was a major cause of discontent among serfs and peasants, and was viewed as increasingly anachronistic by the bourgeoisie, state officials and enlightened members of the nobility. In this context maintaining the extraction of surplus product from peasants and workers as feudalism declined and capitalism developed was a major challenge for the landowning nobility and emerging bourgeoisie (Mooers, 1991: 27–40).

The emergence of capitalism involved, not merely the growing prevalence of capitalist arrangements in agriculture, but early industrialisation and rapid economic growth, accelerating urbanisation and population growth, which created widespread unemployment and social dislocation. This was exacerbated by the serious economic crisis that emerged in Europe from 1845 to 1848. Poor cereal harvests in 1845 and 1846, together with potato blight, led to a substantial rise in food prices (Price, 1988: 18). This undermined the already low living standards of peasants, workers and the petit bourgeoisie, and simultaneously depressed demand for manufactured goods 'with the result that at the very moment that the prices of basic necessities rose, so too did unemployment in both urban and rural industry' (Price, 1988: 18). This contributed to growing misery and discontent amongst wide layers of the population, including peasants, workers and the petit bourgeoisie.

In Ireland the famine resulting from the potato blight killed over half a million people, which explains the absence of popular revolt and also, given the woefully and callously inadequate response of the British government, explains a deepening of opposition to British rule. The conditions associated with the economic crisis led to an increase in strikes, demonstrations, food riots and increased criminality. As Price observes, 'although conditions tended to improve from the autumn of 1847, after a good harvest, unemployment remained high, indebtedness widespread and insecurity intense. The real danger, from the point of view of government, was the politicisation of this discontent' (1988: 20).

With the exception of Britain, Belgium and Holland, states across Europe remained dominated politically by the land-owning nobility. Aristocratic dominance was particularly obvious in the absolute monarchies of Prussia, Austro-Hungary and Russia, but it also characterised, albeit to a lesser extent, the constitutional monarchy of Louis Philippe in France. Among many liberals in the German and Italian states, national unity and autonomy was considered to be 'a prerequisite for political and economic modernisation' (Price, 1988: 29).

The revolutions of 1848 involved all of the major social classes of European societies in transition from feudalism to capitalism, but the classes that were most influential, especially during the first ascendant phase of revolutionary activity, were those that were concentrated in the cities: the bourgeoisie, petit bourgeoisie, students and workers. As Harman observes:

The growing islands of industry across western Europe meant the capitalist class was bigger and more powerful in 1848 than it had been at the time of the French Revolution. Alongside it there was a growing middle class of intellectuals, professors, teachers and civil servants who looked to England as their economic model and the unified national state established by the French Revolution as their political model.

(Harman, 1999: 336–7)

The bourgeoisie and their middle-class allies expressed their demands through liberalism, an ideological orientation that desired 'the end of arbitrary government through a reduction in the power of such traditional institutions as the monarchy and church, a wider sharing of political power by means of the development of parliamentary government, together with guarantees of individual freedoms and the rule of law' (Price, 1988: 21).

The working class was still in the early stages of its historical formation as a distinctive social class with its own interests, communities, organisations and leaders. The labouring poor, Hobsbawm argues, was 'strong enough to make the prospect of social revolution look real and menacing', but 'too weak to do more than frighten their enemies' (1975: 35). This weakness arose because the working class at this time constituted only a small minority of the populations of most European societies, Britain being the obvious exception, and because of its ideological and political immaturity. Nonetheless, members of this class 'were disproportionately effective in so far as they were concentrated in hungry masses in the politically most sensitive spots, the large and especially the capital cities' (Hobsbawm, 1975: 35).

Although the urban bourgeoisie, petit bourgeoisie and working class played key roles in the revolutions of 1848, the landowning nobility and peasantry remained numerically and political predominant throughout Western and Central Europe. Germany, for example, 'expressed many of the contradictions of a society in which, as Engels put it in his assessment of early modern absolutism, "the political order remained feudal, while society became more and more bourgeois"' (Mooers, 1991: 134).

A WAVE OF REVOLUTION SWEEPS EUROPE

The revolutions of 1848, initiated by the successful revolutionary insurrection in Paris from February 22 to 24, spread rapidly and extensively throughout the rest of France, the German Confederation, and the Austrian Empire stretching far into south-eastern Europe and Italy (Hobsbawm, 1975: 23). Indeed, revolution swept through Europe as quickly as the news of events in France, which 'encouraged the holding of public meetings and demonstrations – mainly involving the urban middle classes and skilled artisans – in favour of reforms' (Price, 1988: 37).

In France the revolutionary upheaval was sparked by the government of King Louis Philippe banning a mass banquet in Paris that had been scheduled as the culmination of a national campaign for electoral reform and civil liberties. Radicals in the movement refused to accept the ban and called for a protest demonstration on February 22. Unrest spread though the poorer sections of the city, with barricades being raised, but 'the crisis appeared to be subsiding, until around 10 pm on the 23rd when a fusillade was fired, apparently without orders, by nervous troops guarding the Foreign Ministry' (Price, 1988: 36). Forty or fifty people were killed, and as news of this atrocity spread through the city, the people responded by building over 1,500 barricades (Stearns, 1974: 73; Fasel, 1970: 51). This rapidly developed into a mass insurrection 'against a king who had murdered his people' (Price, 1988: 36). Of the 56,000 members of the National Guard drawn from the 12 *arrondissements* of the city:

> only one legion, that of the wealthy first *arrondissement*, unequivocally supported the government. Of the remaining eleven, a few were politically divided, and six or seven were belligerently anti-government, assembling with cries in favour of reform, calling for the dismissal and even the arrest of [Prime Minister] Guizot.
>
> (Fasel, 1970: 50)

This left the king with little choice other than to abdicate. Popular forces occupied all of the strategic buildings in the city, and on February 24 a new provisional government was proclaimed and took possession of the Hotel de Ville.

The new government was inexperienced politically, and divided socially and politically. As Price observes, its members 'had sympathy for the poor, but like aristocratic and middle class reformers elsewhere, they were unwilling or unable to contemplate changes which might alter the existing social systems significantly' (1988: 44). This meant that although the government enthusiastically introduced a number of radical political changes, only reluctantly and under considerable pressure from the popular movement did it make a number of social reforms, such as setting up national workshops to provide relief for the unemployed and reducing the length of the working day by an hour (from eleven to ten hours in Paris and twelve to eleven hours in the provinces: Price, 1975: 69). Nonetheless, the government introduced manhood suffrage, increasing the number of voters from approximately 250,000 to close to 8 million, and promoted civil liberties such as freedom of speech, the press and association. This contributed to a growing politicisation of the population, and a radicalisation of the inhabitants of the major cities, especially in Paris where workers considered that 'political reform was only the instrument of social reform' (Price, 1988: 54). Mass demonstrations with 150,000 to 200,000 participants in Paris maintained pressure on the government to avoid compromising with the forces of conservative reaction.

On April 23 a national election was held on the basis of manhood suffrage in order to elect a Constituent Assembly. The result was a sweeping victory for conservatives, many of them monarchists, because they enjoyed the support of the church and were better organised and more influential in rural France than the radical supporters of the revolution. Only 70–80 out of the 900 deputies were radical republicans, and another 100 or so were moderate republicans. Socially it was an assembly composed overwhelmingly of provincial notables.

'These included landowners and especially representatives of the traditional bourgeois professions: 261 members of the liberal professions, including 176 lawyers; about 170 public officials; 170 members of the economic professions; 279 [who were] mainly large landowners' (Price, 1988: 56).

The social composition and political orientation of the Assembly made conflict inevitable with members of the working class and petit bourgeoisie, particularly in Paris, where many people had thought the revolution had ushered in a new era in which workers' rights would be recognised.

> The Constituent Assembly, which met for the first time on 5 May, reorganised the government, entrusting executive power to a commission which appointed to its ministries men of the provisional government excluding the socialists. The socialists, angry at losing [a] share in power and relying on the clubs and the Workers' Committee from the Luxembourg, attempted a second revolution by a sudden attack on the Assembly on 15 May. They failed and were obliged to relinquish what posts they still held, such as the Prefecture of Police. Their leaders, Raspail, Blanqui, Barbes, Albert, were arrested.
>
> (Pouthas, 1967: 399)

This strengthened the conservative alliance committed to restoring the old order and monarchy, and further fuelled social tension.

In the 1840s Germany was a confederation of principalities dominated by Prussia. Social and political unrest was widespread because of the economic crisis mentioned above, especially amongst the peasantry, educated middle classes and workers. As news of the revolution in France spread, popular revolt swept through all of the German states, starting in western Germany at the end of February, moving into Bavaria and East Prussia in early March, then northern Germany where events in Berlin were particularly important.

Because of high unemployment and food prices, three days of intense rioting broke out in Berlin in April 1847. Eleven months later the workers and middle classes once rose again in revolt, but this time under the influence of events in France they were determined to force the Prussian king – Friedrich Wilhelm – to introduce a democratic constitution. On March 18, under instructions from the king's ministers, troops in the city moved to suppress the uprising, wounding or killing over 200 civilians, most of these being skilled workers. Although the army appeared to have cleared the barricades successfully, this came at the expense of greatly deepening opposition to the continued absolutist rule of the king. In order to avert the kind of insurrection that swept the French monarch from power, Wilhelm agreed to the establishment of a constitutional monarchy.

On March 30, 600 deputies drawn from the existing state assemblies formed a Pre-Parliament which determined that a national election, with property ownership being a key element of the franchise, was required to elect a new assembly (referred to here as the Frankfurt Parliament) that would draw up a

German constitution.[1] The election created a parliament, which met from May 18 onwards, 'dominated by landowners (60), bourgeois (80), professors (106), lawyers (223), and officials (118)' (Price, 1988: 49). The parliament eloquently debated the unification of the German states and whether or not to include Austria in the new German Empire, the extent of the franchise, and social reform, but achieved little and was ultimately unable to withstand the forces of conservative reaction. When in April of 1849 it finally agreed to create a federal union with a national parliament and a constitutional monarchy in which the monarch retained considerable executive power, the Prussian king who was the most likely candidate decided 'not to accept the imperial crown at the hands of national assembly' (Price, 1988: 50).

The German revolution was not, like the revolutions in France and Austria, heavily concentrated in a capital city. In contrast, revolution engulfed all regions and major cities of the German confederation. In part this was because of the generalised misery caused by the economic crisis. It was also because although formal liberal political parties did not exist, 'liberal and democratic leadership had already emerged in the press, in the various state diets and in the Prussian United Diet in 1847, which largely explains why events in every German capital took a similar course' (Price, 1988: 39). Rural revolt was also more prominent in the German revolution, forcing the governments in the German states to abolish serfdom and protect traditional rights of usage on common land and in forests (Price, 1988: 40). To this extent it was a social as well as a political revolution.

In conjunction with, and under the influence of, the French and German revolutions, revolutionary upheavals developed rapidly in the Austrian Empire. In Austria itself, pressures for democratic and social reform were concentrated in the capital city, Vienna. On March 3, liberal members of the Lower Austrian Estates meeting in Vienna 'called for the election of "a patriotic and enlightened assembly" to advise the Emperor on political reform' (Price, 1988: 37). The revolutionary movement denounced 'the oppression of an absolute government', and wanted Austria to be governed by an assembly in which the bourgeoisie, professional middle class and peasants would be represented, which would form a ministry to govern the country, and usher in a more equitable taxation system, civil liberties, legal reform and the expansion of education.

Not surprisingly this horrified the emperor and his advisers. When a large crowd gathered outside a meeting of the Lower Austrian Diet on March 13, they ordered troops to clear the streets.

The subsequent development of events was similar to that in Paris. [The troops] were met with a hail of missiles and eventually opened fire; in response demonstrators constructed barricades, partly to protect themselves,

---

1 Although it is most commonly referred to as the Frankfurt Parliament, Siemann (1998: 120) more accurately refers to it as the Frankfurt National Assembly.

partly as a means of continuing the struggle. Middle class Civil Guards refused to obey orders, and after two days of mounting disorder the Emperor felt obliged to accept the resignation of Metternich, the symbol of the old order... and to promise a liberal constitution.

(Price, 1988: 38)

Students, numbering around 5000, were the leading radical force in the city, supported by workers. They seized several thousand muskets from an arsenal and forced the government to consent to the formation of a National Guard, with the students forming a distinct Academic Legion. From this point until the election of a new government on July 22, 'the radicals controlled Vienna though the Habsburg-appointed government retained nominal power, while the Hapsburg court itself, cowed but intact, began to marshal its forces in other parts of the empire' (Stearns, 1974: 102). A recurring pattern emerged in which the government made concessions, while students and workers responded by mobilising and forcing the government to make further concessions. This culminated in a huge demonstration on May 15 which forced the government to agree to elections conducted with manhood suffrage to elect a single-chamber parliament. The court fled the city to Innsbruck on May 17, and a Committee of Citizens, Nationals, and Students of Vienna for the Preservation of the Rights of the People effectively controlled the city (Stearns, 1974: 102).

The new government that resulted from the July election had 383 members of whom 60 per cent were bourgeois, 25 per cent peasants and the remainder clergy and nobles (Price, 1988: 52). Political inexperience and bitter internal divisions meant that it achieved little. The bourgeois and educated middle class were moderate and liberal in orientation. They wanted a constitutional monarchy in which they would be able to participate in government, and opposed both social reform and the introduction of a republican form of democracy with full manhood suffrage. In any case, the Habsburg government had already effectively reduced the main source of pressure for social reform – the peasantry – by proclaiming the abolition of serfdom on March 20. 'The landowners who had exercised manorial rights were to be indemnified by the government, which in turn would raise the taxes on the peasants' (Stearns, 1974: 103). This was 'an extremely clever stroke, suggesting the resiliency of the imperial government and the ruling class. A measure that could have been the product of revolution was pre-empted' and it ensured that the radical forces of change in the cities would remain isolated from potential sources of rural revolt (Stearns, 1974: 103).

The collapse of the power of the Hapsburg government in Vienna during March encouraged those people living in Bohemia/Czechoslovakia, Hungary and the Italian provinces of the empire (Lombardy and Venetia) to push for liberal reforms and greater national autonomy. In Hungary liberal modernisers in the Hungarian diet such as Kossuth and Szechenyi drove the revolution forward. They wanted Hungary to become an industrialised society presided over by a democratic government with considerable autonomy within the Hapsburg Empire. They were not enthusiastic about social reform but were prepared to abolish serfdom in order to secure the support of the peasantry for the new regime. The diet discussed Kossuth's plan for reform during the first half of March, and on May 15 agreed to create a new Hungarian state. The diet would be transformed into a parliament elected by property owners. 'A ministry responsible to it was established as the executive branch, and the whole government moved to Budapest, the traditional Hungarian capital. Hungarian units were taken out of the imperial army to form a separate force' (Stearns, 1974: 104). However this government would remain a constitutional monarchy, with the king of Hungary being appointed by the Hapsburgs. In April the new government passed laws that 'provided for equality before the law, the abolition of peasant labour service and tithes – with compensation provided – and of noble tax privileges, and for a liberal political constitution by establishing a property-based franchise which gave the vote to about 1/4 of adult males' (Price, 1988: 80). Not surprisingly, 74 per cent of deputies to the first parliament elected under this franchise were nobles.

Initially events in Italy were largely independent of developments in France and Austria, with the first of the 1848 revolts actually taking place in Palermo, Sicily, on January 12. It spread to the mainland of the kingdom of Naples and forced the king (Ferdinand II) to grant a constitution on January 29. A similar pattern unfolded in Tuscany on February 17, the Papal States on February 21, and Piedmont on March 4. Then in response to news of events in Paris and Vienna, a revolt against Austrian rule began in Milan. 'After five days of particularly bitter street fighting, Radetzky, the Austrian commander, who had remained inadequately prepared in spite of warnings from Vienna, was forced to withdraw his troops' (Price, 1988: 39). The Austrian General Zichy was also forced to capitulate in Venetia, enabling the re-establishment of the Venetian Republic, with a provisional government led by Daniel Manin. Assuming that Austrian power was on the wane, in April Charles Albert, king of Piedmont, Pope Pius IX, the king of Naples and the grand duke of Tuscany jointly decided to commit troops in order to drive Austrian troops beyond the Alps. As we shall see, this attempt ultimately failed because of the inability of these rulers to remain united while waging a military campaign, and the military superiority of the Austrian forces.

THE JUNE INSURRECTION

The key turning point in the revolutions of 1848 took place in Paris in June. The republican government, elected in April and composed mainly of provincial notables, announced on June 22 that the national workshops, which were the major source of support for the unemployed, would be closed, presenting the unemployed with the options of either enrolling in the army or leaving Paris for the provinces. Conservatives in the government clearly wanted to confront the working class and petit bourgeois forces in Paris that had been pushing for further social reform. It appeared to workers and the petit bourgeoisie that the hopes for social reform – for a democratic and social republic – were being dashed. 'A delegation of workers led by a man called Pujol was told, with amazing lack of tact, by Marie on behalf of the [Government's] Executive Commission, that "if the workers do not want to leave, we will send them from Paris by force"' (Price, 1988: 58).

In response, a largely spontaneous uprising began involving 40–50,000 people, which was concentrated in the poorer eastern sections of the city. As Price puts it:

> the insurgents were drawn mainly from the small-scale artisanal trades of the city, such as building, metalwork, clothing and shoes, and furniture, with the addition of some workers from modern industrial establishments such as the railway engineering workshops, as well as a large number of unskilled labourers and a not inconsiderable group of small businessmen. These were not rootless vagabonds as was often claimed by conservative propagandists but mostly skilled workers, well-integrated into their crafts and neighbourhood communities. It was the strength of these loyalties which explained high levels of participation in such *arrondissements* as the 6th, 9th and 12th. Each of the main centres of resistance was dominated by particular trades – carters at La Villette, dockworkers along the St-Martin canal, bronze workers in the Boulevard du Temple, joiners and cabinetmakers in the Faubourg St-Antoine.
>
> (Price, 1988: 59)

Many of these people carried arms as members of the National Guard, and on June 30 they erected barricades to defend themselves and, as they saw it, the revolution. In this manner they successfully took control of a large part of the city. Against them the government was able to mobilise National Guard units from the wealthier *arrondissements* with between 60–80,000 members, around 30,000 troops from the regular army, and up to 25,000 mobile guards (Harman, 1999: 339). After several days of intense and bloody street fighting the workers' insurrection was crushed. As Stearns says:

> National Guardsmen showed themselves particularly vicious, in the sprit of a class war. Approximately 500 insurgents lost their lives in the fighting, as against 1000 soldiers and guardsmen, but after the last barricades were captured the insurgents were hunted throughout the city and almost 3000 more were killed in cold blood. In addition, over 12,000 people were arrested, and about 4,500 of them were ultimately jailed or deported to labour camps in Algeria.
>
> (Stearns, 1974: 92)

THE CONSERVATIVE COUNTER-REVOLUTION

The defeat of the June insurrection in Paris not only strengthened the forces of reactionary conservatism in France, it also encouraged the aristocratic and conservative opponents of revolution to move onto the offensive. Bismarck, for example, 'told the Prussia National Assembly it was "one of most fortunate events in the whole of Europe"' (Harman, 1999: 340). Although the revolution had apparently triumphed with ease, quickly establishing new governments, the difficulties that these governments faced were enormous, especially given the intensification of the economic crisis that took place across Europe from February 1848 onwards, the strength of the conservative forces opposed to social and political reform, and the weak commitment of the bourgeoisie to democracy.

As Price (1988: 85) observes, 'the old social elites soon recovered from the demoralisation they initially experienced with the apparent collapse of the existing institutions of government'. These elites had a number of advantages in countering the revolutionary movements and the governments that these movements had created. They developed a growing appreciation of the need for unity when faced with revolutionary threats to their wealth, status and power, could generally rely on the support of the churches which acted as bastions of conservatism, had entrenched high-level positions in the civil service and army, possessed considerable power as landowners and/or employers, collectively maintained a strong sense of social and cultural superiority, and their leaders typically possessed greater political experience than their opponents. Furthermore, in Austria and Prussia the revolutions had left existing monarchs with a hold on executive power and control over the army. On the other side, revolutionary forces were weakened by the bourgeoisie's commitment to the maintenance of order and constitutional monarchy.

> Once concessions to liberal demands had been made, a political realignment had commenced. The more moderate, especially amongst the better-off and economically secure upper [and middle classes] (landowners, officials, business and professional men) affirmed their fundamental desire to avoid social change, and their willingness to preserve a strong, protective monarchy. This indeed was the general pattern of response throughout Europe to the development of demands for radical political and social change.
>
> (Price, 1988: 53)

In the countryside 'a mixture of concessions to the peasants, and an exaggerated representation of the threat posed by the left to property, religion, the family and nation, all helped to win mass support [for the conservative opponents of liberal reform]' (Price, 1988: 86). In contrast, the left had trouble winning the support of the peasantry.

Drawing on the advantages mentioned above, especially their control of the state bureaucracy and army, counter-revolutionary forces mobilised to roll back the social and political reforms that had been introduced during the first radical phase of the revolution. Conservative propaganda presented the 'reds' as plotting to destroy society in an orgy of looting and violence, 'electoral systems were manipulated, suspect local officials purged, newspapers and meeting places closed, and radicals intimidated. The result in many areas was effectively to demobilise radical political movements and opposition to political reaction' (Price, 1988: 89).

In the wake of the suppression of the June insurrection, the Constituent Assembly in France entrusted the conservative general who had successfully commanded the government's military forces – Cavaignac – with executive control over the provisional government. He was appointed president of the Council of Ministers, a position he held until December 20 when Louis Napoleon Bonaparte was elected president (Denholm, 1972: 142). Under Cavaignac's presidency, the provisional government intensified and generalised the suppression of the political activities of the left, while the Constituent Assembly drafted the constitution of the Second Republic. Among other things, the constitution determined that a single-chamber parliament would be elected by universal manhood suffrage every three years, guaranteed a range of civil liberties, and created an executive branch of government ruled by a president subject to election by universal manhood suffrage every four years who possessed strong powers and to whom ministers were responsible (Stearns, 1974: 213).

In the presidential election held in December 1848 Louis Napoleon, who was a conservative populist, won a landslide victory with 5,534,520 votes (Stearns, 1974: 215). The national election held in April 1849 to create the first government under the new constitution resulted in a sweeping conservative victory, but also a dramatic political polarisation, with radical candidates polling strongly. Of the 750 deputies there were 75–80 moderate republicans; around 200 radicals (*democrate-socialistes*) and over 450 conservatives (Pouthas, 1967: 408; Price, 1988: 64). Radicals gained strong support from working-class voters in major cities and also from the peasantry in the south-east. The left had worked hard in these areas:

> to penetrate their rural hinterlands, encouraging organisation, and distributing propaganda in the form of songs, pamphlets and newspapers. These promised the right to work, free education, support for the establishment of producers' and consumers' cooperatives, cheap credit and reduced taxation for the poor, to be paid for by higher taxes on the rich and the nationalisation of key sectors of the economy.
>
> (Price, 1988: 64)

The strong showing of the radical left appalled conservatives, leading to an intensification of governmental repression and culminating in widespread conservative support for Louis Napoleon's coup in December 1851. Louis Napoleon overturned the constitution of the Second Republic, declared himself president for life, and disbanded parliament. This was a mortal threat to the hope held by large sections of the working class, petit bourgeoisie and peasantry that republican democracy would lead to social reform. This hope had been fostered by the radicals' success in the 1849 election, which many thought would be surpassed by even greater success in the 1852 election. It provoked a massive wave of armed resistance based in the areas of radical republican strength, involving around 100,000 people, with 70,000 of these being armed. Armed insurrections took place 'in the centre (Allier, Nievre), south-west (Lot-et-Garonne, Gers) and especially the south-east (Drome, Ardeche, Basses-Alpes, Herault, Var)' (Price, 1988: 65). Ultimately because these regional and largely rural uprisings lacked national coordination they were defeated by the military, which remained loyal to Bonaparte, who assumed the title of Emperor Napoleon III in 1852 and then ruled as a conservative but populist dictator for 18 years (known as the Second Empire).

In Germany, the Frankfurt parliament began drafting a new liberal constitution in October 1848. It guaranteed civil liberties such as freedom of assembly, speech, the press, religious affiliation and trial by jury. As well as abolishing all manorial rights and other feudal privileges, it provided for 'a two-house national parliament, the upper house representing the states, the lower to be elected by universal suffrage' (Stearns, 1974: 187). Establishing a constitutional monarchy, on March 28 the Frankfurt parliament: 'offered the heredity headship of a united Germany to the king of Prussia. This forced Friedrich Wilhelm to declare himself openly, and he predictably refused what he called a 'crown from the gutter', commenting that 'it would be a dog-collar fastened round my neck by the sovereign German people' (Stearns, 1974: 188). In response, the bulk of the parliament refused to fight against the king's active promotion of an aristocratic counter-revolution. From this point in the revolution the central dynamic was propelled by the growing strength of the forces of reaction, declining political courage of the bourgeoisie, quiescence of the bulk of the peasantry, and the growing radicalisation and political courage of the working class, students and sections of the middle class. Following the departure of Prussian and Austrian deputies, the parliament was effectively dissolved on May 30, and definitively suppressed by military force at the king's behest on June 18. This provoked widespread armed resistance by workers, students and some sections of the middle class. Armed uprisings took place in the Rhineland, Bavarian Palatinate, Baden and finally Saxony. Because these uprisings occurred successively rather than simultaneously, the Prussian army was able to suppress each in turn. It met with fierce resistance in Dresden in Baden, where 'four days of fighting, involving 8,000–10,000 insurgents left 250 dead' (Price, 1988: 70).

After the resistance was defeated, the Prussian king granted a liberal constitution in December 1848 which, although providing him with the power of veto over all legislation, protected civil liberties and provided for a two-house parliament, with the lower house being indirectly elected by a form of universal manhood suffrage. Elections were held on this basis in January 1849, and although the result was a victory for the conservatives (184 seats), the radicals polled well (160). When in April the parliament passed a resolution to the effect that the king should approve the liberal constitution developed earlier by the Frankfurt parliament, he responded by again dissolving the parliament and introducing a new electoral system with a gerrymander that favoured the wealthy. As Stearns observes,

> The new law established three classes of voters, according to the amount of taxes paid. The first class paid a third of all direct taxes but included only the wealthiest 5 percent of the population; it elected a third of the deputies. The second class, about four times as numerous, elected the second third, and the final class, which included the vast majority (approximately 75 percent of taxpayers), along with those who paid no direct tax, elected the remaining third. This ingenious voting system, satisfactory to many liberals as well as conservatives, since neither group had ever favoured a democracy, endured until 1918.
>
> (Stearns, 1974: 190)

Not only did the new electoral system result in a conservative parliament with very limited powers, it also exemplifies a broader pattern in which ruling classes throughout Western and Central Europe promoted and successfully entrenched forms of government that combined some limited democratic features with the largely untrammelled exercise of executive power by monarchs and their ministers.

In Vienna internal division weakened revolutionary forces. On August 23 a workers' protest against wage cuts for the unemployed undertaking relief work was violently suppressed by middle-class National Guards, killing six and wounding many more, and this deepened the division between the workers who desired social reform and an adequate standard of living, and the liberal bourgeoisie and professional middle class who wanted no more than limited political reform. Although estimates of the numbers involved vary, it is clear that at least 30–40,000 and possibly as many as 100,000 were involved in an armed insurrection that broke out in the city on October 6, when crowds protesting against the king's decision to send the Austrian army to suppress the revolutionary government in Hungary stormed the main arsenal in the city and killed the minister of war (Price, 1988: 72; Siemann, 1998: 163). 'The troops which defended the revolution were made up of the Vienna units [of the regular army], the democratic associations, the Workers' Club, the Student Legion and a newly formed Mobile Guard, made up of the unpropertied population, armed with weapons from the storming of the armoury' (Siemann, 1998: 163). Against them, the reactionary General Windischgratz commanded over 70,000 troops that attacked the city on October 26. After seven days of intense fighting Windischgratz's troops took the city, killing over 2000 insurgents. This not only enabled the restoration of the Hapsburg monarchy in Austria, it also led directly to an intensification of the counter-revolutionary efforts of the Austrian armies in Hungary and Italy.

The fate of the insurrection in Vienna was inextricably linked to the fate of the revolution and struggle for national autonomy in Hungary. As Price (1988: 82) observes, 'the German-Austrian dominated imperial bureaucracy thought that the Hungarian reformers had demanded greater autonomy than was compatible with the survival of the empire'. Growing tension between the Austrian imperial government and the Hungarian parliament culminated on September 21 in the formation of a National Defence Committee under the leadership of Kossuth, which became the effective government. The imperial government moved on September 28 to dissolve the Hungarian parliament and declared martial law, effectively declaring war on the Hungarian government. After suffering some initial defeats, the hastily organised Hungarian forces, with mass popular support amongst the Hungarian population, successfully repulsed the Austrian army but failed, through the hesitancy of the conservative Hungarian General Gorgey, to succeed in their attempt to advance on Vienna to support the insurgents at the end of October. This then gave the Austrian imperial government the time that it needed to consolidate the counter-revolution in Austria and call upon the Russian tsar to provide military assistance in the campaign against Hungary. With the aid of over 100,000 Russia troops, the Austrian army successfully defeated the Hungarians and dissolved the revolutionary government in June 1849.

Austrian forces under the command of Radetzky successfully defeated the Piedmont army at Custoza on July 25, 1848, allowing them to reoccupy Lombardy and begin a blockade of Venetia, finally forcing the latter to capitulate on August 22, 1849. Military defeat was in part owing to a lack of peasant support for the forces resisting Austrian reoccupation, which arose because:

> the fundamental unwillingness of the revolutionary governments in Milan and Venice, dominated as they were by property, to concede major agrarian reforms, together with requisitioning by the Piedmontese army as it moved into the Lombard plain, alienated much of the rural population, and isolated the revolutionary movements in the cities.
>
> (Price, 1988: 77)

Revolutionary unrest occurred throughout the Italian states in 1849, but ultimately Austrian forces in the northern states successfully suppressed it, the French army suppressed a revolutionary government in Rome that had been formed in February in opposition to the temporal rule of the pope, and the forces of the king of Naples arrested over 15,000 revolutionary opponents of the monarchy.

SPRINGTIME OF THE PEOPLES

Despite the many differences, a number of common features are apparent in the 1848 revolutions. First, these revolutions displayed a remarkable degree of simultaneity, especially given the slowness of communications in the mid-nineteenth century, and of interconnectedness, with the rise and fall of the revolutionary movement in each country being profoundly influenced by related developments occurring elsewhere in Europe. Second, the revolution in France played a key role both in giving impetus to the first ascendant phase of the revolution and then, following the defeat of the June insurrection in Paris, the counter-revolution. Third, as Hobsbawm observes, the revolutions:

all possessed a common mood and style, a curious romantic-utopian atmosphere and a similar rhetoric ... the beards, flowing cravats and broad-brimmed hats of the militants, the tricolours, the ubiquitous barricades, the initial sense of liberation, of immense hope and optimistic confusion; it was the 'springtime of the peoples' – and like spring, it did not last.
(Hobsbawm, 1975: 26)

Fourth, there were also strong similarities in the positions adopted by radicals, most of whom were students, skilled workers, or else members of either the professional middle class or petit bourgeoisie. Their political agenda was the creation of a centralised democratic republic accompanied by social reform to end feudalism and ameliorate the poverty and suffering of workers who had become unemployed as a result of the economic crisis that had engulfed Europe during the second half of the 1840s. The republic 'was to be built according to the tried principles of the French Revolution on the ruins of all kings and princes, and raising its version of the tricolour which, as usual on the French model, was the basic model of the national flag' (Hobsbawm, 1975: 25).

Apart from the predictably staunch opposition of the forces of the landowning nobility, monarchy, church and conservatism, the major obstacle that the radicals faced was the weak commitment of the bourgeoisie to democracy. In every country the wealthiest members of the bourgeoisie tended to side with the forces of counter-revolution, and even those members of the liberal bourgeoisie who were committed to creation of representative democracy, whether in the form of a constitutional monarchy or republic, were simultaneously 'enmeshed in a web of complex calculations, based essentially on the fear of democracy which they believed to equal social revolution' (Hobsbawm, 1975: 25).

The problem that the bourgeoisie faced was that the 1848 revolutions 'were, in fact or immediate anticipation social revolutions of the labouring poor', and also were the first in which socialists and communists played an important role (Hobsbawm, 1975: 28). 'They therefore frightened the moderate liberals whom they pushed into power and prominence – and even some of the more radical politicians – at least as much as the supporters of the old regimes' (Hobsbawm, 1975: 28; see also Harman, 1999: 336). The workers, artisans and small business owners who were mobilised and radicalised by these revolutions were not just committed to the creation of liberal representative democracies, they wanted republics that were both democratic and socially equalitarian, providing basic material security for all.

In this respect, the decisive confrontation of the 1848 revolutions: 'was not that between the old regimes and the united "forces of progress", but between "order" and "social revolution". Its crucial confrontation was not that of Paris in February but that of Paris in June, when the workers, manoeuvred into isolated insurrection, were defeated and massacred' (Hobsbawm, 1975: 30). The upshot is that during the revolutions of 1848–49 bourgeois liberals 'made two important discoveries in Western Europe: that revolution was dangerous and that some of their substantial demands (especially in economic matters) could be met without it. The bourgeoisie ceased to be a revolutionary force' (Hobsbawm, 1975: 33). As we shall see in Chapter 10, the experience of the Paris Commune confirmed this analysis, and in this respect marked a key historical turning point. Whereas the bourgeoisie played a broadly historically progressive role in the French revolutions of 1789–93, 1830 and 1848, opposing absolutist monarchies and supporting representative democracy (whether in the form of a constitutional monarchy or moderate republic), from 1871 onwards the bourgeoisie opposed any revolutionary movement that pushed for more participatory forms of democracy and threatened the continued existence of capitalism and hence their wealth, power and privilege.

CONCLUSION: THE HISTORICAL LEGACY OF THE 1848 REVOLUTIONS

After the capitulation of the Hungarians and Venetians in August 1849 the revolution was dead. With the single exception of France, all of the old rulers were restored to power – in some instances, as in the Hapsburg Empire, to greater power than ever before – and the revolutionaries scattered into exile. Again with the exception of France, virtually all the institutional changes, all the political and social dreams of the spring of 1848, were soon wiped out, and even in France the Republic had only another two and a half years to live.

(Hobsbawm, 1975: 27)

This interpretation of the 1848 revolutions fails to place sufficient emphasis on the important impact that they had on the subsequent course of European history. First, and most importantly, the 1848 revolutions brought about the end of feudal obligations, payments and serfdom throughout those areas of Central and Western Europe where they had still existed immediately prior to 1848. This often resulted in peasants being no better off because the landowning nobles increasingly transformed themselves into agrarian capitalists charging rents to the tenant farmers who worked their land, and/or because the state hiked up the taxes that peasants had to pay in order to compensate the nobility for the loss of its feudal privileges. But, despite this, the abolition of feudal arrangements in the countryside contributed to the rapid spread of agrarian capitalism and the kind of increase in agricultural productivity necessary in order to sustain rapid industrialisation and urbanisation.

Second, after the revolutions of 1848 the monarchs of Western Europe could no longer rule in a traditional absolutist manner, justified by religion as divinely ordained, and assuming the admiration and consent of their subjects. As Hobsbawm acknowledges, 'henceforth the forces of conservatism, privilege and wealth would have to defend themselves in new ways. The defenders of the social order would have to learn the politics of the people' (1975: 38). Through the experience of the revolution and its aftermath they discovered that the best way of achieving this was to:

> recognise limited political rights while retaining control over bureaucratic and military institutions. In social systems as diverse as those of France, the German States, and Austria-Hungary, an extended suffrage together with representative institutions, was retained, but with severe constraints placed upon the rights of participants.
>
> (Price, 1988: 96)

Third, the 1848 revolutions had a decisive impact on the future development of socialism in Europe, both as a political movement, and with respect to its intellectual development. They were, for example, the only revolutions in which Marx and Engels were direct participants (Nimtz, 2000: 57–81). The conservative and ultimately treacherous role played by the liberal bourgeoisie in the German revolution, and the violent suppression of the workers' insurrection in Paris, led Marx and Engels to stress the importance of the independent political organisation of the working class. The working class needs its own political party because even though the 'democratic bourgeois' will draw upon the support of workers in its struggle to overthrow absolutism, as soon as they have done so, they 'immediately turn their newly acquired power against the workers' (Marx, 1978: 278). Marx further argued that the proletariat can only prevail over the bourgeoisie if they overthrow the bourgeois republic, take state power, and use this power to establish:

> the class dictatorship of the proletariat as the necessary transit point to the abolition of class distinctions generally, to the abolition of all the relations of production on which they rest, to the abolition of the all the social relations that correspond to these relations of production, to the revolutionising of all the ideas that result from these social relations.
>
> (Marx, 1978: 127)

Finally, as Harman (1999: 342) observes, 'the bourgeoisie, looking back in the late 1860s, could reflect that they might have lost the political struggle in 1848, but they won the economic battle'. These revolutions may not have given rise to representative democracies in which sovereign governments were elected by a universal manhood franchise, but they did give rise to constitutional, juridical and political arrangements that were significantly more favourable to the development of capitalism.

GUIDE TO FURTHER READING

For extensive guides to further reading, see: Price (1988: 101–9) and Sperber (1994: 260–9). The best chapter-length Marxist accounts of the 1848 revolutions are by Hobsbawm (1975: 21–40; see also 1962: 359–372) and Harman (1999: 335–44). Non-Marxist chapter-length accounts abound, but Pouthas (1967) is still worth reading, while Gildea (2003: 83–104) and Lyons (2006: 214–37) provide more recent accounts. Price (1988) is a short book that provides an excellent introductory overview, and Sperber (1994) also provides an overview in a book that is longer, more detailed and comprehensive. Other useful books on the 1848 revolutions include: Fasal (1970), Rapport (2009), Sigman (1973), Stearns (1974) and Robertson (1960).

Although not specifically focused on the 1848 revolutions, Mooers (1991) provides an outstanding Marxist account of the wider historical context within which these revolutions took place, with chapters on France (absolutism to Bonapartism) and Germany (Prussian absolutism to Bismarck). Agulhon (1983), Denholm (1972) and Duveau (1967) provide useful accounts of the French revolution of 1848 and the Second Republic. Price (1975) provides a useful set of original documents.

For Marx's (1978) analysis see *The Class Struggles in France* and *The Eighteenth Brumaire of Louis Bonaparte*. Nimtz (2000) provides an excellent account of Marx's and Engels's participation in and analysis of the 1848 revolutions. On the German and Austro-Hungarian revolutions of 1848-9, see Siemann (2001) and Blackbourn (1997: 138–74). Siemann (1998) is very useful, and Blackbourn and Eley (1984) provide a richly insightful discussion Germany's bourgeois revolution. Engels's *The German Revolutions* (1967) is essential reading.

8
Capitalist expansion, globalisation and democratisation

INTRODUCTION

The historical emergence and development of capitalism has created social and economic conditions conducive to the emergence and consolidation of representative democracy. There is widespread scholarly agreement on this point and equally widespread disagreement concerning why capitalist development has, with important exceptions, been positively correlated with democratisation. As established in previous chapters, capitalist development has created social and economic conditions conducive to the emergence of representative democracy because it destroyed feudalism, with its ties of personal obligation and coercive compulsion binding serfs or peasants to landowning nobles, and greatly strengthened the social classes that have most consistently promoted democracy, namely the working class and independent capitalist farmers (Rueschemeyer, Stephens and Stephens, 1992: 6–8; Therborn, 1977: 23–8). This chapter completes the account of the historical emergence of representative democracy by providing an account of the period from the end of the revolutions in which the bourgeoisie played a leading and progressive role, the last being the American Civil War of 1861–65, to the present. Specifically, this chapter focuses on the geographical expansion of capitalism, the extension of the electoral franchise in the advanced capitalist societies, the growing proportion and number of countries that can be categorised as representative democracies, and the aspects of globalisation that are creating significant problems for representative democracy.

CAPITALIST EXPANSION ON A GLOBAL SCALE

Capitalism has sustained a qualitatively higher rate of expansion than any previous mode of production in world history. From its geographically small origins in England and the Netherlands during the fifteenth and sixteenth centuries, capitalism has spread to engulf the planet. As early as 1848 Marx and Engels observed:

> The need of a constantly expanding market for its products chases the bourgeoisie over the whole surface of the globe. It must nestle everywhere,

settle everywhere, establish connections everywhere. The bourgeoisie has through its exploitation of the world market given a cosmopolitan character to production and consumption in every country.

(Marx and Engels, 1998: 39)

Capitalism has a historically unprecedented capacity for growth and geographical expansion, as well as 'space–time compression' (Harvey, 1989: 201–326), because the drive to maximise profits in conditions of market competition propels capitalists continually to invest in technological innovation and the mechanisation of as many forms of production, distribution and exchange as possible. It is this, above all else, that has enabled capitalism to colonise the globe.

In this process of rapid geographical expansion, capitalist economic growth, state formation and territorialisation, and military power are closely interconnected. As Callinicos observes:

the development of the European state system from the late Middle Ages onwards and its world-wide extension in the nineteenth and twentieth centuries, defined by endemic military and territorial conflicts between politically sovereign actors, could be seen as part of the same process as the emergence of a capitalist economic system driven by competition between 'many capitals'.

(Callinicos, 2002b: 250)

Whether states were increasingly influenced by the rising bourgeoisie, as in Belgium, Britain, France and the United States, or led by non-bourgeois state actors who initiated state-led and supported industrialisation in order to be able to compete economically and militarily with the other Great Powers, as in Germany and Japan, they acted on balance in ways that facilitated capitalist development and advanced the interests of their nationally based capitalists. This centrally involved 'a ferocious and continuous process of military and territorial competition among the Great Powers' throughout the nineteenth and twentieth centuries. The advent of capitalist imperialism 'marked the point at which this process fused with, and was subordinated to, the expansion of industrial capitalism .... States' military power now depended directly on their level of industrialisation' (Callinicos, 1994: 23–4; 2009: 146).

A brief overview of the global expansion of capitalism necessarily starts with the capitalist social and property relations that emerged in the English countryside between lords who had obtained full property in the land, capitalist tenant farmers paying fixed rents, and agricultural wage labourers, because these relations generated a revolutionary advance of agricultural productivity and ensured that England experienced unbroken economic and demographic growth right through the seventeenth and eighteenth centuries, eventually leading to the Industrial Revolution (Brenner, 1990: 184). As a result of the Industrial Revolution, Britain emerged during the nineteenth century as the world's economic powerhouse and dominant military power. This forced the other major powers that were Britain's traditional rivals, such as France, Prussia and the Austrian Empire, to develop capitalist relations of production and industrialise. From the time of the American Revolution until the Civil War, the primary basis of economic growth in the United States was the westward expansion of capitalist agriculture, but the north-eastern states industrialised throughout the nineteenth century (Ashworth, 1995: 91). Geographically, capitalism spread from England to encompass the British Isles, white settler colonies in the British empire (American colonies, Australia, Canada, New Zealand, South Africa), France and Germany, then in the second half of the nineteenth century to Japan and Russia.

The expansion of the British empire reached its highest point in 1860 when Britain was 'the workshop of the world'. Having maintained this dominant position during the 1860s, from 1870 a long-term decline commenced in the comparative size of Britain's economy, because France, Germany and the United States grew at a significantly faster rate than Britain from 1870 to 1893. The remarkable acceleration of industrialisation in Germany, which far outstripped that in France and Britain during the boom, ensured that it would become the most economically prosperous and militarily powerful nation-state on the European continent by the 1870s, an achievement forcibly demonstrated by the easy defeat of France in the Franco-Prussian War of 1870–71. The era of classical imperialism thus centrally involved the decline of British hegemony, as Britain ceased to be the world's overwhelmingly dominant superpower, and the rise of inter-imperialist rivalry between the Great Powers (Britain, France, Germany, United States, Russia). However, despite Britain's overall decline, until the early twentieth century it remained the world's dominant military power and had by far the greatest capacity to project this power globally due to the unparalleled superiority of the Royal Navy.

The long economic boom from the late 1840s to the early 1870s was propelled, not only by rapid industrialisation in Belgium, Britain, France, Germany, Holland and the United States, but also by the dramatic expansion of the material infrastructure for communications (the telegraph) and the transportation of people and commodities. As could be expected, since the 'mid-nineteenth century was pre-eminently the age of smoke and steam', this boom centrally involved large increases in coal, iron and fixed engine production in these countries (Hobsbawm, 1987: 55). Advanced scientific knowledge was increasingly applied in technologically innovative ways, especially in the electrical and chemical industries. The progress of industrialisation during this period was much more geographically widespread than earlier in the century; 'The spread of railways and, to a lesser extent, steamships, now introduced mechanical power to all continents and into otherwise un-industrialised countries. The arrival of railway ... was in itself a revolutionary symbol and achievement, since the forging of the globe into a single interacting economy was in many ways the most far-reaching and certainly the most spectacular aspect of industrialisation' (Hobsbawm, 1987: 55, 70).

These developments helped to generate a dramatic growth of world trade (increasing by 260 per cent between 1850 and 1870), international capital flows, and mass migration to colonies around the globe. Hence the boom was fuelled by a tremendous 'lateral extension of the market for both consumer goods and, perhaps above all, the goods required to construct the new industrial plants, transport undertakings, public utilities and cites' (Hobsbawm, 1987: 48). Economic liberalism, which considered that 'the liberation of private enterprise' was the engine propelling the advance of industry, prevailed unchallenged as the economic orthodoxy amongst economists, business leaders and governments. Thus 'the remaining institutional barriers to the free movement of the factors of production, to free enterprise and to anything which could conceivably hamper its profitable operation, fell before a world-wide onslaught' (Hobsbawm, 1987: 50).

The economic boom collapsed in the early 1870s, ushering in the 'Great Depression' of 1874 to 1893. Governments responded by abandoning their earlier commitment to laissez-faire and providing protection to domestic industries. In this context, the Great Powers rushed to colonise the globe in order to obtain raw materials, territory and secure markets.

The great period of growth of the Western empires was the last quarter of the nineteenth century. Some European powers (Britain, Holland, France) already had empires, inherited from a previous phase of capitalist development, but not until the 1880s did they seek to divide ... the world between them. In 1876 no more than 10 per cent of Africa was under European rule. By 1900 more than 90 per cent was colonised. In the same period Britain, France, Russia and Germany established wide spheres of influence extending out from colonial enclaves in China; Japan took over Korea and Taiwan; France conquered all of Indochina; the US seized Puerto Rico and the Philippines from Spain; and Britain and Russia agreed to an informal partitioning of Iran.

(Harman, 2003: 7–8)

As this suggests, the era of classical imperialism is unsurpassed with respect to the use of military power to extend capitalism across vast areas of the planet's surface. Despite often heroic and skilled resistance by indigenous peoples, decimated by the introduction of European diseases and facing professional troops armed with advanced weaponry: 'European colonial possessions rose from 2.7 million square miles and 148 million inhabitants in 1860 to 29 million square miles and 568 million inhabitants in 1914. Colonial conquest was accompanied by a huge increase in European foreign investment, from £2 billion in 1862 to £44 billion in 1913' (Callinicos, 1994: 23). Lenin (1977a: 191) observed in 1920 that 'Capitalism has grown into a world system of colonial oppression and financial strangulation of the overwhelming majority of the people of the world by a handful of "advanced" countries.' In part due to the stimulus provided by European colonisation, a long economic boom took place from the mid-1890s to 1913. The major industrialised capitalist powers:

> now formed an enormous and rapidly growing, and extending, productive mass at the heart of the world economy. They now included not only the major and minor centres of mid-[nineteenth] century industrialization, themselves expanding at a rate ranging from the impressive to the almost unimaginable – Britain, Germany, the USA, France, Belgium, Switzerland, the Czech lands – but a new range of industrializing regions: Scandinavia, the Netherlands, northern Italy, Hungary, Russia, even Japan.
>
> (Hobsbawm, 1987: 49)

The population of Europe and North America grew substantially during this period, partially as a result of the economic growth that it in turn, helped to sustain through the growth of mass consumption. As Hobsbawm (1987: 50) observes with respect to Europe, North America, and the small number of advanced capitalist countries elsewhere, from 1900 to 1913 these countries occupied: 'something like 15 per cent of the planet's surface, containing something like 40 per cent of its inhabitants. These countries thus formed the bulk of the world's economy. Between them they constituted 80 per cent of the international market. What is more, they determined the development of the rest of the world' (Hobsbawm, 1987: 50). The very substantial geographical expansion of capitalism during the boom centrally involved the further development of material infrastructure (steamships, extension of railway and telegraph networks) to enable more efficient and extensive international transportation of commodities, people and money (Held et al., 1999: 291).

The relative economic decline of Britain continued from 1894 to 1913, with Britain's share of the total industrial and mining production of the four largest industrial economies in 1913 being 19.5 per cent compared with the United States's 46 per cent, Germany's 23.5 per cent, and France's 11 per cent (Hobsbawm, 1987: 51). Germany's rise as an economic and military power coincided with Britain's decline. But whereas Britain had already obtained the world's largest empire during the nineteenth century, and was primarily concerned in the twentieth century to hold on to it, Germany's imperialist ambitions were dangerously thwarted by France and Britain's previous gains and the latter's continuing naval supremacy. As Lens puts it, Germany:

> had begun its industrial and imperialist ascent only after defeating France in the 1870–71 war, and had acquired by 1900 a colonial empire of a million square miles and 15 million people, most of it in Africa. While this was substantial, it was meagre compared to the 9.3 million square miles and 309 million people in the British empire, and 3.7 million square miles and 56 million inhabitants in the French empire. This disparity was particularly onerous, in the opinion of Germany's leaders, because their country had forged ahead by leaps and bounds, transforming itself from an agricultural

nation into the world's second largest industrial producer in just a few decades.

(Lens, 2003: 236–7)

Above all else, it was the determination of Germany's rulers to develop substantially larger military forces in order to establish a much larger empire, and the equal determination of Britain's rulers to prevent Germany from doing so, that contributed to the outbreak of the First World War in 1914. The First World War was unprecedented in human history: the systematic industrialisation of warfare, symbolised by artillery and machine guns unleashing 'hurricanes of steel', ultimately resulted in the deaths of somewhere between 9.4 and 11 million people (Briggs and Clavin, 2003: 201).

The capitalist system emerged from the war in a weakened state. The brief global economic recovery of 1924–29 collapsed with the US stock market crash on October 29, 1929 and ensuing collapse of much of the US banking system. This ushered in the deepest and most generalised crisis of the global capitalist economic order in history. Although most governments initially responded to the Depression with 'orthodox' neoclassical policies with an emphasis on balancing government budgets through fiscal austerity and maintaining the soundness of money, as it dragged on they adopted policies that restricted international trade in order to protect their own national industries. Increasingly it became evident that 'those powers, such as Britain and France, which could rely on their colonies for protected markets and raw materials, were able to weather the slump better than those, such as the US and Germany, which lacked empires' (Callinicos, 1994: 25). The shift towards economic protectionism was a key manifestation of the dramatic intensification of inter-imperialist rivalry during the 1930s.

This drive towards economic autarky by the Great Powers served only to exacerbate the tensions among them, since it gave those imperialist states lacking ready access to colonial markets and raw materials – notably Germany and Japan – a powerful incentive to use their military machines to carve out a larger share of the world's resources for themselves. Thus the contradictions which Bukharin had identified between the internationalisation and the statisation of capital produced a second and even more destructive attempt to repartition the globe among the imperialist powers (Callinicos, 1994: 27).

This attempt came when Nazi Germany followed its invasion and occupation of Czechoslovakia in March of 1939 by invading Poland on September 1. Britain and France declared war on Germany two days later. The Second World War had begun, ultimately involving all of the world's major powers together with the medium and small states allied to them. By the time that Germany, Austria, Japan and Italy had been defeated by the Soviet Union, the United States, Britain, China, and their allies, the scale of the carnage dwarfed that of the First World War. In total over 80 million military personnel and civilians had been killed.

By the end of the Second World War the United States had definitively replaced Britain as the dominant world power, finally translating its vast economic strength into overwhelmingly dominant military power. US imperialism was imperialism of a new type – 'less an imposition based on external force than the restructuring of the other advanced economies along lines that mirrored the structures of the dominant capitalism' (Callinicos, 2002b: 256). As Harvey observes,

> An international framework for trade and economic development … was set up through the Bretton Woods agreement to stabilize the world's financial system, accompanied by a whole battery of institutions such as the World Bank, the International Monetary Fund, the International Bank of Settlements in Basle, and the formation of organisations such as GATT (General Agreement on Tariffs and Trade) and the OECD (Organization for Economic Cooperation and Development) designed to coordinate economic growth between the advanced capitalist powers and to bring capitalist-style economic development to the rest of the non-communist world. In this sphere the US was not only dominant but also hegemonic in the sense that its position as a super-imperialist state was based on leadership for propertied classes and dominant elites wherever they existed. Indeed, it actively encouraged the formation and empowerment of such elites and classes throughout the world: it became the main protagonist in projecting bourgeois power across the globe.
>
> (Harvey, 2003: 54–5)

This form of imperialism encouraged an economically multipolar world, but also a world that was divided geopolitically between the West, led by the United States, and the East, led by the Soviet Union.

High profit rates underpinned the post-war long boom from 1945 to 1973, characterised by historically high growth rates in all of the advanced capitalist societies, scientific and technological advancement, low unemployment, rising real wages and an improving material standard of living, and capital accumulation organised on the basis of mass production for mass consumption. This was the greatest economic boom in the history of capitalism, and by the mid-1970s it ensured that capitalism had become a fully global system.

Outside of the advanced capitalist core of the system, one of the most important changes in the global order following the end of the Second World War was the dismantling of the territorially extensive European colonial empires that had been forged during the era of classical imperialism. This change was in part driven by the United States, as it wanted to:

> open other economies, their resources, their labour and their markets, to western, and especially US, capital. This was to be accomplished by the simple means of making the reconstruction of European economies and the development of the 'third world' dependent on their compliance with conditions imposed in the main by the US.
>
> (Wood, 2003: 132)

It was also driven by national liberation movements that successively forced the imperialist powers to grant their independence, such as those that forced France to abandon its former colonies in Indochina (Vietnam, Cambodia and Laos) in 1954 and Algeria in 1962, Britain to grant independence in 1947 to India, and soon after to Ceylon (renamed Sri Lanka) and Burma. It then abandoned its colonies in Africa (including Ghana, Kenya, Sudan, Uganda, Zimbabwe), Asia (Malaysia), the Pacific and Indian oceans, and the Caribbean. France was also forced to abandon its remaining colonies in Africa (Guinea) and Asia, but held on to minor colonies in the Pacific. The Netherlands abandoned Indonesia in 1950. The United States allowed its major colony in Asia, the Philippines, to become formally independent in 1946. In the Middle East, popular nationalist movements successfully pushed for independence in Iran, Egypt, Lebanon, Libya and Morocco. A former British colony – Palestine – was violently colonised by Zionists with British and US support, to form a racist US subimperialist state (Israel).

The list above is by no means comprehensive, but it gives some sense of the scale of decolonisation. One of the major factors that made decolonisation possible was the declining dependence of advanced capitalist countries on raw materials imported from the third world because of substitutes developed from 1914 to 1945, the development of agricultural sectors in Europe, North America and Japan with massive state support, and the emergence of strong internal demand within the advanced capitalist countries in the context of the boom and Keynesian demand management. This meant that 'The Third World, with the exception of a handful of Newly Industrialising Countries was not so much exploited as ignored by … an 'ostracising imperialism'' (Callinicos, 2002b: 256). As this suggests, although most former colonies experienced economic growth during the long boom from 1945 to 1973, the rate of this growth was lower than in the advanced capitalist societies.

The long boom collapsed in the mid-1970s, and the prolonged economic crisis that followed accelerated a series of developments that increased international interconnectedness, including the growing international integration of capital markets, the internationalisation of capital ownership, expansion of international trade, and development of financial circuits largely outside the control of nation-states. The major set of institutional changes that made these developments possible was the breakdown of the Bretton Woods system and the rise of the dollar Wall Street regime (Gowan, 1999: 19–38). In 1971 the Nixon Administration 'shocked world financial markets by announcing that the dollar was no longer to be freely convertible into gold, effectively signalling the end of fixed exchange rates' (Held et al., 1999: 202). The United States gained control over the US dollar's exchange rate and 'thereby enormous leverage over the other advanced capitalist countries' (Callinicos, 2002b: 259).

This leverage was used to promote the global implementation of neoliberal policies. For example, the explosion of foreign currency transactions and international banking following the 1973–74 oil price hikes generated huge cash surpluses in the oil-producing states, surpluses that they invested in Western, and particularly US, financial institutions. These institutions then lent money to Poland and Hungary in Eastern Europe, as well as countries in Africa and Latin America, ultimately creating a major debt crisis in the 1980s and 1990s. More generally:

> Washington and Wall Street were able to manage the greatly increased global flows of private finance to compel other states to adopt neoliberal polices that opened up their economies to foreign capital. The resulting socio-economic restructurings strengthened the domestic constellations of interests aligned to internationally mobile money capital.
>
> (Callinicos, 2002b: 259)

In addition to expediting the implementation of neoliberalism, the collapse of Bretton Woods also led to a dramatic increase in foreign direct investment (FDI). As Harman (2003: 39) observes, the stock of FDI 'had amounted to only 4 per cent of world gross domestic product in 1950 (as against 9 per cent in 1913). In 1999 it reached 15.9 per cent. Total world FDI outflows amounted to $37 billion by 1982. By 1990 they had shot up to $232 billion and in 2000 to $1,150 billion. By 2000 they were equivalent to 1/6th of total world fixed capital formation.' As this suggests, 'what distinguishes the era of globalization since the mid-1970s is not the growth of world trade ... but, rather, the explosion of foreign direct investment and, most crucially, the emergence of the multinational corporations that drive it' (McNally, 2006: 38). In contrast to classical imperialism, flows of FDI were overwhelmingly within the advanced capitalist core of the global capitalist order, and outside the core it was channelled very narrowly; 'ten developing countries received 80 per cent of the total FDI flows to the developing countries' (Harman, 2003: 39).

'Globalisation' – that is, a qualitative increase in international inter-connectivity – is actually specific in key respects to the period of capitalist development following the collapse of the post-war long boom in the mid-1970s. In this period the world's financial markets have become increasingly deregulated and integrated; the advanced capitalist economies have tended to become less protected and more open to international trade; industrial production has become increasingly internationalised; the material infrastructure for communications and media has facilitated the emergence of virtually instantaneous communications and informational and cultural flows on a global scale; and the influence of supranational bodies such as the International Monetary Fund (IMF), World Bank and World Trade Organization (WTO) on national governments has grown substantially.

THE KEY CHARACTERISTICS OF REPRESENTATIVE DEMOCRACY

In order to provide an account of the extension of the electoral franchise within the advanced capitalist societies and the growing proportion and number of countries that can be categorised as representative democracies, first we need to identify the key characteristics of this historically unique form of democracy. Despite the existence of a wide-ranging debate between the left critics and liberal defenders of representative democracy, there is general agreement that representative democracy has several defining characteristics.

First, representative democracy is an exclusively political form of democracy that is constitutionally, institutionally, ideologically and by convention highly circumscribed and separated from the social and economic spheres. There is a clear separation of the polity from civil society. Although the majority of citizens cannot directly participate in the political sphere of governance, they can participate indirectly, in particular through interest groups, parties, media and elections. These are institutional 'transmission mechanisms' through which citizens can exert influence over the process of governance. Regular secret ballot elections, competition between factions, potential leaders and parties, a free press, and majority rule are the institutional bases for establishing the accountability of those who govern (Held, 2006: 78). Although the system of representation is majoritarian, constitutional safeguards protect the rights of individuals and minorities. These guarantee equality before the law and civil liberties ensuring freedom of speech, expression and association, freedom of the press and other media, and protection against arbitrary treatment by the state. This is further enhanced by the constitutional separation of powers between the executive, legislature and judiciary.

As we shall see in the next section, in the advanced capitalist societies the citizenry was tightly circumscribed throughout the nineteenth century, with propertyless workers, women, indigenous peoples and blacks being excluded from the franchise. Largely in response to mass struggles from below, citizenship was eventually extended to the overwhelming majority of adult citizens. As Held observes:

> It was only with the actual achievement of citizenship for all adult men and women that liberal democracy took on its distinctively contemporary form: a cluster of rules and institutions permitting the broadest participation of the majority of citizens in the selection of representatives who alone can make political decisions (that is, decisions affecting the whole community). This cluster includes elected government; free and fair elections in which every citizen's vote has an equal weight; a suffrage which embraces all citizens irrespective of distinctions of race, religion, class, sex and so on; freedom of conscience, information and expression on all public matters broadly defined; the right of all adults to oppose their government and stand for office; and associational autonomy – the right to form independent associations including social movements, interest groups, and political parties.

> (Held, 2006: 94)

This is widely recognised, but it is less commonly recognised that liberal defenders of representative democracy consider that even in its most inclusive form the citizen body is composed of discrete individuals who enjoy juridical equal status, whose interests are conceptualised as expressed policy preferences, and who are not socially organised in distinct and antagonistic social classes. In the liberal tradition, pluralists consider that capitalism creates social and economic conditions that are conducive to the emergence and persistence of representative democracy, in part because advanced capitalist societies are characterised by an extensive differentiation of interests and widespread diffusion of power.

According to liberal pluralists, the transmission mechanisms between the citizenry in civil society and democratic institutions in the polity enable citizens to exert indirect, but real and effective, influence over government. Regular multi-party elections provide citizens with a choice between governing and opposition parties, enabling them to remove an unpopular government from power. Governments in office are constrained by the anticipated reaction of the electorate to the general mix of policies implemented prior to the next election. In the interim, citizens can organise themselves in interest groups in order to exert ongoing influence over government. Freedom of expression in the media ensures that citizens have an additional channel to communicate their views to the rest of the electorate and to government, and can subject government to rigorous criticism. Finally, mass political parties provide citizens with another opportunity to participate in the political direction of a liberal democratic state – either by exerting influence over the policies of the governing party or by participating in an opposition party.

From a liberal perspective these institutional mechanisms ensure that, for the first time in history, the majority of citizens can exert effective influence over the governance of society. While acknowledging that the influence of the citizenry over government is greater in representative democracies than in authoritarian dictatorships, and constitutes a qualitative advance over the coercive exploitation of serfs and peasants by the absolutist state of the late feudal era, Marxists argue that the amount of substantive influence that citizens can exert over government in representative democracies in the normal course of events is limited. This argument is discussed at length in Chapter 9.

THE DEVELOPMENT OF REPRESENTATIVE DEMOCRACY IN THE ADVANCED CAPITALIST SOCIETIES AND THE GROWING GEOGRAPHICAL SPREAD OF REPRESENTATIVE DEMOCRACY

Even a brief overview of the extension of the franchise highlights that what we understand as constituting representative democracy today, namely civil liberties and voting rights for the overwhelming majority of the adult population, is a relatively recent development in the history of democracy. Indeed, it is only from the late nineteenth century onwards that we see for the first time democracies in which the majority of the adult population have such liberties and rights. The extension of the franchise was achieved through mass popular struggles against the major bases of exclusion: class, gender and ethnicity. In most cases, the working class and its allies played a central role in these struggles. Sometimes the franchise was extended after the initial wave of working-class struggle had been defeated, but the scale of these struggles made it clear to ruling classes and their governments that the franchise could not be restricted to property owners indefinitely.

Defining representative democracy is a controversial but necessary prerequisite to determining empirically when a country has become a democracy, and to assessing how democratic it is relative to other countries. For example, Rueschemeyer and colleagues define representative democracy as entailing:

> first, regular, free and fair elections of representatives with universal and equal suffrage, second, responsibility of the state apparatus to the elected parliament (possibly complemented by direct election of the head of the executive), and, third, the freedoms of expression and association as well as the protection of individual rights against arbitrary state action.
>
> (Rueschemeyer et al., 1992: 43)

This definition is based on Therborn's (1977: 4) earlier similar definition. On this basis, Therborn (1977: 11) provides a useful summary of the dates at which representative democracy with a universal franchise was first established in the advanced capitalist societies: Australia (1903), Austria (1918), Belgium (1948), Canada (1920), Denmark (1915), Finland (1919), France (1946), Germany (1919), Italy (1946), Japan (1952), Netherlands (1919), New Zealand (1907), Norway (1915), Sweden (1918), Switzerland (1917), the United Kingdom (1928) and the United States (1970). Obviously if something less than a fully universal adult franchise is used as the criterion, most of these countries became democracies in a more limited sense considerably earlier. But this estimate highlights the relatively recent establishment of the universal franchise, even in the advanced capitalist societies where it emerged earlier than in other parts of the world.

The historical backdrop to and manner in which the universal franchise was introduced varies considerably across different countries, and a comprehensive account is obviously not possible here. Some of the broader patterns and trends are exemplified by the struggles for greater democracy in the four countries that were considered in the accounts of the bourgeois revolutions earlier in this book (Britain, the United States, France and Germany). The central role of the working class in pushing for the extension of the franchise is particularly clear in Britain. The key electoral reforms of 1867 and 1884 were 'in part a delayed response to earlier working-class agitation':

> beginning at least as early as the Chartist movement [which peaked from the late 1830s to the late 1840s], whose main demand was universal suffrage. After forcefully suppressing the immediate threat represented by Chartism, the established bourgeois parties, under the pressure of electoral

competition, later responded to the working-class challenge with attempts to co-opt segments of the working class by politically incorporating them.

(Rueschemeyer et al., 1992: 95–6)

The British situation was unusual in that the majority of the bourgeoisie did not actively oppose suffrage extensions. The next major electoral reform, which established full male suffrage, was passed in the wake of the First World War, in 1918. In part as a response to the women's suffrage movement, all adult women were enfranchised in 1928. Accordingly the electorate increased in size as follows: 1831, 4.4 per cent of the population over 20; 1832, 7.1 per cent; 1864, 9 per cent; 1868 16.4 per cent; 1883, 18 per cent; 1886, 28.5 per cent; 1914, 30 per cent; 1921, 74 per cent; 1931, 97 per cent (Dahl, 1998: 24).

As discussed in Chapter 5 the US Constitution left it to the states to determine the franchise. Indeed, 'not until 1868, with the passage of the Fourteenth Amendment, did the phrase "the right to vote" appear in the federal Constitution, and to this day the nation's fundamental law contains no affirmative embrace of universal suffrage' (Keyssar, 2000: 317). From 1791, when the constitution was ratified by all the states, to the election of Andrew Jackson to the presidency in 1828, women, blacks and Amerindians were excluded, and a variety of property, tax, religious, registration and literacy qualifications prevented the bulk of the white working class from voting as well (Keyssar, 2000: 8–25, 336–402). Nonetheless, because agricultural property ownership was much less concentrated than in Britain and continental Europe, smallholder independent farmers were for the most part enfranchised, and consequently the franchise was more extensive than most European countries during the nineteenth century. It is possible that in the wake of the Revolution somewhere from 60 to 70 per cent of the white adult male population could vote (Keyssar, 2000: 24). Because everyone else was excluded from the franchise, less than 20 per cent of the total population voted in presidential elections from 1824 to 1916 (Dahl, 1967: 68).

Women achieved the franchise for federal elections in 1920, but in the south universal suffrage was only achieved with the passage of the Civil Rights Act of 1964 and the Voting Rights Act of 1965 'which gave the federal government the responsibility of enforcing black voting rights in the South and eventually resulted in the inclusion of southern blacks in the electorate' (Rueschemeyer et al., 1992: 132). Despite the achievement of something approaching a universal franchise by the late 1960s, in recent federal elections, 'only half of all eligible adults have voted in presidential elections, and fewer than 40 per cent generally cast their votes in other contests. Electoral turnout has declined significantly over the last century, and it is markedly lower in the United States than in most other nations' (Keyssar, 2000: 320).

Voter turnout is lowest amongst ethnic minorities, especially blacks, and poorer strata in the working class (Keyssar, 2000: 320).

The 1793 Jacobin Constitution of the French Revolution, unlike the US Constitution, included a provision for universal manhood suffrage, but it was never implemented (see Chapter 6). Nonetheless 'the outcome of the French

Revolution was decisive for the development of democracy in France because it destroyed the seigniorial system and the political power of the landed aristocracy' (Rueschemeyer et al., 1992: 87). The Restoration regime of the Bourbon monarchy was too narrowly based on the nobility to be sustainable, and thus it gave rise to the revolution of 1830 which brought down the Restoration regime and enfranchised the bourgeoisie:

> The upper bourgeoisie, particularly those sectors based in Paris and in finance, and not the artisans who did the street fighting, was the primary beneficiary of the Orleanist July Monarchy that was subsequently installed. The suffrage law enacted, although considerably broader than the Restoration franchise, ensured that this would be so. It enfranchised males paying 200 francs or more in direct taxes and thus gave 1 in 170 inhabitants the right to vote.
>
> (Rueschemeyer et al., 1992: 88)

The French revolution of 1848 was discussed in Chapter 7. Here it will suffice to note that although it introduced a universal manhood franchise, this was subsequently narrowed and once again excluded the majority of working-class voters. Although a broad franchise was retained for presidential elections during the Second Empire of Louis Napoleon Bonaparte (1852–71), there were no other effective democratic constraints on the power of the executive. The Third Republic was established in the wake of the Paris Commune of 1871. Universal male suffrage and cabinet responsibility to parliament were introduced in 1877 following a sweeping electoral victory for the Republicans in 1876. It was not until 1946, however, that the franchise was extended to encompass women.

In Germany, 'the popular conquest in 1848–49 of effectively universal and equal male suffrage was swiftly reversed by pro-capitalist royal reaction' (Therborn, 1977: 14). Two decades later, Bismarck promoted the extension of the franchise in order to expedite his plans to unify Germany. Thus:

> after 1870 a Prussian dominated Germany emerged in which universal male suffrage was granted in the constitution of 1871. However, the German polity was only very partially democratic. Despite such a broad suffrage, broader than that of either Britain or America at the time, power remained highly concentrated and unaccountable in the Second Reich.
>
> (Potter et al., 1997: 53)

Imperial Germany from 1870 to 1918 was politically dominated by a class alliance of wealthy Prussian landowners (Junkers) and the section of the bourgeoisie based in heavy industry, particularly iron, coal, naval shipbuilding and armaments production. This rye–iron alliance was significant because 'the German bourgeoisie were more anti-democratic than their counterparts elsewhere, and that was at least part of the reason for the weakness of democratic impulses and the persistence of the authoritarian features of the Imperial German regime' (Rueschemeyer et al., 1992: 107). The working class was the major social force that was consistently pro-democratic. Germany's defeat in 1918 and the revolution of 1918–19, in which widespread military mutinies, mass strikes, and the establishment in some areas of workers councils forced the monarchy to abdicate and the Kaiser to flee the country, led to the creation of the Weimar Constitution in 1919. 'This provided for universal suffrage, for both men and women, an accountable executive and representative legislature and the constitutional entrenchment of regular elections, changes of power and civil and political liberties' (Potter et al., 1997: 53). Democracy was suppressed by the Nazis and following the Second World War by the Stalinist regime in East Germany, but re-established in West Germany in 1949.

As these cases demonstrate, even in the relatively favourable conditions provided by advanced capitalism, democracy emerged late in human history and was a fragile construction that depended, among other things, on the prevailing balance of power between those class alliances that were either supportive of or opposed to it. The extension of democratic citizenship rights to encompass the majority of the adult populations of the advanced capitalist societies, and the growing geographical spread of representative democracy to encompass an increasing proportion of the world's nation states, advanced very slowly until the late nineteenth century but at a faster pace during the second half of the twentieth century, especially after 1973. Whereas in 1974 only 26.9 per cent of all countries could feasibly be described as representative democracies, by 1997 this had increased to 61.3 per cent (Diamond, 1999: 25). The number of electoral democracies increased from 66 individual countries, or 40 per cent of all countries, in 1987, to 47.6 per cent in 1995, 123 or 64 per cent in 2006, and 60 per cent (117 out of 195 countries) in 2011 (Potter et al., 1997: 9; Freedom House, 2007: 5; 2012: 4).

Representative democracy emerged later in the less developed countries of the so-called 'third world', being largely concentrated in the period from the mid-1970s to the present, because the working class was proportionately smaller, the peasantry much larger, large landowners with authoritarian political proclivities more socially and politically influential, especially in less industrialised and more agrarian developing capitalist societies, and finally, the politically dominant fraction of the bourgeoisie in developing countries is typically aligned with one or more of the ruling classes of the more powerful states. Furthermore, the extent to which these countries can be considered genuinely independent of the major imperialist powers varies enormously according to the strategic importance of the countries concerned to the imperialist powers, and consequently many remain vulnerable to covert or overt external intervention. One of the most important aspects of this relates to the global imposition on less powerful and economically prosperous countries of the neoliberal Washington consensus. For this reason democratisation is often associated with substantial increases in socio-economic inequality (Ross, 2006). Furthermore, given the strength of anti-democratic class forces in many of these countries, typically aligned with coercive and authoritarian sections of the state apparatus, democratic advance in less developed countries remains fragile.

Geographically the trend from authoritarian forms of governance to representative democracy:

> began in Southern Europe in the mid-1970s, spread to the military regimes of South America in the late 1970s and early 1980s, and reached East, Southeast, and South Asia by the mid to late 1980s. The end of the 1980s saw a surge of transitions from ... authoritarian rule in Eastern Europe and the former Soviet Union and a trend toward democracy in Central America as well.
>
> (Diamond et al., 1997: 1–2)

In the 1990s the trend spread to Africa, beginning with the fall of the apartheid regime in South Africa during the early 1990s and the election of an ANC government in 1994. More recently, a wave of pro-democratic revolutionary uprisings against authoritarian dictatorships swept across North Africa and the Middle East from the end of 2010, most prominently in Tunisia, Egypt, Libya and Syria, constituting 'the most significant challenge to authoritarian rule' since the collapse of East European Stalinism (Freedom House, 2012: 1; cf. Callinicos, 2011).

The literature focusing on this trend towards democratisation is vast, and overwhelmingly dominated by those writing within the liberal pluralist tradition of political science. Consequently it is widely assumed that liberal representative democracy is the only historical form of democracy worthy of serious consideration and that there is no realistic and desirable 'alternative political system or ideology competing with [liberal] democracy' (Huntington, 1996: 11). The two most widely cited sources of comparative and historical data on democratization – Polity IV and Freedom House – both define representative democracy in narrowly institutional terms and focus on variables such as the degree of political competition and participation, executive recruitment, constraints on executive authority, electoral process, freedom of expression and belief, associational and organizational rights (Freedom House, 2012: 33; http://www.systemicpeace.org/polity/polity4.htm). Although both of these research institutes can justly be criticised for favouring the United States and its allies in their assessments of the level of democracy prevailing in individual countries, due in part to the funding that they receive from US state agencies including the CIA, they nonetheless provide useful comparative and historical data. For example, Freedom House (2012: 3) states that the number of countries it designated as 'free' in 2011 'stood at 87, representing 45 per cent of the world's 195 polities and 3,016,566,100 people – 43 per cent of the global population' and 'partly free' 'stood at 60, or 31 per cent of all countries ... and they were home to 1,497,442,500 people, or 22 per cent of the world's total'. The fact that an agency like this can with some justification claim that 65 per cent of the world's people are governed by states that are fully or partly democratic indicates clearly just how far democratisation has advanced since 1860, when, according to the eminent liberal pluralist Robert Dahl, only one country had a sufficiently broad franchise to be counted as a democracy (1998: 8).

THE IMPACT OF GLOBALISATION ON REPRESENTATIVE DEMOCRACY

Democratisation has been historically progressive in a number of respects, but it has also been characterised by severe limitations, not least of which is the fact that the shift from an authoritarian to a democratic form of governance is often associated with a substantial increase in socio-economic inequality because of the implementation of neoliberal policies and the exploitative nature of free market capitalism. These and other limitations of representative democracy are discussed in Chapter 9. Here I focus on one specific set of problems for democracy and democratisation that arise because of the impact that 'globalisation' has had on the autonomy of nation-states. In this regard, Held argues that 'the focus of modern democratic theory has been on the conditions which foster or hinder the democratic life of a nation', the major problem being that 'in a world of regional and global interconnectedness, there are major questions about the coherence, viability and accountability of national decision-making entities themselves' (Held, 2006: 290–1).

In one of the most influential scholarly accounts, globalisation is defined as centrally involving 'the widening, deepening and speeding up of worldwide interconnectedness in all aspects of contemporary social life' (Held et al., 1999: 2). The technological advancement of basic material infrastructures, particularly in the areas of production, transportation of commodities and people, communications, media, computing and information technologies, the emergence of English as the world's dominant second language, the growing reach of international law, and the establishment of regional and international networks of governance such as the European Union, Asia-Pacific Economic Cooperation (APEC), the Organization of Petroleum-Exporting Countries (OPEC), the G8, the United Nations, the IMF, World Bank and WTO, have all contributed to the acceleration, intensification and spread of global interconnectedness. Hence:

> globalisation denotes the expanding scale, growing magnitude, speeding up and deepening impact of interregional flows and patterns of social interaction. It refers to a shift ... in the scale of human social organisation that links distant communities and expands the reach of power relations across the world's major regions and continents.
>
> (Held and McGrew, 2003: 4)

This creates problems for the viability of democracy within nation-states because both liberal and radical thinkers assume symmetry and congruence between 'citizen voters and the decision-makers whom they are, in principle, able to hold to account' and 'the 'output' (decisions, policies, etc.) of decision-makers and their constituents – ultimately, 'the people' in a delimited territory' (Held, 2006: 290; 1995: 16). This assumption is problematic because a decision made by a particular government, such as the Bush Administration's decision to invade Iraq in 2003, can have major effects on people living elsewhere in the world. More generally, 'the idea of the democratic state as in principle capable of determining its own future' is being undermined by developments in 'the world economy, international organisations, regional and global institutions, international law and military alliances which operate to shape and constrain the options of individual nation-states' (Held, 2006: 295; 1995: 99–140). The upshot is that the geographical territorialisation of democracy is becoming increasingly complex and is being reconstituted at regional and global levels. This is highly significant because:

> territorial boundaries specify the basis on which individuals are included and excluded from participation in decisions affecting their lives (however limited the participation might be), but the outcomes of these decisions, and of the decisions of those in other political communities and agencies, often stretch beyond national frontiers. The implications of this are troubling, not only for the categories of consent and legitimacy but for all the key ideas of democracy: the nature of a constituency, the meaning of representation, the proper form and scope of political participation, the extent of deliberation, and the relevance of the democratic nation-state as the guarantor of the rights, duties and welfare of subjects.
>
> (Held, 2006: 292)

Since the mid-1970s the world economy has been transformed by the growing internationalisation of production networks, increasing concentration and centralisation of capital ownership embodied in the growth of huge multinational corporations, massive expansion of global financial flows due to the extensive deregulation and international integration of capital markets, and the growth of international trade (Held et al., 1999: 149–282; 2004: 21–33; see also Gowan, 1999: Part I; Harvey, 2005). These and other developments in the world economy have significantly reduced the capacity of nation-states to govern their domestic economies and, in particular, to do so through Keynesian demand management (Held, 2004: 14–16, 30).

International political decision making has been conducted by a growing array of organisations reflecting 'the rapid expansion of transnational links, the growing interpenetration of foreign and domestic policy and the corresponding desire by most states for some form of international governance and regulation to deal with collective policy problems' (Held, 2006: 298). This development is exemplified by the growth of international governmental organisations (IGOs) such as the IMF, World Bank, WTO, European Union, United Nations, G8 and the G20, and international non-governmental organisations (INGOs). In 1909 there were 37 IGOs and 176 INGOs, in 1996 4667 IGOs and 25,260 INGOs (Held, 2006: 298).

During the post-war era, 'the development of international law has subjected individuals, governments and non-governmental organisations to new systems of legal regulation' (Held, 2006: 300). In particular, international policies and conventions on human rights, such as the European Convention on Human Rights (1950) and the UN Declaration on Human Rights (1948) and International Bill of Human Rights, have created sets of international rules that transcend, and to varying degrees constrain, the traditional national sovereignty of states (Held, 2006: 300–1). Global interconnectedness has accelerated dramatically in the areas of transportation, telecommunications, printed and electronic media, and popular culture. Finally, major environmental problems such as non-renewable resource depletion, global warming as a result of deforestation and the growing emissions of greenhouse gases, ozone depletion, and pollution of oceans, lakes and rivers, are clearly transcending the borders of nation-states (Held, 2004: 132–6; Held and McGrew, 2007: 64–72).

These developments combine to restrict the freedom of action of national governments and obscure 'the lines of responsibility and accountability' of these governments by 'blurring the boundaries of domestic politics, transforming the conditions of political decision-making, changing the institutional and organisational context of national polities, [and] altering the legal framework and administrative practices of governments' (Held, 2006: 303). Consent and legitimacy through elections becomes problematical once the autonomy of national governments becomes limited and the definition of their constituency becomes blurred. Furthermore, in recent decades the global order has been characterised by:

> the progressive concentration of power in the hands of multinational capital (productive and financial), and the weakening role of states faced with global market processes and forces. In this context, the risk is that democratic politics will increasingly be reduced to adapting to global markets – second-guessing their tendencies and accommodating to them.
>
> (Held, 2006: 304)

Held contends that the only effective way to counter this is to establish cosmopolitan democracy and implement social democratic policies on a global scale. This contention is problematic because it is unlikely that class inequality, gender and ethnic inequalities, unemployment, poverty, alienation within the workplace, global warming and industrialised military conflict between nations can be eliminated while retaining a modified variant of the capitalist mode of production. For this reason, although a form of cosmopolitan democracy embodying a number of the features that Held describes needs to be created, it needs to be fundamentally anti-capitalist and socialist in nature. So, for example, a cosmopolitan socialist democracy would, as Held suggests, constitutionally entrench an international cluster of rights, including the civil liberties that many people falsely assume is exclusive to liberal democracy, but unlike cosmopolitan social democracy it would remove the major social and economic forces emanating from capitalism that currently systematically undermine the establishment and effective exercise of these rights (Roper, 2011).

CONCLUSION

By way of conclusion four central points are worth emphasising. First, capitalism has a historically unprecedented capacity for both intensive and extensive expansion. In conditions of market competition, capitalist firms must continually invest in new technologies, typically involving increases in the mechanisation and capitalisation of industry, agriculture, transportation, communications, and service provision, in order to reduce costs, enhance product quality and increase market share. In order to maximise profits capitalists also need to obtain raw materials at the lowest possible cost and keep waged and nonwaged labour costs as low as possible. In a nutshell, capitalism is a system that must continually expand in order to survive and prosper. This expansive dynamic explains why it is that, in contrast to all earlier forms of social and economic organisation, capitalism has expanded from its small beginnings in sixteenth and seventeenth-century rural England to encompass the globe.

Second, in the relatively advanced capitalist societies, the historical formation of nation-states, the specific institutional configurations of particular states – ranging from undemocratic monarchies to representative democracies – and the extent of state capacity to shape capitalist development, cannot be explained in simplistic terms by reference to the basic requirements of capital accumulation and/or the instrumental influence of capitalist ruling classes because of the complexity of the processes involved. Nonetheless, there can be little doubt that capitalist nation states in general, and the major imperialist powers in particular, have tended to act in ways that have maintained the conditions necessary for capitalism to expand domestically and internationally. Furthermore, capitalist ruling classes have only been prepared to countenance the extension of the franchise to encompass a majority of the adult population in situations where this is compatible with the basic requirements of capital accumulation, the reproduction of capitalist relations of production, and extensive capitalist influence over state policy formation and decision making.

Third, this is not, however, to deny the historically progressive nature of capitalism with respect to democratisation. Although representative democracy is structured in a manner that prevents the majority of the population from exerting effective influence over government, at least in the normal course of events, nonetheless as a form of government it is vastly superior both to the absolutist monarchies of the late feudal and early capitalist eras and to the fascist and Stalinist dictatorships of the twentieth century. The civil liberties and voting rights of workers and farmers in capitalist societies are indeed remarkable when compared with the politico-juridical and coercive domination and exploitation experienced by slaves in classical antiquity or serfs and peasants in feudalism. Capitalist development has made democratisation possible by creating social and economic conditions and forces that are conducive to the emergence and persistence of representative democracy, at least in settings characterised among other things by organised and powerful working classes.

Fourth, although it is true that capitalism creates social and economic conditions that are necessary for representative democracy to emerge historically, this form of democracy is a historically possible rather than inevitable outcome of capitalist development. For example, when the system is in deep crisis, as it was in Germany during the 1920s and 1930s, capitalists may shift their weight behind authoritarian movements in order to smash working-class organisation, thereby reducing labour costs, boosting profit rates and reviving capital accumulation. Hence from a capitalist viewpoint representative democracy is not necessarily always the best form of governance of capitalism with respect to its systemic reproduction. For this and other reasons democratisation is a vastly more limited and fragile development than most intellectual apologists for capitalism are prepared to acknowledge.

GUIDE TO FURTHER READING

A vast literature on globalisation has emerged during the past decade. The single best chapter-length overview of the debate between 'sceptics' and 'globalists' is the introduction by Held and McGrew (2003: 1–50) to the best edited collection of writings on the subject. Held et al. (1999) is the best non-Marxist book on globalisation. McNally (2006) and Callinicos (2002b, 2003a, 2003b) provide the best book-length accounts of globalisation and the global justice movement from a Marxist perspective. Dahl (1989: 213–24), Held (2006: 56–95), Holden (1993: 49-72) and MacPherson (1977: 1-92) provide clear accounts of the key features of representative democracy. Dahl, Shapiro and Cheibub (2003) provides a comprehensive collection of classical and contemporary writing on democracy within the liberal tradition. The best accounts of democratisation are those provided by Rueschemeyer et al. (1992) and Therborn (1977). Grugel (2002) provides a useful book-length introduction to democratization and Potter et al. (1997) is a very useful collection. For a representative sample of mainstream liberal pluralist writing on democratisation see Dahl (1998), Diamond (1999), Diamond and Plattner (1996), Diamond et al. (1997), Gill (2000), Huntington (1991) and Leftwich (1996). For an exposition and critical discussion of cosmopolitan social democracy see Roper (2011).

9

The Marxist critique of capitalism and representative democracy

ase
INTRODUCTION

INTRODUCTION

In the preceding chapters we considered the revolutionary revival of representative democracy in the broader context of the transition from feudalism to capitalism. The re-emergence of democracy was a development of world-historical significance. As we have seen, the ruling classes in Europe had effectively suppressed democracy throughout the period from 322 BC to 1640 AD. After two or more centuries of absolutist rule by centralised hereditary monarchies in feudal societies, revolutionary struggles established new state forms that embodied a historically novel form of democracy – liberal representative democracy. This particular form of democracy was revived in the context of social and economic conditions associated with the emergence and growth of capitalism within wider societies that remained largely feudal during the seventeenth and eighteenth centuries (with capitalism advancing much more rapidly in England, Holland and the American colonies than in continental Europe). It was further developed throughout the nineteenth and twentieth centuries as the capitalist mode of production completely supplanted feudalism and other pre-capitalist modes of production throughout the world.

Marx acknowledged that the demise of feudalism and the absolutist state and the emergence of representative democracy constituted a major step forward for humankind (and he was himself involved in the German bourgeois revolution of 1848). He celebrated the historical achievements of both capitalism and representative democracy. Nonetheless, Marx argued that this form of specifically bourgeois democracy is extremely limited, with respect to its social and economic foundations in capitalism, and with regard to its specific institutional mechanisms. It is limited for precisely the reason that makes it contrast so dramatically with Athenian democracy: the labouring citizens are systematically excluded from participating in the governance of society.

However, Marx's critique did not focus, in the first instance, on the deficiencies of the institutional mechanisms of liberal representative democracy. His analysis of the limitations of representative democracy is thoroughly grounded in his underlying critique of the capitalist mode of production. This is an extremely important point because, while some liberals (neo-pluralists) and social democrats are prepared to acknowledge elements of the Marxist critique of representative democracy, they still reject the substance of Marx's critique of capitalism. This should not surprise us for Marx's critique of capitalism highlights the extent to which modern representative democracy is the best possible political shell for capitalist exploitation. Further, it shows that the democratisation of the economic and social spheres is antithetical to the continued functioning of capitalist economic systems and the reproduction of capitalist relations of production. Hence this chapter begins with a consideration of Marx's critique of capitalism, and only then moves on to consider his more institutionally focused critique of the limited, restrictive and illusory nature of parliamentary democracy and 'the parliamentary swindle'.

THE MARXIST CRITIQUE OF CAPITALISM

Marx's critique of modern representative democracy ultimately rests on his underlying critique of capitalism. The centrality of Marx's theory of surplus-value to his critique of representative democracy, and his related arguments concerning the possibility and necessity of working-class self-emancipation, are seldom fully recognised in the literature. For example, the considerable body of political science literature generated by defenders and critics of pluralism tends to focus on the effectiveness of institutional channels for citizen influence over government, rather than addressing the question of the extent to which representative democracy is sustained by, and in turn fosters, capitalist exploitation. Yet it is this issue that really distinguishes the classical Marxist critique of the capitalist revival of democracy, both from other bodies of criticism (non-Marxist socialism, feminism, environmentalism, anarchism) and from the disillusioned defence of representative democracy (social democracy, neo-pluralism). Marx's theory of exploitation is essential to develop a sophisticated critical analysis of the strengths and weaknesses of modern representative democracy.

Exploitation and inequality

Perhaps the strongest, and most neglected, empirical support for Marx's theoretical analysis of specifically capitalist exploitation is its general historical realism. For one of the truly great paradoxes of capitalism is the fact that it evidently has a historically unprecedented capacity to generate an enormous social surplus product (surplus product over and above the subsistence needs of the immediate producers), but that it creates the appearance that the production of this surplus product does not involve a process of exploitation. In other words, to a greater extent than any prior mode of production, capitalism is highly successful at simultaneously producing and obscuring the production of a massive surplus.

The contradiction between potential plenty, and actual poverty, for the workers who produce the surplus product in capitalist society, has existed for nearly as long as capitalism, but it has never been more marked than at present.

A small super-rich minority appropriates a rapidly increasing share of the world's wealth while the workers, peasants and their dependants who actually produce this wealth through increasingly internationally enmeshed networks of production, and who constitute the majority of the world's population, experience growing deprivation and poverty (Harman, 2002; 2010: 329–32). As McNally observes:

> while more than a billion people do not have access to clean water or adequate food and shelter, there are now 793 billionaires in the world whose combined wealth ... is an almost incomprehensible $US2.6 trillion – more than the gross domestic product of all but six countries in the world. In fact, the assets of the world's 200 richest people are greater than the combined income of 41 per cent of humankind.
>
> (McNally, 2006: 129)

The share of world income received by the richest 20 per cent of the world's countries relative to the share received by the poorest 20 per cent, increased from a ratio of 30:1 in 1960 to 74:1 in 1997 (2006: 130).

Income and wealth has also become much more unequally distributed within the advanced capitalist societies (Galbraith and Lu, 2001; Harvey, 2010: 12–16; McNally, 2006: 124–31). Since the mid-1970s real incomes for the majority of workers have either increased at a slower rate than from 1945 to 1973 or declined (Armstrong, Glyn and Harrison, 1991: 255; Brenner, 2003b: 8; Callinicos, 2010: 54–7; McNally, 2011: 42–5; Shawki, 2001: 27–9). As governments in the advanced capitalist countries have implemented neoliberal policies, spending on health, housing, education and welfare has been subject to 'fiscal restraint' and reduced in real terms. Poverty, homelessness, malnutrition, drug abuse, crime and violence are widespread in the midst of societies producing massive amounts of wealth for small rich minorities. Furthermore, the majority who live in these societies are wage and salary earners who spend a large part of their lives in workplaces that are typically governed by undemocratic authoritarian administrative and managerial hierarchies.

Apologists for capitalism are quite happy to acknowledge its immense capacity to generate a surplus product. The historically unprecedented growth rates of capitalist economies are a common reference point for those who want to argue that capitalism is superior to any conceivable alternative form of economic organisation, but they vehemently deny that capitalist production is inherently exploitative. It is a denial that flies in the face of historical reality. As we have seen, ancient Greek civilisation, the Roman empire and feudalism all incontrovertibly involved exploitation in the sense that a minority class of land and/or slave owners appropriated the surplus product produced by slaves, serfs and/or peasants. Are we to assume that exploitation suddenly disappeared with the arrival of capitalism? Are we also to assume that the highly unequal distribution of market income and economic wealth in actual capitalist societies is completely unrelated to an underlying process of the production and appropriation of a surplus product? It seems, *prima facie*, highly unrealistic to make such assumptions.

Marx's theory of surplus-value provides a comprehensive and convincing explanation of growing inequality within the advanced capitalist nations and between these nations and the poorer nations. More specifically, the theory of surplus-value explains why capitalism has a historically unprecedented capacity to produce a surplus product over and above the subsistence needs of the workers who produce it. In this way, it explains how inequality in capitalist society originates and is reproduced cumulatively over time. It does this by developing a historically specific analysis of the underlying process of exploitation that is at the core of capitalist production. It also shows how the exploitation that occurs within the sphere of production is obscured by relations in the sphere of circulation that appear to involve free and fair market exchanges between capitalists and workers.

McNally comments:

> Central to the genesis of capitalism are those historical processes which bring about the separation of a large and growing proportion of the labouring population from means of production which could provide them with an adequate subsistence. It follows that the emergence of a *labour market* is central to the rise of capitalism.
>
> (McNally, 1993: 7)

This means that as capitalism develops historically and spreads geographically it destroys non-capitalist forms of production, drives subsistence producers, such as peasants and indigenous peoples, off their land, and forces them to become wage labourers. In the British empire this involved white settler and extractive colonialism, and in the world today it continues in the form of capitalist globalisation. This means that, far from disappearing, on a global scale the working class is increasing in size in both absolute and relative terms.

As Harman observes:

> the working class exists as never before as a class in *itself*, with a core of perhaps two billion people, or a third of the global population. On top of this there are very large numbers of peasants, up to 50 per cent, who do some wage labour and so are subject to much of the same logic of the system as the workers. The global proletariat and semi-proletariat combined are the majority of the population for the first time in history.
>
> (Harman, 2010: 332)

The collective separation of wage labourers from the means of production, which are owned by capitalists, an underlying socio-economic compulsion for workers to sell their labour-power to capitalists so as to subsist at a historically determinate level, and, because of the above, the generalised commodification of labour-power, are basic preconditions of capitalism as a system of production (Mandel, 1976: 47–57; Marx, 1967a: 34–5).

In the capitalist mode of production, labour-power, which is the potential capacity that a person has to labour for a specified period of time, becomes a commodity that appears to be freely exchanged on the labour market. The worker legally owns and is formally free to sell their labour-power to whomever they choose. But this apparent freedom and equality between buyer and seller in the labour market is illusory precisely because workers, lacking ownership of the major means of production, are effectively compelled to sell their capacity to work to an employer in order to subsist. Labour-power is unique because, unlike any other commodity, it can produce value over and above its exchange-value. Marx termed this surplus-value: that is, the difference between the necessary labour-time which the worker performs in order to cover the costs of their own reproduction and the surplus labour-time which is the labour performed in the labour-process over and above this necessary labour-time. Surplus-value is the social form which surplus labour-time assumes in the capitalist mode of production, and capitalists, who own and effectively control the means of production within the labour process, appropriate it. The principal phenomenal forms that surplus-value takes in the capitalist mode of production are profit, interest and rent. Hence Marx's theory of surplus-value demonstrates that 'The historical specificity of capitalism arises from the fact that its relations of exploitation are almost completely hidden behind the surface of its relations of exchange' (Shaikh, 1990: 167).

In general, capitalists are subject to strong competitive pressures in both capital and product markets to maximise profitability. The necessity to remain profitable drives capitalists to battle simultaneously on a number of different but interrelated fronts. First, capitalists engage in an ongoing struggle with workers over the buying and selling of labour-power, in which they try to keep waged and non-waged costs of employing workers to a minimum. Second, in the labour process, capitalist management struggles with workers over the production of surplus-value. Battle on this front essentially involves attempts to maximise managerial control over productive labour in conjunction with the mechanisation of production in order to increase the productivity of labour and hence the production of relative surplus-value (Rosdolsky, 1977: 224–9). As Shaikh (1990: 75) observes, 'Mechanization becomes the dominant form of technical change precisely because it is the production of surplus-value, not use value, which is the dominant aspect of the labour process under capitalism.' Third, in the circulation process or sphere of market competition, capitalists struggle against other capitalists over the realisation of surplus-value in the form of profits through the sale of commodities (Shaikh, 1991: 185). Battle on this front essentially involves the increased capitalisation of production in order to reduce unit production costs and thereby obtain a larger market share – assuming that a lower cost-price is achieved without any deterioration in product quality (Shaikh, 1991: 185). Beyond the level of the individual firm, capitalists battle on a fourth front, in the political sphere, by placing as much pressure as they can, individually and/or collectively, on governments to deliver policies favourable to their interests (tax cuts, subsidies, anti-union industrial relations legislation, free trade agreements, and so forth) (Roper, 2005: ch.4; 2006).

The battles waged on these fronts between capitalists and workers are crucial in determining the distribution of income and wealth in the society as a whole. Increasing inequality is thus ultimately a result of generalised capitalist victories over workers and their allies. As this suggests, Marx's theory of surplus-value has a considerable degree of political efficacy. After all, Marx interpreted the world in order to change it. The theory of surplus-value enables us to identify a common enemy, which all those subject to exploitation and oppression share in a capitalist society – the capitalist class. It demonstrates that the overwhelming majority of people who inhabit advanced capitalist societies have a sufficiently broad range of shared social, economic and political interests to make large-scale collective struggles against the capitalist class and state both possible and necessary. In this respect, it is a theoretical critique of capitalism that can be used, by those seeking to improve the lives of working class people, to justify and guide mass protest, militant trade unionism, and the quest for emancipatory social and political change.[1]

For Marx, and the classical Marxists who followed him, trade unions are an essential, and at the same time a limited, means of pursuing working-class ends. Workers need to organise collectively in trade unions in order to overcome their vulnerability as individuals and to use their collective power to push for better pay and conditions of employment through strikes and/or protests. Although vitally important, union struggles are inherently limited because they ultimately do no more than ameliorate, rather than fundamentally alter, the terms on which capitalists exploit workers. This suggests that an egalitarian distribution of income and wealth can only be achieved if capitalism is eliminated. As Marx puts it: 'Instead of the conservative motto, "A fair day's wage for a fair day's work!" [workers] ought to inscribe on their banner the revolutionary watchword, "Abolition of the wages system!"' (1973b: 78). Hence the theory of surplus-value also remains at the absolute heart of the revolutionary socialist critique of social democratic reformism. Any strategy that accepts the continued existence of capitalism thereby also accepts the continued exploitation of workers, who produce the world's wealth, by capitalists, who appropriate it.

The global justice movement has been centrally concerned with the growth of global inequality, focusing on the role played by the neoliberal structural adjustment programmes, pushed by the International Monetary Fund (IMF)

---

1   This is why Marx's theory is so dangerous from the viewpoint of capitalists and also the major reason that intellectual defenders of capitalism have repeatedly tried to demolish the theory ever since Volume 1 of *Capital* was published in 1867. For vigorous defences of the theory see Freeman and Carchedi (1996), Mandel and Freeman (1984) and Shaikh (1977, 1982, 1984).

and World Bank, in increasing this inequality (Bello, Cunningham and Rau, 1999; Chossoduvsky, 1997). For example, in Africa 'Debt amounts to $US230 billion and has increased 400 per cent since 1980 when the IMF and World Bank started imposing structural adjustment programmes' (Fisher, 2001: 199). Poverty has increased dramatically, with 48.5 per cent of the 630 million people living in sub-Saharan Africa living on less than US$1 per day (Fisher, 2001: 199). At the same time in India, '47 per cent of Indian girls and boys, aged four and under, are malnourished, as are 48.5 per cent of adults' (McNally, 2006: 102–3). In 2005, according to the United Nations, 'more than one billion people live on less than $US1 per day. Another 1.5 billion struggle to survive on between one to two dollars daily. That's 40 per cent of humankind condemned to unrelenting poverty and hardship' (McNally, 2006: 51–2).

The growth of poverty in the third world is because output and income growth has been much lower than in the advanced capitalist countries. Whereas per capita income rose by 73 per cent in Latin America and 34 per cent in Africa from 1960 to 1980, from 1980 to 2000 the respective figures are 7 per cent and -23 per cent. The relatively poor performance of these two regions – Africa and Latin America – where IMF structural adjustment has been most extensively imposed, speaks volumes about one of the real outcomes of the past three decades of capitalist globalisation. As McNally (2006: 55) astutely observes, globalisation centrally involves a 'massive transfer of wealth from poor to rich'. Although the capitalist governments that have been imposing neoliberal policies on the developing countries always have money for war and weapons, they will not spend the equivalent of a small fraction of their military budgets to eliminate mass starvation in the third world. In fact, western aid to Africa is only a small percentage of the total amount paid each year by African governments to western financial institutions in interest payments on debt (Altvater et al., 1991; Barratt Brown, 1996; Herman, Ocampo and Spiegel, 2010; Jochnick and Preston, 2006; Pettifor, 2001). At the same time that hundreds of millions suffer from malnutrition, food stockpiling and dumping is common in Europe and North America.

Marxism explains this global inequality, at the most basic level of analysis, by reference to the central dynamics of capitalist exploitation and accumulation. Hundreds of millions of the world's people go hungry, despite there being enough food to feed them, because food is produced for profit rather than need. The world's agricultural and fishing industries are driven by corporate greed rather than human need. Massive third world debt not only yields a huge net surplus for western financial institutions, it enables the World Bank and the IMF to force third world governments to shift agricultural production away from food production for the domestic market, towards the production of cash crops for export.

How is this discussion relevant to a consideration of Marx's critique of representative democracy? For Marx the historically distinctive characteristics of representative democracy are to be understood and explained primarily, but by no means exclusively, in terms of the constantly changing, and internally contradictory, social and economic relations with which it is thoroughly enmeshed, and which, in turn, the institutional ensemble of the liberal democratic state attempts to govern. More particularly, the theory of surplus-value is central to Marx's critique of the capitalist revival of democracy, because it is capitalist exploitation which generates class inequality, fosters and sustains other related forms of oppression based on gender and ethnicity, creates serious social problems, and is central to economic dynamics which culminate in economic and environmental crises. In these respects, capitalist exploitation creates a social and economic environment that systematically circumscribes democratisation from extending beyond a narrowly defined political sphere. These issues are discussed on pages 236–9.

Environment

Capitalism centrally involves exploitation, not just of workers by capitalists and of the workers and peasants of poor countries by the transnational corporations and financial institutions of rich countries, but also of the natural environment to the maximum extent possible (Bellamy Foster, 1999). In fact, no previous system of production has had such a damaging effect on the natural environment. After three centuries of capitalist development, we are confronted by a mounting environmental crisis which, if current trends continue, may lead to the extinguishment of human life on this plant (Bellamy Foster, 1999: 11–33). Global warming caused by the 'double whammy' of steadily increasing atmospheric pollution which is building up carbon dioxide (CO_2) and chlorofluorocarbons (CFCs), combined with massive deforestation which is reducing the natural absorption of CO_2 and release of oxygen, is melting the polar ice caps, raising ocean levels, and could culminate in catastrophic climate change (Neale, 2008: 13–25; Williams, 2010; Wolf, 2001). In addition, vital non-renewable resources, such as oil, are being rapidly depleted, and hazardous and destructive pollutants continue to be released into waterways and oceans (Boardman, 2010; Jones and Hollier, 1997; Peet, Robbins and Watts, 2010). Genetically modified organisms are being released into the environment before adequate scientific research has been conducted to ascertain the long-term impacts on the environment and human health (Peet et al., 2010; Rapien, 2002).

While all of this is widely recognised, the real causes of capitalist destruction of the environment are not. Central to capitalism is the privatisation of the benefits of economic production through the appropriation of profits and the accumulation of wealth, and the socialisation of the environmental costs. These costs assume a wide variety of different forms, but in general they are borne by the workers who produce the profits capitalists accumulate, people in the wider society who are exposed to the resulting pollution, and the inhabitants of third-world countries adversely affected by the climate change caused by atmospheric pollution, the bulk of which is generated by the world's most advanced capitalist countries. More specifically, when large corporations run plants that pump pollutants into the sky and/or waterways, the costs of this pollution are externalised or pushed onto others. The profits, however, go to the executives, directors and major shareholders who own and control these corporations. It is not a case of the odd business being 'irresponsible', as Green parties often claim, but of *all* businesses seeking to maximise profits by minimising costs. Because recycling and technology that reduces pollution add to production costs and reduce profits, businesses generally try to avoid investing in these areas (Dale, 2007: 118–27). Far from having nothing interesting to say about these issues, the Marxist tradition provides rich, interesting and fruitful explanations of the major environmental problems generated by capitalism (see Bellamy Foster, 2000; Burkett, 1999, 2006; Dale, 2007; Hughes, 2000; Kovel, 2007; McNally, 2006: 113–22; Neale, 2008; Pepper, 1993; Wolf, 2001; Williams, 2010).

Competition, imperialism and war

Capitalism is based on competition. Neoclassical economics textbooks present this as centrally involving the harmonious and universally beneficial workings of the 'hidden hand' that allocates resources within market economies through the operation of the law of supply and demand. In reality, the global implementation of neoliberalism, with its promotion of free-market capitalism, frequently requires that the hidden hand becomes a hidden fist (Callinicos, 2003a: 50–66; McNally, 2006: 83–136). A neo-conservative defender of George W. Bush's geopolitical strategy for world domination accurately observes in this regard that:

> Because we are the biggest beneficiaries of globalisation we are unwittingly putting enormous pressure on the rest of the world ... producing a powerful backlash from all those brutalized or left behind .... The hidden hand of the market will never work without a hidden fist. Markets function and can flourish only when property rights are secured and can be enforced, which, in turn, requires a political framework protected and backed by military power .... Indeed, McDonald's cannot flourish without McDonnell Douglas, the designer of the US Air Force F15. And the hidden fist that keeps the world safe for Silicon Valley's technologies to flourish is called the US Army, Air Force, Navy and Marine Corps.
>
> (Friedman, 2000: 464)

It is important to recognise that the world's largest transnational corporations remain solidly based in particular countries (especially the United States, Japan and countries in the European Union) and have very close ties to the governments of these countries. As Harman (2003: 41) observes, 'a big portion of the sales and bulk of the investments of the major multinationals remain concentrated in their home country'. Furthermore, the world's biggest companies 'remain dependent to a high degree on their ability to influence "their" national government. This is because ... they need a state to protect their web of international interests, and the only states that exist are national states' (Harman, 2003: 43–4). Thus, in the era of globalisation from 1974 to the present, imperialism centrally involves competition between capitalist elites, and the nation-states that do their bidding on a global scale, for markets, resources and territory (Callinicos, 2009: 188–227).

From this perspective, Bush's 'war on terror' was, in reality, an attempt to use the military superiority of the United States in order to shape the world in a manner most likely to curtail the advance of competitors such as China, Russia, Japan and the European Union, while advancing the global dominance of US capitalism (Callinicos, 2002b, 2003b; Harman, 2003; McNally, 2006: 237–66; Sepehri, 2002). Surprisingly little changed under the Obama administration, which also explicitly stated that current US military supremacy was to be maintained and projected throughout the world to maintain US geo-political and economic supremacy. It is merely the most recent example of capitalist competition breeding inter-imperialist rivalry and war.

Crisis

The global capitalist economy from the mid-1970s to the present has been characterised, in contrast to the prosperity of the post-war long boom from 1945 to 1973, by prolonged stagnation and mass unemployment in the advanced capitalist core of the system. This prolonged crisis has ultimately been determined by a long-term generalised decline in average profitability (Callinicos, 2010: 50–60; Duménil and Lévy, 2011; Dunne, 1991; Harman, 2007, 2010; Mandel, 1995; Mosely, 1991; Shaikh, 1992; Shaikh and Tonack, 1994; for alternative Marxist interpretations see Brenner, 2003b; Glyn, 2006; McNally, 2011: 25–84). As profitability declines, spending on investment in productive sectors of the advanced capitalist economies declines, output growth rates decline and unemployment rises. This has happened in all of the major capitalist economies since the mid-1970s.

The onset of this generalised crisis of the global capitalist system has greatly intensified the pressures on capitalist ruling classes in the advanced capitalist countries to increase the exploitation of workers in their own countries, the extraction of profits and resources from the rest of the world, the exploitation of natural resources, and to oppose measures that would help to preserve the environment but that would also increase costs and reduce profits. At the same time, the crisis has prompted capitalist elites to devote more resources to exerting influence on policy-makers at every level of governance – from regional to national to supranational – in order to promote the neoliberal policies and geopolitical strategies, often involving military conflict, that they consider to be in their interests. This is why the implementation of neoliberal policies on a global scale, and the ensuing growing global integration of national economies into the global economy, has been so contentious. The rich capitalist minority that dominates the governance of the world, has been busily promoting neoliberal policies, geopolitical strategies, covert operations and bloody military adventures, which have the effect of making the rich even richer and the majority of the world's people poorer.

Marx's critique of representative democracy rests, not only on his underlying theory of surplus value, but also on the theory of capitalist crisis that he articulates in the third volume of *Capital*. This is so because such crises tend to fuel mass class struggles because the ruling class responds to a generalised decline in profitability by becoming more industrially militant and attacking workers directly – seeking to cut wages and conditions, while at the same time boosting labour productivity. In conjunction with these direct attacks, the ruling class also places increased pressure on the state to introduce a gamut of measures aimed at counteracting the tendency of the rate of profit to fall (tax cuts for business, fiscal austerity, labour market flexibility and so on). So there can be no question of liberal democratic states acting as 'neutral referees' between the conflicting claims of the contending parties in the class struggle. On balance, these states side with capitalists against workers and the oppressed.

The continuing relevance of Marxian and Marxist theories and empirical studies of the tendency of capitalism to generate recurrent economic crises is currently particularly clear in the midst of the most serious global economic crisis since the Great Depression of the 1930s. The crisis started in 2007 with the subprime mortgage crisis in the United States but soon spread to engulf the global financial system by the end of 2008. Even those who advocate neoliberal policies, and present the global capitalist economy as being inherently self-adjusting and the best of all possible economic systems, acknowledge the severity of the crisis. The head of the IMF pronounced that 'We were very close in September [2008] to a total collapse of the world economy' (Strauss-Kahn, 2009: 1–2). The secretary-general of the Organisation for Economic Co-operation and Development (OECD) similarly argued that 'sound, counter-cyclical, fiscal policies' are required to counter the 'severest financial and economic crisis in decades' (Gurria, 2009: 3). US treasury secretary Tim Geithner said of the 2008 crisis that 'Our economy stood on the brink' and 'the United States risked a complete collapse of our financial system' (quoted by McNally, 2011: 13). Governments around the world initially responded by pumping vast sums of money into the advanced capitalist economies, spending billions on corporate welfare to bail out failing banks and financial institutions, then followed this up with sweeping programmes of fiscal austerity, cutting social spending on health, housing, education, welfare and pensions, public sector employment and so forth. In this historical conjuncture, it is not hard to find an abundance of empirical support for the central thrust of the Marxist critique of capitalist exploitation, class inequality, economic crisis, and the pro-business, anti-working class, role that liberal democratic states generally play in managing serious crises of the capitalist system.

Oppression

Horizontal and vertical gender segregation of the workforces of the advanced capitalist societies means that women are over-represented in a narrow range of relatively poorly paid occupations, and within particular occupations tend to be stuck at the bottom of managerial hierarchies (Scott, Crompton and Lyonette, 2010). Women's incomes are substantially lower than men's, women possess less wealth, and are more likely to have insecure employment (Banyard, 2010; Power, 2009). Female participation in paid employment continues to be adversely affected by inadequate, or nonexistent, employer and government provision of childcare (Orr, 2010; Scott et al., 2010). Within the family-household an unequal gender division of labour prevails (Addabbo, Arrizabalaga and Borderías, 2010; Crompton et al., 2007). Surveys show that even where both partners are also working in paid employment, women perform most of the domestic labour and childcare (Bullock, 1994: 30–2; Delphy and Leonard, 1992: 75–104, 226–53; Hartman, 1996; Scott et al., 2010). Far from being a 'haven in a heartless world', the family-household is the primary site of male violence and sexual abuse. Sexuality remains channelled within narrow heterosexual limits and other sexualities are repressed (Levy, 2005: ch.1).

Gender inequality in the social and economic spheres is both intrinsically important and significant because of the impact that it has on women's participation in politics and government. Marx wrote little on the oppression of women within capitalist society; this he left to his intellectual partner – Engels. In 'The origin of the family, private property and the state' Engels developed the first systematic Marxist account of women's oppression. There is a clear recognition of the existence of gender inequality existing within as well as between social classes. Even in the case of working-class families, 'he is the bourgeois; she is the proletariat' (Engels, 1968: 501). But perhaps the greatest strength of Engels's account is the attempt to draw upon the available anthropological and historical sources to trace the origins and development of women's oppression throughout history. This enables gender inequality within capitalist society to be contextualised appropriately, and its historical origins identified. Further, he fruitfully restated the materialist conception of history in a manner that enabled him to engage in systematic analysis of the relationship between class, gender and the state.

> According to the materialistic conception, the determining factor in history is, in the last resort, the production and reproduction of immediate life. However, this itself is of a twofold character. On the one hand, the production of the means of subsistence, of food, clothing and shelter and the tools requisite therefore; on the other, the production of human beings themselves, the propagation of the species. The social institutions under which men of a definite historical epoch and of a definite country live are conditioned by both kinds of production; by the stage of development of labour, on the one hand, and of the family, on the other.
>
> (Engels, 1968: 449)

This was written in 1884. Since then classical Marxists, feminists and contemporary Marxists have developed a vastly enriched understanding of the historical origins of women's oppression, the profound transformation of gender relations involved in the transition from feudalism to capitalism, and the underlying causes of gender inequality within capitalist society. Clearly it is not possible to review these bodies of literature here, but let me make a few brief observations about the transformation of gender relations involved in the transition from feudalism to capitalism and the underlying social structural causes of gender inequality within capitalist society.

Gender and class relations have been profoundly intertwined throughout history. In feudalism this is clear in every area of society. Two examples include the use of patrilineal descent, and hence systematic control of women's sexual activity through the institution of monogamous marriage, to determine the intergenerational distribution of property through inheritance within the nobility, and the sexual division of labour that prevailed in the productive activity of the subordinate classes (serfs, peasants, artisans). Gender relations were transformed in the transition from feudalism to capitalism because *inter alia* productive labour became spatially and temporally separated from reproductive labour, and as part of this process the family-household ceased to be a primary site of both productive labour (as was the case with the peasant household) and productive labour (Seccombe, 1992). In short, 'work' and home became divided.

The nature of women's oppression altered fundamentally with the emergence of capitalism. Brenner (2000) provides the best historical account of this. The social relations governing the process of reproduction established an unequal division of labour between women and men within the family-household. Women bear the primary responsibility for the labour necessary to reproduce labour-power as a commodity. The advent and persistence of this unequal gender division of labour cannot be explained exclusively in terms of its functionality for capital because, while undoubtedly it is in the interests of capital to have labour-power reproduced cheaply by unpaid labour within the working class family-household, there is nothing in the economic logic of capital per se which can explain why it is specifically *women* who perform this labour. The social allocation of women to this role can only be explained adequately by reference to the 'production and reproduction of immediate life' understood, not as biological reproduction, but as an inescapably and pervasively *social* process. In short, the underlying causes of gender inequality in capitalist society are located within a system of production governed by historically specific relations of production and reproduction.

The social relations that govern human reproduction, a process encompassing sexuality, fertility, pregnancy, birth and childcare, are configured in a manner that assigns the primary responsibility for the bearing and rearing of children to women. This is crucially important because the primary involvement of women in bearing and rearing children is the major determinant of the unequal division of labour within the family-household. The primary and unequal involvement of women in childcare and domestic labour, given the inadequate provision of childcare facilities and paid parental leave, is also a major determinant of the gender differentiation of social production in general, and female participation in paid employment in particular.

Once established, gender inequality in the closely related spheres of the family-household and paid employment becomes mutually reinforcing because decisions about which partner is to sacrifice their career in order to bring up the children are influenced by the relative income levels of male and female partners. In view of the fact that men are likely to be earning a higher income than their partner, often there is a powerful financial pressure on women who become mothers to either leave paid employment all together, or else move from full-time to part-time employment.[2] Once they do this, women with children become financially dependent on their male partners and often are subject to a lack of viable financial alternatives if the relationship starts to become unhealthy. Compared with women who are living with heterosexual or lesbian partners, women who are sole parents find that their capacity to participate in paid employment is even more tightly circumscribed by their parental responsibilities.

In sum, the differences in women and men's participation in paid employment are a key determinant of gender income inequality because these differences mean that it is more likely that women will withdraw completely from paid employment, or will shift from full to part-time employment, in order to care for children. Women are also more likely to interrupt their career paths, meaning that they are less likely than their male counterparts to be promoted. In turn, the fact that women bear an unequal share of the burden of childcare and domestic labour, generally earn less money and possess less wealth, is a key determinant of other related patterns of gender inequality in the wider society, such as women's over-representation amongst welfare beneficiaries and under-representation in the political sphere.

In capitalist society gender is not the only axis of oppression. Ethnicity, sexual orientation, disability, religious belief and age are also the bases for highly significant forms of inequality and oppression. Unfortunately the need for brevity means that these forms of inequality cannot be discussed here. It is important to note, however, that the Marxist tradition has produced a particularly rich set of accounts of the emergence and persistence of ethnic inequality and racism focusing on eighteenth and nineteenth-century slavery

---

2 The propensity for women to withdraw from paid employment when they have children is not biologically determined. It is due to the social, economic and political
   organisation of childcare and domestic labour in our society. This systematically
   discourages men from sharing equally in childcare and, given that the supply of
   affordable high-quality childcare is extremely limited, and largely unsupported
   financially by employers and the state, simultaneously discourages women from
   participating in full-time paid employment. This is clear from the age variations of
   female participation in paid employment, and explains why gender income inequality starts to increase dramatically from the mid-twenties onwards in the advanced
   capitalist societies.

(Blackburn, 1988, 1997), white settler colonialism (Poata-Smith, 1997; Roper, 2005: 56–68; Steven, 1989; McMichael, 1984), ethnic patterns and consequences of labour migration (Callinicos, 1993a: 16–39; Loomis, 1990; Miles, 1984; Shelley, 2007), empirical patterns of ethnic inequality, and the overt racism of the far right (Renton, 1999).

Alienation

The relevance of Marx's conception of alienation to his critique of representative democracy and his conception of socialist democracy is often overlooked. Ollman (1976: 131) usefully refers to Marx's theory of alienation 'as a grand summing up' of his critique of class society in general and capitalist society in particular. Stripped of its Hegelian trappings, the core of the conception as Marx employs it is the notion that:

> Alienation is a historically created phenomenon. Its origin and continuing basis in civilized society arises from the alienation of labour that characterizes all systems of private property from slavery to capitalism. Alienation expresses the fact that the creations of [human] hands and minds turn against their creators and come to dominate their lives. Thus, instead of enlarging freedom, these uncontrollable powers increase human servitude and strip [humans] of the capacities for self-determination and self-direction which have raised them above the animals.
>
> (Mandel and Novack, 1973: 7)

At the absolute heart of Marx's general critique of capitalism is the notion that alienation is an inevitable effect of capitalist social relations because these relations systematically deprive the majority of access to the means of production (and hence subsistence) and subject them to domination from above, not just within the workplace, but also throughout society. Hence the struggle for working class self-emancipation and socialism is simultaneously a struggle to transcend alienation.

Let us explore this in a little more depth. First, as we have seen, it is only with the arrival of capitalism that the immediate producers become fully separated from the means of production. Hence they are subject to an ongoing socio-economic compulsion to sell their capacity to work for a specified period of time to a capitalist employer. Yet is vitally important to recognise that the selling of one's labour power involves far more than a mere economic transaction in the narrow sense of neoclassical economics. Mandel puts this eloquently:

> What does it mean to sell your labour power to a boss? In Marx's analysis, both in his youthful and his mature work, behind this purely formal and legal contractual relation – you sell your labour power, part of your time, to another for money to live on – is in reality something that has profound consequences for all human existence and particularly for the life of the

wage labourer. It first of all implies that you lose control over a large part of your waking hours. All the time which you have sold to the employer belongs to him [or her], not to you. You are not free to do what you want at work. It is the employer who dictates what you will and will not do during this whole time. He will dictate what you produce, how you produce, how you produce it, where you produce it.

(Mandel and Novack, 1973: 21)

Hence the selling of our capacity to work for a specified period of time has profound implications for our entire life experience. For those of us who are in full-time paid employment our experience of life is dominated, to a considerable extent, by the time we spend working under the authority of those above us in our workplace – whether that be in the public or private sector, in a factory or an office, a building site or a university, a supermarket or a hospital.

This is not the only form of alienation that we experience within our workplace – we also become alienated from the products of our labour. In an immediate economic sense they become the products of the employer. If we labour to assemble a car, we do not thereby become entitled to possess one of the many thousands of cars we may produce each year – we have to buy one. This stands in marked contrast to the situation prevailing in classical antiquity, European feudalism, as well as in the indigenous cultures of North America and Australasia, where the producers typically retained at least part of their product. Hence the complete alienation from the products of our labour that we take for granted is actually something that is specific to capitalism.

The clearest form of domination by the products of our labour is the domination of the labourer by the machine in industrial production. The machine is a remarkable product of human ingenuity which 'becomes a source of tyranny against the worker when the worker serves as an appendage of the machine and is forced to adapt the cadence of his life and work to the operation of the machine' (Mandel and Novack, 1973: 22). This can be illustrated from my own experience of working in an industrial plant – a frozen food factory. In this factory we collectively produced approximately 150 metric tonnes of frozen product per twelve-hour shift. For six years I worked in an area of the factory referred to as 'the tunnel'. This was the area where the frozen peas we were producing poured out of shoots from huge blast freezers. We were responsible to ensure that large bins that we continually assembled were placed under the shoots by forklift. If we failed to keep up with the line, then the peas would cascade down from an overflow shoot near the ceiling like a green waterfall. The entire rhythm of our work effort appeared to be (and in a certain sense actually was) set by this large and tremendously noisy industrial apparatus. This kind of experience is shared daily by millions of process workers in industrial plants around the world.

This points to another manifestation of alienation within the workplace – caused not only by being subject to managerial authority from above, but also by the often extreme degree of occupational specialisation generated by the extensive division of labour (across and within specific workplaces) that characterises advanced capitalism. Work is typically experienced as drudgery and boredom, as pressure and stress, rather than creative self-expression. While we are working it is not 'our time' and we cannot 'be ourselves'; we have to assume the role of the employee and perform our allocated tasks in a manner and a period of time dictated by the managers above us. We cannot develop our talents, in anything other than a narrow range of work-related skills, through education, artistic or musical practice, physical training, or work on our own projects.

Beyond the workplace, economic coordination and resource allocation are governed by market relations and market forces, rather than by conscious collective planning. Here Marx's broad theory of alienation is informed by his analysis of commodity fetishism. Capitalist production is generalised commodity production, and the ideological mystification of capitalist relations of production stems, in part, from its most elemental social form: the value of commodities. A commodity is, Marx suggests, a mysterious thing:

> simply because in it the social character of [women and] men's labour appears to them as an objective character stamped upon the product of that labour; because the relation of the producers to the sum total of their own labour is presented to them as a social relation, existing not between themselves, but between the products of their labour.
>
> (Marx, 1967a: 72)

This has the effect that 'the value-relation between the products of labour which stamps them as commodities ... is a definite social relation between [women and] men, that assumes, in their eyes, the fantastic form of a relation between things' (Marx, 1967a: 72). 'To the [producers], therefore, the relations connecting the labour of one individual with that of the rest appear, not as direct social relations between individuals at work, but what they really are, material relations between persons and social relations between things' (Marx, 1967a: 73).

Since 'things' as commodities exchanged on the market govern the working activity of persons engaged in the production process, the relations of producers to each other within the social division of labour takes the form, not of direct conscious social regulation, but of 'material relations between persons'. In more concrete terms, workers relate to each other within and between sectors of industry largely in terms of the immediate physical processes involved in production. There is no democratically centralised process involved through which the producers can consciously reach collective decisions about what to produce, how much to produce, where to produce, to whom the product should be distributed, and so forth. Instead, the allocation of labour-power in the economy is determined independently of conscious social regulation through exchange relations (so-called 'market forces').

Because the coordination and regulation of productive units takes place

234 THE HISTORY OF DEMOCRACY

through exchange relations on domestic and international markets, plant closures, retrenchment, rationalisation, pay-cuts and speed-ups, relocation of factories to countries with comparatively low real wage rates, and so forth, all appear to be determined, not by the capitalist imperative to maximise profits, but by 'blind market forces', which act with the inexorable necessity of laws of nature.

At the same time that social relations between producers are governed by the exchange of the products of their labour, the things that are exchanged between production units as well as those things employed directly in production acquire certain social characteristics, the most elemental of which is the exchange-value of the particular commodities involved. In this way, the division of labour is characterised by material relations between persons but the social coordination and allocation of labour-power within that division of labour only takes place through 'social relations between things', that is, via the exchange-value of commodities.

Returning to the general conception of alienation, market competition not only has the effect of ideologically disguising the real social determinants of economic phenomena like crises of overproduction and unemployment, it also divides individuals in an immediate and direct way– both within and between classes. In the working class, individuals are divided by the frequently intense struggle for jobs and publicly provided resources (for example, public housing and health). In the capitalist class, there is intense competition between firms, and for individual promotion within the firm. Antagonistic interests arising from their locations in the class structure generate distance, tension and conflict between individuals of different classes.

Commodity fetishism does not just affect workers – members of all classes experience their lives as being dominated by alien economic forces over which they have little control. Individual capitalists exercise effective control over the activities of their own firms, but do not, and cannot, exercise effective control over macroeconomic dynamics. Hence the business cycle and associated fluctuations on the markets for fictitious capital appear as essentially ungovernable and 'natural' features of 'the economy'.

Alienation pervades our experience, not just of paid work, but the other areas of our lives as well. As consumers we are bombarded with multimedia propaganda in order to cultivate an insatiable desire to purchase ever more commodities – clothes, food, houses, household appliances, cars, travel, sports equipment, luxury items: the list goes on. Enough is never enough, and the quality could always be better. Each model of car, TV, DVD player, computer, cell phone, iPod and so forth is better than the model before. Whatever combination of these things that we come to possess, we are constantly encouraged to be dissatisfied with them, so that we might buy more and better.

As part of this process, 'our time' – that is our leisure time – becomes increasingly commodified as capitalism develops. To entertain ourselves we purchase audiovisual equipment, sports equipment, luxury food items, drugs, concert tickets and so forth. We go on holiday and spend money on travel, accommodation and entertainment. Almost every aspect of sexuality, including sexual intimacy, can and often does become commodified. Major industries provide cosmetics, cosmetic surgery, hairdressing, contraceptives, erotic lingerie, sexual aids, romantic novels, filmic love stories, women's magazines, as well as the sex industry itself – pornography, prostitution, strip shows and raunch culture. Organised sport is big business. We pay to see 'our' teams play – either through admission to the games themselves, or through subscriptions to pay TV. We buy sport magazines, T-shirts and jerseys, paraphernalia and other sundry items. We go to bars and cafes, pay for entertainment, and buy alcohol, coffee, food and so forth. But we have no control, as consumers, over the provision of services and commodities in these areas. The supporters of sports teams generally have no real influence over the major decisions made by the club administration, regular patrons in bars and cafes have little say over their organisation or management, and we have virtually no influence over television and radio programming, film production or the music industry.

One of the most elementary and important aspects of human existence, at all times and in all cultures, is communication between individuals. But in capitalist society all of the major forms of communication are provided and controlled by large corporations and/or governments: telecommunications, mail, electronic and printed media, computers, email and the internet, film, music, advertising, book publishing and so forth. So we are alienated from exercising effective control over the major means, apart from direct face-to-face speech, by which we communicate with each other. And our use of the major forms of communication that are available to us nearly always is dependent on our ability to pay.

Although of declining significance in many capitalist societies, religion is another manifestation of alienation:

Alienation is a condition in which human creations escape conscious control and instead become forces which govern their creators. ... The clearest example is furnished by religious institutions. God is a human creation and has no other basis for existence than in the imagination of the devout. Nevertheless, once created, His dictates actually govern the activity of His creators and operate as an alien force independent of them.

(Howard and King, 1985: 18)

The central promise of most major religions – a better life after the misery of this one – is itself a sad commentary on the extent of alienation in all class societies, including our own. While the significance of religion may be declining due to increasing secularisation in many capitalist countries, arguably other social institutions (organised sport) and ideologies (nationalism) have ended up performing similar functions.

From this summary, it should be clear that Marx's theory of alienation is a highly inclusive one. In capitalist society every individual experiences it

– capitalist and worker, woman and man, black and white, young and old. Finally, and this brings us to the subject of the next section, the experience of alienation extends to politics and the state. Workers and the oppressed feel systematically alienated from the governance of society. We shall now see why Marx held that this specific form of alienation was a necessary characteristic of the representative form of democracy.

THE DEMOCRATIC SWINDLE

Having identified the key elements of Marx's critique of capitalism we are now in a position to outline the central thrust of the Marxist critique of representative democracy. This critique focuses, as we have seen, both on the broad socio-economic context of modern representative democracy, and on the actual constitutional and institutional mechanisms of representative democracy. Liberals contend that institutional mechanisms and constitutional principles such as regular secret ballot elections, competition between factions, potential leaders and parties, a free press, and majority rule ensure that, for the first time in history, the majority of citizens can exert effective influence over the governance of society (see pages 204–6). Although acknowledging that the influence of the citizenry over government is greater in representative democracies than in modern fascist and/or authoritarian dictatorships, and constitutes a qualitative advance over the coercive exploitation of serfs and peasants by the absolutist state of the late feudal era, Marxists argue that the amount of substantive influence that citizens can, in the normal course of events, exert over government in representative democracies is limited.

The social and economic context of representative democracy

At the centre of Marx's critique of representative democracy is his observation that 'the specific economic form, in which unpaid surplus-labour is pumped out of direct producers, determines the relationship of rulers and ruled' (1967b: 791). This is primarily because it is the process of exploitation that is at the heart of social structuration and profoundly shapes the polity. In particular, exploitation in class societies generates massive inequalities in the distribution of income and wealth. This is most pronounced in capitalism, where the irony is that an economic system that has a vastly superior capacity to generate surplus product over and above the subsistence needs of the direct producers (compared with all previous modes of production) appears to be non-exploitative. As we have already seen, this is because the relationship between capitalists and workers appears to be regulated by 'free and fair' market exchanges.

The existence of massive inequalities in the distribution of income and wealth, the persistence and trans-generational reproduction of these inequalities (*inter alia* through inheritance, elite schooling, 'old school tie' networks, familial patronage and so forth), and the heavy concentration of control over economic resource allocation, production and distribution in the hands of a relatively small minority of capitalists, combine to ensure that different categories of citizens have markedly unequal capacities to exert influence over government.

There is now a well-established literature highlighting the disproportionate influence that business can wield over government through funding well-resourced interest groups, making regular donations to the major parties, controlling all major non-state media, and 'bending' electoral constraints in a direction favourable to its interests (Lindblom, 1977: 170–90; Roper, 2006). The research underpinning this literature provides considerable empirical support for central elements of Marx's critique of representative democracy.[3] But it has also tended to gloss over what is really distinctive about the Marxist critique. Exploitation is at the heart of the complex historical process through which the major social classes form within the totality of capitalist society. In particular, the capitalist class, which composes a small minority of the citizenry, and the working class, which constitutes a large majority, are conjoined in relations of exploitation, and these relations of exploitation not only give rise to inequalities of income and wealth, but also generate distinctive and antagonistic sets of class interests. Most of the major 'interest groups' evident in the capitalist societies can be conceptualised as political and organisational crystallisations of class interests. Further, the relations of exploitation or production entail a social structural relationship of domination and subordination, and generate distinctive logics of collective action (Offe, 1985: ch.7).

The theory of surplus-value provides a rigorous analytical foundation both for the critique of representative democracy and for explaining the evident unequal capacities of different categories of citizen to exert effective influence over the governance of society. For it is the process of exploitation that ensures business groups are better resourced than, for example, trade unions, women's groups and environmentalists. Exploitation creates and perpetuates major disparities of socio-economic status across the citizenry. Class struggle, capitalist control of the media, and business influence over the major political parties are further illustrations of the political ramifications of the underlying process of exploitation.

Liberal democratic states are profoundly influenced by changing economic conditions, being subject to economic pressures that vary widely according to whether capitalism is booming or stuck in the mire of stagnation associated with a prolonged crisis phase of capitalist development. When capitalism is in the midst of a strong growth phase, governments can make concessions to the working class, hence strengthening the apparent neutrality of the so-called 'liberal democratic state' with respect to social conflict. The opposite is the

3 This has led McLennan (1989) and others to suggest that a convergence has taken place between Marxists and neopluralists. While there is an element of truth in this claim, the degree of convergence has been overstated, in no small part because of the failure to recognise the centrality of Marx's theory of exploitation to his critique of representative democracy.

case during prolonged economic crises when the pro-business bias of the state becomes more evident.

The final point to emphasise here is the inherently and necessarily undemocratic nature of capitalist relations of production. The generalised commodification of labour power disguises the authoritarian nature of social relations in the sphere of production (workplaces are generally organised hierarchically and undemocratically), and also the undemocratic nature of resource allocation by market mechanisms. In other words, the relations of production that are constitutive of the capitalist mode of production are necessarily undemocratic precisely because they rest on the systematic exclusion of the immediate producers from exercising effective control over the means of production, labour-power and resource allocation.

In sum, the global social and economic context in which liberal democratic states operate is characterised by exploitation, inequality, alienation, oppression, recurrent crises, violence and war, mass starvation in the so-called third world, and environmental destruction. The exploited and oppressed (who form the overwhelming majority of citizens) are excluded from directly participating in processes of governance, and furthermore have little indirect influence over government. The democratic citizenship associated with capitalism not only alienates power from citizens and concentrates it in the hands of their representatives, it also 'leaves untouched the whole new sphere of domination and coercion created by capitalism, its relocation of substantial powers from the state to civil society, to private property and the compulsions of the market' (Wood, 1995: 234). Representative democracy, even in its most fully developed form, leaves untouched vast areas of our daily lives – in the workplace, in the distribution of labour and resources – that are not subject to democratic accountability, but are governed by the powers of property, 'market forces' and the exigencies of profit maximisation.

The institutional mechanisms of representative democracy

As Draper (1977: 306) demonstrates, Marx criticises representative democracy as constituting a 'democratic swindle' not because it is democratic but, on the contrary, because it utilises democratic institutional forms to frustrate genuine popular control over the state from below. Thus representative democracy constitutes a swindle not because it is undemocratic, but because this specific form of democracy is inherently limited: it systematically and necessarily excludes the majority of labouring citizens from exerting effective control over their workplaces, resource allocation, social institutions and the state. Representative democracy is also a swindle because ideologically it creates and sustains the illusion of popular sovereignty and influence, while actually acting to undermine and limit the latter.

But even purely in terms of its constitutional principles, key institutional mechanisms and operating procedures, representative democracy is an extremely limited and restrictive form of democracy. Elections are, according to liberals, the linchpin of representative democracy since they help to maintain the ongoing accountability of government to the citizenry. Yet they are clearly defective mechanisms in this regard. Parliamentary elections are held infrequently, and most parliamentary terms range from three to five years. The degree of real choice offered to voters is limited because the social structural constraints described above operate to ensure that all major parliamentary parties remain committed to the social and economic arrangements of capitalism. There is no right of recall built into the system: once elected, representatives can completely disregard the wishes of their constituencies with no fear of being withdrawn from office and replaced. The process of secret ballot voting itself tends to atomise the electorate. Voters spend five minutes once every three, four or five years filling out a ballot paper in the seclusion of a private booth and then deposit the ballot paper in a box.

Not only is the effectiveness of the electoral constraint on government extremely limited, in the institutional ensemble of the state itself, power is heavily concentrated in the executive. In reality, the constitutional separation of powers in liberal democratic states does not effectively constrain the power of the executive. It is presidents, prime ministers and cabinets that actually rule liberal democratic states, not representative assemblies. These assemblies are not, as is well known, in any way accurately representative in their composition of the wider citizenry that elects them; they are disproportionately composed of wealthy white men.

With respect to equality before the law and civil liberties, in reality the wealthy are most able to use the judiciary to seek protection from arbitrary and unfair treatment by the state. Further, members of the capitalist class, and the middle classes, are better placed to utilise their citizenship rights to exert influence over the political sphere. Rupert Murdoch has a vastly superior capacity to utilise the right of free speech and the principle of a free press to communicate his views to the citizenry and to government, than a waged worker, welfare beneficiary, anti-racist activist or feminist.

The formation and implementation of policy by liberal democratic states is controlled by the executive in conjunction with the upper echelons of the state bureaucracy. High-ranking bureaucrats, most of whom share the same privileged backgrounds and educational training as those in business, are not elected and are not subject to effective democratic accountability to the citizenry.

CONCLUSION: EXPLOITATION, ALIENATION AND DEMOCRACY

In sum, Marx established a central theme of socialist (and much feminist and anarchist) criticism of liberal democracy: capitalism limits and undermines democracy of anything more than a highly indirect, tightly circumscribed and elitist form. The major contrast between Marxism and liberalism concerns the positive and negative view that each tradition holds of the relationship between capitalism and democracy. Liberals consider that capitalism underpins and buttresses representative democracy, while Marxists argue that it imposes strict limits on democratisation.

The central thrust of the Marxist critique of liberal principles of representation is that they are far too limited: direct participation is preferable to indirect representation; power should remain with, rather than being alienated from, labouring citizens; elections should be held frequently and the right of recall instituted at all levels; the standing police and army should be disbanded and replaced by a popular militia; representatives should be paid no more and enjoy privileges no greater than those enjoyed by the average worker; the freedom of the press should be extended by making the media much more accessible to, and democratically controlled by, the majority of citizens, and so forth. Perhaps the only liberal democratic citizenship right that would be rescinded, rather than transcended, would be the right to own private property, a right that is in reality a right to own and control an unequal share of property and productive resources.

As this implies, socialist participatory democracy centrally involves extending democracy from the political to the social and economic spheres through giving labouring citizens effective democratic and collective control over the means of production, resource allocation, workplaces, social institutions and all major state institutions. This kind of socialist participatory democracy is central to the classical Marxist vision of working class self-emancipation. In the final chapter we consider the two most significant attempts in history to establish this form of democracy, the Paris Commune of 1871 and the Russian revolutions of 1905 and 1917.

GUIDE TO FURTHER READING

The best general critique of capitalism and representative democracy in the Marxist tradition that I have read in recent years is McNally (2006). Also very useful in this regard are Callinicos (2003a), D'Amato (2006) and Harman (2007). Wood (1995: 181–237) provides an outstanding Marxist critique of representative democracy. Miliband (1969) is a modern classic, and despite the factual information being somewhat dated, is still well worth reading (see also Miliband, 1994: 7–42). He also provides a useful book-length introduction to the Marxist critique of capitalism and representative democracy (Miliband, 1977), as does Moore (1957). For a chapter-length introduction see Callinicos (1984). The best comprehensive accounts of Marx and Engels's critique of capitalism and representative democracy are Draper (1977) and Nimtz (2000). Although the bulk of Marx and Engels's writings are relevant to the themes of this chapter, the following sources are particularly important: Marx and Engels (1998), Marx (1978), Marx (1967a) and Marx (1974a). The global justice and Occupy movements have adopted, developed and applied many of the central elements of the Marxist critique of capitalism and representative democracy (Bircham and Charlton, 2001; Roper, 2004; Saad-Filho, 2003; Saad-Filho and Johnston, 2005; Singsen, 2012; Trudell, 2012).

10

Precursors of socialist participatory democracy: the Paris Commune of 1871 and Russian Revolutions of 1905 and 1917

INTRODUCTION

Three distinctive forms of democracy have emerged thus far in history: Athenian democracy, liberal representative democracy and socialist participatory democracy. This book has focused in the main on Athenian democracy and representative democracy. Accordingly Chapters 3 to 7 focused on the transition from feudalism to capitalism, the historical emergence of representative democracy through the English, American, French and 1848–9 revolutions, and the global spread of this form of democracy during the past century.

As discussed in the previous chapter, Marx and Engels provide a systematic critique of capitalism and representative democracy. From this critique, Marx and Engels derived an analysis of why, how and by whom capitalist society could be changed, and argued for a democratic and socialist alternative to it. In this chapter I explore this set of issues through a consideration of the most important attempts thus far in history to create political forms of working-class self-emancipation – the Paris Commune of 1871 and the Russian revolutions of 1905 and 1917. The aim is to show how the classical Marxist conception of socialist participatory democracy emerged in the context of, and was developed in relation to, these revolutionary struggles of the working class.

Marx's advocacy of socialist participatory democracy and communism as an alternative to capitalism was based on an analysis of all of the fundamental contradictions of the capitalist mode of production which we considered in the previous chapter: the antagonism between bourgeoisie and proletariat generated by exploitation, the contradiction between the increasing socialisation of production and privatisation of appropriation, the frenzied chaos of recurrent capitalist crises generated by the underlying tendency for the rate of profit to fall, and the profound alienation experienced by everyone inhabiting a capitalist society. But it is not just that capitalism tends towards increasingly intractable economic crises and intense class struggles; it also produces the principal collective agent of its transformation, and lays the economic foundations for a qualitatively superior form of society. For Marx it is capitalism that makes the socialist transformation of society 'both historically possible, and historically necessary' (Callinicos, 1995: 160).

In order to be clear about what Marx and Engels did, and did not, say about working class self-emancipation it is vitally important to recognise that the *Communist Manifesto* provides only a partial and incomplete guide to their mature view of proletarian social revolution and 'the political form of working class emancipation'. The revolutions of 1848–9 broke out in the weeks following the publication in February of the *Manifesto*. As leading protagonists on the left of the democratic movement in Germany, where Marx became the editor of the *Neue Rheinische Zeitung*, Marx and Engels further developed their ideas concerning the role of the proletariat in the struggle against absolutism and for representative democracy, concluding that 'the liberal bourgeoisie in Germany was incapable of leading the charge for bourgeois democracy and that only an alliance of workers and peasants would ensure the institution of democratic rule' (Nimtz, 2000: 111; Marx, 1973c).

Furthermore, it was the workers of Paris who, through their own efforts, invented key institutional mechanisms of a radically democratic workers' state in the concrete form of the Commune of 1871. It was only by reflecting on the world historic achievement of the Parisian proletariat that Marx could fully develop his mature view of socialist democracy and articulate it clearly in *The Civil War in France*.

The institutional embodiment of democracy in the Paris Commune was the municipal assembly. Although this assembly constituted an historic advance over parliamentary forms of democracy (see pages 243–52), it came to be overshadowed by the new form of working-class and peasant democracy that emerged in the Russian Revolution of 1905 – the workers' council or soviet. In August and September of 1917 Lenin drew upon the experience of the soviets and Marx's analysis of the Paris Commune in order to write *State and Revolution*. In this work Lenin (1980a: 324) argues that the establishment of socialism involves 'an immense expansion of democracy, which *for the first time* becomes democracy for the poor, democracy for the people, and not democracy for the money-bags'. In a similar vein, he emphasises that 'democracy is of enormous importance to the working class in its struggle against the capitalists for its emancipation' and 'the way out of parliamentarism is not, of course, the abolition of representative institutions and the elective principle, but the conversion of the representative institutions from talking shops into "working" bodies' (Lenin, 1980a: 332, 294).

The section starting on page 252 focuses on the positive achievements of the Russian workers and peasants in creating a participatory form of democracy that, albeit for a tragically brief period, allowed the labouring masses to exert a greater degree of influence over the governance of society than at any other time since the Athenian democracy.

The brief achievement of democratic working-class self-rule in Russia remains a key touchstone highlighting fundamental ideological differences between conservative, liberal and social democratic defenders of capitalism from its revolutionary opponents. But although the Russian Revolution of 1917–18 constitutes a high point in the struggle for working-class self-emancipation, the Stalinist degeneration of the revolution during the 1920s and 1930s without doubt constitutes a low point, rivalled only by the defeat of the workers' movement by the Nazis in Germany. On pages 252–69 I outline very briefly why the revolution failed, and I argue against the view that this constitutes the definitive failure of any realistically possible attempt to overthrow capitalism and create a democratic socialist alternative.

THE PARIS COMMUNE 1871

The Paris Commune lasted 72 days from March 18 to May 28, 1871. It was 'the biggest urban insurrection of the nineteenth century, an anticipation of the revolutions that were to follow' (Edwards, 1971: 9). Most importantly, it was the first revolutionary upheaval in history in which the working class played a central role throughout. This led *The Times* on March 29 to describe the revolution as 'the predominance of the Proletariat over the wealthy-classes, of the working man over the master, of Labour over Capital' (quoted in Edwards, 1971: 39). Not surprisingly, the Paris Commune had a decisive impact on Marx's and Engels's ideas concerning the political form of working-class self-emancipation. It also had a profound impact on the subsequent development of the classical Marxist tradition, especially in Russia, where it remained a key reference point in the thinking and debates of the socialist movement. As Hobsbawm (1975: 200) observes, 'the Paris Commune was ... important not so much for what it achieved as for what it forecast; it was more formidable as a symbol than as a fact.'

In France the monarchy was overthrown and a republic declared on February 24, 1848. Louis-Napoleon Bonaparte (1808–1873) was elected president of the Second Republic in December 1848, took power in a coup d'état in 1851, and assumed the title 'Emperor Napoleon III' in 1852. He then ruled as a conservative but populist dictator for 18 years. This is referred to as the Second Empire. Becoming increasingly unpopular, he played the 'war card' against Prussia in July 1870. A series of defeats during August culminated during the first days of September in a catastrophic defeat at Sedan, where Napoleon and the French army led by General MacMahon were captured. In response:

> The republican deputies for Paris, elected in 1869, then went to the Hotel de Ville, symbol of popular Parisian power ... they proclaimed a republic [on September 4 1870] and installed themselves as the Government of National Defence, acting deliberately to forestall the possibility that the revolutionary Left might try to seize power.
>
> (Toombs, 1999: 43)

The Prussian army continued to advance towards Paris, laying siege to the city from September 18 onwards. The remaining French army led by Bazaine became besieged at Metz and surrendered on October 27.[1]

Popular unrest in Paris grew rapidly because of severe material hardship and food shortages, general economic crisis, rising unemployment and the half-hearted prosecution of the war by the government. It became increasingly clear to the Parisian masses that the government was more concerned to avert revolutionary challenges to the prevailing order than it was to defend France against the reactionary Prussians. On October 31, in response to news of the surrender at Metz, the government was nearly overthrown as insurgent National Guards led by revolutionaries such as Flourens, Blanqui and Delescluze stormed into the Hotel de Ville where it was meeting. Although the government successfully defused this near-insurrection, the city remained in a state of seething unrest. A January 22 demonstration against the government outside the Hotel de Ville had to be dispersed by gunfire, killing five and leaving 18 wounded. The government's signing of an armistice with the Prussians on January 28 further outraged the Parisian masses.

An election of a new National Assembly was staged to endorse the armistice and sanction the Third Republic (a peace treaty was signed with the German government on February 28). As Edwards observes:

the composition of the new assembly … gravely aggravated the situation. The monarchist majority of the Assembly, elected by rural France against the republican aspirations of the big cities, only further alienated the capital with open talk of restoring the monarchy and of removing the seat of government from Paris.

(Edwards, 1973a: 18)

On March 1, Parisians who had endured the privations caused by the siege sullenly watched the Prussian army stage a victory parade through the city. Then on March 11 and 12 the National Assembly passed four bills that Parisians dubbed 'measures against Paris' (Sowerwine, 2001: 17). As well as moving the seat of government to Versailles, these measures demobilised the National Guard, ending the small daily payment on which guardsmen and their families depended for survival in the context of the economic dislocation and mass unemployment caused by the Prussian siege of the city; made overdue rent and bills repayable with interest; and lifted the moratorium on the sale of goods at pawnshops. These measures impacted negatively on all but the very rich, and created a potentially explosive political mood amongst the Parisian working masses.

Adolphe Thiers led the national government. He had played a leading role in the violent and bloody suppression of the workers' uprising in June 1848 and

---

1 According to Horne (1965: 106) the surrender occurred on October 29, but most sources date the surrender on October 27 (Edwards, 1971: 373; Sowerwine, 2001: 14; Williams, 1969: 96).

was elitist, ruthless and right-wing. He referred to the Parisian masses as 'the vile multitude' and stated, 'businessmen were going around repeating constantly that financial operations would never be started up again until all those wretches were finished off and their cannons taken away. An end had to be put to all that, and then one could get back to business' (Edwards, 1973a: 25).

Disarming the Parisian masses was easier said than done. On September 6 the new government under popular pressure authorised the expansion of the Paris National Guard. Proletarian and lower-middle-class men joined en masse: 'Within a week, 78 new battalions had been formed, 194 by the end of the month .... The Paris National Guard thus became a popular army ... of over 340,000 men, with 280,000 rifles, many of them modern breech-loaders, and eventually with artillery too, partly paid for by public donations' (Toombs, 1999: 45–6). The National Guard was about to become, as Marx aptly described it, 'the revolution armed' (1974b: 188). The now fully armed Parisian masses were not going to take kindly to being forcibly disarmed by the government. As Edwards puts it:

The Government's attempt to capture the National Guard's guns early on the morning of Saturday, 18 March 1871, sparked off the revolution. The plan was to occupy strategic points throughout the city, capture the guns, and arrest known revolutionaries. Thiers himself and some of his ministers went to Paris to supervise the operation. At first, Paris being asleep, all went well. But soon crowds began to collect, jeering at the soldiers, the women particularly remonstrating with hungry soldiers even while offering them food. The National Guard began to turn out, though surely not in support of the Government. The regular troops, still waiting for transport to arrive to cart away the guns, began to find themselves isolated. Events first took a serious turn at Montmartre, when the troops refused to fire on the crowd and instead arrested their own commander, who was later shot. Elsewhere throughout the city officers found they could no longer rely on their men, and in the early afternoon Theirs decided to abandon the capital. Jumping into a waiting coach he scribbled an order for the complete evacuation of the army to Versailles, and summoned the rest of his ministers to follow him.

By 11 pm that night the Central Committee of the National Guard finally mustered up enough members and enough courage to take over the abandoned Hotel de Ville, while other National Guard commanders and men occupied the remaining public buildings in the capital. This revolution was a spontaneous uprising throughout the city, there having been no central direction by any of the various National Guard committees.

(Edwards, 1973a: 26–7)

The Central Committee of the National Guard then assumed power until the Commune was formed through a municipal election held on Sunday March 26.

246 THE HISTORY OF DEMOCRACY

At this election, 227,000 votes elected 81 delegates from the 20 *arrondissements* (geographical sectors) of Paris. These delegates were relatively young, with average age of 38. Approximately 35 members were from the manual working class; the rest were predominantly middle class. About 40 had experience in the French labour movement. 'The results showed an overwhelming swing to the Left, only about fifteen to twenty moderate republicans being elected, and they soon resigned. The most solidly working-class *arrondissements* were the most strongly pro-Communard' (Edwards, 1973a: 26).

The Commune held 57 sessions. It was headed by a seven-person Executive Commission in order to 'execute decrees and orders', and:

it also set up nine commissions to preside over administration: War; Finance; Public Services (including post, telegraph, roads, public assistance etc.); Supply; General Security (police); Justice; Education; Labour, Industry and Exchange (which was to consider social and Economic reform); and External Relations (to deal with the Prussians, other foreign powers, and the rest of France).

(Toombs, 1999: 80-1)

It is important to note that 'those elected to represent the people [in the Commune] were to act as delegates, not as parliamentary members', they were subject to recall by the constituencies that elected them, and they were expected to 'report back and remain in constant touch with sources of popular sovereignty' (Edwards, 1973a: 31). In this regard, the delegates acted simultaneously as delegates to the Commune from the *arrondissements*, and as mayors in the *arrondissements* with responsibilities for local administration. They were paid no more than the average working person's wage.[2]

Public participation in politics was facilitated by the numerous clubs in which there was wide-ranging political discussion of the issues of the day, by the reorganisation of the National Guard into geographical sections corresponding to the *arrondissements* and the continuing democratic organisation of the National Guard itself, and by the many newspapers that allowed all of the major shades of opinion within the Commune to be freely expressed (Gluckstein, 2006: 14–31, 112–16).

As Edwards (1971: 277) observes, 'The Commune was indeed a "festival of the oppressed", as Lenin once described it, in which the whole city became a public forum of political discussion and action. However short its duration, the Commune lasted long enough to show the possibility of new forms of association.' The clubs were particularly important in this regard, since they facilitated the participation of workers, the petit bourgeoisie and women in political discussion and debate, and provided an avenue through which their

2 Toombs (1999: 85–6) claims that in fact they were paid approximately four times the average wage, but this still effectively represents the abolition of high official salaries (cf., Gluckstein, 2006: 21).

views could be communicated to the Commune. A federation of clubs was proposed in late April, and the central committee of this federation met for the first time on May 5. Thereafter this committee met daily, and moved to the Public Assistance building close to the Hotel de Ville where the Commune met. The committee of this federation aimed to 'maintain daily communication with the Commune in order that it may transmit daily news of activity and military events to us for distribution to the clubs by their respective delegates' and also to 'discuss proposals made among ourselves and forward these on to the Commune' (Edwards, 1971: 281). A speaker at the club in the church of Saint-Eloi declared, 'We are going to found a new society, a truly social and democratic society, where there will never be poor nor rich, since the rich, should there be any, will be forced to give up their goods to the poor' (Edwards, 1971: 287–8).

In principle all leading public administrators were to be elected, although in practice there often was not time to do this. Instead they were authorised by the Commune to oversee and direct city administrations such as posts and telegraphs, roads, museums, libraries, hospitals, public assistance and the state tobacco monopoly. The hated Prefecture of Police was abolished and units of the National Guard conducted routine policing in the localities in which they were based.

The Commune delegated Leo Frankel to lead the Commission of Labour and Exchange. According to Frankel, 'the Revolution of 18 March was accomplished solely by the working-class. If we do nothing to assist this class, we who believe in social equality, I can see no reason for the Commune's existence' (Edwards, 1973a: 35). In fact, the social measures introduced by the Commune were moderate, incomplete and largely anticipatory, even when viewed as a programme of social reform rather than as a programme of revolutionary social transformation. It was particularly conservative in financial matters, much to the consternation of Marx, leaving the Bank of France largely untouched on the proviso that it would advance the funds needed by the Commune to pay the National Guard and maintain public services. Arrears in rents that most working and middle-class Parisians had incurred during the Prussian siege were cancelled. After heated debate, a three-year delay in the payment of bills was decreed, but debtors remained liable to pay these debts after this delay. One of the major avenues of credit for the working and middle classes of Paris was the state-owned pawnshop, the Mont-de-Pieté. During the siege many had been forced to pawn their trade tools and household items in order to survive. The terms disadvantaged the poor because the rate of interest was higher for small loans than for large loans. Rather than abolishing the institution altogether and replacing it with a Workers Bank, as advocated by Frankel and the Commission of Labour and Exchange, 'it granted the free restitution of household articles and work tools up to the value of twenty francs' (Edwards, 1971: 256).

The Commune did not promote generalised cooperative production in the form of the 'socialisation of the means of production, distribution and exchange'. But it did encourage workers to take over and run those factories that had been abandoned by their bourgeois owners. For example, an April 16 decree entitled the trade unions to take over abandoned workshops and form cooperative associations to run them. By May 14, 43 producers' cooperatives had been formed among the many craft industries of the city.

In the area of education, the Commune took steps to eliminate the church's involvement, address the problem of widespread illiteracy amongst the working class and promote an 'integral' form of education that combined practical trades-related training with academic learning. It also paid particular attention to the education of women, which had hitherto been largely restricted to teaching by poorly trained nuns in church schools. In contrast, 'during the Commune the prevailing view was … in favour of public education for both sexes' (Edwards, 1971: 272). As the popular newspaper *Le Pere Duchêne* put it, 'In a good Republic we have to take even more care of girls' education that of boys'! Because you know, patriots, that it's on a citizeness's knee … that we put together our first ideas' (cited by Sowerwine, 2001: 23; the full text is in Edwards, 1973b: 116–17).

As well as attempting to make public education freely accessible to women, 'day nurseries, to be situated near the factories, were also proposed as a means to help working women', and a pension of 600 francs was introduced to be paid to partners (married or not) and children (legitimate or not) of members of the National Guard who had died in battle (Edwards, 1971: 272–3; 1973b: 117–20). In part, these measures reflected the central role that women played in the Commune, whether as political leaders (Mink, Leo, Dmitrieff, Michel), participants in the various political clubs and the Women's Union for the Defence of Paris and for Aid to the Wounded, or increasingly as soldiers in the National Guard. Of course, to this should be added the labour of women in caring for children, the sick and wounded, and in the productive industries that were vital to the survival of Paris.

Despite the sound of gunfire that could be heard for much of the duration of the Commune, and the deprivations caused by the second successive siege of the city, a celebratory and festive atmosphere prevailed in working-class *arrondissements*. Although theatre and opera changed little, many public concerts were staged, and the painter Courbet formed a pro-Communard federation of artists. 'This festivity, this gayness of the capital in the revolution and despite the siege, was typified by the concerts given in the Tuileries Palace' (Edwards, 1971: 308). Tragically, one of the largest of these concerts, with an audience of over 6,000, was conducted on May 21 at the same time as the government's troops stormed into the city to violently suppress the Commune.

The most important issue for the Commune, on which its very survival depended, was the conduct of the civil war against the National Government at Versailles. The National Government's army, with the tacit support of the Prussians who still surrounded over half of the perimeter of the city to the north and east, began its assault on May 1, by artillery bombardment of the city's outer fortifications and gradually advancing its trenches closer to these fortifications (Horne, 1965: 357). Unfortunately, the Commune was at its weakest in undertaking its most important task – organising and directing the military defence of the city. The National Guard, although nominally a formidable military force, in reality was a poorly organised volunteer army with no effective centralised direction. The Central Committee of the National Guard, rather than the Commune, formally retained the power to direct the various units of the Guard, but in reality these units remained largely autonomous of each other. Officers were elected locally and their first loyalty was to the members of the unit who had elected them. Orders were debated and adhered to only if a majority in the unit concerned agreed with them. Artillery, despite its vital strategic significance for the defence of the city as a whole, remained under the control of the local unit of the Guard rather than the Central Committee (this ultimately resulted in a large number of cannon being captured by the enemy without even being used in the defence of the city). Further, despite its huge nominal size, by May 21 the National Guard constituted an effective fighting force of around 30,000. This diminished force was up against Thiers' army of 130,000 troops (which had been greatly bolstered by the Prussian decision to release over 100,000 prisoners of war to assist in the suppression of the Commune). In response to news that government troops had invaded the city, Delescluze issued an inspiring exhortation to 'the people and the National Guard' to take up arms in defence of the city:

> Citizens, enough of Militarism, no more staff-officers with their gold-embroidered uniforms! Make way for the people, the combatants, the bare arms! The hour of revolutionary war has struck. The people know nothing of planned manoeuvres, but when they have a rifle in their hand, cobblestones under their feet, they do not fear all the strategists of the monarchist school. To arms! Citizens, to arms!
>
> (Edwards, 1971: 311–12)

Thus began the 'week of blood'. The government troops entered the bourgeois districts of Auteuil and Passy in the south-west of Paris and then pushed eastwards towards the working-class districts of Montmartre, La Villette, Belleville, Roquette and Bercy. Resistance became increasingly staunch and courageous as it become clear to the Communards that the government troops were intent, not merely on recapturing the city, but on exterminating all active supporters of the Commune (Horne, 1965: 408). Those who surrendered to the advancing forces were shot, women defenders of the Commune often being raped first. Despite the increasingly heroic resistance of the women, men and children in the working-class eastern quarters of Paris, the government army finally achieved victory on May 28.

The genocide of Communards continued in the days that followed. The Prussians colluded by refusing to allow Communards to escape through their lines. Estimates of the scale of the killing vary widely, but the most reliable suggest that somewhere between 20,000 and 37,000 were killed (Edwards,

1971: 346; Gluckstein, 2006: 177; Horne, 1965: 418; cf. Toombs, 1999: 180). In addition, at least 40,000 were arrested, possibly as many as 50,000, several died while awaiting trial, 23 were executed, and many were imprisoned and/or deporting to penal colonies (over 4,000 to New Caledonia) (Gluckstein, 2006: 177; Toombs, 1999: 181).

Classical Marxist interpretations of the Commune

The revolutionary uprising of workers and brief establishment of the Paris Commune in 1871 had a decisive impact on Marx's and Engels's ideas concerning the political form of working-class self-emancipation. They considered that the commune was:

> a thoroughly expansive political form, while all previous forms of government had been emphatically repressive. Its true secret was this. It was essentially a working-class government, the produce of the struggle of the producing against the appropriating class, the political form at last discovered under which to work out the economic emancipation of labour.
>
> (Marx, 1974b: 212)

The establishment of the Commune showed that 'the working class cannot simply lay hold of the ready-made state machinery, and wield it for its own purposes' (Marx, 1974b: 206). Rather the working class had to build a thoroughly democratic 'political form' characterised by a number of principles that became central to the classical Marxist vision of socialism. First, the bourgeois parliament had to be overthrown and replaced by directly representative and participatory institutions. Marx's account of the Commune illuminates his conception of the possible form that the institutions of participatory working-class self-governance might take. It is worth quoting at length:

> The Commune was formed of the municipal councillors, chosen by universal suffrage in the various wards of the town, responsible and revocable at short terms. The majority of its members were naturally working men, or acknowledged representatives of the working class. The Commune was to be a working, not a parliamentary body, executive and legislative at the same time. Instead of continuing to be the agent of central government, the police was at once stripped of its political attributes, and turned into the responsible and at all times revocable agent of the Commune. So were the officials of all other branches of the administration. From members of the Commune downwards, the public service had to be done at *workmen's wages*. The vested interests and the representation allowances of the high dignitaries of state disappeared along with the high dignitaries themselves. Public functions ceased to be the private property of the tools of the central government. Not only municipal administration, but also the whole initiative hitherto exercised by the state was laid into the hands of the Commune.
>
> (Marx, 1974b: 209)

Although this account is not, as we have seen above, entirely historically accurate, nonetheless it accurately highlights some of the central conclusions that Marx drew from his analysis of the Commune. Workers' power is to be exercised democratically through the establishment of district and municipal assemblies, which then send delegates to a national assembly. These assemblies are to be held accountable to their constituencies by the right of recall and frequent elections. Delegates to these assemblies are 'to be at anytime revocable and bound by the ... [formal instructions]' of their constituents (Marx, 1974b: 210). This means that 'instead of deciding once in three or six years which member of the ruling class [is] to misrepresent the people in Parliament, universal suffrage [is] to serve the people' (Marx, 1974b: 210). The standing army and other 'repressive organs of the old governmental power were to be amputated' and replaced by a popular militia (Marx, 1974b: 210, 187–8). Finally, the Commune sought the abolition of private property but this did not, for Marx, mean that it would be simply replaced by state ownership: it centrally involved the exercise of *effective control* over the means of production by the associated producers through democratic assemblies. The relations of production, *definitive of Marxian socialism*, centrally involve democratic working-class control of the means of production that become 'mere instruments of free and associated labour' (Draper, 1977: 253–4).

The scale of the repression of the Commune led Marx (1974b: 231) to observe that 'the conquering and conquered hosts [the German leader Bismarck and Thiers] ... fraternize for the common massacre of the proletariat'.

> The civilisation and justice of the bourgeois order comes out in its lurid light whenever the slaves and drudges of that order rise against their masters. Then this civilization and justice stand forth as undisguised savagery and lawless revenge.
>
> (Marx, 1974b: 226)

Furthermore, 'the bourgeois of our days considers himself the legitimate successor to the baron of old, who thought every weapon in his own hand fair against the plebeian, while in the hands of the plebeian a weapon of any kind constituted in itself a crime' (Marx, 1974b: 230–1). The bloody suppression of the Communards highlights just how high the stakes are in revolution – the cost of failure is not merely the re-establishment of the previous order, but death.

As we shall see shortly, this lesson was learned well by Lenin (who considers Marx's analysis of the Commune at length in *State and Revolution*), Trotsky and other leading figures in the Bolsheviks. They also learned from the experience of the Commune that no revolution can be made in the capital alone, if the capital city remains politically and militarily isolated from the rest of the country. (Although there were revolts in other major cities, these were suppressed, and Paris isolated.) The failure of the National Guard to press its tactical advantage immediately after the March 18 uprising, and proceed to overthrow the National Government at Versailles, was also a lesson learned and applied by the Bolsheviks during 1917. Finally, the experience of the Commune highlighted the need for a centralised revolutionary party to exercise leadership within the working class during the course of the revolution in order to ensure that capitalism and parliamentary democracy are successfully overthrown and replaced by socialist democracy.

THE RUSSIAN REVOLUTIONS OF 1905 AND 1917: WORKERS' POWER

The experience of the Commune was extremely important because it showed that it was possible for the working class to take power and run society. But what occurred in Russia during 1917 was incomparably more significant. The Russian Revolution of 1917 is of world historic significance because for the first time in history the working class, allied with the peasantry, took power at a national level. For the first time since Athenian democracy the labouring citizens ruled, albeit for a tragically brief period. This is why the Russian Revolution continues to be a touchstone that highlights the fundamental ideological differences dividing conservative and neoliberal defenders of the status quo, social democrats who accept the status quo but push for reforms within the system, and revolutionary socialists who reject the status quo altogether. Consequently, the history of Russian Revolution is hotly contested, with historical accuracy and truth being a casualty of the ideological war waged against the socialist defenders of the positive achievements of the revolution by conservatives, neoliberals and social democrats intent on simultaneously defending capitalism and discrediting the socialist alternative.

In view of this, the central objective of this section is to identify, through an examination of the Russian experience, the key features of the classical Marxist vision of socialist democracy. At the same time, I will also engage with contemporary historical critiques of the Bolsheviks, not always directly, but indirectly and (sometimes) implicitly. The section will, however, decisively rebut the right-wing argument that what took place in Russia was not really a revolution at all, but a Bolshevik coup. In addition, it will also critique the argument that the Bolsheviks were wrong to close down the Constituent Assembly.

Historical context

At the beginning of the twentieth century Russian society was characterised by what Trotsky referred to as combined and uneven development. In the cities a process of industrialisation which accelerated during the 1890s resulted in the construction of some of the largest and most advanced factories in the world. By 1914, '54 percent of workers in Russia were employed in factories of over 500 [workers], whereas in the US the figure was 32.5 percent' and '76 percent of Russian workers were employed in factories with more than 100 employees' (Shawki, 1997: 8; Liebman, 1970: 28–9). The Putilov factory in the working-class Vyborg district of Petrograd employed around 35,000. Consequently although the working class remained a small minority of 3–4 million in the total Russian population of around 160 million, it was concentrated in large factories and strategically located in the major cities. In the vast rural expanse of the country, and in stark contrast to the comparatively advanced nature of production in the cities, semi-feudal relations continued to prevail in agricultural production. Although Tsar Alexander II had formally abolished serfdom in 1861, the peasantry, which constituted the bulk of the population, continued to live in grinding poverty, under-fed and over-taxed. As Liebman observes, 'Towards the end of the nineteenth century, the total amount raised by direct taxation was 208 million roubles, of which the starving peasantry contributed 195 million' (1970: 27).

The productive efforts of the peasantry sustained the opulent lifestyles of the land-owning nobility, which was headed by the absolutist monarch who believed himself divinely ordained to rule over Russia – Tsar Nicholas II. An unusually high proportion of Russian industry was foreign owned (41 percent of capital in joint-stock companies in 1915), and the indigenous bourgeoisie was politically cowardly and weak. The majority of this class favoured, at most, 'a liberal constitutionalist regime' introduced by reform from above 'in order to create a modernised capitalist Russia' (Haynes, 2002: 20). But it was too closely socially interconnected with the nobility and the tsarist regime, and frightened by the prospect of working-class revolt, to play a leading role in the popular movement to overthrow the tsar and establish a democratic form of government.

The 1905 Revolution

This is the social background to the Russian Revolution of 1905, which unfolded in the wake of Russia's defeat in the war on Japan (declared by the tsarist regime in February of 1904). On January 4, 1905 workers at the Putilov metal work factory went on strike. As Wright observes,

> Stifled and oppressed for years by harsh working conditions and the regime's secret police, the workers at Putilov now tasted freedom. They began to discuss other important matters. Most pressingly, they began to demand a reduction in the hours of work, and improvements in sanitary conditions and health treatment. Visiting other Petersburg factories to win support for their action, they sparked off more discussion: throughout St Petersburg workers began angrily to air their grievances. Soon the talk was not only of bread, work and survival, but also of freedom; of elections, the right to free speech, and an end to censorship. On the 9th of January, 200,000 workers marched to the Winter Palace to petition the Tsar on these matters. Within one week, a minor trade union dispute had become a mass political movement.
>
> The Tsar himself now took a hand in the political development of his subjects. His troops fired into the peaceful and unarmed crowd, then horsemen charged with sabres, wounding and killing more than 1,000. Gapon, a priest who had marched at the end of the demonstration,

expressed the horror that this action aroused: 'A river of blood divides the Tsar from his people.' And Lenin grimly drew the political conclusion: 'The revolutionary education of the working class made more progress in one day than it could have done in months and years of drab, humdrum, wretched existence.'

(Wright, 1984: 5)

The violent suppression of the January 9 protest became known as 'Bloody Sunday', and it generated waves of popular unrest, with strike action spreading to all the major cities, peasant revolt sweeping large areas of the countryside, and sailors mutinying at the Kronstadt and Sevastopol naval bases.

This unrest culminated in the formation of the Petrograd Soviet (workers' council) on October 13. Although it only lasted 50 days until December 3, it played a key role in leading and coordinating workers' struggles for better pay, work conditions and democratic rights (calling two general strikes in October and November), and increasingly took on the form and functions of a workers' government. It was an all-embracing organisation of the proletariat which 'immediately acquired an enormous authority as both a political focus for the popular movement and an institution that could meet their needs' (Haynes, 2002: 27). According to Trotsky, elected president of the Petrograd Soviet just prior to its suppression by the Tsarist regime,

> It was an organisation which was authoritative and yet had no traditions; which would immediately involve a scattered mass of hundreds of thousands of people while having virtually no organisational machinery which united the revolutionary currents within the proletariat; which was capable of initiative and spontaneous self-control– and, most of all, which could be brought from underground within twenty-four hours.
>
> (Trotsky, 1973: 122)

The Soviet centrally involved a direct and participatory form of democracy based on elected delegates from the factories and workplaces:

> Originally proposed by the Menshevik wing of Russian socialism, the Soviet met the spontaneous demands of workers for mass organisation. Within three days it had assembled 226 delegates, chosen on the basis of one delegate per 500 workers in the factories. ... the Soviet was undisputed as the mass collective organisation of Petersburg workers.
>
> (Gluckstein, 1985: 16)

Soviets were also formed in Moscow and the other major cities.

The tsarist regime was finally able, with the assistance of a generalised campaign of lockouts by the employers, to suppress the Petrograd Soviet on December 3 and the Moscow Soviet shortly thereafter. Nonetheless, although the suppression of the 1905 revolution dispersed the soviets, they 'remained in the memory of Russian workers' (Gluckstein, 1985: 18).

Revolutionaries learned a great deal from the 1905 revolution. The industrial working class, despite constituting such a small minority of the population, showed that it was strategically located in large factories in the cities and therefore could play a leading role in any future revolutionary challenge to Tsarist absolutism. The poor peasantry demonstrated a capacity to break out of entrenched habits of deference and superstition and rise up against the nobility in rural revolt. The liberal bourgeoisie, which had meekly accepted the very limited reforms introduced by the Tsarist regime to stave off revolution (particularly the creation of a thoroughly unrepresentative and largely powerless parliament, or duma) had shown that it was incapable of playing a forceful and leading role in revolutionary events. Although the revolution failed to overthrow the repressive tsarist regime, it did highlight the profound unpopularity and fragility of this regime when confronted by a mass revolutionary movement encompassing workers, peasants and sections of the army and navy. It also highlighted the extent to which Russian society was riddled with contradictions and tensions, intensified because of Russia's economic and military weakness relative to its major rivals, which threatened to unleash another revolutionary uprising in the future. Finally, the 1905 revolution demonstrated the importance of the leadership role played by revolutionaries. On the basis of his experience of the 'dress rehearsal' of 1905, Lenin argued that the role of a socialist organisation during the course of a revolution is to 'reveal to [the masses] our democratic and socialist ideal in all its magnitude and splendour, and show them the shortest and most direct route to complete, absolute, and decisive victory' (1977b: 113).

Perhaps most importantly of all, the 1905 revolution made leading figures in classical Marxism acutely aware of the importance of rapid shifts in collective consciousness. In Luxemburg's brilliant analysis of this revolution in *The Mass Strike*, she graphically demonstrates why and how revolutionary working-class consciousness develops through participation in mass struggles. Thus in order to overthrow absolutism in Russia 'the proletariat requires a high degree of political education, of class-consciousness and organization. All these conditions cannot be fulfilled by pamphlets and leaflets, but only by the living political school, by the fight and in the fight, in the continuous course of the revolution' (Luxemburg, 1970a: 172; see also Geras, 1976: 111–31, 1986: 133–41). Lenin makes a similar point: 'The real education of the masses can never be separated from their independent political, and especially revolutionary, struggle. Only struggle educates the exploited class. Only struggle discloses to it the magnitude of its own power, widens its horizon, enhances its abilities, clarifies its mind, forges its will' (Lenin, 1981: 241). It is these rapid and dramatic shifts in working-class consciousness that ultimately make revolution possible because it is only in the context of mass struggles that workers and the oppressed can become fully aware, not only of what is wrong with the world, but also of why it is like this, of their collective capacity to change it, and of the socialist and democratic alternative to capitalism.

The Menshevik and Bolshevik interpretations of the 1905 revolution foreshadowed the positions that they would adopt during the course of the 1917 revolution. According to the Mensheviks, Russian society was insufficiently developed socially and economically, and the working class too small, for the revolution to build socialism. The role of socialists was to push for a bourgeois revolution to overthrow the tsar and exact major concessions from the new democratic government for the proletariat, while avoiding measures that would alienate the liberal bourgeoisie. Lenin and the Bolsheviks agreed that Russia was insufficiently advanced for the creation of socialism to be possible, but they rejected the idea that the weak and cowardly liberal bourgeoisie, with its many ties to the tsarist regime and land-owning nobility, could be trusted to play a leading role in this regard. Instead, Lenin envisaged a revolutionary government of workers and peasants which would smash the remnants of feudalism in the countryside and introduce bourgeois democracy.

Trotsky was the only major intellectual figure in the Russian revolutionary movement to reject both of these positions. He argued that 'in the event of a decisive victory of the revolution, power will pass into the hands of that class which plays a leading role in the struggle – in other words, into the hands of the proletariat' (1969: 69). Furthermore:

> The political domination of the proletariat is incompatible with its economic enslavement. No matter under what political flag the proletariat has come to power, it is obliged to take the path of socialist policy. It would be the greatest utopianism to think that the proletariat, having been raised to political domination by the internal mechanism of a bourgeois revolution, can ... limit its mission to the creation of republican-democratic conditions for the social domination of the bourgeoisie. [This political domination], even if it is only temporary, will weaken to an extreme degree the resistance of capital, which always stands in need of the support of the state, and will give the economic struggle of the proletariat tremendous scope.
>
> (Trotsky, 1969: 102–3)

The strategic location of the proletariat in large industries in the cities would enable it to recognise and support 'all revolutionary changes (expropriations) in land relationships carried out by the peasants' and, therefore, to stand before the peasantry 'as the class which has emancipated it' (Trotsky, 1969: 71). In view of these considerations, the role of socialists is to help make the revolution permanent and push not only for the overthrow of the Tsarist regime, but the building of socialism. Trotsky considered this to be possible, despite Russia's backwardness, because the triumph of revolution in Russia would spark a wave of revolution that would sweep across Europe, creating socialist republics in the more advanced West European countries which would then aid the building of socialism in Russia. I have outlined Trotsky's theory of permanent revolution at some length because, as we shall see, Lenin's adoption of this theory in April 1917 was to have a decisive impact on the revolution.

War, crisis and revolution

Following the period from 1907 to 1911, which was dominated by greatly increased political repression by the tsarist regime, a decline of working-class struggle, and a dramatic decline in the membership and organisational strength of the Mensheviks and Bolsheviks, a major revival in the struggle took place following the violent suppression of a miners' strike in Siberia (killing over 170). This provoked sympathy strikes and demonstrations in Petrograd and Moscow, initiating much higher levels of strike activity in the years immediately prior to the entry of Russia into the First World War on August 1, 1914.

In response to the outbreak of the First World War, the major socialist parties of Europe affiliated to the Second International (including the German Social Democratic party, which was the largest with close to one million members), ditched their principles, ignored the anti-war resolutions of the International, and backed their own ruling classes and governments. In Russia only the Bolsheviks and internationalist Mensheviks opposed the war. Lenin argued for revolutionary defeatism – socialists should welcome the defeat of their own government and turn the imperialist war into a civil war between the workers and the real ruling-class enemy at home. An initial wave of patriotic fervour soon gave way to widespread disillusionment as the relatively poorly equipped, trained and led Russian army suffered massive losses at the hands of superior German forces (1.7 million dead by 1917), and wartime privations and shortages impacted on the working masses while leaving the wealthy largely untouched (Harman, 1999: 408). Not surprisingly, the Tsarist regime quickly became massively unpopular.

The February Revolution and dual power

On February 23, 1917, on International Women's Day, women textile workers in the militant Vyborg district of Petrograd went on strike and sent delegates to the large engineering works calling on them for support. This action, like those that would quickly unfold, was spontaneous. As Trotsky (1980a: 101) observes, none of the socialist organisations called for action to be taken on that day, 'even a Bolshevik organisation, and a most militant one – the Vyborg borough-committee ... was opposing strikes' because they considered 'the time unripe for militant action – the party not strong enough and the workers having too few contacts with the soldiers'.

> Thus ... the February revolution was begun from below, overcoming the resistance of its own revolutionary organisations, the initiative being taken of their own accord by the most oppressed and downtrodden part of the proletariat – the women textile workers .... The overgrown breadlines had provided the last stimulus. About 90,000 workers, men and women, were

on strike that day. The fighting mood expressed itself in demonstrations, meetings, and encounters with the police. The movement began in the Vyborg district with its large industrial establishments; thence it crossed over to the Petersburg side …. A mass of women, not all of them workers, flocked to the municipal duma demanding bread. It was like demanding milk from a he-goat. Red banners appeared in different parts of the city, and inscriptions on them showed that the workers wanted bread, but neither autocracy nor war.

(Trotsky, 1980a: 102)

In the five days that followed strike activity skyrocketed and the mass demonstrations against the tsarist regime grew increasingly large and militant. The regime violently tried to suppress the uprising, killing 433 and injuring 1214, but this succeeded only in further fanning the flames of revolt (Haynes, 2002: 16). Soon Petersburg was paralysed by a general strike involving the overwhelming majority of the workforce.

If the bulk of the army had been hostile to the striking workers, and if it had remained under the regime's control, then the uprising would eventually have been defeated. But as Trotsky observes in his brilliant account of the growing influence of the masses of workers over the soldiers, 'no deep national crisis can fail to affect the army to some extent. Thus along with the conditions of a truly popular revolution there develops a possibility – not, of course, a guarantee – of its victory' (1969: 120). In these historic days the workers, and especially women workers, ensured that throughout the city there were 'arguments, approaches, appeals' in the seething interaction of the army with the people the army has been commanded to suppress. By February 27 the bulk of the army in Petrograd had either joined the uprising, or adopted a position of benign neutrality towards it. As this suggests, although there is an important sense in which the uprising was initially spontaneous, it was fuelled by the kind of rapid transformations of consciousness that had also characterised the 1905 revolution. In this respect, 'Elements of experience, criticism, initiative, self-sacrifice, seeped down through the mass and created, invisibly to a superficial glance but no less decisively, an inner mechanics of the revolution as a conscious process' (Trotsky, 1980a: 151).

On February 28 the tsar abdicated, centuries of tsarist rule being ended by five days of mass revolutionary struggle. As newspapers carried word of the tsar's overthrow, the revolution spread like wildfire to Moscow and then the remainder of the country. Soviets combining delegates of workers, soldiers and peasants were formed not only in Petrograd and Moscow but also throughout the country; 'By 17 March 49 cities had soviets; five days later the number was 77 and by June 519' (Gluckstein, 1985: 21). The Petrograd Soviet in full plenary session was composed of over 1100 delegates, who elected a smaller Executive Committee, in which all the major parties were represented according to their level of support, to conduct the day-to-day tasks of government.

At the same time that the Petrograd Soviet was being convened, bourgeois liberal members of the Duma formed the provisional government, with the active support of the Mensheviks and Social Revolutionaries. The provisional government was not an elected body; its members were co-opted and it had no democratic mandate to govern. It claimed legitimacy as a transitional body which would eventually organise the democratic election of a Constituent Assembly, but it moved at a snail's pace in this regard because its members feared that if elected freely and fairly such a body would be too radical. Furthermore, as Haynes observes:

> in the months of its existence [the Provisional Government] proved unequal to the task of consolidating a degree of order in society and stabilising the legitimacy it had in March. It talked of ending the war but could not break with the Allies [Britain, France, Italy and the United States]. It remained trapped from within by its links to Russia's traditional interest groups, and trapped from without by pressures from Britain and France. It proved no more able to inspire the workers with confidence than it could supply them with food and respect, and develop workplace democracy. Promising land to the peasants, it continually prevaricated and lost support too with the biggest group in Russian society .... The consequence was that when the slogan 'Bread, peace, land' was raised it came to symbolise the things that the Provisional Government could not deliver.
>
> (Haynes, 2002: 29)

Under the pressure of events, the composition of the government changed four times from February to October, with the representation of the moderate socialists (Mensheviks and Social Revolutionaries) increasing on each occasion. Throughout its power was limited because, as minister of war Guchkov observed:

> The Provisional Government possesses no real power and its orders are executed only in so far as this is permitted by the Soviet of Workers' and Soldiers' deputies, which holds in its hands the most important elements of actual power, such as troops, railroads, postal and telegraph service. It is possible to say directly that the provisional Government exists only while this is permitted by the Soviet of Workers' and Soldiers' deputies.
>
> (quoted in Gluckstein, 1985: 21)

On July 7, Alexander Kerensky, a member of the Social Revolutionary party, replaced Prince Lvov who was a member of the Cadet party, and formed a cabinet made up of six 'capitalist' and nine 'socialist' ministers (Gluckstein, 1985: 29). They were united by their shared commitment to the creation of a bourgeois constitutional democracy which would preside over the capitalist modernisation of Russian society.

The February revolution had thus created two distinctive forms of government – the provisional government, which was closely aligned with the liberal bourgeoisie, and the soviets, which were the organisational expression of a revolutionary movement encompassing workers, peasants and soldiers. Initially both operated from different wings of the Tauride Palace in Petrograd, but the soviet relocated to the Smolny building in July. According to Trotsky this situation of dual power, around which the course of the revolution was to turn, arose because:

> The historic preparation of a revolution brings about, in the pre-revolutionary period, a situation in which the class which is called to realize the new social system, although not yet master of the country, has actually concentrated in its hands a significant share of state power, while the official apparatus of the government is still in the hands of the old lords.
>
> (Trotsky, 1980a: 207)

Dual power is inherently unstable because:

> it arises where the hostile classes are already each relying upon essentially incompatible governmental organisations – the one outlived, the other in the process of formation – which jostle against each other at every step in the sphere of government. The amount of power which falls to each of these struggling classes ... is determined by the correlation of forces in the course of the struggle.
>
> (Trotsky, 1980a: 207–8)

Throughout 1917 the Mensheviks continued to adhere to the view that the revolution was essentially a bourgeois revolution in which the ultimate goal was the creation of a republican constitutional democracy. In practice, this committed them to supporting the provisional government, continuing the war, prevaricating on the crucial question of land reform, and opposing the transfer of all state power to the soviets. As a result, their support amongst workers, peasants and in the army and navy declined precipitously.

Until Lenin arrived in Petrograd on April 3, the Bolsheviks applied the line developed by Lenin in the wake of the 1905 revolution. However, on April 4 Lenin presented his *April Theses* to the Bolshevik party. 'Lenin's theses produced the impression of an exploding bomb', observed Trotsky (1980a: 312). In essence, Lenin articulated the main line of Trotsky's theory of permanent revolution, although he developed the *Theses* independently and without acknowledgement to Trotsky, who at this time was still outside the party – joining in July. He argued that 'the country is *passing* from the first stage of the revolution – which, owing to the insufficient class-consciousness and organisation of the proletariat, placed power in the hands of the bourgeoisie – to its second stage, which must place power in the hands of the proletariat and the poorest sections of the peasants' (Lenin, 1980b: 22). 'The masses must be made to see' through 'a patient, systematic, and persistent *explanation* of the errors of their tactics', that 'the Soviets of Workers' Deputies are the only possible form of revolutionary government' (Lenin, 1980b: 23).

Although initially in a minority in the party, Lenin successfully pushed for a fundamental change in party policy during April. Henceforth the Bolsheviks urged 'transferring the entire power to the Soviets of Workers' Deputies' and added the slogan – 'All Power to the Soviets' – to their other major slogan – 'Peace, Bread, Land' (Lenin, 1980b: 23–5). Lenin was able to win the party over to his views because they coincided 'with the practical experience of the most advanced and militant sections of workers' (Wright, 1984: 259).

From the end of April until October, the provisional government consistently failed to provide peace, bread and land. It was committed to continuing the war, was unable to prevent the meagre standard of living of urban workers from being undermined by rampant inflation, and refused to introduce land reform. The masses continually pushed for change from below and desired an end to the war, a better standard of living, land reform, and a democratic system of government. As Haynes observes:

At the heart of the process of revolution in 1917 were the actions of ordinary Russians who, for a time, became the freest people in the world. Russia was alive with politics because politics mattered. It mattered because the radicalisation promised more than just the occasional vote for a distant government. It opened up the possibility of democratic control of society from the bottom up.

(Haynes, 2002: 21)

The Bolshevik party grew massively from 10,000–20,000 members in February to between 200,000–350,000 in October because it was the only major party that demonstrated in practice its commitment to achieving peace, bread and land, and also because it provided the most astute leadership for the workers, soldiers and peasants during the twists and turns in the struggle between the revolution and counter-revolution in these months (Haynes, 2002: 30; Liebman, 1970: 176).

During these months the revolution passed through four distinctive phases. The first was marked by massive demonstrations in Moscow and Petrograd against the provisional government in the wake of the disastrous defeat of the army in an offensive ordered by the government. Over 500,000 marched in Petrograd on June 18 in a demonstration which Lenin described as 'more than a demonstration and less than a revolution'. 'Judging by the placards and slogans', observed the independent socialist newspaper edited by Gorky, 'the Sunday demonstration revealed the complete triumph of Bolshevism among the Petersburg proletariat' (quoted in Trotsky, 1980b: 454). Tensions continued to mount, and in early July the workers, Kronstadt sailors and soldiers in Petrograd pushed hard for an insurrection. But the Bolsheviks had learned one of the major lessons of the failure of the Paris Commune – although the masses in Moscow and Petrograd were ready to overthrow the provisional government and transfer all power to the Soviets, the bulk of the army and the peasantry were not yet ready for this. Accordingly, the Bolsheviks threw their weight behind restraining the movement in order to prevent a premature revolutionary insurrection that could have politically isolated Petrograd and Moscow from the rest of the country, and made the revolution vulnerable to counter-revolutionary forces.

Once the Bolsheviks had successfully restrained the movement, the provisional government moved from July 3 onwards to suppress the Bolsheviks, sacking their HQ, smashing the printing press and offices of *Pravda*, arresting hundreds of members including Trotsky, and instituting plans to place Lenin, Zinoviev and other leading members on trial for being German agents. Trotsky referred to July as the month of the 'great slander' – the provisional government, Mensheviks, Social Revolutionaries and Cadets all joined together to accuse the Bolsheviks of working on the payroll and at the behest of the Germans. This was completely untrue, but in the short term large numbers of workers and soldiers believed the accusation, and political conditions became more difficult for the Bolsheviks.

The forces of counter-revolution, including the Cadet party of the liberal bourgeoisie and reactionary officers in the army, were given a great boost by this. The third phase of the revolution during these months involved a political shift to the right, culminating in an attempt at a counter-revolutionary coup led by General Kornilov, who was supreme commander of the army, from August 28 to 31. This threatened both sets of governmental institutions created by the February revolution – the provisional government and the soviets – because Kornilov aimed to install himself in power as a military dictator who would restore order.

'It is high time we seized all these German agents and spies with Lenin at their head,' he confided to his chief aide, General Lukomsky. 'And for the rest, we shall hit this Soviet of workers and soldiers so hard that it will never dare to come out again.' ... With the Provisional Government he was somewhat more lenient. All that was needed there was a purge of the more unreliable elements, and the best way of ensuring this was to place himself at the head.

(quoted by Liebman, 1970: 206)

The Bolsheviks, so recently slandered by Kerensky and the provisional government as German agents and provocateurs, now turned quickly to defend this government militarily while simultaneously remaining sharply critical of it politically. The Bolsheviks did so, not in order to save the provisional government as such, but rather 'to defend the revolution and its true objectives: the victory of the workers, the victory of the poor, the victory of peace' (Lenin quoted by Liebman, 1970: 211).

The Red Guards were a Bolshevik-influenced workers' militia which had formed in the wake of the February revolution but that had been disarmed during the July Days. The Bolsheviks ensured that they were mobilised rapidly (within a few days they numbered 25,000) and rearmed, that workers were prepared and organised to resist the advance of counter-revolutionary troops, particularly the railway workers who in the event did successfully sabotage Kornilov's entire operation, and that the Kronstadt sailors and troops under Bolshevik influence were also prepared to enter the fray when called upon. In response to questions from the latter about why the Bolsheviks were now apparently defending the provisional government, Trotsky replied, 'Use Kerensky as a gun rest to shoot Kornilov. Afterward we will settle with Kerensky' (1980c: 233). As it turned out, the Kornilov coup was something of a non-event – the troops under his command were not convinced of the legitimacy of the enterprise and were easily disarmed politically by delegates from Petrograd and the workers they encountered en route, action by railway workers brought the rail network to a standstill, and the advance was poorly planned and led.

The Bolsheviks and the October Revolution

The key role of the Bolsheviks in successfully defending the revolution led to a massive upsurge in their popularity, and the further decline in popular support for the Mensheviks. It enabled the Bolsheviks to win a majority in the Petrograd Soviet on August 31, with Trotsky being elected as chairperson, and the Moscow soviets on September 5. By mid-September they had achieved a majority in the soviets of most major cities.

Throughout September Lenin fought with all his might for the Bolsheviks to lead an insurrection to overthrow the provisional government and give all power to the soviets. His strongest and most consistent supporter in this struggle was Trotsky. Trotsky agreed with Lenin's argument for the insurrection, but disagreed with Lenin's proposal that Bolshevik Party itself should stage the insurrection. He argued that:

it was technically and politically desirable that the insurrection should coincide with the meeting of the All-Russian Congress of Soviets. In this way the impression would be given that the uprising had been ordered, in the name of the workers' institution, by a broad section of the proletariat and not simply by a political party, thus increasing the prestige and the chances of success of the revolutionary movement.

(Liebman, 1970: 238)

Two leading members of the Bolshevik Central Committee – Kamenev and Zinoviev – strongly opposed the calling of an insurrection in any form. Eventually, at a ten-hour meeting held on October 10, the Central Committee of the Bolsheviks carried by ten votes to two Lenin's resolution that '"an insurrection is inevitable" and called on the party to prepare it' (Liebman, 1970: 242). In effect, Lenin had won the party leadership over to the view that the party should lead an insurrection provided that the insurrection was staged in the name of the soviet, not the party itself. This decision was confirmed at an expanded Central Committee meeting on October 16, which encompassed delegates from a number of important party organisations, and Trotsky was put in charge of organising the insurrection.

Zinoviev and Kamenev still could not accept this decision, and 'in flagrant violation of the rules of party discipline bordering on sabotage', Kamenev wrote an article for a non-party newspaper published on October 18 announcing that the 'problem of insurrection had been the subject of important discussions in the Bolshevik Party' (Liebman, 1970: 244). Lenin was outraged and, describing them as 'strike-breakers' of the revolution, called for their expulsion from the party (Lenin, 1977c: 216). In fact, Trotsky was the chief organiser, orator, and poet of the insurrection. As Liebman observes:

> It was he who at meeting after meeting, in proclamation after proclamation, gave voice to the enthusiasm and fury of the people; he who had his finger on the people's pulse; he who made it beat faster; he who showed the entire nation that their actions had a scope far beyond the narrow confines of Russia.
>
> (Liebman, 1970: 245)

On October 9 the Petrograd Soviet formed a 'Committee of Revolutionary Defence' to defend the city against a German offensive, which seemed increasingly likely. Trotsky, as chairperson of the Soviet, played a leading role in the committee, which was soon renamed the Military Revolutionary Committee. The Bolsheviks dominated the committee's composition but it also included Left Social Revolutionaries. With Trotsky at the helm, this soviet committee planned, organised and led the insurrection. The Red Guards were rapidly expanded, trained and equipped for the task. The insurrection was scheduled to take place immediately prior to the convening of the Second All-Russian Congress of Soviets on October 26.

Having been made aware of the Bolsheviks' intentions, on October 24 Kerensky and the provisional government moved to suppress the Bolsheviks and forestall the possibility of the insurrection. Trotsky used this as the pretext to order the insurrection, which took place largely according to plan and with remarkably little bloodshed on the night of October 24 and 25. The Red Guards, bolstered by sailors from the Baltic Fleet, quickly occupied all of the key strategic points in the city. When the garrison at the Peter and Paul Fortress, whose guns overlooked the Winter Palace which housed the provisional government, refused to recognise the orders of the Military Revolutionary Committee, Antonov-Oveseenko, the Bolshevik secretary of the committee, argued for a military assault on the fortress.

> Trotsky said that the job could be done much better by political persuasion. He accordingly went to the fortress, called for a general meeting, and so fired those present with his own zeal that he swung them round completely.

As a result the Bolsheviks gained not only the fortress itself, but also the near-by Kronverksky arsenal containing 100,000 rifles – all without firing a single shot.

This feat was typical not only of the October insurrection but of the entire Bolshevik Revolution. It involved no brilliant displays of military strategy, no spectacular show of force – the seizure of power was a political rather than a military achievement. It was compounded not of a tissue of dark, Machiavellian plots but of thousands of acts of persuasion and propaganda repeated with indefatigable patience. By refusing the temptation of a frontal attack, by going unarmed to the Peter and Paul Fortress to plead with soldiers in person, Trotsky did the work of a true revolutionary: he chose conversion rather than conspiracy, argument rather than guns, agitation rather than bludgeoning.

(Liebman, 1970: 259–60)

On the night of October 25, supported by the cruiser *Aurora* in the Neva, whose sailors fired a volley of blanks from its guns as a warning against armed resistance, the Red Guards stormed the Winter Palace and arrested the cabinet of the provisional government at 2 am.

Lenin, in his speech to the Congress of Soviets on the night of October 26, promised to end the war, give the land to the peasants, and announced that 'we shall now proceed to construct the socialist order' (Trotsky, 1980c: 324). Trotsky summed up the central thrust of the politics and policy of the new Congress of Soviets, headed by an Executive Committee composed of Bolsheviks and left-wing Social Revolutionaries: 'The soviet government proposes immediate peace. It will transfer land to the peasant, democratize the army, establish control over production, promptly summon the Constituent Assembly, guarantee the right of the nations of Russia to self-determination' (1980c: 317).

Was the Russian Revolution a 'Bolshevik coup'?

One of the most common criticisms of the October Revolution contends that it amounted to little more than a 'Bolshevik coup'. Thus Richard Pipes, a former US National Security Council member and Harvard historian, argues in *The Russian Revolution* that October 1917 constituted 'a model of a modern coup d'état' (1990: 491), and portrays the Bolsheviks as a ruthless, violent, evil conspiratorial minority taking power illegitimately through military means. This criticism is generally the preserve of right-wing revisionist historians, although some anarchists and social democrats also adhere to it.

In my view, this criticism is one of the weakest of all, and it trades historical truth for ideological gain. It does so in a number of ways. First, it ignores the fact that the Bolshevik leadership, including Lenin and Trotsky, were explicitly opposed to an insurrection unless the Bolsheviks had the support of a majority in the soviets. As Lenin argued in his letter to Central Committee on September 27:

> The Bolsheviks, having obtained a majority in the Soviets of Workers' and Soldiers' Deputies of both capitals, can and *must* take power into their own hands. ... The majority of people are *on our side*. This was proved by the long and painful course of events from May 6 to August 31 and September 12. The majority gained in the Soviets of the metropolitan cities *resulted* from the people coming over to *our side*.
>
> (Lenin, 1977d: 19)

In other words, the growing popularity of Bolsheviks because of their commitment to 'Peace, Bread, Land', their effectiveness in leading the fight against Kornilov's attempted counter-revolutionary coup, and their call for all power to be transferred to the soviets, had resulted in the Bolsheviks gaining a democratic mandate to make the power transfer. In contrast, the contemporary critics of the insurrection conveniently ignore the complete absence of a meaningful democratic mandate for the provisional government to continue prevaricating on all of the important issues, not least of which was bringing Russia's bloody involvement in the First World War to a swift end.

Second, if the Bolsheviks' central concern was simply taking power into their own hands, they could have done this, at least in the major cities, during the upheaval in June. The fact that, in contrast, they held the movement back highlights the extent to which they were committed to the insurrectionary overthrow of the provisional government only if they had the support of a majority of workers, peasants and soldiers in the country as a whole.

Third, as we have seen, the insurrection was coordinated and led by the Military Revolutionary Committee of the Petrograd Soviet. Although around 50 out of 80 members of this committee were Bolsheviks, it also included left Social Revolutionaries and thus was by no means an exclusively Bolshevik body. Furthermore, the Red Guard of the Petrograd Soviet was not a small section of the army loyal to a clique of officers wanting to stage a coup, but a mass militia composed of militant workers.

Fourth, Zinoviev and Kamenev openly announced the looming insurrection and, despite Kerensky's confident assertion that he commanded sufficient military forces to 'put them [i.e. the Bolsheviks] down' and ensure that 'they will be beaten for once and all', the insurrection was strongly supported and weakly opposed (Liebman, 1970: 251). In reality the majority of troops in Petrograd clearly supported the Bolsheviks. As Liebman observes, at the conference of the Petrograd Garrison, held when preparations for the insurrection were in full swing:

> every Bolshevik speaker received a standing ovation while the Menshevik and Social Revolutionary delegates could not even make themselves heard. If the Petrograd garrison had by no means completely gone over to the Bolsheviks, the latter could at least count on its benevolent neutrality. In any case – and this was the decisive factor – no regiment was prepared to lift a finger in support of the Provisional Government.
>
> (Liebman, 1970: 249–51)

In this, as in so many of its aspects, recall that the insurrection 'was compounded not of a tissue of dark, Machiavellian plots but of thousands of acts of persuasion and propaganda repeated with indefatigable patience' (Liebman, 1970: 259–60). A 'coup' is not a political phenomenon that is openly debated in mass democratic soviets and conferences; a revolutionary insurrection is.

Fifth, the central openly stated objective of the insurrection was conveyed by the widely known and popular Bolshevik slogan 'All power to the soviets!' The All-Russian Second Congress of Soviets was composed of delegates from Bolsheviks, Mensheviks, Menshevik Internationalists, Left Social Revolutionaries, Right Social Revolutionaries, other socialists and some anarchists. The Executive Committee that was elected by approximately 670 delegates consisted of 14 Bolsheviks, 7 Social Revolutionaries, 3 Mensheviks and 1 socialist from the group associated with Maxim Gorky (Liebman, 1970: 272). It is quite frankly absurd to suggest that a party staging a conspiratorial coup behind the backs of the masses would then, having overthrown the government, agree to share power with two other major parties.

Sixth, the insurrection received overwhelming post-facto endorsement: 505 out of 670 delegates to Second All-Russia Congress of Soviets voted for 'All power to the soviets' (Haynes, 2002: 32). As the left-wing Menshevik leader Martov observed, 'Understand please, what we have before us is a victorious uprising of the proletariat – almost the entire proletariat supports Lenin and expects its social liberation from the uprising' (quoted by Haynes, 2002: 33). Sukhanov, the best Menshevik historian of the 1917 revolution, observed in a similar vein that 'To talk about military conspiracy instead of national insurrection, when the party was followed by the overwhelming majority of the people, when the party had already de facto conquered all real power and authority – was clearly an absurdity. On the part of the enemies of Bolshevism it was a malicious absurdity' (quoted by Rees, 1991: 17).

The new workers' state: constructing socialism?

Based on the textual evidence, as well as the actual political practice of the Bolsheviks prior to and immediately following the insurrection, it is possible to identify the central features of the socialist society that the Bolsheviks thought could be constructed in Russia *if and only if* the international isolation of revolutionary Russia was broken by the success of socialist revolutions elsewhere in Europe, and particularly in Germany.

Fundamentally, the construction of socialism was to be governed by a directly democratic workers' state. Recall that in *State and Revolution*, Lenin (1980a: 466) argued that the establishment of socialism involves 'an immense expansion of democracy, which *for the first time* becomes democracy for the poor, democracy for the people, and not democracy for the money-bags.' Trotsky (1980c: 302) described the Second All-Russian Congress of Soviets as 'the most democratic of all parliaments in the world's history'. It was more democratic than bourgeois parliaments because it centrally involved a *direct participatory* form of democracy based on workplaces, units of army and navy, and peasant communities. It constituted a federal system of government that simultaneously decentralised and centralised power and decision making, in that the Executive Committee elected by the All-Russian Congress became the national government, while the regional soviets acted as local or state governments in their regions. It was a multi-party form of democracy, with delegates from the Bolsheviks, Mensheviks and Social Revolutionaries being elected to the Executive Committee. The right of recall of delegates by their constituencies was a fundamental of soviet democracy, as was holding frequent elections. The army and navy were placed under the control of the soviet government. In contrast to bourgeois parliaments, the majority of delegates were workers or peasants. For the first time since the Athenian democracy, 'the poor, being in the majority, rule'. In these and many other respects, the Russian soviets established key features of the socialist participatory model of democracy, even if many of these were never fully realised for reasons that we shall consider shortly.

The new soviet government immediately proposed that the governments of all countries involved in the war meet for peace talks. All of the western powers refused to participate in peace talks, declared their determination to fight the war to the bitter end, and warned Russia not to sign a separate peace treaty with the Central powers. The soviet government, at this time involving a coalition between the Bolsheviks and the Left Social Revolutionaries, signed a peace treaty with Germany at Brest-Litovsk on March 3, 1918, despite the German government imposing extortionately harsh terms, as a result of which the Germans gained '34 percent of the population of Old Russia and 32 percent of her arable land' (Liebman, 1970: 312). This honoured the Bolsheviks' promise to end Russia's involvement in the First World War, albeit at a very high price.

The government recognised the right of peasants to appropriate the estates of nobility without compensation. In doing so it implemented the land policy of the Left Social Revolutionaries rather than the Bolsheviks who had previously been committed to the nationalisation of land ownership, and a shift towards more collective forms of farming. This policy was, at least in the short term, highly effective in cementing the loyalty of the bulk of the peasantry to the soviet government.

As Wright observes, the government passed many revolutionary decrees:

> to co-ordinate and strengthen workers' control [of industry] through elected committees; to abolish secret diplomacy and to call on workers abroad to demand a just peace; to abolish private ownership in land and confiscate all estates without compensation; to proclaim the right of all the nations of Russia to independence if they desired it; to establish the freedom to practice any, or no, religion; to introduce the freedom of divorce.

(Wright, 1984: 262)

Women were enfranchised, equal pay legislated for, universal paid maternity leave introduced, the legal distinction between legitimate and illegitimate children was eliminated, abortion was legalised and made available on demand, and moves were made to introduce communal kitchens, laundry facilities and childcare centres (Rowbotham, 1972: 136–62). Proscriptions against homosexuality were removed from the criminal code. A range of measures was introduced to make education at all levels more available to workers and peasants, and a major literacy campaign was launched. The governance and production of art, music, theatre and opera, and literature was also transformed.

The Bolsheviks' commitment to internationalism and spreading the revolution throughout the world led to the formation of the Third International. This brought together anti-imperialist revolutionary socialist parties from around the world (Hallas, 1985: 27–53).

THE STALINIST DEGENERATION OF THE RUSSIAN REVOLUTION

Most of the high hopes and fine aspirations of the Bolsheviks and the masses in making the Russian Revolution were not to be realised. Limitations of space prevent more than a brief discussion here; rather I will outline the key points generally made by those socialists who defend the positive achievements of the October Revolution, while recognising its limitations and explaining its eventual degeneration.

First, when participating in the provisional government from February to October, the Mensheviks and Social Revolutionaries had displayed much more interest in working cooperatively with the liberal bourgeois Cadet Party than in ending the war and introducing land reform. It was the consistent failure of these parties to act in accord with the wishes of their own members and supporters, and those of the broad mass of workers, peasants and soldiers, that led to the decline in their popularity and the growing popularity of the Bolsheviks. Unfortunately, the very weak commitment to democracy that this revealed became even weaker from the night of the insurrection (October 25/26) onwards.

The real test of a political party's commitment to democracy can be ascertained from an examination of how it behaves when it loses its majority and has to cope with being in opposition rather than holding the reins of governmental power. Both the Mensheviks and the Right Social Revolutionaries failed this test dismally. Rather than accept that the two parties that had been involved in staging the insurrection – the Bolsheviks and Left Social Revolutionaries – now held a large majority in the Second All-Russian Congress of Soviets, and that therefore the Mensheviks and Right Social Revolutionaries would have to assume the role of opposition parties, they walked out of the congress. As Liebman observes:

This walkout, received with catcalls, proved to be of decisive importance in the subsequent course of events. It meant a definite break between the

Bolsheviks and a large section of their socialist adversaries. Henceforth the two camps would be set apart not merely by ideological differences and by personal quarrels but also by profound constitutional differences – during the night of October 25th, 1917, the Bolsheviks had established a new legal order, and by refusing to accept it the [Right] Social Revolutionaries and right-wing Mensheviks deliberately disqualified themselves from playing the part of the official opposition. Worse still, they carried the dispute between Russian Bolsheviks and Social Democrats far beyond the old divisions – they challenged the very basis of the new Soviet Regime during the first hours of its life. From the very start, therefore, these men did not act as opponents but as rebels, and inasmuch as the October insurrection was the logical and revolutionary extension of February – at least in the eyes of the Bolsheviks and broad masses – the socialist Right became transformed into an agent of counter-revolution.

(Liebman, 1970: 272–3)

The left Mensheviks led by Martov also walked out of the Soviet. Sukhanov, who was a left Menshevik, later considered this to be a major mistake because the Menshevik actions:

meant a formal break with the masses and with the revolution. And why? Because the congress had proclaimed a soviet regime in which the minute Menshevik–[Right]SR minority would not be given a place! ... The Bolsheviks, not long ago ... themselves constituted the same impotent minority as the Mensheviks and SRs now, but they did not and could not draw the conclusion that they had to leave the soviet.

(Quoted by Haynes, 2002: 34)

In essence, the Mensheviks and Right SRs demonstrated contempt for the wishes of the majority of workers and peasants as expressed in the elections of delegates to the congress.

Even worse, after months of delaying a national election to allow the formation of the Constituent Assembly when they were members of the provisional government, the Mensheviks and SRs demanded that elections be held immediately. The Bolshevik–Left SR soviet government, unlike the provisional government, in fact did hold the election to the Constituent Assembly without delay on November 12 to 14. The result of the elections, in which only half those eligible voted, gave the SRs 58 per cent of the vote and 410 seats in the Assembly out of a total of 707, Bolsheviks 25 per cent of the vote and 175 seats, the Cadets and other bourgeois parties 13 per cent and 17 seats, and the Mensheviks 4 per cent and 16 seats (Liebman, 1970: 315). This result was somewhat misleading because both the Right and Left SRs appeared on the same party list even though they constituted hostile factions with very different policies. Furthermore, the right-wing SR leadership manipulated the party list in favour of the Right SRs. The Left SRs, who enjoyed the support of a majority of SR voters (as subsequent elections to the Congress of Soviets would show), only got 40 out of 410 seats. The Right SR leader, Chernov, was elected president, and the Constituent Assembly immediately became a rallying point for all the forces of the counter-revolution.

In response, the Bolshevik and Left SR Executive Committee of the Soviet requested that the provisional government accept the primacy of the soviet government and accept that the right of recall be applied to the members of the Constituent Assembly as well as delegates to the soviets. When the Right SRs and the Mensheviks refused this, the Constituent Assembly was dissolved. As Victor Serge observes, 'The dissolution of the Constituent Assembly made a great sensation abroad. In Russia, it passed almost unnoticed' (quoted by Rees, 1991: 27). In truth, there was very little support for the Constituent Assembly because it was clear to a large section of the masses that it was going to be largely unresponsive to their wishes and would continue the policies of the provisional government. Popular endorsement for the disbanding of the Constituent Assembly is evident from the results of the elections to the all-Russian congresses of soviets; Bolshevik support increased from 51 per cent in October of 1917 to 61 per cent in January of 1918, and 66 per cent in July of 1918 (1991: 26). In the Third All-Russian Congress of Soviets on January 10 the Bolsheviks and Left SRs enjoyed the support of 74 per cent of the delegates (Haynes, 1997: 48). Continuing the convocation of the Constituent Assembly would have re-established dual power; disbanding it decisively asserted the primary of direct socialist participatory democracy over indirect bourgeois parliamentary democracy.

The Left SRs departed from the soviet government because they were opposed to the peace treaty signed with the Germans at Brest-Litovsk on March 3, 1918, contributing to the shift towards one-party rule. One of the major tragedies of the revolution was the fact that the Bolsheviks were soon left as the sole party that was consistently committed to ending Russia's involvement in the war, defending the revolution against counter-revolution, and building socialism beyond capitalism.

Second, in view of the overall social and economic backwardness of Russian society, both Lenin and Trotsky recognised that a socialist society could not be built in Russia unless it was aided by proletarian revolution in other countries, particularly Germany. According to Trotsky (1969: 105), 'If the peoples of Europe do not arise and crush imperialism, we shall be crushed – that is beyond doubt. Either the Russian revolution will raise the whirlwind of struggle in the West, or the capitalists of all countries will stifle our struggle.' Similarly Lenin observed, 'It is not open to the slightest doubt that the final victory of our revolution, if it were to remain alone, if there were no revolutionary movement in other countries, would be hopeless .... Our salvation from all these difficulties, I repeat, is an all-European revolution' (quoted by Carr, 1966: 53). The failure of this revolution to eventuate is owing, not to the absence of a series of spontaneous revolutionary upheavals that actually did sweep across Europe in 1917–23, but to the absence of mass revolutionary socialist parties in other European countries. As Rees rightly argues, 'What was lacking [in these revolutionary upheavals] was a leadership of sufficient clarity and an organisation with a core of sufficiently experienced members to successfully lead these movements to power. This was the decisive difference between the German and Russian revolutions' (1991: 9).

The failure of the leaders of the revolutionary socialist wing of German Social Democracy (SPD), including Karl Liebknecht and Rosa Luxemburg, to break from the SPD earlier and begin building a Communist Party during the war was crucial (Cliff, 1986a: 13–17; Harman, 1982: 37–8, 306–7). Equally significant was the abject failure of German Marxist intellectuals and political leaders, like Karl Kautsky of the Independent Social Democratic Party (USPD), to push for a socialist revolution in their own country, where the advanced economic conditions and political crisis made a specifically socialist revolution possible. Kautsky pronounced that the socialist revolution in Russia was 'premature' given the backward social and economic conditions of the country, but in reality he was opposed to socialist revolution anywhere no matter how advanced the social and economic conditions (Harman, 1982: 16; Rees, 1991: 10).

Third, right-wing academics who are inexhaustibly critical of the Bolsheviks, consistently fail to criticise the actions of the 14 governments, including all of the major western powers, to provide military support, including equipment, munitions and more than 200,000 troops, for the White armies simply because they were opposed to the Bolshevik government and fearful that socialist revolution might spread to other countries. Poland, with the backing of the western powers and an army of 740,000, invaded the Ukraine in October 1920. Prior to this foreign intervention the soviet government had easily defeated the small-scale military forces of the counter-revolution; after it they were compelled to mobilise what was left of the meagre resources of the country to defend the revolution against counter-revolutionary and imperialist foreign armies. The meagreness of the resources at the soviet government's disposal was greatly exacerbated by the Allied trade blockade of Russia. By the beginning of 1919, 'not one letter, not one food parcel, not one package of goods, not one foreign newspaper could enter Red Russia' (Rees, 1991: 33).

The combination of civil war, foreign invasion and trade blockade had a devastating impact on the economic infrastructure of the country and decimated the working class. As Haynes observes:

Behind the rapidly changing fronts revolutionary Russia struggled to survive a growing social catastrophe as hunger and cold grew. Life was trapped in a vicious circle of decline that changed both the priorities and the form of the regime. Denied fuel, food and raw materials, factories closed and workers starved. By 1920 industrial output was 31 percent of the 1913 level, and total output 38 percent. Supplying the army from the diminishing resources became the first priority. In areas that were short of food the towns emptied. Petrograd's population fell from 2.3 million in 1917 to 1.5 million in 1918, and 740,000 in 1920 – only 32 percent of the 1917 level .... Petrograd in the winter of 1918 was 'starving ... bitten through by polar winds, a town without coal and bread, its factory chimneys extinguished, a town like a raw human nerve'.

(Haynes, 2002: 50)

In these conditions:

the working class base of the workers' state, mobilised time and again to defeat the Whites, the rock on which Bolshevik power stood, had disintegrated. The Bolsheviks survived three years of civil war and wars of foreign intervention, but only at the cost of reducing the working class to an atomised, individualised mass, a fraction of its former size, and no longer able to exercise the collective power that it had done in 1917.

(Rees, 1991: 65)

The revolution would never fully recover, and eventually Stalin would rise to power as a dictator by drowning all of the basic principles of the revolution in the blood of the Bolsheviks (such as those involved in the Left Opposition from 1926–28), workers and peasants who opposed him.

Trotsky staunchly opposed Stalin's rise to power until at Stalin's behest an agent murdered him in 1940. In 1935, Trotsky wrote, 'I think that the work in which I am engaged now, despite its extremely insufficient and fragmentary nature, is the most important work of my life – more important than 1917, more important than the period of the Civil War or any other' (quoted by Cliff, 1993: 17). The importance of Trotsky's work resided above all in his insistence that the Stalinist regime was essentially inconsistent with the ideals of those who had made the revolution. In *The Revolution Betrayed*, published in 1937, he argued: 'The present regime in the Soviet Union provokes protest at every step, a protest the more burning in that it is repressed. The bureaucracy is not only a machine of compulsion but also a constant source of provocation. The very existence of a greedy, lying and cynical caste of rulers inevitably creates a hidden indignation' (Trotsky, 1972: 284–5). This situation was likely to lead to the revolutionary overthrow of the Stalinist regime. However, this revolution was a matter not simply of 'substituting one ruling clique for another, but of changing the very methods of administering the economy and guiding the culture of the country' (1972: 289). Trotsky's commitment to the restoration of democracy can hardly be doubted:

Bureaucratic autocracy must give place to Soviet democracy. A restoration of the right of criticism, and a genuine freedom of elections, are necessary conditions for the further development of the country. This assumes a revival of the freedom of Soviet parties, beginning with the party of Bolsheviks, and a resurrection of the trade unions. The bringing of democracy into industry means a radical revision of plans in the interests of the toilers.

(Trotsky, 1972: 289)

Unfortunately, the power of Trotsky's critique was severely undermined by his insistence that state ownership of the means of production combined with centralized planning meant that the soviet economy was in some sense 'socialist'. This involved a conflation of property ownership and relations of effective control. The notion that a 'political revolution' was all that was required to re-establish genuine socialism in Russia ignored the reality that a fundamental transformation of the relations of production was required. From the late 1920s onwards, the Stalinist bureaucracy became a new ruling class, exploiting and dominating workers, in a system of bureaucratic state capitalism.

In view of the social and economic backwardness of Russia, the international isolation of the revolution, civil war, foreign invasion and economic blockade, it is hardly surprising that the Bolsheviks were unable to build the kind of socialism envisaged by Marx and Engels in *The Communist Manifesto* and in their writings on the Paris Commune and by Lenin in *State and Revolution*. But if this helps us to understand and explain the degeneration of the revolution, it also highlights how much easier it would be to build socialism in the advanced capitalist societies today – where, among other things, the proletariat constitutes a substantial majority of the population and is better educated than any subordinate social class to have appeared thus far in history. Economic production, transportation networks, communication technologies and scientific knowledge are much more developed, and consequently the general material standard of living is much higher, than Russia in 1917. Furthermore, foreign invasion would be more difficult if a revolution occurred in a state possessing nuclear weapons. All this suggests that a future socialist revolution would not be doomed to degenerate in a similar manner to the Russian Revolution. Socialist participatory democracy, in which the majority is directly involved in the self-governance of society, will be vastly easier to establish and maintain in the twenty-first century, given the economically, culturally and scientifically advanced conditions created by contemporary capitalism, than it was in the relatively under-developed conditions prevailing in Russia during the First World War (Callinicos, 1991).

CONCLUSION: SOCIALISM AND DEMOCRACY BEYOND CAPITALISM

Socialist participatory democracy emerged in an embryonic form during the course of the Paris Commune, and in a more developed form after the Russian revolutions of 1905 and 1917. What are the central characteristics of this particular form of democracy? It is a historically novel form of democracy that has the potential to transcend both Athenian democracy and representative democracy because it incorporates some of the strengths of these earlier forms of democracy, such as the civil liberties associated with representative democracy and the participatory methods of governance, administration, and judicial decision making that were pioneered by Athenian democracy.

Socialist participatory democracy is more than an abstract and utopian philosophical manifesto; its coming into being is simultaneously historically determined and actively created by the broad mass of working-class people through the revolutionary transformation of the existing society and the political institutions that govern it. This is a socialism that can only be built from below by a movement of the immense majority acting in the interests of the majority. In socialist participatory democracy, control over production and distribution is achieved through the institutional mechanism of a network of councils and assemblies that combines elements of centralisation, for example, a national assembly making major investment decisions, and decentralisation with respect to decisions within the workplace and the governance of local communities (Albert and Hahnel, 2002a, 2002b; Callinicos, 1991: 110–18, 1993b, 1993c; Campbell, 2002; Cockshott and Cottrell, 2002; Devine, 1988, 2002; Mandel, 1986; Molyneux, 1991). The right of recall, frequently held elections, regular mass assemblies, constitutional extension of liberal democratic citizenship rights, democratization of the judiciary, and if necessary the establishment of a popular militia to defend the revolution, would ensure the accountability of delegates to the constituencies who elect them.

Such a system of democracy can only be achieved through elimination of all major forms of exploitation, inequality and oppression, and this in turn necessitates the overthrow of capitalism and the parliamentary form of democracy which simultaneously manages and legitimates capitalism. This is also necessary in order to reduce the average hours each person needs to spend performing productive labour and in order to ensure that there is adequate provision of, and equal responsibility for, childcare. By creating more 'free time' socialism ensures, not only that participatory democracy can work, but also that individual liberty, diversity and self-development are maximised.

GUIDE TO FURTHER READING

Callinicos (1996: 160–202) and Draper (1978: 33–48) provide useful accounts of the working class and its collective capacity to overthrow capitalism and create socialism. Callinicos (1996) also provides a useful general introduction to the revolutionary ideas of Marx and Engels. The best general account of Marx's and Engels's conception of socialist democracy is Nimtz (2000). The most important works in which the Marxian vision of socialism and democracy is articulated are Marx and Engels (1998), Marx in Marx and Engels (1978: 45–146) and Marx (1974b: 187–268).

On the Paris Commune, Gluckstein (2006) is essential reading, and the best chapter-length account is still Edwards (1973a) in the introduction to his compendium of primary documents (1973b). Edwards (1971) has also written an excellent book on the subject. Harman (1999: 368–74) provides a condensed overview. Horne (1965) provides a meticulously detailed account, as well as a shorter illustrated history (1971). Descriptions and analysis of the role of women in the Commune are provided by Cliff (1984: 34–45), Eichner (2004) and Rowbotham (1972: 103–7). Other accounts of the Commune include Lissagray (1976), Mason (1967) and Schulkind (1972).

The best short introductions to the history of the Russian revolutions of

1905 and 1917 take the form of pamphlets produced by socialist organisations. In this vein, Wright (1984) provides a superb introductory overview of the making of the Russian Revolution. Other excellent short introductions include Harman (1999: 405–29), Haynes (2002: 15–41), Mandel (1979a: 103–11), Shawki (1997) and Trotsky (1993). Luxemburg (1970b), Lenin (1981) and Trotsky (1969) provide classical Marxist accounts of the 1905 Revolution.

Trotsky's (1980a, 1980b, 1980c) *History of the Russian Revolution* ranks alongside *Capital* as one of the most important works in the Marxist tradition. Widely neglected because of the influence of Stalinism and social democratic reformism on Western academic Marxism, it is essential reading. Of the many books published on the Revolution, Carr (1966) and Liebman (1970) are among the very best. Sukhanov (1984) is the best Menshevik account. Reed's (1997) eyewitness account is justifiably considered a classic. Gluckstein (1985) provides a valuable account of the Russian and Western soviets. For accounts of the roles played by Lenin and the Bolsheviks in making the revolution see Liebman (1975) and Cliff (1985, 1986b, 1987). Hallas (1984) and Mandel (1979a) provide accounts of Trotsky's Marxism from the perspectives of the two largest Trotskyist currents. Haynes (1997) and Rees (1991) rebut the revisionist claim that the October Revolution was a 'Bolshevik coup'. Trotsky's (1972) critique of the Stalinist degeneration of the revolution is essential reading on the subject. The best contemporary accounts of the degeneration of the Russian Revolution are Callinicos (1991) and Haynes (2002), both writing in the tradition founded by Cliff (1988). For an orthodox Trotskyist analysis of Stalinist Russia as a degenerated workers' state see Mandel (1979b: 112–15). Callinicos (1990) provides an overview of the various Trotskyist interpretations of the degeneration of the revolution. Resnick and Wolff (2002) provide an interesting Marxist, but non-Trotskyist, state capitalist analysis of Stalinist Russia.

Bibliography

Addabbo, T., Arrizabalaga, M.-P. and Borderías, C. (2010). *Gender Inequalities, Households and the Production of Well-Being in Modern Europe*. Farnham: Ashgate.

Agulhon, M. (1983). *The Republican Experiment, 1848–1852*, trans. J. Lloyd. Cambridge: Cambridge University Press.

Akamatsu, P. (2010). *Meiji Restoration 1868*. Hoboken, N.J.: Taylor & Francis.

Albert, M. and Hahnel, R. (2002a). 'In defence of participatory economics', *Science and Society*, 66(1), 7–21.

Albert, M. and Hahnel, R. (2002b). 'Participatory planning through negotiated coordination', *Science and Society*, 66(1), 72–87.

Alexander, A. (2011). 'Revolution shakes the Middle East: the battle of Tunis', *Socialist Review*, 355, 10–14.

Altvater, A. and Rojas, R. (eds) (1991). *The Poverty of Nations: A guide to the debt crisis from Argentina to Zaire*, trans. T. Bond. London and New Jersey: Zed.

Anderson, P. (1974a). *Passages from Antiquity to Feudalism*. London: New Left Books.

Anderson, P. (1974b). *Lineages of the Absolutist State*. London: New Left Books.

Appleby, J. (1984). *Capitalism and a New Social Order*. New York and London: New York University Press.

Arblaster, A. (1994). *Democracy*, 2nd edn. Minneapolis, Minn.: University of Minnesota Press.

Archer, M., Bhaskar, R., Collier, A., Lawson, T. and Norrie, A. (eds) (1998). *Critical Realism*. London and New York: Routledge.

Aristotle. (1962). *The Politics*. Harmondsworth: Penguin.

Armstrong, P., Glyn, A. and Harrison, J. (1991). *Capitalism Since World War Two*, 2nd edn. Oxford: Basil Blackwell.

Ashworth, J. (1995). *Slavery, Capitalism, and Politics in the Antebellum Republic*, Vol. 1. Cambridge: Cambridge University Press.

Aston, T. H. and Philpin, C. H. E. (1985). *The Brenner Debate*. Cambridge and New York: Cambridge University Press.

Aylmer, G. E. (1975). *The Levellers in the English Revolution*. London: Thames & Hudson.

Bang, P. F. (2008). *The Roman Bazaar*. Cambridge and New York: Cambridge University Press.

Banyard, K. (2010). *The Equality Illusion*. London: Faber & Faber.

Barratt Brown, M. (1996). *Africa's Choices After Thirty Years of the World Bank*. Boulder, Colo.: Westview Press.

Beard, C. (1913). *An Economic Interpretation of the Constitution of the United States*. New York: Free Press.

Beard, M. and Crawford, M. H. (1985). *Rome in the Late Republic*. London: Duckworth.

Beier, A. L. and Finlay, R. (1986). *London 1500–1700*. London and New York: Longman.

Bellamy Foster, J. (1999). *The Vulnerable Planet*. New York: Monthly Review Press.

Bellamy Foster, J. (2000). *Marx's Ecology*. New York: Monthly Review Press.

Bello, W., Cunningham, S. and Rau, B. (1999). *Dark Victory*, 2nd edn. London: Pluto.

Benjamin, W. (1992). *Illuminations*. London: Fontana.

Bhaskar, R. (1989). *Reclaiming Reality*. New York and London: Verso.

Bircham, E. and Charlton, J. (eds) (2001). *Anti-capitalism*. London: Bookmarks.

Blackbourn, D. (1997). *The Fontana History of Germany, 1780–1918*. London: Fontana.

Blackbourn, D. and Eley, G. (1984). *The Peculiarities of German History*. Oxford and New York: Oxford University Press.

Blackburn, R. (1988). *The Overthrow of Colonial Slavery, 1776–1848*. London and New York: Verso.

Blackburn, R. (1997). *The Making of New World Slavery*. London and New York: Verso.

Bloch, R. (2000). 'The construction of gender in a republican world', pp. 610–16 in J. Greene and J. Pole (eds), *A Companion to the American Revolution*. Malden, Mass. and Oxford: Blackwell.

Boardman, P. R. (2010). *Governance of Earth Systems*. Basingstoke: Palgrave Macmillan.

Bois, G. (1984). *The Crisis of Feudalism*. Cambridge: Cambridge University Press.

Bonwick, C. (1991). *The American Revolution*. London: Macmillan.

Braddick, M. J. (1996). *The Nerves of State*. Manchester and New York: Manchester University Press.

Brailsford, H. N. (1983). *The Levellers and the English Revolution*, 2nd edn. Nottingham: Spokesman.

Brandon, P. (2007). 'The Dutch revolt: a social analysis', *International Socialism*, **116**, 139–64.

Brennan, T. C. (2004). 'Power and process under the republican "constitution"', pp. 31–65 in H. I. Flower (ed.), *The Cambridge Companion to the Roman Republic*. Cambridge: Cambridge University Press.

Brenner, J. (2000). *Women and the Politics of Class*. New York: Monthly Review Press.

Brenner, R. (1985). 'Agrarian class structure and economic development in pre-industrial Europe', in T. H. Aston and C. H. Philpin (eds), *The Brenner Debate*. Cambridge: Cambridge University Press.

Brenner, R. (1989). 'Bourgeois revolution and transition to capitalism', in A. L. Beier (ed.), *The First Modern Society*. Cambridge: Cambridge University Press.

Brenner, R. (1990). 'Feudalism', pp. 170–85 in J. E. A. Eatwell (ed.), *The New Palgrave Marxian Economics*. London: Macmillan.

Brenner, R. (2003a). *Merchants and Revolution*. London and New York: Verso.

Brenner, R. (2003b). *The Boom and Bubble*. London: Verso.

Brenner, R. (2006). 'What is, and what is not, imperialism?' *Historical Materialism*, **14**(4), 79–106.

Brenner, R. (2007). 'Property and progress: where Adam Smith went wrong', pp. 49–111 in C. Wickham (ed.), *Marxist History Writing for the Twenty-first Century*. Oxford: Oxford University Press.

Briggs, A. and Clavin, P. (2003). *Modern Europe, 1789–Present*. London: Longman.

Brockway, F. (1980). *Britain's First Socialists*. London and New York: Quartet.

Brown, R. (ed.) (2000). *Major Problems in the Era of the American Revolution, 1760–1791*, 2nd edn. Boston, Mass.: Houghton Mifflin.

Brunt, P. A. (1971a). *Social Conflicts in the Roman Republic*. London: Chatto & Windus.

Brunt, P. A. (1971b). *Italian Manpower, 225 B.C.–A.D. 14*. Oxford: Clarendon Press.

Brunt, P. A. (1988). *The Fall of the Roman Republic and Related Essays*. Oxford: Clarendon Press.

Bullock, S. (1994). *Women and Work*. London: Zed.

Burkett, P. (1999). *Marx and Nature*. New York: St Martins Press.

Burkett, P. (2006). *Marxism and Ecological Economics*. Leiden, Netherlands, Boston, Mass. and Tokyo: Brill.

Callinicos, A. (1983). *Marxism and Philosophy*. Oxford: Oxford University Press.

Callinicos, A. (1984). 'Marxism and politics', pp. 62–85 in A. Leftwich (ed.), *What is Politics?* Oxford: Basil Blackwell.

Callinicos, A. (1987). *Making History*. Cambridge: Polity Press.

Callinicos, A. (1988). 'The foundations of Athenian democracy', *International Socialism*, 40, 113–72.

Callinicos, A. (1989). 'Bourgeois revolutions and historical materialism', *International Socialism*, 43, 113–72.

Callinicos, A. (1990). *Trotskyism*. Buckingham: Open University Press.

Callinicos, A. (1991). *The Revenge of History*. Cambridge: Polity Press.

Callinicos, A. (1993a). *Race and Class*. London: Bookmarks.

Callinicos, A. (1993b). 'Socialism and democracy', pp. 200–13 in D. Held (ed.), *Prospects for Democracy*. Cambridge: Polity Press.

Callinicos, A. (1993c). 'What will socialism be like?' *Socialist Review*, 160, 18–20.

Callinicos, A. (1994). 'Marxism and imperialism today', pp. 11–66 in A. Callinicos, J. Rees, C. Harman and M. Haynes (eds), *Marxism and the New Imperialism*. London: Bookmarks.

Callinicos, A. (1995). *Theories and Narratives*. Cambridge: Polity Press.

Callinicos, A. (1996). *The Revolutionary Ideas of Karl Marx*, 2nd edn. London: Bookmarks.

Callinicos, A. (2002a). 'The grand strategy of the American empire', *International Socialism*, 97, 3–38.

Callinicos, A. (2002b). 'Marxism and global governance', pp. 249–66 in D. Held and A. McGrew (eds), *Governing Globalization*. Cambridge: Polity.

Callinicos, A. (2003a). *An Anti-Capitalist Manifesto*. Cambridge Polity Press.

Callinicos, A. (2003b). *The New Mandarins of American Power*. Cambridge: Polity Press.

Callinicos, A. (2009). *Imperialism and Global Political Economy*. Cambridge: Polity Press.

Callinicos, A. (2010). *Bonfire of Illusions*. Cambridge: Polity Press.

Callinicos, A. (2011). 'The return of the Arab revolution', *International Socialism*, 130, 3–32.

Callinicos, A., Rees, J., Harman, C. and Haynes, M. (1994). *Marxism and the New Imperialism*. London: Bookmarks.

Campbell, A. (2002). 'Democratic planned socialism: feasible economic procedures', *Science and Society*, 66(1), 29–42.

Carlin, N. (1999). *The Causes of the English Civil War*. Oxford and Malden, Mass.: Blackwell.

Carr, E. H. (1966). *The Bolshevik Revolution, 1917–1923*, Vol. 3. Harmondsworth: Penguin.

Centre for Responsive Politics (2011), 'Business–labor–ideology split in PAC and individual donations to candidates and parties.' Retrieved August 3, 2012 from <www.opensecrets.org/bigpicture/blio.php?cycle=2008>.

Chossoduvsky, M. (1997). *The Globalisation of Poverty*. London: Zed.

Cliff, T. (1984). *Class Struggle and Women's Liberation, 1640 to Today*. London: Bookmarks.

Cliff, T. (1985). *Lenin: All Power to the Soviets, 1914–17*. London: Bookmarks.

Cliff, T. (1986a). *Rosa Luxemburg*. London: Bookmarks.

Cliff, T. (1986b). *Lenin: Building the Party, 1893–1914*. London: Bookmarks.

Cliff, T. (1987). *Lenin: The Revolution Besieged, 1917–1923*. London: Bookmarks.

Cliff, T. (1988 (1948)). *State Capitalism in Russia*. London: Bookmarks.

Cliff, T. (1993). *Trotsky: The Darker the Night the Brighter the Star, 1927–40*. London: Bookmarks.

Cobban, A. (1964). *The Social Interpretation of the French Revolution*. Cambridge: Cambridge University Press.

Cockshott, P. and Cottrell, A. (2002). 'The relation between economic and political instances in the communist mode of production', *Science and Society*, **66**(1), 50–63.

Collier, A. (1989). *Scientific Realism and Socialist Thought*. Herfordshire: Harvester Wheatsheaf.

Comminel, G. (1987). *Rethinking the French Revolution*. London: Verso.

Constable, N. (2003). *Historical Atlas of Ancient Rome*. New York: Thalamus.

Countryman, E. (1985). *The American Revolution*. New York: Hill & Wang.

Coward, B. (2003). *The Stuart Age: England, 1603–1714*, 3rd edn. Harlow: Longman.

Crane, E. (1987). 'Dependence in the era of independence: the role of women in a republican society', pp. 253–75 in J. Greene (ed.), *The American Revolution: Its character and limits*. New York and London: New York University Press.

Crawford, M. (1978). *The Roman Republic*. Sussex: Harvester Press.

Crawford, M. and Whitehead, D. (eds) (1983). *Archaic and Classical Greece*. Cambridge: Cambridge University Press.

Crompton, R., Lewis, S. and Lyonette, C. (2007). *Women, Men, Work and Family in Europe*. New York: Palgrave Macmillan.

Culham, P. (2004). 'Women in the Roman republic', pp. 139–59 in H. I. Flower (ed.), *The Cambridge Companion to the Roman Republic*. Cambridge: Cambridge University Press.

D'Amato, P. (2006). *The Meaning of Marxism*. Chicago: Haymarket.

Dahl, R. (1967). *Pluralist Democracy in the United States: Conflict and Consensus*. Chicago: Rand McNally.

Dahl, R. (1989). *Democracy and its Critics*. New Haven, Conn.: Yale University Press.

Dahl, R. (1998). *On Democracy*. New Haven, Conn. and London: Yale University Press.

Dahl, R., Shapiro, I. and Cheibub, J. (eds) (2003). *The Democracy Sourcebook*. Cambridge and London: MIT Press.

Dale, G. (2007). 'Corporations and climate change', *International Socialism*, **116**, 117–38.

Davies, J. K. (1978). *Democracy and Classical Greece*. London: Fontana.

Delphy, C. and Leonard, D. (1992). *Familiar Exploitation*. Cambridge: Polity Press.

Denholm, A. (1972). *France in Revolution: 1848*. Sydney: John Wiley & Sons.

Devine, P. (1988). *Democracy and Economic Planning*. Cambridge: Polity Press.

Devine, P. (2002). 'Participatory planning through negotiated coordination', *Science and Society*, **66**(1), 72–85.

Diamond, L. (ed.) (1999). *Developing Democracy*. Baltimore, Md.: Johns Hopkins University Press.

Diamond, L. and Plattner, M. (eds) (1996). *The Global Resurgence of Democracy*, 2nd edn. Baltimore, Md.: Johns Hopkins University Press.

Diamond, L., Plattner, M., Tien, H.-M. and Tien, Y.-H. (eds) (1997). *Consolidating the Third Wave Democracies*. Baltimore, Md.: Johns Hopkins University Press.

Diamond, M., Fisk, W. and Garfinkel, H. (1966). *The Democratic Republic*. Chicago, Ill.: Rand McNally.

Dobb, M. (1963). *Studies in the Development of Capitalism*. New York: International Publishers.

Draper, H. (1977). *Karl Marx's Theory of Revolution, Vol. 1*. New York and London: Monthly Review Press.

Draper, H. (1978). *Karl Marx's Theory of Revolution, Vol. 2*. New York and London: Monthly Review Press.

Dry, M. (2000). 'The debate over ratification of the Constitution', pp. 482–94 in J. Greene and J. Pole (eds), *A Companion to the American Revolution*. Malden, Mass. and Oxford: Blackwell.

Duby, G. (1972). 'Medieval agriculture 900–1500', pp. 175–220 in C. M. Cipolla (ed.), *The Fontana Economic History of Europe: The Middle Ages*. Glasgow: Collins/ Fontana.

Du Plessis, R. (1997). *Transitions to Capitalism in Early Modern Europe*. Cambridge: Cambridge University Press.

Duménil, G. and Lévy, D. (2011). *The Crisis of Neoliberalism*. Cambridge, Mass.: Harvard University Press.

Dunne, P. (ed.) (1991). *Quantitative Marxism*. Cambridge: Polity Press.

Dupont, F. (1992). *Daily Life in Ancient Rome*. Oxford: Basil Blackwell.

Duveau, G. (1967). *1848: The Making of a Revolution*, trans. A. Carter. London: Routledge & Kegan Paul.

Eagleton, T. (1999). 'Utopia and its opposites', pp. 31–40 in L. Panitch and C. Leys (eds), *Socialist Register 2000*. New York: Monthly Review Press.

Edwards, S. (1971). *The Paris Commune 1871*. London: Eyre & Spottiswoode.

Edwards, S. (1973a) 'Introduction', pp. 9–42 in S. Edwards (ed.), *The Communards of Paris, 1871*. Ithaca, N.Y.: Cornell University Press.

Edwards, S. (ed.) (1973b). *The Communards of Paris, 1871*. Ithaca, N.Y.: Cornell University Press.

Eichner, C. (2004). *Surmounting the Barricades*. Bloomington, Ind.: Indiana University Press.

Engels, F. (1967). *The German Revolutions*. Chicago, Ill.: University of Chicago Press.

Engels, F. (1968). 'The origin of the family, private property and the state', in K. Marx and F. Engels, *Selected Works in One Volume*. Moscow: Progress.

Eyck, F. (1972). *The Revolutions of 1848–9*. Edinburgh: Oliver & Boyd.

Farrar, C. (1988). *The Origins of Democratic Thinking*. Cambridge: Cambridge University Press.

Farrar, C. (1992). 'Ancient Greek political theory as a response to democracy', pp. 17–39 in J. Dunn (ed.), *Democracy: The Unfinished Journey*. New Jersey: Humanities Press.

Fasel, G. (1970). *Europe in Upheaval*. Chicago, Ill.: Rand McNally.

Federal Electoral Commission. (2011). *The FEC and the Federal Campaign Finance Law*. Brochure retrieved April 10, 2012, from www.fec.gov/pages/brochures/fecfeca. shtml#Contribution_Limits

Finley, M. I. (1973). *Democracy*. London: Chatto & Windus.

Fisher, J. (2001). 'Africa', pp. 199–211 in E. Bircham and J. Charlton (eds), *Anti-capitalism*. London: Bookmarks.

Flower, H. I. (ed.) (2004). *The Cambridge Companion to the Roman Republic*. Cambridge: Cambridge University Press.

Foner, E. (1976). *Tom Paine and Revolutionary America*. New York: Oxford University Press.

Foner, E. (1998). *The Story of American Freedom*. New York and London: W.W. Norton.

Foot, P. (2006). *The Vote*. London: Penguin.

Fornara, C. W. and Samons, L. J. (1991). *Athens from Cleisthenes to Pericles*. Berkeley, Calif. and Oxford: University of California Press.

Foyster, E. (2003). 'Gender relations', pp. 111–86 in B. Coward (ed.), *A Companion to Stuart Britain*. Oxford: Basil Blackwell.

Freedom House. (2007). 'Freedom in the world 2007.' Retrieved April 14, 2012, from www.freedomhouse.org/report/freedom-world/freedom-world-2007

Freedom House. (2012). 'Freedom in the world 2012.' Retrieved April 14, 2012, from www.freedomhouse.org/report/freedom-world/freedom-world-2012

Freeman, A. and Carchedi, C. (eds). (1996). *Marx and Non-Equilibrium Economics*. Cheltenham: Edward Elgar.

Frey, S. (2000). 'Slavery and anti-slavery', pp. 402–12 in J. Greene and J. Pole (eds), *A Companion to the American Revolution*. Malden, Mass. and Oxford: Blackwell.

Friedman, T. (2000). *The Lexus and the Olive Tree*. New York: Anchor.

Fukuyama, F. (1989). 'The end of history?' *The National Interest* (Summer), 3–18.

Fukuyama, F. (1992). *The End of History and the Last Man*. New York: Free Press.

Furet, F. (1981) *Interpreting the French Revolution*. Cambridge: Cambridge University Press.

Galbraith, K. and Lu, J. (2001). 'Measuring inequality in the global economy', pp. 16–32 in K. Galbraith and M. Berner (eds), *Inequality and Industrial Change*. Cambridge: Cambridge University Press.

Geras, N. (1976). *The Legacy of Rosa Luxemburg*. London: Verso.

Geras, N. (1983). *Marx and Human Nature*. London: Verso.

Geras, N. (1986). *Literature of Revolution*. London: Verso.

Gildea, R. (2003). *Barricades and Borders: Europe, 1800–1914*, 3rd edn. Oxford and New York: Oxford University Press.

Gill, G. (2000). *The Dynamics of Democratization*. New York: St Martins Press.

Gluckstein, D. (1985). *The Western Soviets*. London: Bookmarks.

Gluckstein, D. (2006). *The Paris Commune*. London: Bookmarks.

Glyn, A. (2006). *Capitalism Unleashed*. Oxford: Oxford University Press.

Godineau, D. (1998). *The Women of Paris and their French Revolution*. Berkeley, Calif.: University of California Press.

Gowan, P. (1999). *The Global Gamble*. London: Verso.

Green, P. (1993). 'Democracy as a contested idea', pp. 2–18 in P. Green (ed.), *Democracy: Key concepts in critical theory*. New Jersey: Humanities Press.

Greene, J. and Pole, J. (eds) (2000). *A Companion to the American Revolution*. Malden, Mass. and Oxford: Blackwell.

Grugel, J. (2002). *Democratization: A critical introduction*. Basingstoke and New York: Palgrave.

Guérin, D. (1977). *Class Struggle in the First French Republic*. London: Pluto.

Gurria, A. (2009). 'Economic crisis: the long term starts now', *OECD Observer* (270–1), 1–2.

Hallas, D. (1984). *Trotsky's Marxism*. London: Bookmarks.

Hallas, D. (1985). *The Comintern*. London: Bookmarks.

Hallas, D. (1988). 'The decisive settlement', *Socialist Worker Review* (113), 17–20.

Hansen, M. H. (1987). *The Athenian Assembly in the Age of Demosthenes*. Oxford and Cambridge: Basil Blackwell.

Hansen, M. H. (1991). *The Athenian Democracy in the Age of Demosthenes*. Oxford and Cambridge: Blackwell.

Hanson, P. R. (2009). *Contesting the French Revolution*. Chichester and Malden, Mass.: Wiley-Blackwell.

Hardman, J. (ed.) (1981). *French Revolution: The fall of the Ancien Regime to the Thermidorian reaction 1785–95*. London and New York: Edward Arnold.

Harman, C. (1982). *The Lost Revolution*. London: Bookmarks.

Harman, C. (1998). *Marxism and History*. London: Bookmarks.

Harman, C. (1999). *A People's History of the World*. London: Bookmarks.

Harman, C. (2002). 'The workers of the world', *International Socialism*, **96**, 3–45.

Harman, C. (2003). 'Analysing imperialism: from the scramble for Africa to the attack on Iraq', *International Socialism*, **99**, 3–82.

Harman, C. (2006). 'Debate: the origins of capitalism', *International Socialism*, **111**, 127–62.

Harman, C. (2007). 'The rate of profit and the world today', *International Socialism*, **115**, 141–61.

Harman, C. (2007). *Revolution in the 21st Century*. London: Bookmarks.

Harman, C. (2008). 'An age of transition? Economy and society in England in the later Middle Ages. The field and the forge: population, production and power in the pre-industrial west', *Historical Materialism*, **16**(1), 185–99.

Harman, C. (2010). *Zombie Capitalism*. Chicago, Ill.: Haymarket.

Harrison, R. (1993). *Democracy*. London and New York: Routledge.

Hartman, H. (1996). 'The family as the locus of gender, class, and political struggle: the example of housework', pp. 470–97 in N. Folbre (ed.), *The Economics of the Family*. Cheltenham UK: Elgar.

Harvey, D. (1989). *The Condition of Postmodernity*. Oxford and Cambridge, Mass.: Blackwell.

Harvey, D. (2003). *The New Imperialism*. Oxford: Oxford University Press.

Harvey, D. (2005). *A Brief History of Neoliberalism*. Oxford: Oxford University Press.

Harvey, D. (2010). *The Enigma of Capital and the Crises of Capitalism*. New York: Oxford University Press.

Haynes, M. (1997). 'Was there a parliamentary alternative in Russia in 1917?' *International Socialism*, **76**, 3–66.

Haynes, M. (2002). *Russia: Class and power, 1917–2000*. London: Bookmarks.

Haynes, M. and Wolfreys, J. (2007). *History and Revolution*. London and New York: Verso.

Held, D. (1995). *Democracy and the Global Order*. Cambridge: Polity Press.

Held, D. (2004). *Global Covenant*. Cambridge: Polity Press.

Held, D. (2006). *Models of Democracy*, 3rd edn. Cambridge: Polity Press.

Held, D. and McGrew, A. (eds) (2003). *The Global Transformations Reader*. Cambridge: Polity Press.

Held, D. and McGrew, A. G. (2007). *Globalization/Anti-globalization: Beyond the great divide*, 2nd edn. Cambridge: Polity Press.

Held, D., McGrew, A., Goldblatt, D. and Perraton, J. (1999). *Global Transformations*. Stanford, Calif.: Stanford University Press.

Heller, H. (2006). *The Bourgeois Revolution in France, 1789–1815*. New York: Berghahn.

Herman, B., Ocampo, J. A. and Spiegel, S. (eds) (2010). *Overcoming Developing Country Debt Crises*. Oxford: Oxford University Press.

Hill, C. (1941). *The English Revolution, 1940*. London: Lawrence & Wishart.

Hill, C. (1980). 'A bourgeois revolution? pp. 109–40 in J. Pocock (ed.), *Three British Revolutions: 1641, 1688, 1776*. New Jersey: Princeton University Press.

Hill, C. (2002). *The Century of Revolution 1603–1714*, 2nd edn. London: Routledge.

Hilton, R. (1976). *The Transition from Feudalism to Capitalism*. London: Verso.

Hilton, R. H. (1985). *Class Conflict and the Crisis of Feudalism*. London: Hambledon.

Hilton, R. H. (1992). *English and French Towns in Feudal Society*. Cambridge: Cambridge University Press.

Hinderaker, E. (2000). 'The Amerindian population in 1763', pp. 94–8 in J. Greene and J. Pole (eds), *A Companion to the American Revolution*. Malden, Mass. and Oxford: Blackwell.

Hirst, D. (1975). *The Representative of the People?* Cambridge and New York: Cambridge University Press.

Hobsbawm, E. (1962). *The Age of Revolution: Europe 1789–1848*. London: Abacus.

Hobsbawm, E. (1975). *The Age of Capital, 1848–1875*. London: Abacus.

Hobsbawm, E. (1987). *The Age of Empire, 1875–1914*. London: Weidenfeld & Nicolson.

Hobsbawm, E. (1990a). 'The making of a "bourgeois revolution"', in F. Feher (ed.), *The French Revolution and the Birth of Modernity*. Berkeley, Calif.: University of California Press.

Hobsbawm, E. (1990b). *Echoes of the Marseillaise*. New Brunswick, N.J.: Rutgers University Press.

Hobsbawm, E. (1995). *Age of Extremes: The short twentieth century*. London: Abacus.

Holden, B. (1993). *Understanding Liberal Democracy*, 2nd edn. New York: Harvester/ Wheatsheaf.

Hollister, C. W. (1998). *Medieval Europe: A short history*, 8th edn. Boston, Mass.: McGraw-Hill.

Hornblower, S. (1992). 'Creation and development of democratic institutions in Ancient Greece', pp. 1–16 in J. Dunn (ed.), *Democracy: The unfinished journey*. Oxford: Oxford University Press.

Horne, A. (1965). *The Fall of Paris: The siege and the commune, 1870–1*. London, Melbourne and Toronto: Macmillan.

Horne, A. (1971). *The Terrible Year: The Paris commune, 1871*. London: Macmillan.

Howard, M. and King, J. (1985). *The Political Economy of Marx*, 2nd edn. London and New York: Longman.

Hughes, A. (1991). *The Causes of the English Civil War*. Basingstoke: Macmillan.

Hughes, A. (2003). 'Religion, 1640 to 1660', pp. 350–373 in B. Coward (ed.), *A Companion to Stuart Britain*. Oxford: Blackwell.

Hughes, J. (2000). *Ecology and Historical Materialism*. Cambridge: Cambridge University Press.

Huntington, S. (1991). *The Third Wave*. Oklahoma City, Okla.: University of Oklahoma Press.

Huntington, S. (1996). *The Clash of Civilizations and the Remaking of World Order*. New York: Simon & Schuster.

Jack, S. M. (1996). *Towns in Tudor and Stuart Britain*. New York: St Martin's Press.

Jansen, M. (ed.) (1995). *The Emergence of Meiji Japan*. New York: Cambridge University Press.

Jessop, B. (1990). *State Theory*. Cambridge: Polity Press.

Jochnick, C. and Preston, F. A. (eds) (2006). *Sovereign Debt at the Crossroads*. Oxford and New York: Oxford University Press.

Jones, A. H. M. (1957). *Athenian Democracy*. Oxford: Basil Blackwell.

Jones, C. (1988). *The Longman Companion to the French Revolution*. London and New York: Longman.

Jones, G. and Hollier, G. (1997). *Resources, Society and Environmental Management*. London: Paul Chapman.

Jones, P. M. (1995). *Reform and Revolution in France: The Politics of Transition, 1774–1791*. Cambridge and New York: Cambridge University Press.

Kamenka, E. (1972). *Paradigm for Revolution?* Canberra: Australian National University Press.

Kaplanoff, M. (2000). 'The Federal Convention and the Constitution', pp. 470–81 in J. Greene and J. Pole (eds), *A Companion to the American Revolution*. Malden, Mass. and Oxford: Blackwell.

Keane, J. (2009). *The Life and Death of Democracy*. London and New York: Simon & Schuster.

Keen, M. H. (1991). *The Penguin History of Medieval Europe*. London: Penguin.

Keyssar, A. (2000). *Right to Vote*. New York: Basic Books.

Kishlansky, M. A. (1986). *Parliamentary Selection*. Cambridge and New York: Cambridge University Press.

Korsch, K. (1971). *Three Essays on Marxism*. New York: Monthly Review Press.

Kovel, J. (2007). *The Enemy of Nature*. London: Zed.

Kramnick, I. (2000). 'Ideological background', pp. 88–93 in J. Greene and J. Pole (eds), *A Companion to the American Revolution*. Malden, Mass. and Oxford: Blackwell.

Landes, J. B. (1988). *Women and the Public Sphere in the Age of the French Revolution*. Ithaca, N.Y.: Cornell University Press.

Le Glay, M., Voisin, J.-L. and Le Bohec, Y. (2001). *A History of Rome*. Oxford: Basil Blackwell.

Lefebvre, G. (1962a). *The French Revolution: From its origins to 1793*, Vol. 1, trans. E. Evanson. New York: Columbia University Press.

Lefebvre, G. (1962b). *The French Revolution: from 1793 to 1799*, Vol. 2, trans. E. Evanson. New York: Columbia University Press.

Lefebvre, G. (1989). *The Coming of the French Revolution*, trans. R. R. Palmer. Princeton, N.J.: Princeton University Press.

Leftwich, A. (ed.). (1996). *Democracy and Development: Theory and Practice*. Cambridge: Polity Press.

Lenin, V. (1977a [1917]). 'Imperialism: the highest stage of capitalism', pp. 185–304 in S. Apresyan and J. Riordan (eds), *V. I. Lenin: Collected works*, Vol. 22. Moscow: Progress.

Lenin, V. (1977b [1905]). 'Two Tactics of Social Democracy in the Democratic Revolution', trans. A. Fineberg, G. Hana and J. Katzer, pp. 13–140 in G. Hana (ed.), *V. I. Lenin: Collected works*, Vol. 26. Moscow: Progress.

Lenin, V. (1977c [1927]). 'Letter to Bolshevik Party members', trans. Y. Sdobnikov and G. Hana, pp. 216–19 in G. Hana (ed.), *V. I. Lenin: Collected works*, Vol. 26. Moscow: Progress.

Lenin, V. (1977d [1921]). 'The Bolsheviks must assume power', trans. Y. Sdobnikov and G. Hana, pp. 19–21 in G. Hana (ed.), *V. I. Lenin: Collected works*, Vol. 26. Moscow: Progress.

Lenin, V. I. (1980a [1918]). 'State and revolution: the Marxist theory of the state', trans. S. Apresyan and J. Riordan, pp. 385–497 in S. Apresyan and J. Riordan (eds), *V. I. Lenin: Collected works*, Vol. 25. Moscow: Progress.

Lenin, V. I. (1980b [1917]). 'The tasks of the proletariat in the present revolution', pp. 20–6 in B. Isaacs (ed.), *V. I. Lenin: Collected works*, Vol. 24. Moscow: Progress.

Lenin, V. I. (1981 [1925]). 'Lecture on the 1905 revolution', trans. M. S. Levin and J. Fineberg, pp. 236–53 in M. S. Levin (ed.), *V. I. Lenin: Collected works*, Vol. 23. Moscow: Progress.

Lens, S. (2003). *The Forging of the American Empire*. Chicago, Ill.: Haymarket.

Levy, A. (2005). *Female Chauvinist Pigs*. New York: Free Press.

Lewis, G. (1993). *The French Revolution: Rethinking the debate*. London and New York: Routledge.

Liebman, M. (1970). *The Russian Revolution*. London: Jonathan Cape.

Liebman, M. (1975). *Leninism under Lenin*. London: Jonathan Cape.

Lindblom, C. (1977). *Politics and Markets*. New York: Basic Books.

Lindley, K. (1997). *Popular Politics and Religion in Civil War London*. Aldershot and Brookfield, Vt.: Scolar Press/Ashgate.

Linebaugh, P. (2008). *The Magna Carta Manifesto*. Berkeley, Calif. and London: University of California Press.

Lintott, A. W. (1999). *The Constitution of the Roman Republic*. Oxford and New York: Clarendon Press.

Lissagaray, P. (1976). *History of the Paris Commune of 1871*. London: New Park.

Locke, J. (1966). *The Second Treatise of Government*, 3rd edn. Oxford: Basil Blackwell.

Loomis, T. (1990). *Pacific Migrant Labour, Class and Racism in New Zealand*. Aldershot: Avebury.

Lukacs, G. (1971). *History and Class Consciousness*. Cambridge, Mass.: MIT Press.

Luxemburg, R. (1970a). *Rosa Luxemburg Speaks*. New York: Pathfinder Press.

Luxemburg, R. (1970b [1918]). 'The Russian Revolution', in M.-A. Waters (ed.), *Rosa Luxemburg Speaks*. New York: Pathfinder.

Lyons, M. (2006). *Post-Revolutionary Europe, 1815–1856*. Basingstoke: Palgrave Macmillan.

MacKenzie, K. (1950). *The English Parliament*. Harmondsworth: Penguin.

MacPherson, C. B. (1977). *The Life and Times of Liberal Democracy*. Oxford, London and New York: Oxford University Press.

Maddicott, J. R. (2010). *The Origins of the English Parliament, 924–1327*. Oxford and New York: Oxford University Press.

Mandel, E. (1976) 'Introduction', in K. Marx (ed.), *Capital*, Vol. 1. Harmondsworth: Penguin.

Mandel, E. (1979a). *Trotsky*. London: New Left Books.

Mandel, E. (1979b) *Introduction to Marxism*. London: Pluto.

Mandel, E. (1986) 'In defence of socialist planning', *New Left Review*, 159, 5–38.

Mandel, E. (1995). *Long Waves of Capitalist Development*, 2nd edn. London: Verso.

Mandel, E. and Freeman, A. (eds) (1984). *Ricardo Marx Sraffa*. London: Verso.

Mandel, E. and Novack, G. (1973). *The Marxist Theory of Alienation*, 2nd edn. New York: Pathfinder.

Mann, M. (1986). *The Sources of Social Power*, Vol. 1. Cambridge: Cambridge University Press.

Mann, M. (1993). *The Sources of Social Power*, Vol. 2. Cambridge: Cambridge University Press.

Manning, B. (1991). *The English People and the English Revolution*, 2nd edn. London: Bookmarks.

Manning, B. (1996). *Aristocrats, Plebians and Revolution in England 1640–1660*. London: Pluto.

Manning, B. (1999). *The Far Left in the English Revolution, 1640–1660*. London, Chicago, Ill. and Sydney: Bookmarks.

Manning, B. (2003). *Revolution and Counter-Revolution in England, Ireland and Scotland 1658–60*. London: Bookmarks.

Marshall, P. (2000). 'The West and the Amerindians, 1756–1776', pp. 157–64 in J. Greene and J. Pole (eds), *A Companion to the American Revolution*. Malden, Mass. and Oxford: Blackwell.

Marx, K. (1967a [1867]). *Capital*, Vol. 1. New York: International Publishers.

Marx, K. (1967b [1894]). *Capital* , Vol. 3. New York:International Publishers.

Marx, K. (1970 [1859]). *A Contribution to the Critique of Political Economy*. Moscow: Progress.

Marx, K. (1971 [1863]). *Theories of Surplus Value*, Part III. Moscow: Progress.

Marx, K. (1973a [1858]). *Grundrisse*. Harmondsworth: Penguin.

Marx, K. (1973b). *Wages, Prices and Profit*. Peking: Foreign Languages Press.

Marx, K. (1973c). *The Revolutions of 1848: Political Writings*, Vol. 1. Harmondsworth: Penguin/New Left Review.

Marx, K. (1974a [1875]). 'The critique of the Gotha Programme', pp. 339–59 in K. Marx (ed.), *The First International and After – Political Writings*, Vol. 3. Harmondsworth: Penguin.

Marx, K. (1974b). *The First International and After – Political Writings*, Vol. 3. Harmondsworth: Penguin/New Left Review.

Marx, K. (1975a [1880]). 'Marginal notes on A. Wagner', in T. Carver (ed.), *Texts on Method of Karl Marx*. Oxford: Blackwell.

Marx, K. (1975b [1847]). *The Poverty of Philosophy*. Moscow: Progress.

Marx, K. (1978 [1850]). 'The class struggles in France', pp. 45–145 in K. Marx and F. Engels, *Collected Works*, Vol. 10. Moscow: Progress.

Marx, K. and Engels, F. (1961). *The Civil War in the United States*. New York: International Publishers.

Marx, K. and Engels, F. (1975 [1844–1895]). *Selected Correspondence*. Moscow: Progress.

Marx, K. and Engels, F. (1976 [1846]). *The German Ideology*. Moscow: Progress.

Marx, K. and Engels, F. (1978). *Collected Works*, Vol.10. Moscow: Progress.

Marx, K. and Engels, F. (1998). *The Communist Manifesto*. London and New York: Verso.

Mason, E. (1967). *The Paris Commune*. New York: Howard Fertig.

McGarr, P. (1989). 'Marxism and the great French Revolution', *International Socialism*, **43**, 15–110.

McKitterick, R. (2001). 'Politics', pp. 21–58 in R. McKitterick (ed.), *The Early Middle Ages: Europe 400–1000*, 1st US edn. Oxford: Oxford University Press.

McLennan, G. (1989). *Marxism, Pluralism, and Beyond*. Cambridge, UK and Cambridge, Mass.: Polity Press and Blackwell.

McMichael, P. (1984). *Settlers and the Agrarian Question*. Cambridge and New York: Cambridge University Press.

McNally, D. (1993). *Against the Market*. London: Verso.

McNally, D. (2006). *Another World is Possible*, 2nd edn. Winnipeg: Arbeiter Ring.
McNally, D. (2011). *Global Slump: The economics and politics of crisis and resistance*. Oakland, Calif.: PM Press.
McPhee, P. (2002). *The French Revolution, 1789–1799*. Oxford: Oxford University Press.
McPherson, J. (1982). *Ordeal by Fire*. New York: Alfred A. Knopf.
McPherson, J. (1988). *Battle Cry of Freedom*. New York: Oxford University Press and Ballantine.
Mepham, J. and Ruben, D. H. (eds). (1979). *Issues in Marxist Philosophy*, Vol. 3. Sussex: Harvester Press.
Merrell, J. H. (2000). 'Amerindians and the New Republic', pp. 413–18 in J. Greene and J. Pole (eds), *A Companion to the American Revolution*. Malden, Mass. and Oxford: Blackwell.
Miles, R. (1984). 'Summoned by capital: the political economy of labour migration', pp. 223–43 in P. Spoonley (ed.), *Tauiwi: Racism and ethnicity in New Zealand*. Palmerston North, New Zealand: Dunmore Press.
Miliband, R. (1969). *The State in Capitalist Society*. London, Melbourne and New York: Quartet.
Miliband, R. (1977). *Marxism and Politics*. Oxford: Oxford University Press.
Miliband, R. (1994). *Socialism for a Skeptical Age*. Cambridge: Polity Press.
Millar, F. (1998). *The Crowd in Rome in the Late Republic*. Ann Arbor, Mich.: University of Michigan Press.
Millett, P. (2000). 'The economy', pp. 23–51 in R. Osborne (ed.), *Classical Greece*. Oxford: Oxford University Press.
Molyneux, J. (1991). *Arguments for Revolutionary Socialism*, 2nd edn. London: Bookmarks.
Mooers, C. (1991). *The Making of Bourgeois Europe*. London and New York: Verso.
Moore, S. (1957). *The Critique of Capitalist Democracy*. New York: Paine-Whitman.
Moseley, F. (1991). *The Falling Rate of Profit in the United States Economy*. New York: St Martins Press.
Mosse, C. (1973). *Athens in Decline, 404–86 B.C.* London and Boston, Mass.: Routledge & Kegan Paul.
Mouritsen, H. (2001). *Plebs and Politics in the Late Roman Republic*. Cambridge and New York: Cambridge University Press.
Muldrew, C. (2003). 'Economic and urban development', pp. 148–65 in B. Coward (ed.), *A Companion to Stuart Britain*. Oxford: Blackwell.
Neale, J. (2008). *Stop Global Warming: Change the world*. London: Bookmarks.
Nicholas, D. (1992). *The Evolution of the Medieval World*. London and New York: Longman.
Nimtz, A. (2000). *Marx and Engels: Their contribution to the democratic breakthrough*. New York: SUNY Press.
North, J. A. (1990). 'Democratic politics in Republican Rome', *Past and Present*, **126**, 3–21.
North, J. A. (2006). 'The Constitution of the Roman Republic', pp. 256–77 in N. Rosenstein and R. Morstein-Marx (eds), *A Companion to the Roman Republic*. Oxford: Blackwell.
Novack, G. (1971). *Democracy and Revolution*. New York: Pathfinder.
Novack, G. (ed.) (1976). *America's Revolutionary Heritage*. New York: Pathfinder.
Obama, B. (2010). *2010 National Security Strategy*. Washington: The White House.
Ober, J. (1996). *The Athenian Revolution*. Princeton, N.J.: Princeton University Press.

Ober, J. (2007). '"I besieged that man": democracy's revolutionary start', pp. 83–104 in K. A. Raaflaub, J. Ober and R. W. Wallace (eds), *Origins of Democracy in Ancient Greece*. Berkeley, Calif. and London: University of California Press.

Ober, J. and Hedrick, C. (eds) (1996). *Demokratia: A conversation on democracies, ancient and modern*. Princeton, N.J.: Princeton University Press.

Offe, C. (1985). *Disorganised Capitalism*. Cambridge: Polity Press.

Ollman, B. (1976). *Alienation*, 2nd edn. London and New York: Cambridge University Press.

Ollman, B. (1990). 'Putting dialectics to work: the process of abstraction in Marx's method', *Rethinking Marxism*, 3(1), 26–74.

Ollman, B. (2003). *Dance of the Dialectic*. Urbana and Chicago, Ill.: University of Illinois.

Orr, J. (2010). 'Marxism and feminism today', *International Socialism*, **127**, 25–57.

Osborne, R. (1985). *Demos: The Discovery of Classical Attika*. Cambridge: Cambridge University Press.

Osborne, R. (ed.) (2000). *Classical Greece*. Oxford: Oxford University Press.

Osborne, R. (2004). *Greek History*. London: Routledge.

Osborne, R. (2010). *Athens and Athenian Democracy*. New York: Cambridge University Press.

Parker, G. (1977). *The Dutch Revolt*. London: Allen Lane.

Peet, R., Robbins, P. and Watts, M. (eds) (2010). *Global Political Ecology*. Hoboken, N.J.: Taylor & Francis.

Pepper, D. (1993). *Eco-Socialism*. London: Routledge.

Perkins, E. (2000). Socio-economic development of the colonies', pp. 51–60 in J. Greene and J. Pole (eds), *A Companion to the American Revolution*. Malden, Mass. and Oxford: Blackwell.

Pettifor, A. (2001). 'Debt', pp. 199–211 in E. Bircham and J. Charlton (eds), *Anti-capitalism*. London: Bookmarks.

Phillips, A. (1991). *Engendering Democracy*. Cambridge: Polity Press.

Pipes, R. (1990). *The Russian Revolution*. New York: Knopf.

Plato (1977). 'The Republic VIII', in *The Portable Plato*. Harmondsworth: Penguin.

Poata-Smith, E. (1997). 'The political economy of inequality between Maori and Pakeha', in C. Rudd and B. S. Roper (eds), *The Political Economy of New Zealand*. Auckland: Oxford University Press.

Potter, D., Goldblatt, D., Kiloh, M. and Lewis, P. (eds) (1997). *Democratization*. Cambridge: Polity Press.

Pouthas, C. (1967). 'The revolutions of 1848', pp. 389–415 in J. P. Bury (ed.), *The New Cambridge Modern History*, Vol. 10. Cambridge: Cambridge University Press.

Power, N. (2009). *One-Dimensional Woman*. Winchester and Washington: Zero.

Price, R. (ed.) (1975). *1848 in France*. New York: Cornell University Press.

Price, R. (1988). *The Revolutions of 1848*. London: Macmillan Education.

Purvis, T. (2000). The Seven Years' War and its political legacy', pp. 112–17 in J. Greene and J. Pole (eds), *A Companion to the American Revolution*. Malden, Mass. and Oxford: Blackwell.

Raaflaub, K. A. (2005). *Social Struggles in Archaic Rome*, rev. edn. Oxford: Basil Blackwell.

Raaflaub, K. A. (2007a) 'Introduction', pp. 1–21 in K. A. Raaflaub, J. Ober and R. W. Wallace (eds), *Origins of Democracy in Ancient Greece*. Berkeley, Calif. and London: University of California Press.

Raaflaub, K. A. (2007b). 'The breakthrough of demokratia in mid-fifth-century Athens', pp. 105–54 in K. A. Raaflaub, J. Ober and R. W. Wallace (eds), *Origins of Democracy in Ancient Greece*. Berkeley, Calif. and London: University of California Press.

Raaflaub, K. A., Ober, J. and Wallace, R. W. (2007). *Origins of Democracy in Ancient Greece*. Berkeley, Calif. and London: University of California Press.

Rakove, J. (2000). 'The Articles of Confederation, 1775–1783', pp. 281–6 in J. Greene and J. Pole (eds), *A Companion to the American Revolution*. Malden, Mass. and Oxford: Blackwell

Raphael, R. (2001). *The American Revolution: A people's history*. London: Profile.

Rapien, M. (2002). 'Frankenfoods: what's wrong with genetic engineering?' *International Socialist Review*, **21**, 80–5.

Rapport, M. (2009). *1848: Year of revolution*. New York: Basic Books.

Rawls, J. (1993). *Political Liberalism*. New York: Columbia University Press.

Reed, J. (1997). *Ten Days that Shook the World: The Illustrated Edition*. Stroud: Sutton.

Rees, J. (1991) 'In defence of October', *International Socialism*, **52**, 3–79.

Rees, J. (1998)'. *The Algebra of Revolution*. London and New York: Routledge.

Renton, D. (1999). *Fascism: Theory and practice*. London: Pluto.

Resnick, S. and Wolff, R. (2002). *Class Theory and History*. New York and London: Routledge.

Richardson, R. C. (1998). *The Debate on the English Revolution*. Manchester: Manchester University Press.

Roberts, J. T. (1994). *Athens on Trial*. Princeton, N.J.: Princeton University Press.

Robertson, P. (1960). *Revolutions of 1848*. New York: Harper.

Robinson, E. W. (ed.) (2004). *Ancient Greek Democracy*. Malden, Mass.: Blackwell.

Roper, B. (2004). 'The globalisation of revolt: exploitation, agency and democracy', *Red and Green*, **3**, 13–36.

Roper, B. (2005). *Prosperity for All? Economic, social and political change in New Zealand since 1935*. Melbourne: Cengage.

Roper, B. S. (2006). 'Business political activity in New Zealand, 1990–2005', *Kotuitui*, **1**, 161–83.

Roper, B. (2011). 'Reformism on a global scale? A critical examination of David Held's advocacy of cosmopolitan social democracy', *Capital and Class*, **35**(2), 253–73.

Rosdolsky, R. (1977). *The Making of Marx's 'Capital'*. London: Pluto.

Rose, R. B. (1998). *Tribunes and Amazons: Men and women of revolutionary France, 1789–1871*. Sydney: McCleay Press.

Rosenstein, N. and Morstein-Marx, R. (eds) (2006). *A Companion to the Roman Republic*. Oxford: Blackwell.

Ross, M. (2006). 'Is democracy good for the poor?' *American Journal of Political Science*, **50**(4), 860–74.

Rowbotham, S. (1972). *Women, Resistance and Revolution*. Harmondsworth: Penguin.

Rudé, G. (1959). *The Crowd in the French Revolution*. Oxford: Clarendon Press.

Rudé, G. (1980). *Ideology and Popular Protest*. London: Lawrence & Wishart.

Rudé, G. (1988). *The French Revolution*. London: Phoenix.

Rueschemeyer, D., Stephens, E. and Stephens, J. (1992). *Capitalist Development and Democracy*. Chicago, Ill.: University of Chicago Press.

Russell, C. (1990). *The Causes of the English Civil War*. Oxford and New York: Clarendon Press.

Saad-Filho, A. (Edn. (2003). *Anti-Capitalism: A Marxist introduction*. London: Pluto.

Saad-Filho, A. and Johnston, D. (eds) (2005). *Neoliberalism: A critical reader*. London: Pluto.

Sarson, S. (2000). 'Chronology', pp. 707–44 in J. Greene and J. Pole (eds), *A Companion to the American Revolution*. Malden, Mass. and Oxford: Blackwell.

Sayer, A. (1998 'Abstraction', pp.120–43 in M. Archer, R. Bhaskar, A. Collier, T. Lawson and A. Norrie (eds), *Critical Realism*. London and New York: Routledge.

Sayer, D. (1983). *Marx's Method*. Brighton: Harvester.

Sayer, D. (1987). *The Violence of Abstraction*. Oxford: Basil Blackwell.

Scheidel, W. and Friesen, S. J. (2009). 'The size of the economy and the distribution of income in the Roman empire', *Journal of Roman Studies*, **99**(00754358), 61–91.

Schulkind, E. (1972). *The Paris Commune of 1871*. London: Jonathan Cape.

Scott, D. (2004). *Politics and War in the Three Stuart Kingdoms, 1637–49*. Basingstoke and New York: Palgrave Macmillan.

Scott, J., Crompton, R. and Lyonette, C. (2010). *Gender Inequalities in the 21st Century*. Cheltenham: Edward Elgar.

Seccombe, W. (1992). *A Millennium of Family Change*. London and New York: Verso.

Selfa, L. (2006). 'Is the crisis over? The crisis of the GOP', *International Socialist Review*, (48), 17–24.

Sellers, M. N. S. (1994). *American Republicanism: Roman ideology in the United States Constitution*. London: Palgrave Macmillan.

Sepehri, S. (2002). 'The geopolitics of oil', *International Socialist Review*, **18**, 79–84.

Shaikh, A. (1977). 'Marx's theory of value and the "transformation problem"', pp. 106–39 in J. Schwartz (ed.), *The Subtle Anatomy of Capitalism*. Santa Monica, Calif.: Goodyear.

Shaikh, A. (1982). 'Neo-Ricardian economics: a wealth of algebra, a poverty of theory', *Review of Radical Political Economics*, **14**(2), 67–84.

Shaikh, A. (1984). 'The rransformation from Marx to Sraffa', in E. Mandel and A. Freeman (eds), *Ricardo Marx Sraffa*. London: Verso.

Shaikh, A. (1990). 'Exploitation' and 'Surplus value', pp. 167, 344–9 in J. Eatwell, M. Milgate and P. Newman (eds), *The New Palgrave Marxian Economics*. London: Macmillan.

Shaikh, A. (1991). 'Falling rate of profit', pp. 185–6 in T. E. A. Bottomore (ed.), *The Dictionary of Marxist Thought*, 2nd edn. Oxford: Basil Blackwell.

Shaikh, A. (1992). 'The falling rate of profit as the cause of long waves: theory and empirical evidence', in A. Kleinknecht, E. Mandel and I. Wallerstein (eds), *New Findings in Long-Wave Research*. New York: St Martins Press.

Shaikh, A. and Tonack, A. (1994). *Measuring the Wealth of Nations*. Cambridge: Cambridge University Press.

Shawki, A. (1997). '80 years since the Russian Revolution', *International Socialist Review*, 3, 7–24.

Shawki, A. (2001). 'Between things ended and things begun', *International Socialist Review*, **18**, 25–42.

Shelley, T. (2007). *Exploited: Migrant labour in the new global economy*. London: Zed.

Shotter, D. (1994). *The Fall of the Roman Republic*. London and New York: Routledge.

Singsen, D. (2012). 'A balance sheet of Occupy Wall Street', *International Socialist Review*, **81**, 7–16.

Siemann, W. (1998). *The German Revolution of 1848–49*, trans. C. Banerji, New York: St Martin's Press.

Siemann, W. (2001). 'The revolutions of 1848–1849 and the persistence of the old regime in Germany (1848–1850)', pp. 117–37 in J. Breuilly (ed.), *19th Century Germany: Politics, Culture and Society, 1780–1918*. London: Arnold.

Sigman, J. (1973). *Eighteen-Forty Eight*. London: Allen & Unwin.

Sinclair, R. K. (1988). *Democracy and Participation in Athens*. Cambridge: Cambridge University Press.

Sinnigen, W. and Boak, A. E. (1977). *A History of Rome to A.D. 565*, 6th edn. New York: Macmillan.

Soboul, A. (1972). *The San-Culottes*, trans. A. Frost and C. Jones. New York: Ancho.

Soboul, A. (1974). *The French Revolution 1787–1799: From the storming of the Bastille to Napoleon*, trans. A. Frost and C. Jones. New York: Random House.

Soboul, A. (1977). *A Short History of the French Revolution*. Berkeley, Calif.: University of California Press.

Soboul, A. (1988). *Understanding the French Revolution*. London: Merlin.

Sowerwine, C. (2001). *France Since 1870*. Basingstoke and New York: Palgrave.

Sperber, J. (1994). *The European Revolutions, 1848–1851*. Cambridge: Cambridge University Press.

Starr, C. (1990). *The Birth of Athenian Democracy*. New York and Oxford: Oxford University Press.

Ste. Croix, G. E. M. de (1972). *The Origins of the Peloponnesian War*. Ithaca, N.Y.: Cornell University Press.

Ste. Croix, G. E. M. de (1981). *The Class Struggle in the Ancient Greek World*. London: Duckworth.

Ste. Croix, G. E. M. de (2004). *Athenian Democratic Origins and Other Essays*. Oxford: Oxford University Press.

Stearns, P. (1974). *The Revolutions of 1848*. London: Weidenfeld & Nicolson.

Stedman Jones, G. (1983). 'The mid-century crisis and the 1848 revolutions', *Theory and Society*, **12**(4), 505–19.

Steven, R. (1989). 'Land and white settler colonialism', pp. 21–35 in D. Novitz and B. Willmott (eds), *Culture and Identity in New Zealand*. Wellington: GP Books.

Stockton, D. (1990). *The Classical Athenian Democracy*. Oxford and New York: Oxford University Press.

Stone, L. (1965). *The Crisis of the Aristocracy, 1558–1641*. Oxford: Clarendon Press.

Strauss, B. S. (1986). *Athens After the Peloponnesian War: Class, Faction and Policy 403–386 BC*. London and Sydney: Croom Helm.

Strauss-Kahn, D. (2009). 'World growth grinds to virtual halt, IMF urges decisive global policy response', *IMF Survey Magazine: IMF Research*.

Sukhanov, N. (1984). *The Russian Revolution: A personal account*. Princeton, N.J.: Princeton University Press.

Taylor, L. R. (1966). *Roman Voting Assemblies from the Hannibalic War to the Dictatorship of Caesar*. Ann Arbor, Mich.: University of Michigan Press.

Teschke, B. (2003). *The Myth of 1648*. London: Verso.

Therborn, G. (1977). 'The rule of capital and the rise of democracy', *New Left Review*, **103**, 3–45.

Therborn, G. (1978). *What Does the Ruling Class Do When it Rules?* London: New Left Books.

Thorley, J. (1996). *Athenian Democracy*. London and New York: Routledge.

Tocqueville, A. d. (1955). *The Old Regime and the French Revolution*, 1978 edn. Gloucester, Mass.: Peter Smith.

Toombs, R. (1999). *The Paris Commune 1871*. London and New York: Longman.

Trotsky, L. (1969). *The Permanent Revolution & Results and Prospects*. New York: Pathfinder.

Trotsky, L. (1972 [1937]). *The Revolution Betrayed*. New York: Pathfinder.

Trotsky, L. (1973). *1905*. Middlesex: Pelican.

Trotsky, L. (1980a [1932]). *History of the Russian Revolution*, Vol. 1. New York: Pathfinder.

Trotsky, L. (1980b [1932]). *History of the Russian Revolution*, Vol. 2. New York: Pathfinder.

Trotsky, L. (1980c [1932]). *History of the Russian Revolution*, Vol. 3. New York: Pathfinder.

Trotsky, L. (1993). *Lessons of October*. London: Union Books.

Trudell, M. (2012). 'The Occupy Movement and class politics in the US', *International Socialism*, **133**, 39–53.

Underdown, D. (1996). *A Freeborn People*. Oxford and New York: Clarendon Press.

Van Der Linden, M. (1997). 'Marx and Engels, Dutch Marxism and the "model capitalist nation of the seventeenth century"', *Science and Society*, **61**(2), 161–93.

Wallerstein, I. (1974). *The Modern World System*, Vol. 1. New York and London: Academic Press.

Wallerstein, I. (1980). *The Modern World System*, Vol. 2. New York and London: Academic Press.

Wallerstein, I. (1989). *The Modern World System*, Vol. 3. London and New York: Academic Press.

Ward, A. M., Heichelheim, F. and Yeo, C. A. (1999). *A History of the Roman People*, 3rd edn. New Jersey: Prentice-Hall.

Ward-Perkins, B. (2005). *The Fall of Rome and the End of Civilization*. New York: Oxford University Press.

Wheeler, J. S. (1999). *The Making of a World Power*. Stroud: Sutton.

White, L. (1972). 'The expansion of technology 500–1500', pp. 143–76 in C. M. Cipolla (ed.), *The Fontana Economic History of Europe: The Middle Ages*. Glasgow: Collins/Fontana.

Wickham, C. (2001). 'Society', pp. 59–96 in R. McKitterick (ed.), *The Early Middle Ages: Europe 400–1000*, 1st US edn. Oxford: Oxford University Press.

Wickham, C. (2005). *Framing the Early Middle Ages*. Oxford: Oxford University Press.

Wickham, C. (2009). *The Inheritance of Rome*, 1st US edn. London: Penguin.

Williams, C. (2010). *Ecology and Socialism*. Chicago, Ill: Haymarket.

Williams, R. (1969). *The French Revolution of 1870–1*. New York: W.W. Norton.

Williams, R. (1993). 'Democracy', pp. 19–23 in P. Green (ed.), *Democracy: Key concepts in critical theory*. New Jersey: Humanities Press.

Williamson, C. (1960). *American Suffrage from Property to Democracy, 1760–1860*. Princeton, N.J.: Princeton University Press.

Wolf, S. (2001). 'Climate chaos: can global warming be stopped?', *International Socialist Review*, **18**, 79–84.

Wolff, R. (2000). 'Marxism and democracy', *Rethinking Marxism*, **12**(1), 112–22.

Wolfreys, J. (2007). 'Twilight revolution: Francois Furet and the manufacturing of consensus', pp. 50–70 in M. Haynes and J. Wolfreys eds), *History and Revolution: Refuting Revisionism*. London and New York: Verso.

Wood, E. (1988). *Peasant-Citizen and Slave*. London: Verso.

Wood, E. (1991). *The Pristine Culture of Capitalism*. London: Verso.

Wood, E. (1995). *Democracy Against Capitalism*. Cambridge: Cambridge University Press.

Wood, E. (2002). *The Origin of Capitalism: A longer view*. New York: Monthly Review Press.

Wood, E. (2003). *Empire of Capital*. London and New York: Verso.

Wood, E. and Wood, N. (1978). *Class Ideology and Ancient Political Theory*. Oxford: Basil Blackwell.

Wood, E. and Wood, N. (1997). *A Trumpet of Sedition*. New York: New York University Press.

Wood, G. (2003). *The American Revolution: A history*. New York: Modern Library.

Woolf, G. (ed.) (2003). *The Cambridge Illustrated History of the Roman World*. Cambridge: Cambridge University Press.

Woolrych, A. (2002). *Britain in Revolution 1625–1660*. Oxford: Oxford University Press.

Wright, S. (1984). *Russia: The making of the revolution*. London: Bookmarks.

Wrightson, K. (1982). *English Society, 1580–1680*. London: Routledge.

Yakobson, A. (1999). *Elections and Electioneering*. Stuttgart: F. Steiner.

Yakobson, A. (2006). 'Popular power in the Roman Republic', pp. 383–400 in N. Rosenstein and R. Morstein-Marx (eds), *A Companion to the Roman Republic*. Oxford: F. Steiner.

Zinn, H. (1999). *A People's History of the United States*, 20th anniv. edn. New York: HarperCollinss.

Index

compatibility with democracy, ix, 129, 215–16

crises of, xiii, 227 (*see also* global financial crisis; *under* economic)

emergence of, 78, 81–5

expansion on global scale, 196–204, 215

expedited by revolution, 117, 176

facilitating socialist transformation, 242

fall considered inevitable, 10

forces for change in, xiii

global resistance to, ix

Marxist critique of, 3, 217–40

possible trajectories beyond, 3, 9, 10–11

spread of, xiii, 178

state capitalism, 274

struggles within, 234

undemocratic nature of relations of production, 238

uneven development in Europe, 178

vs pre-capitalist societies, 6, 123

Carolinigian empire, 65–6, 95

Carthage, 38, 39

Case of the Army Truly Stated, The, 110

Cavaignac, Louis-Eugene, 188

censors (in ancient Rome), 46

censorship, 114, 254

Centre for Responsive Politics, xiii

Charlemagne, 65

Charles I, king of England, 89, 93, 96, 98–101, 104–5, 111–12

arrest and execution of, 107, 112

Charles II, king of England, 113, 114, 115

Charles Albert, king of Piedmont, 185

Chartists, 35, 117, 207

Chernov, Viktor, 271

childcare, 228–30, 248, 275

church, Christian, 59, 77

education by, 248

in eighteenth-century America, 125–6

in eighteenth-century France, 156, 164, 165, 168

as landowner, 70

Papacy, 76

prayer books, 98

Protestant work ethic, 125–6

Reformation of, 93

Roman Catholic, 94

in seventeenth-century England and Scotland, 92–4, 97–8, 100, 102, 103, 108, 114

tithes demanded by, 78, 79, 93, 156

as upholder of class system, 70, 98, 116, 187

Cicero, 52, 56, 125

Citizens United v. Federal Election Commission, xiii

citizens

of ancient Athens, 31–2

of ancient Rome, 41

of the United States, 147–8

civil liberties, 12, 168, 180, 181, 183, 188, 189, 205, 206, 214–15, 275

Civil Rights Act (US), 208

Clarendon Code, 114

class

in American society, 144

conflict and economic development, 145

contemporary struggles, 227, 234

contempt of upper for lower, 57

definitions of, 5

and ethnic/gender issues, 121–2

factors in the American Revolution, 124

factors in the English civil war, 91–2, 94, 102, 107, 114

factors in the French Revolution, 171

factors and the US Constitution, 138

four classes in ancient Athens, 19

issues and representative democracy, 206

Marxist conception of, 7

in pre-revolutionary France, 154–8

Roman derivation of term, 40

in Roman society and army, 40, 52, 57

struggles in the American colonies, 128–30

struggles in ancient Athens, 20, 30–1

struggles in ancient Rome, 42, 45

struggles in improving democracy, 206–8